Gatherings in Diaspora
*Religious Communities
and the New Immigration*

Gatherings in Diaspora

Religious Communities and the New Immigration

Edited by

R. Stephen Warner
Judith G. Wittner

Temple University Press: *Philadelphia*

Temple University Press, Philadelphia 19122

∞ The paper used in this publication meets the requirements of the
American National Standard for Information Sciences—
Permanence of Paper for Printed Library Materials,
ANSI Z39.48-1984

Text design by Susan Gutnik

Library of Congress Cataloging-in-Publication Data

Gatherings in diaspora : religious communities and the new immigration /
edited by R. Stephen Warner and Judith G. Wittner.
    p.   cm.
  Includes bibliographical references and index.
    ISBN 1-56639-613-1 (alk. paper).—ISBN 1-56639-614-X (pbk. : alk. paper)
    1. Religious communities—United States. 2. South Asians—United States.
  3. Immigrants—United States—Religious life. I. Warner, R. Stephen.
  II. Wittner, Judith G.
  BL632.5.U5G37   1998
  305.6′0973—dc21   97-38147

Contents

III

Institutional Adaptations

IV

Internal Differentiation

Conclusion

Introduction

Immigration and Religious Communities in the United States

R. Stephen Warner

Gatherings in Diaspora brings together the latest chapters in the long-running chronicle of religion and immigration in the American experience. Today, as in the past, people migrating to the United States bring their religions with them, and gathering religiously is one of the ways they make a life here. Their religious identities often (but not always) mean more to them away from home, in their diaspora, than they did before, and those identities undergo more or less modification as the years pass. To a greater or lesser extent, immigrants and their offspring adapt their religious institutions to American conditions, and in the process they often interact with religious communities already established here. The religious institutions they build, adapt, remodel, and adopt become worlds unto themselves, "congregations," where new relations among the members of the community—among men and women, parents and children, recent arrivals and those longer settled—are forged.

Later generations, not to mention historians of the late twenty-first century, will have reason to thank the authors of these chapters for documenting the struggling early years of what by then may have become established institutions, or, alternatively, for preserving records of failed projects long forgotten.[1]

With the exception of Native American religion, the religions of the United States are imports, and the most Americanized of religious communities in the United States still bear signs of their foreign heritage in the hymns they sing, the languages they use for prayer, the special garments their members wear, the architecture of their places of worship, and the names of the saints they venerate and the prophets they follow. Until recently—that is to say, until the 1960s—the foreign

3

origins of American religion were primarily European and African, with major streams from England, Ireland, the Netherlands, France, Germany, Scandinavia, Poland, Russia, Italy, Greece, and the historic kingdoms of west and central Africa, and only a small presence from such Asian countries as Japan. To the home-country list today we must add the Philippines, China, Korea, Vietnam, Thailand, India, Iran, Lebanon, Egypt, Sudan, Haiti, Jamaica, the Dominican Republic, Cuba, Guatemala, and Mexico. Although Christians, in their staggering variety, are still by far the largest religious group in the United States, millions of adherents of other religions—Islam, Hinduism, Buddhism, and more—have joined Jews to expand the boundaries of American religious pluralism to an extent unimaginable only forty years ago. At the same time, Christians from Asia, the Middle East, and Latin America are de-Europeanizing American Christianity.

The increased numbers and an enhanced appreciation of diversity have also rendered the presence of earlier religious minorities retrospectively more visible. Japanese Buddhists in California, a community over one hundred years old (Kashima 1977); Filipinos, who began to gather in California in the 1920s (San Buenaventura 1996); Mexican American Presbyterians with roots in Texas going back a century and a half (Brackenridge and García-Treto 1974); and Puerto Rican Catholics in New York (Díaz-Stevens 1993) are merely four examples. Immigration and multicultural awareness have also emboldened legatees of previously hidden religious streams to make themselves heard. Thus, Americans are freshly hearing old stories of crypto-Jews in New Mexico, descendants of *conversos* who were forced to adopt Catholicism during the Spanish inquisition (Alexy 1993, 281–292), and of Santeria, a religion developed in Cuba from African and European elements, which has found new appeal among Americans of African and Caribbean descent (Stevens-Arroyo and Pérez y Mena 1995).

Signs of the cultural shift in American religion are everywhere. It is hard not to be aware of Korean immigrant churches in cities and suburbs—some of them sharing space with English-speaking Protestant churches, some freestanding; some imposing, most modest. In inner cities, Spanish-language Protestant storefront churches, most of them very modest, abound. Less numerous but more visible are the grand mosques and Hindu and Buddhist temples that now dot the suburbs of many American cities and frequently receive respectful mention in the Sunday papers. Outdoor religious processions drawing thousands of Mexicans or Haitians for a passion play or a saint's festival also receive attention from the media in places like San Antonio and New York City.

But it is easy to ignore other, equally significant aspects of the new religious diversity in the United States, including Catholic parishes that feature one or more weekly masses in Spanish and white Protestant churches that provide a religious home for one or another minority. Most Muslim and Buddhist centers in the United States are small and inconspicuous, except on Friday and Sunday, respectively, when the surrounding streets are crowded with the cars of those who have come for prayer and devotions. Few college students, for example, know that scores of Muslims gather every Friday for noon prayer in a room of the student union or elsewhere on campus.

Still other manifestations of the new religious diversity are tucked away in private homes, where families and friends gather to practice their own rituals—Christian, Jewish, Muslim, Hindu, Buddhist, Vodou, Rastafarian, and more. Without benefit of clergy, yellow-page listings, or nonprofit status, such gatherings are the functional equivalent of churches for many of their participants.

The subjects of this book are the churches, temples, and mosques, home meetings and outdoor processions, official organizations and informal gatherings, through which today's immigrants and newly emerging ethnic groups express their religions—as previous waves of immigrants long have done. There are thousands of such places. To cite some realistic estimates of the more formal of such places, today there are some 3,500 Catholic parishes where mass is celebrated in Spanish and 7,000 Hispanic/Latino Protestant congregations, most of them Pentecostal or evangelical in theology. By actual count in 1988, there were 2,017 Korean immigrant churches, and in 1994 there were an estimated 700 Chinese Protestant churches in the United States. Two different research projects counted between 1,000 and 1,200 mosques and other Islamic centers in the early 1990s, and at the same time Buddhist temples and meditation centers (many of the latter having white American constituencies) numbered between 1,500 and 2,000. Hindus could worship in some 400 temples.[2]

Gatherings in Diaspora concerns the religious institutions not of all immigrant and ethnic groups but only of those we call the "new" groups, people with origins in East and South Asia, the Middle East, the Caribbean, and Latin America—what in Cold War days was called the Third World. Other than their common humanity, these people share little except for their new but unrecognized place in the United States. Some, like the majority of Asian Indians, are immigrants properly speaking, who have voluntarily come to the United States in search of a better life. Others, like Vietnamese boat people and Guatemalan highlanders, are refugees, who have sought asylum here from deathly circumstances at home. Some may be thought of as colonized people, residing in the United States not because they crossed the border but because, like Tejanos, Chicanos, and Puerto Ricans, the border crossed them, with their descendants never quite making peace with the conquest.[3] (Such "colonized" people, like African Americans, have ancestors who did not come to the United States of their own volition.) Others, like many Haitians, may reside in the United States sporadically, maintaining simultaneous residences in this county and abroad, in a pattern called "transnationalism." Many, among them Chinese and Jamaicans, think of themselves as part of a "diaspora," adapting a historically Jewish self-understanding of people with roots in one place who are scattered around the world.

From the point of view of this book, these "new" ethnic and immigrant peoples share two things: a greatly expanded presence in the United States since the 1960s, and a nearly complete neglect of their burgeoning religious institutions by researchers and the public. For this reason, although immigration from Poland and Ireland is once again sizable, we do not focus here on Polish or Irish churches, for they have received and will continue to receive significant scholarly attention. Similarly, although religion is the most prominent institution in the African American community, black churches have been studied in depth and were not encompassed by our project. So also for Native American religions. But the communities represented in this book—Chinese and Indian Christian congregations worshiping in the home-country language, Korean American congregations worshiping in English, Hispanic Pentecostal churches, Vodou and Rastafarian gatherings, Guatemalan and Hindu house groups, and immigrant mosques—previously have been overlooked in the literature.[4] With this work, these and other nascent religious institutions will begin to receive the attention that is their due.

The effort that produced this book—the New Ethnic and Immigrant Congregations Project—was premised on the following fact: the religious presence of the these groups, some 15 percent of the U.S. population, has been ignored by scholars. That unrecognized presence, a form of scholarly discrimination, is what these groups otherwise diverse have in common.

It is conventional to cite 1965 as a watershed year marking the end of an ethnoreligious regime of European American Protestants, Catholics, and Jews and mostly Protestant African Americans (Warner 1994, 56–57), and it is true that the abolition of 1920s-era country-of-origin quotas in the Immigration Act of 1965 made possible an unprecedented (and largely unintended) diversification of the American population over the subsequent thirty years.[5] For example, the number of Asian Indians in the United States jumped from fewer than 9,000 in 1960 to nearly 400,000 in 1980 (Leonard 1992, 175). Of the 5 million immigrants who arrived between 1985 and 1990, only 13 percent were born in Europe, Canada, Australia, or New Zealand, "whereas 26 percent came from Mexico, 31 percent from Asia, [and] 22 percent from other parts of the Americas" (Chiswick and Sullivan 1995, 216–217).

But the story of the Latin American, Caribbean, and Asian presence in the United States cannot be simply explained as the result of the 1966 law (Heer 1995, 27–76), for it is also the result of wars, revolutions, and American needs for labor. For example, Mexicans became residents of the United States first through the war of 1846–48 and later through flight from the 1911–23 revolution, but their numbers greatly increased through the *bracero* (guest worker) program of 1942–64, which was initiated during a period of little immigration because agricultural interests in the American West successfully argued their need for cheap labor. Thus was established a pattern of labor migration that later restrictions have not stemmed.

Beginning in the 1860s, Chinese, then Japanese, and then Koreans were brought to California and Hawaii first as railroad workers and later as agricultural laborers, with each group encountering nativist and racist reaction. Each was eventually barred from immigration, whether by law, as in the 1882 Chinese Exclusion Act, or diplomacy, as in the 1907 "gentlemen's agreement" with Japan (but not before the Japanese in the United States had established religious institutions that persist to this day). Beginning in 1899, after the United States took possession of the Philippines in the war with Spain, Filipinos were U.S. nationals, as Asians ineligible for citizenship but qualified for work, and between 1907, when Japanese immigration was barred, and 1934, when Congress authorized eventual Philippine independence, over 100,000 Filipino laborers came to work in the plantations of Hawaii and fields of California (Melendy 1980). The 1990 census reports that 1.4 million Americans now claim Filipino national origin.

The Cold War significantly affected immigration patterns. Conservative politicians' desire to accommodate Chinese refugees from the 1949 revolution made the 1882 Exclusion Act an embarrassment. Soon thereafter, thousands of anticommunist Hungarians were granted presidential "parole" after their failed 1956 revolution, and that precedent was used to admit over a half-million Cubans in the twenty years following the 1959 revolution in their country. Hundreds of thousands of Vietnamese and other Southeast Asians were admitted under similar provisions after the fall of their U.S.-backed governments in 1975. Although communists were not the victors in the Iranian revolution of 1979, the losers, the Pahlevi regime, had been U.S. allies during the Cold War, and those who had flourished under that regime had good reason to leave. Thus, the 1990 census reported 285,000 Iranians in the United States, most of them recently arrived. In Los Angeles alone, "the Iranian population grew sixfold in the 1970–80 decade, mainly because of the massive influx of exiles after 1978" (Bozorgmehr et al. 1996, pp. 351, 376). Refugees from Central America and the Caribbean—El Salvador, Guatemala, Nicaragua, Haiti—often came to escape wars in their countries that had a Cold War agenda, but *their* pleas for political asylum fell on systematically deaf ears in Washington. As an indication of the vulnerability of this largely refugee population, the 1990 census recorded 565,000 individuals of Salvadoran descent in the United States, and 269,000 of Guatemalan descent; in 1992 the Immigration and Naturalization Service estimated unauthorized Salvadorans at 327,000 (or 58 percent of the 1990 population) and Guatemalans at 129,000 (or 48 percent of the 1990 population) (Lopez, et al. 1996, pp. 281, 287).

This brief sketch shows that the diverse profile of the U.S. population today is not a simple matter of foreigners taking advantage of the genuinely more evenhanded 1965 immigration law. It was more often the case that the United States had intervened in their countries' affairs and had work for them and their ancestors to do. In the last third of the twentieth century, many of these old chickens have come home to roost.

Another aspect of the book's focus—its emphasis on gatherings, or congregations—must be explained. Books abound on "Eastern religion," especially the diverse forms of Buddhism, which is one of the religions that new immigrants have brought to the United States. Indeed, many cities have entire bookstores devoted to Eastern and "new age" religion. Yet most of this abundant literature expounds philosophy and doctrine or coaches the reader in spiritual and self-help practices, and very little narrates the history of Buddhists in the United States or analyzes the communities they have built. (For an outstanding exception, see Fields 1992.)

In contrast, the studies in this book focus on *congregations*—local, face-to-face religious assemblies—rather than on teachings, private devotions, scriptures, buildings, or national umbrella organizations. Our task was to discover what new ethnic and immigrant groups were *doing together religiously* in the United States, and what manner of religious institutions they were developing *of, by, and for themselves.*

Behind this focus on the congregation stand several presuppositions. First of all, as just implied, religion as understood here exists in the form not of texts but of living communities. This sociological principle stands opposed to a historically Protestant attitude, deeply seated in much of American culture, that holds that true religion is found only in the Bible and stands outside the world. (Some secular thinkers employ this fundamentally Protestant principle by quoting the sayings of Jesus, for example, to expose the hypocrisies of organized religion.) Catholic theologians have clarified the matter by theorizing the necessary "inculturation" of religion (Schreiter 1985, 1–6). Whatever may be true of God, they point out, the human institution of religion always takes one or another here-and-now form. This point is made unmistakably in the American immigrant experience, when mutually incomprehensible forms of the same world religion come in contact for the first time, as, for example, Sri Lankan Buddhists encounter Korean Buddhists in Los Angeles or Indian Orthodox Christians meet Serbian Orthodox Christians in Chicago.

Second, the process through which a religion takes on an expression specific to one or another community—whether we call it inculturation, contextualization, or indigenization—is ongoing. Especially when people cross a significant boundary, as they do when they migrate, these processes are dramatic and visible. Thus, although I have spoken of American religions as "imports," bearing the stamp of their foreign origins, they are also adapted to this country. Although the authors of these chapters represent several disciplines, the perspective on contextualization is another fundamental sociological presupposition of this text. Unlike anthropology, which began a century ago with efforts to salvage disappearing customs of Native Americans and to document Oceanic cultures untouched by Western influence, the field work tradition of sociology got its start in Chicago with studies of the adaptations of immigrant communities and did not expect to find cultural purity. Following in the sociological tradition, our project set out to analyze adaptations, not to dismiss or deplore them as inauthentic.

Third, the focus on congregations means that we look at what the various communities do religiously for themselves, not what others do or do not do on their behalf. This does not mean that the United States and its churches are necessarily inhospitable. Although many churches are self-satisfied, prejudiced, and otherwise closed off to newcomers, other religious groups in the United States work hard to welcome them. Some aspire to integrate immigrants within a preexisting American congregation. In other cases—notably the Southern Baptist Convention—an American denomination facilitates immigrants' establishment of their own congregations. Historically, the Catholic church has made the greatest effort to serve immigrants, and its many "apostolates" are designated for today's immigrants—notably those from Mexico, the Philippines, Vietnam, Cuba, Haiti, and the Dominican Republic (Christiano 1991). The studies in this book document interactions between immigrant groups and established American groups (whom we call their "proximal hosts," using a concept of Mittelberg and Waters [1992]), but the cases are defined from the point of view of the immigrants, not of the hosts or missionaries. We look not at this or that denomination's missions *to* immigrant groups but rather at congregations *of* such groups.

The New Ethnic and Immigrant Congregations Project

Gatherings in Diaspora is the product of a research training and support program—the New Ethnic and Immigrant Congregations Project—which in turn had its origins in plans for another book, tentatively entitled *Communities of Faith,* which I began to write nearly ten years ago. That still-incomplete book examines American religious communities under a theory that the increased decentralization, pluralism, and voluntarism of American religious life are signs not of religion's demise but of its vitality (Warner 1993b, 1995). In writing a chapter of that book on churches and mosques of new immigrants, I ran into a snag. To add texture to the theory, I had intended to use notes I had taken on field trips to the home churches (and other religious institutions) of students in my sociology of religion classes at the University of Illinois at Chicago, an inner-city state university with a diverse student body. For analytic weight, I intended to supplement these notes with the findings of scholars in the field. However, the problem was that such a literature hardly existed. With a few, notable exceptions (which I shall presently draw upon), almost nothing was "known" about new immigrant congregations in the sense that social scientists and humanists want to "know" things. These religious communities had simply been ignored by scholars.

Upon reflection, I recognized three general reasons for the neglect (see Warner in press). One was the practical matter that such informa-

R. Stephen Warner

tion is hard to come by. We do know quite a bit about where the new immigrants come from, where they are settling, how they are faring in the economy, and how their children are doing in school (Chiswick and Sullivan 1995, Heer 1996, Portes and Rumbaut 1996, Rumbaut and Cornelius 1995). But we have such information largely because scholars can use data collected by government agencies, such as the Bureau of the Census, the Immigration and Naturalization Service, the Bureau of Labor Statistics, and state boards of education. But government agencies in the United States, unlike those in Canada, cannot ask people about their religion, and therefore reliable data are scarce. Thus for numerical information (including the basic question of how many members of various religious groups live in the United States), scholars of religion must rely on the public records of religious organizations themselves or on the results of sample surveys. The former vary in quality from meticulous, regularly updated rosters to wishful, inflated guesstimates. The latter, such as the General Social Survey, an annual face-to-face survey of about 1,500 Americans, serve well for large sub-populations (such as European-origin Catholics and Baptists), but poorly for small ones (including Jews and Muslims) and miserably for groups whose members are not fluent in English.[6]

Given that research must be conducted by scholars motivated to overcome these barriers and scholars fluent in the languages of the respective communities, a second problem is that such individuals are still few in number (Kivisto 1993). The literature is abundant on European American Catholics, white evangelicals, black Protestants, and Jews, but much of it is the work of men and women with generations-deep roots in the traditions they study, such as Jay Dolan and Robert Orsi, scions respectively of Irish and Italian Catholicism; Nancy Ammerman and Randal Balmer, born into white evangelical families; Cheryl Townsend Gilkes and Evelyn Higginbotham, African American Protestants; and Lynn Davidman and Samuel Heilman, Jews. The problem is that new immigrant groups have not yet spawned the critical mass of United States–based scholars who will write their religious stories.[7]

Yet there are ethnic studies departments at many American universities that have attracted Asian American and Latino/a scholars to their faculties. However, although one might expect that some of them would have devoted their energies to the study of the religious institutions of their respective peoples, in fact few have (Leong 1996, vii–ix). So we must mention a third factor that has contributed to the sparseness of the literature: an antireligious bias in much of the social science research devoted to new ethnic and immigrant communities. Religion in general was "cast as an opiate of the masses and as ephemeral in nature," and Christianity in particular (which, in one or another form, the great majority of American Hispanics and many Asian Americans practice) was seen as an aspect of an illegitimate "imperial apparatus" (Yoo 1996, xv). The most legitimate focus of research was identified as indigenous, pre-Columbian, pre-Christian, even pre-Buddhist and pre-Muslim, religion. Especially because of its intimate connection with colonial powers and its more or less complete ideological hegemony, the Catholic church in particular was seen by many Latin Americanists as the very paradigm of inauthentic "institutional" religion. Thus even among scholars who did focus on religion, studies of religious institutions were disfavored, despite the enormous popular involvement in Catholic and Protestant churches.[8]

Despite these barriers, my literature search for the book—which extended into monographs, thematic collections, journal articles, theses, conference papers, and term papers—let me know that a few pioneers were beginning the needed research, some of them outsiders (e.g., Denny 1987, Fenton 1988, Mullins 1988, Williams 1988, Burns 1994, Waugh 1994) and some with the same ethnicity as the groups they studied (e.g., Hurh and Kim 1990, Kashima 1977, Shin and Park 1988). I learned that other studies were in process, notably the Pluralism Project at Harvard, headed by Diana Eck; the Notre Dame History of Hispanic Catholics in the United States, managed by Jay Dolan and his associates; and the Program for the Analysis of Religion Among Latinos (PARAL), led by Anthony Stevens-Arroyo.

Scattered across the country, across disciplines, and across universities, and often unbeknownst to each other, a few scholars were beginning to take notice of the huge, overlooked world of new ethnic and immigrant religion. Program officers for religion at the Lilly Endowment and the Pew Charitable Trusts agreed with me that a well-designed, well-funded, and well-publicized research training and support program might help accelerate the process by bringing together a dozen such researchers—graduate students, and postdoctoral scholars, co-ethnics, and outsiders. Judith G. Wittner, who had far more experience than I in field research methodology, agreed to sign on as faculty associate, and the foundations came through with generous funding. The New Ethnic and Immigrant Congregations Project (NEICP) was announced in the fall semester of 1993, with a direct mailing of five thousand poster-brochures to sociologists, anthropologists, historians, and scholars in ethnic studies and religious studies.

We cast a wide net, receiving hundreds of inquiries and eventually more than fifty full proposals. At length, we chose the most promising of the applicants—graduate students and recent Ph.D.s—whom we designated NEICP "fellows," to conduct the research represented in the ten chapters below.[9] I was surprised that we received no proposals to study Filipino American religion and distressed that none of the Buddhist-focused proposals was strong enough to pass the committee's scrutiny, and I am relieved that some studies have recently appeared to fill these gaps (San Buenaventura 1996, Numrich 1996).

Such gaps aside, the religious communities represented in this book—five Christian (Protestant, Catholic, and Orthodox), one each Hindu, Jewish, Muslim, and Rastafari, and one mixed Vodou-Catholic—are broadly representative of the religions of new immigrants, to the best of my knowledge. It is very likely that the great majority of what we call new ethnic and immigrant populations are at least nominally Christian, having origins in such western Hemisphere nations as Mexico, the Dominican Republic, Cuba, Haiti, Jamaica, El Salvador, Guatemala, and Colombia, as well as such dominantly Christian countries of the Eastern Hemisphere as the Philippines. Because immigration is a self-selected process, immigrants from mixed-religious countries like Korea, Vietnam, and Lebanon are disproportionately drawn from the Christian sector of their home country. For example, three-quarters of Korean Americans are church members, compared with one-quarter in Korea.

The NEICP fellows convened in Chicago in the summer of 1994 for a six-week ethnographic training institute directed by Wittner and me. We were a diverse lot: graduate students and Ph.D.s; representatives of sociology, anthropology, and religious studies; women and men; persons of color and whites; Christians, Muslims, Jews, a Rastafari sympathizer, an initiate in Vodou, and those professing no religion; United States-born, immigrants, and international scholars. We studied a syllabus of common theoretical, methodological, and topical readings, including a sampling of the pioneering literature, and we worked on such techniques of ethnographic research as participant observation, interviews, and analysis of documents and material culture.

Over the following academic year, the fellows did field research in their communities, where, between September and March, I joined them for weekend site visits. In the summer of 1995, we reconvened for a workshop in Jamaica to begin work on writing and editing the chapters. In August 1996 the fellows presented their reports at the annual meeting of the Association for the Sociology of Religion in New York,[10] and after some additional editing, we were ready for press.

Immigrants and Their Religions: Old Ideas and New Realities

Having read H. Richard Niebuhr's 1929 classic *The Social Sources of Denominationalism* in 1978, shortly before my first visit to an Indian immigrant church in Chicago, I sensed in that congregation the same dynamics Niebuhr had analyzed fifty years earlier, with India substituted for Scandinavia as the place of origin, Malayalam for Norwegian as the language, and Mar Thoma for Lutheran as the religious communion. Since then, I have been inclined to stress the continuity of the immigrant religious experience between the nineteenth century and the present, and I brought corresponding literature to the 1994 seminar.

Several of the fellows saw matters differently, and they brought readings to the seminar to support their view that new realities call for new ideas. Two issues in particular stand out, and they remain unresolved not only in this book but in the field generally. The first is the question of "race." From a "white American" point of view, it is obvious that many of the new immigrants—from Mexico, China, the Philippines, and so on—are phenotypically different from those of a century ago—from Italy, Poland, Russia, and Greece—not to mention more diverse among themselves. They are "Asian" and "Hispanic" rather than "white." Latinos and Latinas, Asian Americans, and Afro-Caribbeans—in the United States generally and among the fellows in particular—experience racist discrimination. Too often, when Asian American youth, no matter how acculturated, are asked, "Where do you come from?" and answer with the name of their American home town, they are asked again, "No, where are you *really* from?" Mexican American youth receive special, suspicious attention when they go shopping in suburban malls. These are unpleasant, inexcusable realities, and many of the fellows, both whites and persons of color, argued that "race" must be a basic category of our analyses, along with ethnicity and religion. Yet all of us in the seminar recognized that "race" is a socially constructed concept (Omi and Winant 1994). Wittner and I argued that it required a protracted social process for Jews and the Irish, to take two examples, to be included firmly among today's "whites," and that the irreducibility of "race" applies primarily to the African American experience (Hollinger 1995). There is no consensus among us whether the descendants of the groups we focus on will maintain in the middle of the next century the same racial status that they occupy today.

The second unresolved issue concerns the concept of "immigrants," a matter that I touched on earlier. Once again the argument involved seminar participants from all points of the racial/ethnic/nationality compass, who argued that the criteria that define just who is an "immigrant" have become blurry. They promoted the concept of "transnationalism" (Schiller et al. 1992, Basch et al. 1994), which is critical of an older idea that people who cross borders necessarily stay to adopt the new country as their home. Transnational theory fits those groups who travel frequently between the United States and their countries of origin, and it is applied most often to Haitians, Jamaicans, Dominicans, and Afro-Caribbeans generally, but also to Mexicans and even, because of their easy access to communications media and air travel, Indians. One strand of the argument is that frequent travel, rich cultural contact (for example, adolescents often being sent "home" to be raised by an aunt out of American harm's way), and continued streams of migration impede assimilation. Another strand looks at the effect of imported American culture on the immigrants' countries of origin. Once again, Wittner and I joined other fellows to argue that many of the immigrants of a century ago also returned to their home countries, disappointed with their sojourn in the United States, and that still others wished to return but for various reasons did not. Moreover, although resources to maintain country-of-origin identities have increased, so also have the factors—especially youth cultures—that erode those identities into various "American" identities (cf. Bankston and Zhou 1996). Once again, this book as a whole leaves this issue open, and the authors were free to adhere to whatever theory they found most cogent. Nonetheless, to save space I will speak generically of "immigrants" in the text that follows.

Despite all of these continuing and fruitful theoretical tensions among the NEICP fellows, we looked together at several themes common to immigrant religious communities, and this text is organized around four of them: (1) religion and the negotiation of identities; (2) immigrants' relations with religious host communities; (3) institutional adaptations; and (4) internal differentiation in congregations.

Religion and the Negotiation of Identities

The project was premised on the assumption that religion would be highly salient for today's immigrant groups, an idea I found at the heart of the classic sociological study of immigration and religion—Will

Herberg's *Protestant, Catholic, Jew.* Looking back from his vantage point in the 1950s to the immigrant streams that were shut off in the 1920s, Herberg (1960, 27–28) wrote:

> *Of the immigrant who came to this country it was expected that, sooner or later, either in his own person or through his children, he would give up virtually everything he had brought with him from the "old country"—his language, his nationality, his manner of life—and would adopt the ways of his new home. Within broad limits, however, his becoming an American did not involve his abandoning the old religion in favor of some native American substitute. Quite the contrary, not only was he expected to retain his old religion, as he was not expected to retain his old language or nationality, but such was the shape of America that it was largely in and through his religion that he, or rather his children and grandchildren, found an identifiable place in American life.*

A generation later, reflecting on the experiences of immigrants from India and Pakistan in the 1980s, Raymond Williams (1988, 29) found much the same thing:

> *Immigrants are religious—by all counts more religious than they were before they left home—because religion is one of the important identity markers that helps them preserve individual self-awareness and cohesion in a group. . . . In the United States, religion is the social category with clearest meaning and acceptance in the host society, so the emphasis on religious affiliation and identity is one of the strategies that allows the immigrant to maintain self-identity while simultaneously acquiring community acceptance.*

From the point of view of the host society, in other words, religion mediates difference (Warner forthcoming). From the point of the view of immigrants, the process of movement itself is often a "theologizing experience" (Smith 1978), raising questions of meaning that religion may be able to answer, if not for immigrants themselves, then for their children. Many immigrants find that when they become parents and want to pass on their heritage, religion is their key to cultural reproduction.

Our project was not designed to test the Herberg-Williams thesis. After all, we set out to study groups who had chosen to organize their lives in the United States to some degree around their religion and would therefore have been "sampling on the dependent variable," as sociologists would put it. Yet several applicants offered indirect evidence for our thesis when they expressed relief that such a project was underway. These were anthropology graduate students who had no prior interest in religion yet who, for one reason or another, had been unable to go abroad to conduct their field research in Indonesia, Cambodia, or Laos. As a fall-back plan, they had located a community of people from one of these countries residing in the United States and had been surprised to find what I would have predicted—that the group met in a church (or temple or mosque).

Yet to say that religion is salient for immigrants is not to say that they merely cling to what they had before they left their home countries. As religion becomes less taken for granted under the pluralistic and secular conditions prevailing in the United States, adherents become more conscious of their tradition and often more determined about its transmission. Religious identities nominally assigned at birth become objects of active persuasion. "In a Muslim country one is naturally a Muslim, whether or not one takes seriously the practice of Islam. In North America, Islam becomes a conscious element in the sense of identity" (Booth 1988, 729). Such seems to be the experience of the Hindu group chronicled by Prema Kurien in Chapter 1.

To highlight the open-ended and ongoing process by which people construct identities, we speak of identities as "negotiated" (Leonard 1992, Nagel 1994). This is the central focus of Part I, but the topic recurs throughout the book, and is never far from the surface of consciousness of both the groups and their chroniclers.

For many children, a newly gained "American" identity competes with other identities their parents bear, and some sloughing seems inevitable. When Herberg spoke of "the immigrant" securing "an identifiable place" through "his religion," he glossed a lengthy process of "transmutation," by which a new religious identity survives the demise of regional, national, and linguistic identities. The Iranian Jews Shoshanah Feher spoke with seem to have decided on just this course (see Chapter 2). Sensing that they will not be able to pass on their Persian language and customs, they hope their children will at least embrace their Judaism.

I was witness to a similar determination by a southeast Asian Muslim, when, in the company of NEICP fellow Keng-Fong Pang, I visited a family-centered Qur'an study in a home in Orange County, California, in October 1994. One of the parents—a member of a minority group within a minority group, Muslim Cham speakers from Vietnam and Cambodia—matter-of-factly told me that he was the last speaker of the Cham language in his family. It was difficult enough to raise the children as Muslims, he said, which he and the other Cham fathers intended to accomplish through the English-based instruction in classical Arabic that they led their children through at these Friday night meetings. Yet their children—in general, members of the second generation—may later undo such intentions by searching for their roots among the national, linguistic, or racial identities they attribute to their parents' origins. Time will tell.

Not all immigrants maintain a country-of-origin religious identity. Some join convert congregations, whose members have turned away from the dominant tradition of the country of origin. Many Hispanic Protestants and Chinese Christians have done this, as represented in the essays by Luís León (Chapter 5) and Fenggang Yang (Chapter 10), respectively. Questions that should be asked about such congregations are the extent to which the conversion was the act of its members or their predecessors, and whether the conversion took place in the country of origin or in the United States. Another issue to consider is the ways in which the new religious identity maintains continuity while simultaneously aiding adjustment, which both León and Yang find that it does.

Immigrants and Religious Hosts

If there was ever a linear process by which immigrants assimilated to American culture, it no longer exists. If in the past immigrants (or more likely their children) first became ethnics and later plain Americans, today the picture is more complex. Assimilation has become "segmented," as Alejandro Portes and Rubén Rumbaut (1996) put it, so that there is no longer just one "America" that newcomers enter nor only one "American identity" that they may adopt. Newcomers encounter a pluralistic social context rich with types and categories to which they may be assigned.

Thus people coming to Chicago from Ireland and Poland arrive in a city that thinks it knows how to deal with the Irish and Polish, and Mexicans and Guatemalans come to a Los Angeles ready and waiting with identities to be assigned to them. In our racialized society, these assignments are often crude and unwanted, and immigrant Koreans are lumped together with long-resident Chinese and Japanese as "Asians" (or "Orientals" and a host of less polite names). Jamaicans and Haitians are often classified with African Americans as "blacks," and Salvadorans and Guatemalans with "Hispanics." Immigrants who scorn such labels may not have the resources—especially the income and freedom from racial discrimination—to resist their effective imposition on their children (Portes and Rumbaut 1996, chap. 7).

David Mittelberg and Mary Waters (1992) use the term "proximal

host" to refer to the racial-ethnic category of the receiving society—
"American Jew" and "African American"—to which, respectively, Israeli and West Indian immigrants are often assigned in the United
States. We found the "proximal host" concept helpful for our work on
religion. After all, the word "host" may connote the welcoming aspirations of the many American religious groups that intend to be more
than passive recipients of newcomers and actively seek them out.

The proximal host concept is defined from the point of view of the
receiving society, in this case the United States, for assignment does
not depend on the consent of the assigned. Thus the relationship between host and newcomer is often strained, as it typically is between
Israeli immigrants and the American Jewish community that is their
proximal host. It seems that Israelis living in the United States want
to be Jewish in a way that is different from that understood by American Jewry. The same is true of many Russian Jews, whose exodus from
the former Soviet Union American Jewry worked so hard promote
(Gold 1992). In Evanston, Illinois, a group of Haitian immigrants
established their own French-language Baptist church in part to distinguish themselves from a proximal host, the large African American
minority in that city (Woldemikael 1989).

In Chapter 3, Nancy J. Wellmeier reports that the Guatemalan
Mayans she met in Los Angeles are seen by the priests of the Catholic
parishes where they go to mass as "Hispanics" or "Latinos," that is,
as part of the vast Mexican immigrant population of that city. The
Mayans are Catholic, but they insist that they are Indian, not Hispanic
or Latino, and much of their collective religious life takes place in their
homes, outside the church.

On the other hand, some newcomers may appreciate the place
waiting for them. For example, Williams (1988) reports that Indian
Hindu immigrants were glad to accept the hospitality and to use the
facilities of the local ISKCON (Hare Krishna) temple when they first
began to arrive in Chicago. I myself have seen Muslim immigrants
from the Middle East earning the respect of African American leaders
of the Chicago mosque where they prayed because of their knowledge
of Islam. The Mexican immigrants Luís León spoke with in a Pentecostal church in Los Angeles seem grateful for the guidance the
church gives them, even if they are not ready to follow their pastors
in abandoning the Catholic identity they brought with them.

Elizabeth McAlister's essay (Chapter 4) examines the ambivalent
relationship between Haitians and the Catholic church in East Harlem
through a close study of Haitians' participation in the historically

Italian *festa* of Our Lady of Mount Carmel. Evidently, the Haitians accept the Italians' domination of the annual event because it provides them with the opportunity to experience their own mixed Vodou and Catholic spirituality in New York when it is impractical or dangerous to return to the island. For their part, the Italians seem pleased to have a massive constituency for the rite when their own people have long ago left the parish for the suburbs. This symbiosis may be a way for each group to avoid contact with another perceived as being too close for comfort—the Puerto Ricans who moved into what had been the Italians' parish and the African Americans who are the Haitians' neighbors in Brooklyn. In the end, like the Guatemalans in Los Angeles, the Haitians in New York succeed in being Catholic on their own terms.

The proximal host may not be a religious group at all, but one that competes with religious, national, and other identities. Thus, Mexican-origin youth in California encounter an American population of "Chicanos," whose own ancestors immigrated two, three, or four generations ago, and sometimes disparage the newcomers' old-country religiosity. This or similar encounters may occur on the streets or in school, and the terms of the engagement differ between southern California, south Texas, and Chicago. For some youth, it may be first through university courses in Chicano studies that they discover this secular ethnic identity. Similarly, children of Korean, Japanese, Chinese, and Filipino immigrants are courted by pan-Asian hosts. Karen J. Chai writes in Chapter 9 about competition for the loyalties of Korean American students between campus-based Korean religious and cultural organizations in New England. Some of those students come to perceive that the Protestant churches that monopolized the organizational field for their parents are not the only place where they, the second generation, can express their simultaneous Korean and American identities.

Adaptations in Religious Organizational Form

To say that religion is salient for immigrants as, among other things, an instrument of cultural conservation, is not to say that their religion is preserved pristinely, without change. Indeed, the opposite is more nearly the case. Because religion is so important to an immigrant group, and because the group's circumstances have been changed so drastically by the migration, the religion must take on new forms to be capable of survival in the new land. Speaking particularly of previous immigrant groups' experience, historian Timothy Smith (1978,

1178) writes that "immigrant congregations . . . were not transplants of traditional institutions but communities of commitment and, therefore, arenas of change. Often founded by lay persons and always dependent on voluntary support, their structures, leadership, and liturgy had to be shaped to meet pressing human needs." On a visit in 1994 to a meeting of a group of Malayalee Hindus, Prema Kurien and I were told by one of its leaders that the way they met—periodically, in homes, inducting the children into the rituals by intentional instruction in English—was "an experiment" intended to ensure the future of their religion in the strange land of southern California. This man was explicit about a phenomenon more often suppressed in consciousness or deplored in conversation than so openly acknowledged.

The most characteristic adaptation I expect to encounter among immigrant religious groups is the development of congregational forms (Warner 1994), using "congregation" now in a stronger sense than we did in defining the project. Using "congregation" in a minimal sense, the project welcomed studies of local, face-to-face religious assemblies. But "congregation" also has a particular meaning within the world of American religious organizations. Among American Protestants and Jews the "congregation" is a local religious body *constituted by the group itself* rather than by administrative or geographic definition, which is what "parishes" are. "Congregational" organization is one of three types of "church polity," or governance structure, which places human authority in the hands of the local body rather than in the hands of bishops ("episcopal" polity) or regional groups of elders ("presbyterian" polity). As such, congregational polity is the historic norm among dissenting Protestants, above all the Baptists. The congregation is a local *voluntary religious association,* usually culturally homogeneous and often legally constituted as a nonprofit corporation controlled by its laity and administered by professional clergy. The organizational history of European American religion includes the assimilation of congregational forms by other bodies, de jure by Jews and de facto (I claim) by Presbyterians and even Catholics (Warner 1994, 73–82).

Studies of new immigrant communities that were available when our work began provided evidence that congregationalism was developing among some of them: Korean American Presbyterians (Warner 1994, 76–77), Japanese American and Korean American Buddhists (Kashima 1977, Yu 1988), Canadian and American Muslims (Waugh 1994; Denny 1987, 113; Haddad and Lummis 1987, 54–59), and Hindus in Chicago, Houston, and Atlanta (Williams 1988, Fenton 1988). Although these groups seemed to be adopting an organizational form typical of the host country, the reasons for the change had less to do with their assimilation to American culture than their discovery that congregationalism suited their circumstances. Thus, on surveying Asian Indian religious communities in Atlanta, John Fenton (1988, 179) observed that

> *in America, Hindu temples tend to become like other American voluntary associations, and in time they will begin to resemble American synagogues and churches. . . . Lay leadership is strong in Hindu temples as it is in Protestant churches and as in American religious organizations generally. Financing is broad-based, and major donors receive public recognition by having their names displayed on plaques. Governance tends to be broad-based also. Cultural halls encourage nonreligious activities, as in ethnic churches and synagogues. Priests perform a variety of functions not normal in India—junketing around the country to perform weddings, to do pujas, to teach children's schools, and so forth.*

In the country of origin, the center of religious activity, be it a temple, a mosque, or a church, may well have existed from time out of mind, originally established by a prince or prominent family, supported thereafter by a landed endowment, government subvention, or some other means. There are many organizational patterns, but most differ from that in the United States, where, upon immigrants' arrival, there may be no suitable place of worship at all within a reasonable distance, or, if there is one nearby (as there is for most Christian immigrants), the language spoken or the ritual practiced is likely to be alienating. Mindful of this experience, many U.S. denominations attempt to open themselves to the new ways that immigrants bring. Yet frequently the immigrant community finds it necessary to organize their own religious center, and the fund-raising effort often leads to the establishment, sooner or later in law, of a board of directors, usually the most reliable contributors of time and money. Another pattern is the founding of a congregation by someone who feels called to ministry and succeeds in gathering a group around himself (occasionally herself), in a case of religious entrepreneurship (Warner 1993b, 1081).

Whereas the chapters in Part IV focus on the internal dynamics of Asian Christian groups organized into more or less conventional congregations, those in Part III narrate processes of innovation whereby congregational forms are adopted by Chicano Pentecostals in Los Angeles and Rastafarians and Muslims in New York, through the efforts of people I call entrepreneurs. Asento Foxe, the "Rasta pioneer" whose

story is told by Randal L. Hepner (Chapter 6), formed social movement organizations in several countries before settling in New York to
found what is, for all its ideological strangeness, a remarkably familiar
congregation. The youthful Jesus Figueroa, whom Luís León saw taking over the helm of Alcance Victoria in East Los Angeles, was one
of the newer recruits to a religious organization that might have been
modeled on Amway or Mary Kay Cosmetics (Biggart 1989). A product
is sold—in this case salvation from life on the street—to a group from
whom the next generation of salespeople will themselves be recruited.

The founding of the New York mosque studied by Rogaia Mustafa
Abusharaf (Chapter 7) might better be thought of as a case of noblesse
oblige, a public offering made by a man of wealth sixty years ago to
a nascent Muslim community. Once the community was constituted,
it could and over time did develop congregational forms consistent
with the culture of a newly dominant ethnic group, in this case Yemenis. In a further convergence toward congregational forms, the mosque
now employs a professional imam. Although he leads the group in
prayer, he is not their organizational leader but instead serves at the
pleasure of a board of directors.

Not all of the case studies in this book center on congregations in
the strong sense. The Mayan Catholics and Malayalee Hindus were
accustomed to church- or temple-centered rites in their home countries,
and their home-based gatherings in southern California, as creative
and well attended as they are, do not yet appear to have sacred sanction. Neither the Haitians' involvement in the saint's day nor the association of Iranian Jews, as meaningful as they are to their participants, is a body autonomously organized for worship. But these
studies, respectively, by Nancy Wellmeier, Prema Kurien, Elizabeth
McAlister, and Shoshanah Feher, are sociology "from the bottom up,"
written from the point of view of people coming together of their own
volition for their own purposes, including religious. As such, the chapters add to our knowledge of the role of religion in immigrants' lives.

Internal Differentiation in Congregations

When a group does organize itself for worship (or any other purpose,
for that matter), it also creates a space for the play of social dynamics,
where questions of interest to sociologists as well as to participants—
Who runs the show? Who defines the agenda? Who gets the benefits?
Who does the work?—can be addressed. In some fashion or other, all
our studies ask questions like these, but those in Part IV, all written
by observing participants, are particularly focused on the sociological

perennials of differences within the group according to gender, generation, and immigration cohort.

In the introduction to the project that was sent to applicants, I stated an expectation, based on the available literature, that gender relations would likely be renegotiated in U.S. congregations. Here is what I wrote then:

> We might hypothesize that religious institutions will be salient for women precisely to the extent that men in the immigrant community attempt to uphold "traditional," sheltered roles for women, for under those circumstances the religious association may be one of the few opportunities women have to venture outside the home and thus to meet one another (Warner 1993a, 13).

Thus, I expected that women would be found to assume roles in these immigrant congregations that would not have been available to them in the home country.

The chapters below provide a few instances of such dynamics. Women members of the Church of Haile Sellasie I in New York have rejected the label "Rastawomen" in favor of "Daughters of Zion" and have turned the focus of their religion toward family matters. In southern California, Hindu women lead the *bhajan* singing and freely contribute to the *bala vihar* religious instruction of the children. Yet the essays contain more instances of the active exclusion of women and girls from religious life. According to Abusharaf, Yemenis, the ethnic group newly dominant in Brooklyn's "Islamic Mission," have withdrawn the welcome previously offered to women in this sixty-year-old mosque. Among the Santa Eulalia Mayans in Los Angeles, women, including anthropologist Wellmeier, are not allowed to play the marimba that is so central to the religious and cultural life of the community. Indeed, it would seem that women are disfranchised or silenced in many of the congregations portrayed here. To hear the women's thoughts, one would need to leave the church and accompany them to their own preserves, their kitchens, nurseries, and places of work. According to McAlister, Haitian women's religious visibility is part of the Vodou culture they bring with them to New York rather than an adaptation to the setting in the United States.

One clue to the persistence, indeed the enhancement, of patriarchy in immigrant congregations is provided by Sheba George's study of gender struggles in an Indian Orthodox congregation (Chapter 8). George, herself the daughter of an immigrant family from Kerala,

India, found that the busy, educated, and well-employed women of her mother's generation deliberately sat on the sideline, relative to their husbands, in the affairs of the church. For the men, the church offered an arena to reclaim the honor they were deprived of by the immigrant experience, coming to the United States to find what work they could years after their wives had established themselves here as nurses. Studies of Korean immigrant churches (Shin and Park 1988, Hurh and Kim 1990) had earlier suggested this dynamic, and a pioneering study of immigrant mosques observed that "in some cases the mosque may be the only avenue available for positions of leadership in society" (Haddad and Lummis 1987, 38). For such reasons, the renegotiation of gender in immigrant congregations, at least in the short run, may be to the advantage of men.

A prime motivation for immigrants to found religious organizations is to pass on their heritage to their children. Thus, Williams (1988, 287) writes, "religious organizations are usually formed at the time when the children of immigrants reach the point of significant socialization outside the home. That is not a sufficient cause, but it is the major cause." Kurien's interviews with Hindu Malayalees and Feher's with Iranian Jews testify to this motivation. Yet just as the church grows up so also do the children, and often the very religious institutions that are intended to serve the presumed cultural needs of youth instead alienate them. For the first generation, the immigrant congregation is a home away from home, a remembrance of Zion in the midst of Babylon, but precisely because of this, the congregation can feel oppressive to an inevitably Americanizing second generation. Ever since Niebuhr's study, it has been clear that, at a minimum, the transition to English presented a crisis.

In 1990, I was invited as an outside speaker to a conference of Korean-American educators and religious leaders, where they voiced their concern that their children were leaving the church (see Pai et al. 1987; Warner 1990), and over the years I have spoken with second-generation students at the University of Illinois at Chicago who were happy to be away at college and no longer required to attend their "mother's church." Thus, I have looked forward to studies of generational transitions.

Such studies are rare. The first priority in the study of immigrant congregations must be scholars' engagement with the immigrant/host society cultural difference. Yet difference, at least as the first generation wishes to define it, is often what second-generation youth seek to escape (Cha 1996). Thus some of the intellectual challenge of and political urgency for the engagement with difference may seem compromised by a focus on the second generation, and it is surely no coincidence that the three chapters in this book paying significant attention to the second generation are the work of the three fellows (Karen J. Chai [Chapter 9], George, and León) who grew up in the immigrant and ethnic religious worlds they decided to study.

Chai's chapter stands out as a rich and well-grounded study of a flourishing second-generation Korean American congregation. One factor in its success is its effective autonomy from its parent congregation, which in turn is attributable to the fact that the second-generation members of the church are largely not the children of the first generation but grown-up college students who come on their own. Chai's church provides an instructive contrast to George's, which is unlikely to manage the generational transition unless it learns how to welcome youth initiative.

A third axis of internal difference is what sociologists call immigration "cohort." In the cases of Japanese Buddhists in Canada (Mullins 1987, 1988) and Iranian Jews in Los Angeles (Feher, Chapter 2), the people came to the United States all at once, as it were, and they and their children suffer misunderstanding and undergo acculturation as a cohort. More typically, pioneer immigrants of one generation are joined years and decades later by flows of new immigrants. Sometimes matters are complicated by the fact that newer arrivals are also new converts to the religion, as is the case among many Chicano Pentecostals.

On the one hand, continuing immigration (and conversion) help maintain the vitality of ethnic and immigrant congregations. On the other hand, newcomers and forerunners may feel alienated from and threatened by each other, as happened with American Jews a century ago when an earlier German community confronted a later Russian and Polish one. Speaking of Muslim institutions in the United States today, Gutbi Mahdi Ahmed (1991, 22) writes that "whenever the second Muslim generation assumed the leadership and it seemed possible for Muslims to be integrated into American society, a new wave of fresh immigrants overtook the older wave. The Islamic presence was again a foreign presence of first-generation immigrant Muslims." Today, newly arrived Muslims are frequently critical of "innovations" adopted by earlier generations, and Abusharaf was surprised by the conservative regime of Yemeni immigrants at the mosque in Brooklyn where some of her fellow Sudanese had comfortably prayed for years.

But the conflict is not always between conservative newcomers and liberalized forerunners. In some cases, particularly among refugees, a conception of tradition may be more rigidly adhered to in the United States than in a home country undergoing rapid change.

In his essay, Yang analyzes the astounding internal heterogeneity of a Chinese Protestant church, whose members represent the complexity of the Chinese diaspora—Chinese and their descendants who left different regions of their homeland for indentured servitude in North America and Southeast Asia a century ago, for refuge in Taiwan and Hong Kong after the 1949 revolution, and to the United States for high-tech jobs today. Yang's church (he was himself a member) is the setting for struggles among such diverse people, many of them new converts to Christianity, who bring with them into the church different primary languages, different places or origins, different politics, different denominational backgrounds, and different agendas corresponding to those identities. Yang traces the "tenacious unity" they maintain in the face of these differences to the Chinese and Christian identities that they have in common.

The chapters below are the fruit of work proposed by the authors in response to the invitation from the New Ethnic and Immigrant Congregations Project. On the basis of these proposals, the authors were chosen as NEICP fellows by an advisory committee I appointed. Some of the authors disagree with my own emphasis on the continuity of immigrant experience over the past century. Some, anthropologically inclined, spend more time on culture and less on organization than I would as a sociologist. However, we all agree primarily that books of this sort are long overdue. Each of the chapters represents its author's own sense of pertinent issues and research priorities regarding the community she or he studied. I have had the first word; now, the authors will speak for themselves.

These studies begin what I hope will grow into a library of literature. Much more needs to be done. We need especially to put congregations like these into the context of other associations and other countries, looking, for example, at the effects on them of events abroad and the reverse, such as the role of American congregations in sending missionaries to Mexico and China and remittances to Guatemala and India. In her conclusion, Judith Wittner sets out other agenda items for further study. This book is only a start, but I hope it will draw attention to the enormous, unwisely neglected, and increasingly diverse world of religious communities in the United States.

ACKNOWLEDGMENTS

Thanks to Paul Numrich for advice, Elise Martel for research assistance, and Michael Ames, James Hall, Anne Heider, Elizabeth McAlister, and Judith Wittner for comments on a previous draft.

NOTES

1. The communities studied in this book are defined with reference to the United States and the respective home country. Due to a complex of cultural and legal factors, religious patterns elsewhere in North America, whether Canada or Mexico, are sufficiently different from those in the United States to require their own extended treatment. "America" will be used sparingly as a synonym for the United States, and, for necessary stylistic convenience, "American" will refer to things and persons pertaining to the United States.

2. The estimate for Catholic parishes is based on a survey conducted by the Office of Hispanic Affairs, U.S. Catholic Conference, and was provided in private correspondence (April 16, 1997) by Professor by Dean Hoge of the Catholic University of America. The estimate for Hispanic Protestant congregations is found in Tapía 1995, and it is credible for reasons I articulate elsewhere (Warner 1994, p. 90, note 13). The count of Korean churches is found in Lee and Moore 1993 (pp. 285–286), and that of Chinese churches is reported in Yang 1996 (p. 79). The counts of mosques were done by projects under the directorships of Ihsan Bagby (Bagby 1994) and Diana Eck (Ostling 1993, Eck 1996, 1997); those of Buddhist centers and Hindu temples are reported in Ostling 1993.

3. Puerto Ricans, whose homeland was acquired from Spain by the United States in the war of 1898, have been American citizens since 1917, free to come and go from the island to the mainland, and therefore legally are not immigrants, but they were included in our "new ethnic and immigrant" category. "Because the island language and culture are foreign to most of the mainland, migration involves a cultural transition differing little from that experienced by immigrants coming from Europe or Asia" (Fitzpatrick 1980, 858).

4. As our citations to the literature will attest, the neglect is not total, and some pioneering researchers should be acknowledged, especially Raymond Brady Williams, Yvonne Yazbeck Haddad, John Y. Fenton, Frederick Denny, Won Moo Hurh and Kwang Chung Kim, Pyong Gap Min, Mark R. Mullins, and Anthony M. Stevens-Arroyo and his associates.

5. Aside from abolishing origin quotas, the 1965 revision of immigration law made special provision for immigration under two circumstances, "family reunification," and "occupational preference." It was assumed that family reunification would serve primarily to replicate the racial-ethnic composition of the U.S. population, whereas the occupational preference provision (welcoming members of the professions of exceptional ability and workers in occupations in which laborers were in short supply) would strengthen the U.S.

labor force. Yet over time, relatives of immigrants admitted under the occupational preference provisions have been admitted under the family reunification provisions.

6. The massive survey conducted by Barry A. Kosmin and Seymour P. Lachman (1993) attempted to overcome these problems by contacting 113,000 households through random-digit dialing. Yet inhibitions about revealing one's religion to a stranger on the telephone probably led to an underestimation of Muslims, among other groups. In addition, not all cultures regard religious identities as mutually exclusive in the manner presupposed by both Christian denominations and standard survey questions (see Stevens-Arroyo and Cadena 1995, Lin 1996). Elizabeth McAlister's chapter in this volume (Chapter 4) explains in detail why it would be misleading to present Haitian respondents with a survey question asking whether their religion was Protestant, Catholic, *or* Vodou.

7. Welcome exceptions to these generalizations are increasing (see, for example, Goizueta 1995, Yoo 1996). Meanwhile, the work of Williams (1988), Paul David Numrich (1996), Samuel G. Freedman (1993), among many others, refutes the notion that one must be an ethnic insider to study religious communities.

8. Roberto Goizueta (1995, p. 52) clarifies the situation in his interpretation of U.S. Hispanic religiosity as communal and popular but not anti-institutional: "Despite their tendency to ossification and corruption, institutions, like the family or church, are essentially structures which perpetuate a community, its identity, and values over time. . . . Institutions are in constant need of criticism, reformation, and transformation, but they are, at least, a necessary evil; they are by definition an extension of community, a 'patterned way of living together' not only here and now but through time."

9. Proposals were read by the NEICP advisory committee, whose members, in addition to Wittner and me, were David Badillo (Latin American Studies), Richard Barrett (Sociology), Xiangming Chen (Sociology), Kathleen Crittenden (Sociology), Luin Goldring (Latin American Studies and Sociology), James Hall (African American Studies and English), Lansiné Kaba (African American Studies and History), Lowell Livezey (Office of Social Science Research), A. G. Roeber (History), and Sylvia Vatuk (Anthropology), all of whom were members of the University of Illinois at Chicago faculty at the time, and Assad Busool (American Islamic College) and Hearn Chun (McCormick Theological Seminary). In addition to the 10 authors represented in this book, Susana L. Gallardo (Religious Studies) and Keng-Fong Pang (Anthropology) were appointed NEICP fellows, and Haider Bhuiyan (Religious Studies) and Brian Steensland (Sociology) participated as "summer fellows" in the 1994 training institute, which therefore had a roster of 14 fellows.

10. We are indebted to Ana-María Díaz-Stevens, Lawrence Mamiya, Pyong Gap Min, and Mary Waters for serving as discussants at the 1996 conference. Two papers presented there—"Who Are the Chams? Maintaining

Dual Congregations as an Adaptive Strategy in Cultural Identity Management Among Vietnamese/Cambodian Refugee Muslims in America," by Keng-Fong Pang, and "'Sal Si Puedes': Reform and Resistance in a Chicano Catholic Parish," by Susana Gallardo—were not made ready for this volume.

REFERENCES

Ahmed, Gutbi Mahdi. 1991. "Muslim Organizations in the United States." Pp. 11–24 in *The Muslims of America,* edited by Yvonne Yazbeck Haddad. New York: Oxford University Press.

Alexy, Trudi. 1993. *The Mezuzah in the Madonna's Foot.* New York: Simon and Schuster.

Ammerman, Nancy. 1987. *Bible Believers: Fundamentalists in the Modern World.* New Brunswick, N.J.: Rutgers University Press.

Bagby, Ihsan. 1994. *Directory of Masjids and Muslim Organizations of North America, 1994/1415.* Fountain Valley, Calif.: Islamic Resource Institute.

Balmer, Randall. 1993. *Mine Eyes Have Seen the Glory: A Journey into the Evangelical Subculture in America.* 2nd ed. New York: Oxford University Press.

Bankston, Carl L., III, and Min Zhou. 1996. "The Ethnic Church, Ethnic Identification, and and the Social Adjustment of Vietnamese Adolescents." *Review of Religious Research* 38 (September): 18–37.

Basch, Linda, Nina Glick Schiller, and Cristina Szanton Blanc. 1994. *Nations Unbound: Transnational Projects, Postcolonial Predicaments, and Deterritorialized Nation-States.* Langhorne, Pa.: Gordon and Breach.

Biggart, Nicole Woolsey. 1989. *Charismatic Capitalism: Direct Selling Organizations in America.* Chicago: University of Chicago Press.

Booth, Newell S., Jr. 1988. "Islam in North America." Pp. 723–729 in *Encyclopedia of the American Religious Experience: Studies of Traditions and Movements,* vol. 2, edited by Charles H. Lippy and Peter W. Williams. New York: Scribner's.

Bozorgmehr, Mehdi, Claudia Der-Martirosian, and Georges Sabagh. 1996. "Middle Easterners: A New Kind of Immigrant." Pp. 345–378 in *Ethnic Los Angeles,* edited by Roger Waldinger and Mehdi Bozorgmehr. New York: Russell Sage Foundation.

Brackenridge, R. Douglas, and Francisco O. García-Treto. 1974. *Iglesia Presbiteriana: A History of Presbyterians and Mexican Americans in the Southwest.* San Antonio: Trinity University Press.

Burns, Jeffrey M. 1994. "¿Qué es esto? The Transformation of St. Peter's Parish, San Francisco, 1913–1990." Pp. 396–463 in *American Congregations,* vol. 1, *Portraits of Twelve Religious Communities,* edited by James Lewis and James Wind. Chicago: University of Chicago Press.

Cha, Peter T. 1996. "Ethnic Identity and Participation in Immigrant Churches:

Second Generation Korean-American Experiences." Paper presented at the Sixth North Park College Korean Symposium, Chicago, October 12.

Chiswick, Barry R., and Teresa A. Sullivan. 1995. "The New Immigrants." Pp. 211–270 in *State of the Union: America in the 1990s,* vol. 2, *Social Trends,* edited by Reynolds Farley. New York: Russell Sage Foundation.

Christiano, Kevin J. 1991. "The Church and the New Immigrants." Pp. 169–186 in *Vatican II and U.S. Catholicism: Twenty-Five Years Later,* edited by Helen Rose Ebaugh. Greenwich, Conn.: JAI Press.

Davidman, Lynn. 1991. *Tradition in a Rootless World: Women Turn to Orthodox Judaism.* Berkeley and Los Angeles: University of California Press.

Denny, Frederick. 1987. *Islam and the Muslim Community.* San Francisco: Harper and Row.

Díaz-Stevens, Ana-María. 1993. *Oxcart Catholicism on Fifth Avenue: The Impact of the Puerto Rican Migration upon the Archdiocese of New York.* Notre Dame, Ind.: Notre Dame University Press.

Dolan, Jay P. 1985. *The American Catholic Experience: A History from Colonial Times to the Present.* Garden City, N.Y.: Doubleday.

Dolan, Jay P., and Allan Figueroa Deck, S. J., eds. 1994. *Hispanic Catholic Culture in the U.S.: Issues and Concerns.* Notre Dame, Ind.: University of Notre Dame Press.

Eck, Diana. 1996. "Neighboring Faiths: How Will Americans Cope with Increasing Religious Diversity?" *Harvard Magazine* 99 (September–October): 38–44.

———. 1997. *On Common Ground: World Religions in America.* New York: Columbia University Press.

Fenton, John Y. 1988. *Transplanting Religious Traditions: Asian Indians in America.* New York: Praeger.

Fields, Rick. 1992. *How the Swans Came to the Lake: A Narrative History of Buddhism in America.* 3rd ed. Boston: Shambhala.

Fitzpatrick, Joseph P. 1980. "Puerto Ricans." Pp. 858–867 in *Harvard Encyclopedia of American Ethnic Groups,* edited by Stephan Thernstrom. Cambridge: Harvard University Press.

Freedman, Samuel G. 1993. *Upon This Rock: The Miracles of a Black Church.* New York: Harper Collins.

Gilkes, Cheryl Townsend. 1985. "'Together and in Harness': Women's Traditions in the Sanctified Church." *Signs* 10 (Summer): 678–699.

Goizueta, Roberto S. 1995. *Caminemos con Jesús: Toward a Hispanic/Latino Theology of Accompaniment.* Maryknoll, N.Y.: Orbis Books.

Gold, Steven J. 1992. *Refugee Communities: A Comparative Field Study.* Newbury Park, Calif.: Sage.

Haddad, Yvonne Yazbeck, and Adair T. Lummis. 1987. *Islamic Values in the United States: A Comparative Study.* New York: Oxford University Press.

Heer, David. 1996. *Immigration in America's Future: Social Science Findings and the Policy Debate.* Boulder, Colo.: Westview Press.

Heilman, Samuel C. 1976. *Synagogue Life: A Study in Symbolic Interaction.* Chicago: University of Chicago Press.

Herberg, Will. 1960. *Protestant, Catholic, Jew: An Essay in American Religious Sociology.* 2nd ed. Garden City, N.Y.: Doubleday.

Higginbotham, Evelyn Brooks. 1993. *Righteous Discontent: The Women's Movement in the Black Baptist Church, 1880-1920.* Cambridge: Harvard University Press.

Hollinger, David A. 1995. *Postethnic America: Beyond Multiculturalism.* New York: Basic Books.

Hurh, Won Moo, and Kwang Chung Kim. 1990. "Religious Participation of Korean Immigrants in the United States." *Journal for the Scientific Study of Religion* 29 (March): 19-34.

Kashima, Tetsuden. 1977. *Buddhism in America: The Social Organization of an Ethnic Religious Institution.* Westport, Conn.: Greenwood Press.

Kivisto, Peter A. 1992. "Religion and the New Immigrants." Pp. 92-107 in *A Future for Religion? New Paradigms for Social Analysis,* edited by William H. Swatos, Jr. Newbury Park, Calif.: Sage.

Kosmin, Barry A., and Seymour P. Lachman. 1993. *One Nation Under God: Religion in Contemporary American Society.* New York: Harmony Books.

Lee, Sang Hyun, and John V. Moore. 1993. *Korean American Ministry: A Resource Book.* Expanded ed. Louisville, Ky.: Presbyterian Church (U.S.A.).

Leonard, Karen. 1992. *Making Ethnic Choices: California's Punjabi Mexican-Americans.* Philadelphia: Temple University Press.

Leong, Russell. 1996. "Racial Spirits: Between Bullets, Barbed Wire, and Belief." *Amerasia Journal* 22 (Spring): vii-xi.

Lin, Irene. 1996. "Journey to the Far West: Chinese Buddhism in America." *Amerasia Journal* 22 (Spring): 106-132.

Lopez, David E., Eric Popkin, and Edward Telles. 1996. "Central Americans: At the Bottom, Struggling to Get Ahead." Pp. 279-304 in *Ethnic Los Angeles,* edited by Roger Waldinger and Mehdi Bozorgmehr. New York: Russell Sage Foundation.

Melendy, H. Brett. 1980. "Filipinos." Pp. 354-362 in *Harvard Encyclopedia of American Ethnic Groups,* edited by Stephan Thernstrom. Cambridge: Harvard University Press.

Min, Pyong Gap. 1992. "The Structure and Social Functions of Korean Immigrant Churches in the United States." *International Migration Review* 26 (4): 1370-1394.

Mittelberg, David, and Mary C. Waters. 1992. "The Process of Ethnogenesis Among Haitian and Israeli Immigrants in the United States." *Ethnic and Racial Studies* 15 (July): 412-435.

Mullins, Mark R. 1987. "The Life-Cycle of Ethnic Churches in Sociological Perspective." *Japanese Journal of Religious Studies* 14 (4): 321-334.

———. 1988. "The Organizational Dilemmas of Ethnic Churches: A Case Study of Japanese Buddhism in Canada." *Sociological Analysis* 49 (Fall): 217-233

Nagel, Joane. 1994. "Constructing Ethnicity: Creating and Re-creating Ethnic Identity and Culture." *Social Problems* 41 (February): 152–176.

Niebuhr, H. Richard. 1929. *The Social Sources of Denominationalism.* New York: Henry Holt.

Numrich, Paul David. 1996. *Old Wisdom in the New World: Americanization in Two Immigrant Theravada Buddhist Temples.* Knoxville: University of Tennessee Press.

Omi, Michael, and Howard Winant. 1994. *Racial Formation in the United States, from 1960 to 1980.* 2nd ed. New York: Routledge.

Orsi, Robert Anthony. 1985. *The Madonna of 115th Street: Faith and Community in Italian Harlem, 1880–1950.* New Haven: Yale University Press.

Ostling, Richard. 1993. "One Nation Under God: Not Without Conflict, An Unprecedented Variety of Faiths Blooms Across the Land." *Time* 142 (special issue, Fall): 62–63.

Pai, Young, Deloras Pemberton, and John Worley. 1987. *Findings on Korean-American Early Adolescents and Adolescents.* Kansas City: University of Missouri School of Education.

Portes, Alejandro, and Rubén G. Rumbaut. 1996. *Immigrant America: A Portrait.* 2nd ed. Berkeley and Los Angeles: University of California Press.

Rumbaut, Rubén G., and Wayne A. Cornelius, eds. 1995. *California's Immigrant Children: Theory, Research, and Implications for Educational Policy.* San Diego: Center for U.S.–Mexican Studies, University of California.

San Buenaventura, Steffi. 1996. "Filipino Folk Spirtuality and Immigration: From Mutual Aid to Religion." *Amerasia Journal* 22 (Spring): 1–30.

Schiller, Nina Glick, Linda Basch, and Cristina Blanc-Szanton, eds. 1992. *Towards a Transnational Perpective on Migration: Race, Class, Ethnicity, and Nationalism Reconsidered.* Annals of the New York Academy of Sciences, vol. 645. New York: New York Academy of Sciences.

Schreiter, Robert J. 1985. *Constructing Local Theologies.* Marynoll, N.Y.: Orbis Books.

Shin, Eui Hang, and Hyung Park. 1988. "An Analysis of Causes of Schisms in Ethnic Churches: The Case of Korean-American Churches." *Sociological Analysis* 49 (Fall): 234–248.

Smith, Timothy L. 1978. "Religion and Ethnicity in America." *American Historical Review* 83 (December): 1155–1185.

Stevens-Arroyo, Anthony M., and Gilbert R. Cadena. 1995. *Old Masks, New Faces: Religion and Latino Identities.* New York: Bildner Center of the City University.

Stevens-Arroyo, Anthony M., and Ana-María Díaz-Stevens, eds. 1994. *An Enduring Flame: Studies on Latino Popular Religiosity.* New York: Bildner Center of the City University.

Stevens-Arroyo, Anthony M., and Andres I. Pérez y Mena. 1995. *Enigmatic Powers: Syncretism with African and Indigenous Peoples' Religions Among Latinos.* New York: Bildner Center of the City University.

Tapía, Andrés. 1995. "Growing Pains: Evangelical Latinos Wrestle with the Role of Women, Generational Gaps, and Cultural Divides." *Christianity Today* 39 (February 6): 38–42.

Warner, R. Stephen. 1990. "The Korean Immigrant Church in Comparative Perspective." Paper presented at the colloquium "The Korean Immigrant Church: A Comparative Perspective," Princeton Theological Seminary, February 16–18.

———. 1993a. "Introduction to the New Ethnic and Immigrant Congregations Project." Working Paper, Office of Social Science Research, University of Illinois at Chicago.

———. 1993b. "Work in Progress Toward a New Paradigm for the Sociological Study of Religion in the United States." *American Journal of Sociology* 98 (March): 1044–1093.

———. 1994. "The Place of the Congregation in the American Religious Configuration." Pp. 54–99 in *American Congregations,* vol. 2, *New Perspectives in the Study of Congregations,* edited by James P. Wind and James W. Lewis. Chicago: University of Chicago Press.

———. 1995. "The Metropolitan Community Churches and the Gay Agenda: The Power of Pentecostalism and Essentialism." Pp. 81–108 in *Sex, Lies, and Sanctity: Religion and Deviance in Contemporary North America,* edited by Mary Jo Neitz and Marion S. Goldman. Greenwich, Conn.: JAI Press.

———. forthcoming. "Changes in the Civic Role of Religion." *Common Values, Social Diversity and Cultural Conflict,* edited by Jeffrey C. Alexander and Neil J. Smelser. Princeton: Princeton University Press.

———. in press. "Approaching Religious Diversity: Barriers, Byways, and Beginnings." *Sociology of Religion* 59.

Waugh, Earle H. 1994. "Reducing the Distance: A Muslim Congregation in the Canadian North." Pp. 572–611 in *American Congregations,* vol. 1, *Portraits of Twelve Religious Communities,* edited by James Lewis and James Wind. Chicago: University of Chicago Press.

Williams, Raymond Brady. 1988. *Religions of Immigrants from India and Pakistan: New Threads in the American Tapestry.* Cambridge: Cambridge University Press.

Woldemikael, Teklé Mariam. 1989. *Becoming Black American: Haitians and American Institutions in Evanston, Illinois.* New York: AMS Press.

Yang, Fenggang. 1996. "Religious Conversion and Identity Construction: A Study of a Chinese Christian Church in the United States." Ph.D. dissertation, Catholic University of America.

Yoo, David. 1996. "For Those Who Have Eyes to See: Religious Sightings in Asian America." *Amerasia Journal* 22 (Spring): xiii–xxii.

Yu, Eui-Young. 1988. "The Growth of Korean Buddhism in the United States, with Special Reference to Southern California." *The Pacific World: Journal of the Institute of Buddhist Studies,* n.s. 4 (Fall): 82–93.

I

Religion and the Negotiation of Identities

1 | Becoming American by Becoming Hindu: Indian Americans Take Their Place at the Multicultural Table

Prema Kurien

> As I kept learning [about my heritage and religion], I be-
> came more confident and sure of myself. With a wealth of
> knowledge by my side, I felt strong. . . . I felt a sense of be-
> longing, but not sameness, as though I were an individual
> piece adding color to the complete picture. I could fit in but
> still be different.—Hema Narayan, school essay

Introduction

How to "fit in" but still maintain one's cultural and personal integrity
is the challenge that most immigrants in the United States face in their
transition from immigrants to ethnics. Indian immigrants from a
Hindu background have achieved this end by using Hinduism, albiet
a Hinduism that has been recast and reformulated to make this transition possible. Religion has conventionally defined and sustained ethnic life in this country, and thus while "becoming Hindu" may on the
surface appear to be the antithesis of "becoming American," these
Indian immigrants have made the transition from sojourners to citizens
by developing a Hindu American community and identity. Asserting
pride in their Hindu Indian heritage has also been their way of claiming a position for themselves at the American multicultural table.

This chapter is based on an ethnographic study of two Hindu Indian
religious groups in and around Los Angeles. Their two new forms of
collective religious worship and education represent two different strategies of sustaining Hinduism that Hindus have developed in the United
States. I shall show how such transformations of Hindu practice take
place as Indian immigrants adapt Hinduism to fit the American context.

New Forms of Hindu Practice

Satsang

It is a pleasant Saturday evening. In a suburban area, a row of expensive cars are parked in front of an upper-middle-class house. Shoes and sandals are placed neatly outside on the porch. Inside, the furniture has been cleared from the large living room and sheets spread over the carpet. In the center is a makeshift shrine with pictures of several Hindu deities arranged against the wall. Several of the deities are adorned with fresh flower garlands. Tall brass oil lamps with flickering flames stand on either side of the shrine. Baskets containing fruit and flowers have been placed in front. A man dressed in traditional South Indian clothes is seated on the floor before the shrine, his wife beside him in a silk saree. Around the couple are seated about fifty people, the men and boys in casual Western clothes largely on one side of the room, and the women and girls in rich and colorful Indian clothes on the other. This is the monthly devotional meeting of the Organization of Hindu Malayalees (OHM), a *satsang* (congregation of truth) of Hindu immigrants from the state of Kerala in South India. The states in India have generally been formed on the basis of language, and thus Kerala constitutes a distinct linguistic and cultural unit. Its people are Malayalees, speaking the language Malayalam. The OHM, established in 1991, is a religiocultural organization of around fifty to seventy-five Hindu Malayalee families. Members meet on the second Saturday of the month in different locations (mostly in people's houses) around the region for the *pooja* (worship) and *bhajans* (devotional songs). Around forty to sixty people attend each *pooja*. Since the members are scattered over a wide area, except for the "regulars," it is a changing group that attends each meeting, depending on the locality. The OHM meeting starts with the lay worship leader chanting an invocation (in Sanskrit) to the deities. This is followed by the singing of *bhajans* accompanied by cymbals, played by the leader's wife. The leader of the *bhajan* sings a line, and the rest of the group repeats it. Occasionally, there is a brief lull, and the leader and his wife call for volunteers to start new *bhajans*. Different members of the group, including a teenage girl, take turns leading the singing. Some fifteen to twenty *bhajans* are sung, each lasting around five minutes.

A few months before my fieldwork with the group ended, a Gita discussion period was introduced toward the end of the *pooja,* where two verses from the *Bhagavad Gita* were translated and explained by Mrs. Kala Menon, a university professor, followed by a group discussion (in English). During one such meeting, a member of the group wanted to know why bad things happened to good people, and why people should bother to be good if that was the case. Mrs. Menon's reply was that the bad thing may have been caused by something bad that the person had done in a past incarnation. "Good deeds will be rewarded, if not in this life, then at least in the next," she answered firmly. Two of the teenage girls in the group also became involved in the discussion at this point, one pointing out that the Hindu conception of good and evil is more complicated than the Christian, since "good does not always give place to good." The other elaborated, "Yes, a person may lead a good life and then be rewarded in the next life with a lot of money, but the money may make him arrogant. So he will be punished in the following life."

After the teenagers complained that they felt alienated from the OHM meetings since they were largely Sanskrit-based and adult-oriented, the group has been making special efforts to try to involve them through discussions and youth activities. If the participation in the Gita sessions is any indication, this effort seems to be yielding results.

The two-and-a-half-hour worship concludes with further invocations and devotions by the lay priest and a group chant. A potluck vegetarian South Indian meal follows, during which there is a lot of joking and teasing as people catch up on the month's news. Relatives and jobs are enquired after, clothes and jewelry admired, and recipes and professional information are traded, while those who have recently visited India regale the others with their accounts. Youngsters go off and form their own groups. In the adult clusters, children are discussed in great detail by the parents—their health, educational progress, extracurricular accomplishments, and, in the case of older children, parental concerns about finding appropriate marriage partners for them.

Bala Vihar

On a Sunday afternoon in another suburban South Indian household in the same region, twelve Hindu families with school-age children from Tamil Nadu, another state in South India, get together for their monthly *bala vihar* (child development) meeting, also led by a lay leader, the father of two children in the group. After they sing some familiar *bhajans* and learn a new one, taught by one of the mothers, there is a discussion of Hindu philosophy and values (also in English) and how they can be practiced in everyday life in American society. The first issue discussed is the need for each individual to do his or her allotted tasks, however small, to the best of his or her ability, for the well-being and smooth functioning of society. Children and parents together discuss the problems involved in maintaining the delicate balance between working toward the good of the whole and achieving individual success. One of the young girls gives an example of this tension: "Like, you know, I may want all my friends to get good grades, but my effort is spent in studying to get a good grade for myself." The group nods in agreement. At this point one of the men comes forward to make a further point. He cautions the children that in the work world people are often not given credit for their efforts. "Let me give you an example," he says. "I am a scientist, and a common problem that comes up in my field regards who gets to be first author for publications." He goes on to explain the significance of first authorship and gives examples of unfair decisions. He ends by saying, "So you should also be aware of your rights and fight for them."

The leader then discusses how to deal with disappointment when results fall below one's expectations despite hard work. Here his point is that the children should do their very best and then accept whatever they get as a result of their work, "even" if it is a B grade. "Don't care too much about the grade as such," he says. "But how can you not care about grades?" one young girl bursts out. Another teenager tries to explain to her, "Yes, you work really hard but a B somewhere in your transcript prevents you from getting into Harvard, and you feel really bad. But sometime later you may realize that the place you did get into was better for you than Harvard." One of the women adds, "Not getting the end that you think you deserve is very hard. I used to get very depressed when that happened to me and still do sometimes, but over time I have tried to cultivate a certain detachment. You should try to recognize that your effort is the only thing that you have control over, so do your very best but then stop thinking about it, go out and have a good time to rejuvenate yourself"—she pauses and then explains—"for the next big effort." There is laughter at this. She continues, "But the effect of this attempt to better yourself is that it results in an expanding sphere of influence. Take Gandhi for instance. He was at first only trying to better himself, but soon that started affecting others, and finally it resulted in his having a major effect on the whole world."

After a snack break, the group divides into two for the Tamil language class. The junior class focuses on vocabulary, while the senior class is taught to appreciate the beauty of classical devotional Tamil poetry. The group reconvenes in the living room for the story session led by yet another woman. The stories are taken from the Hindu epics.

Here again the moral of each story is expounded and discussed. One of the day's stories had a message about the sanctity of marriage and family, and the evils of extramarital sex. Particular Hindu practices deriving from the stories are explained, and the children are encouraged to follow them since they have been "time tested over thousands of years." The eagerly awaited crossword puzzle of the month is given out next. The puzzle has questions about Hinduism, Tamil vocabulary, and the history, geography, and culture of India. The three-and-a-half hour *bala vihar* concludes with the "host family time," when a child of that family makes a presentation to the group. This month the teenage daughter shows a video of the family's trip to South India, during which they made a pilgrimage to several temples that ended with their family temple. She gives an emotional account of the trip and its meaning for her, ending with a beautiful *bhajan* that she said was the favorite of the deity in their family temple. Several in the group are visibly moved. Finally, there is a lavish potluck meal to end the gathering.

Satsang groups and *bala vihars* have proliferated among the immigrant Indian community in the United States. They represent two different strategies adopted by Indian immigrants to re-create a Hindu Indian environment on foreign soil. The first, which largely targets adults, celebrates and reenacts religious practice. The second is directed at teaching the children about the religion.[1] Both options come with their own problems. In the first case, many of the children in the OHM have expressed dissatisfaction with not being meaningfully included in the organization. Again, having a dedicated core of members willing to take on the extra responsibilities of being the planners and organizers is crucial for the survival of groups such as the OHM. *Bala vihars* are even more difficult to organize and sustain since they involve a heavy investment of time and energy by both adults and children. As a much smaller group (compared to a *satsang*), the *bala vihar* depends on members making the commitment to attend most of the monthly meetings. Besides cooking for the dinners and making sure that the children attend regularly and do their homework, parents also have to be willing to share in the responsibility of planning and running the various classes. Many *bala vihars* disband after a few months or years, when the adults and children in the group get too busy. Even if the group is successful in sustaining the *bala vihar* over a long period (as this Tamil group did), they have to deal with the constant attrition of college-bound children and their parents. These are just some of the dilemmas Indian immigrants face in their attempts to institutionalize Hinduism in the United States.

In this process of institutionalization, however, Hinduism is also "reinvented." Both *satsangs* and *bala vihars* are forms of religious practice that do not typically exist in India. In fact, group religious activity does not exist in "traditional" Hinduism.[2] In India, Hindus worship largely as families or as individuals, in their homes or a temple. Larger groups at the temple may be present to witness the *pooja* performed by the priest on behalf of the community. Only festivals are celebrated communally by a village. At temple festivals, groups of devotees might sing songs, and individuals take turns to be part of the group so that the singing can be continued uninterrupted for the whole period. As an Indian woman I spoke to mentioned, "I grew up in India, I consider myself a good Hindu, but I'd never heard of many of these things [the *satsangs, bala vihars,* and Hindu youth camps] until I came here."

Religious innovations have frequently taken place among American immigrants. To quote Timothy Smith's (1978, 1178) classic statement regarding religion and ethnicity in America, "Immigrant congregations . . . [are] not transplants of traditional institutions but communities of commitment and, therefore, arenas of change. Often founded by lay persons and always dependent on voluntary support, their structures, leadership and liturgy . . . [have] to be shaped to meet pressing human needs". He continues: "Pastors, rabbis, and lay officers respond . . . to this challenge to make religion more personal by reinterpreting scriptures and creeds to allow ancient observances to serve new purposes." What these "pressing human needs" are for Indian immigrants and how the OHM and the Tamil *bala vihar* shape and reinterpret Hinduism to fit the American context will be the subject of the next two sections.

Indian Immigrants in the United States

The 1990 U.S. Census reported over eight hundred thousand people of Indian origin in the country,[3] of whom around 65 percent probably came from a Hindu background (Fenton 1988, 28). Having arrived largely in the wake of the 1965 immigration act, Indians are a fairly recent ethnic group in the United States. It is common now to talk about two waves of post-1965 Indian migration. Since there were very few people of Indian origin residing in the country before the act, most of the first wave of immigrants came under the "special skills" provision of the law, and thus were highly educated people who entered professional or managerial careers. Once here, however, they sponsored the immigration of relatives under the family reunification aspect of the 1965 act, and thus the second wave of immigrants, coming since the early 1980s, often do not have the same educational or professional status as the first wave. Socially, too, their experiences are different, since they come to join relatives and an already established ethnic community.

The first-wave immigrants came in search of better economic prospects and often planned only a temporary stay. Thus, in the early years, they were generally preoccupied with building their careers and establishing an economic foothold. They socialized primarily with other members of their community (who were not very many in this period) during any spare time that they had, and thus, except in work-related contexts, American culture and society did not impinge on their personal lives to any great extent. But as their children became older and a return to India grew less and less likely (Fenton 1988, 39),[4] it became important for them to have a more structured means of interacting with co-ethnics.

Smith (1978, 1174–1175) poetically describes the reason for the "intensification of the psychic basis of religious commitment" among immigrants as

> loneliness, the romanticizing of memories, the guilt for imagined desertion of parents and other relatives, and the search for community and identity in a world of strangers. . . . Separation from both personal and physical associations of one's childhood community drew emotional strings taut. . . . Friendships, however, were often fleeting, and the lonely vigils—when sickness, unemployment, or personal rejection set individuals apart—produced deep crises of the spirit. At such moments, the concrete symbols of order or hope that the village church or priest and the annual round of religious observances had once provided seemed far away; yet the mysteries of individual existence as well as the confusing agonies of anomie cried out for religious explanation. For this reason, I shall argue, migration was often a theologizing experience.

Most of the members of the OHM are first-wave immigrants, and its secretary offered an equally poetic explanation about why the group was formed:

> Before we established OHM, many of the true lovers of Kerala heritage and culture were lost in the congested wilderness of Southern California without having any communication with other Kerala members who shared similar interests. Some of them felt lonely in the crowded streets of this faraway land, and hungry and thirsty, in this land of plenty, for company of people who recognized and under-

stood them. They searched everywhere for some familiarity, to prove to their beloved children that the usual bedtime stories of their motherland and her heritage were not some fairy tales but existed in reality (Vellatheri 1992).

The teaching of Indian culture and values to the children was an important reason for the formation of the *satsangs* and the primary reason for the formation of *bala vihars*. Indian parents were concerned about the environment within which their children were growing up, which they perceived to be filled with unstable families, sexual promiscuity, drug and alcohol abuse, and violence. The attitudes and values that the children were picking up from school in many ways seemed completely alien to the parents, and created a frightening feeling that the second-generation was growing up to be total strangers with whom parents and other relatives could not even communicate. One of the members of the OHM told me about her friend, whose child came home from school one day and asked, "Why don't I have a white mommy like everyone does? I want a white mommy." Another described how her child, when younger, would dissociate herself from anything Indian and would refuse to walk with her father, acting like she didn't know him, when he wore Indian clothes.

The children in turn had to deal with the difficult issue of negotiating their personal and cultural identity between the values and practices learned at home and those of the American society they faced outside[5] In the process they raised questions about their own culture and religion to which parents discovered they had no answers: "[W]e are forced to articulate over and over again what it means to be a Hindu and an Indian to our friends and to our children, and one feels ill-equipped for the task. . . . [In India] one was never called upon to explain Deepavali or Sankaranti [festivals], and least of all, 'Hinduism' (Narayan 1992, 172). In India, children "breathe in the values of Hindu life" (Fenton 1988, 127). In the United States, on the other hand, parents realized that unless they made a deliberate effort, children would never learn what their "Indianness" meant.

As R. Stephen Warner (1993, 1044–1093) points out, even in the assimilationist era, cultural pluralism was tolerated in and expressed through religion. The tendency to express cultural pluralism through religion has only increased with the range and diversity of backgrounds now in the United States. Recent immigrant groups such as the Indians, Pakistanis, and Koreans appear to follow this pattern even more strongly (Warner 1993, 1062; Fenton 1988, 50–51).[6] According to Raymond Brady Williams (1988, 11), "Immigrants are religious—by all counts more religious than they were before they left home—because religion is one of the important identity markers that helps them preserve individual self-awareness and cohesion in a group."

Thus, for Indian immigrants, particularly non-Christians, religion has become the key symbol of identity and of difference from American society, and has come to represent their Indian heritage.

Hindu religiocultural associations like the OHM and *bala vihars* have sprung up in all the major metropolitan areas around the country. These groups are not just narrowly "religious" and do far more than organize congregational worship. In the absence of the residential concentration characteristic of many of the other immigrant groups, the *satsangs* and *bala vihars* of Indian Americans are often the only place at which they meet other members of the community.[7] It is through their activities that the second generation is socialized into their Indian American identity and meet other young people whom the parents hope will provide a source of support. As Mr. Radha Krishna Sharma, a member of the OHM put it, "You know that children here go in search of their roots. We did not want our children to lose their heritage in a foreign environment and then have to re-create Alex Haley's journey!"

Besides the needs of children, there are also increasing numbers of retirees, older immigrants who have now "made it" (and therefore have more leisure time), and parents of immigrants (brought over under the family reunification provision) who enjoy such congregational activities. Usha R. Jain (1989, 168–169), for instance, notes that religious and philanthropic activities (usually involving collecting money for a cause in India) have become increasingly important for the older generation. In addition, such organizations are important to the large numbers of second-wave Indians who have been continuously arriving, since, "they provide a renewable continuity with religious organizations and traditions in India" (Williams 1992b, 252).[8] Most scholars who have studied Indian immigrants point out that contrary to conventional expectations that the cultural identities and practices of the home country will be gradually abandoned over time, Indians in the United States have tended to become more community-oriented, more religious, and more "Indianized" over time.[9] As the number of Indians in the major metropolitan areas of the country have increased, the Indian organizations have given way to more regional and sectarian groups such as the OHM, and thus the first-generation Indians in the United States are also becoming more "parochialized."[10] In areas where there are large groups of Indian immigrants from a particular region, it is not uncommon for the different castes to form separate organizations.[11] The second generation is simultaneously becoming "Indianized" in the colleges and universities, where there are many pan-Indian organizations. At home, however, the community with which they identify is the subcultural one, since most family-level interaction is within the regional group. What the relationship between the regional and national identity will be for this generation remains to be seen.[12]

The Organization of Hindu Malayalees

In addition to the monthly meeting described above, the OHM celebrates the major Kerala Hindu festivals with religious and cultural programs. Cultural programs are also sponsored several times during the year, when music and dance-dramas are performed by community members or by visiting artists from Kerala. Member contributions are used for various projects—local charities as well as a women's shelter in Kerala and disaster relief in various parts of India. The group has also managed to raise $42,000 to build a shrine to Lord Aiyappa, a popular deity whose abode is in a mountain on the Kerala border, in the local pan-Indian temple.

My findings are based on a two-year ethnographic study of this group. In addition to attending the monthly meetings, I visited the homes of many of the members and conducted semistructured interviews with them. I also participated in more informal activities with individuals in the group. My own status as a Malayalee immigrant helped me considerably, although the fact that I came from a Christian background did lead to some initial discomfort on both sides and to a lesser extent continued to result sporadically in delicate situations. This happened particularly when I was introduced to people in the group, since my last name clearly identifies my background. My being non-Hindu also most certainly affected many of the statements members have made to me regarding their ideas and feelings about religion. It has also meant that I have had to proceed slowly and carefully with my research. After the centuries of mockery and harassment that Hindus have had to endure from Christians and the negative stereotypes that exist in this society regarding Hinduism, many of the members were understandably wary of my intentions and the purpose of my study. They were particularly anxious that I did not perceive or characterize them as "fanatic" Hindus and wanted me to give them a copy of "my report" before I submitted it to the editors. (I gave copies of a draft of this chapter to the current president, Ravi Vellatheri, who in turn circulated it among the executive committee members and obtained their approval.) Despite their concerns, most members have been very warm, welcoming, and hospitable.

The OHM is a fairly elite group in class and occupational terms, a fact that they have repeatedly emphasized to me and to R. Stephen Warner on the two occasions that he met with some of the group. In contrast to the Kerala Christians that Sheba George writes about in Chapter 8, most members of the OHM, both male and female, are professionals—mainly doctors, engineers, scientists, and accountants. I was particularly struck by the fact that the women were as well educated and well placed as their husbands. In fact, there seemed to be only one case where the woman was currently not working or studying. But even in this instance, the woman had given up her career to raise two small children.

Formation

The founder-president, and chief initiator of the OHM, Mr. Govindankutty Nair, described how the idea of forming an association occurred to him:

> *During that time [the late 1980s] we used to go occasionally for various [Indian] get-togethers. But it all seemed so superficial. You know the way Americans say, "How are you?" and rush past without even waiting for your reply. It is a meaningless question. The person doesn't care whether you are ill or have lost your job or if your mother just died. Well, that's the way I felt about those parties. The same jokes recycled, the same trivial conversation. And generally the women would be in one room, the men in another, there would be a few people playing cards and the children would be somewhere else. Except for the fact that the different groups were within the four walls of same house, there was nothing gained from everyone being together.*

He hurried to add, however, that "I am not saying such get-togethers are bad. I still go sometimes—it just left me feeling unsatisfied." Mr. Nair paused and then went on:

> *I had been thinking about it for a while, and I had also talked to some of my other friends. My idea was to develop a support group for Hindu Malayalees. Christians have the church as a support group, Hindus don't have anything.*

Mr. Vellatheri, another of the founding members of the group, had made the same point regarding Christian Malayalees earlier, using much the same words. Thus, the Christian congregational model seemed to be an important influence for this group.

A little later in the conversation, Mr. Nair stated:

> *I also wanted it to be a group that did some social service. We are all in a good position here so I wanted us to contribute to support some worthwhile causes in Kerala. Preserving the culture was another goal. And then when our relatives and parents from Kerala came to visit, I wanted them to have a group where they would feel comfortable. These were my long-term goals. But I also had to think of something that would have short-term results and that would hold the group together in a more meaningful way than just a potluck party. That's how I came up with the idea of having a pooja and bhajan monthly meeting. So, the intention was always that the OHM be much more than just a bhajan group.*

To emphasize this, he told me that he had been thinking of organizing a workshop for women in the coming year, open to all but led by the OHM, to impart some basic financial, legal, medical, and child care knowledge relevant to life here. Referring to Indira, a woman who had been widowed several years before, he described the difficulty she had experienced having to deal with all the practical details that her husband had previously looked after and added, "Some of our group may lose their husbands, and when that happens they should know how to deal with the many issues that will come up." He also wanted the OHM to get involved in planning a retirement home for Indians: "We are all getting older, and in ten to twenty years there will be a big need for it. And particularly then, we would prefer to be with others from our own background."

While Mr. Nair played down the religious aspect of the OHM, it was obviously an important reason for its formation: "Growing up as Hindus in a Judeo-Christian environment can be difficult. There are so many misconceptions here about Indians and Hindus. People ask us about the cows roaming the streets—they think we are all vegetarians, that India is full of snake charmers." Mr. Sharma, an executive member of the group, said that one of the reasons that the OHM was founded was to correct such misconceptions. Mrs. Kala Ramachandran, another executive member, continued: "We are not fanatics, but being a Hindu organization, we believe very strongly that the Hindu religion and faith should be preserved forever. We believe that Hindu values have a big role to play in the future world and we are all proud of being Hindus."

The Social Community

Members of the OHM have developed a close-knit community, even though they are scattered over an area with a radius of around 125 miles. Mr. Vellatheri told me that the

> *OHM is like an extended family. It helps to alleviate problems—it helps in crisis management, stress management. There are many problems here—job related, domestic. Before OHM I had around four or five people to turn to, but now I have around twenty families that I can trust. I have several close friends, and we call each other one or two times a week for personal conversation, quite apart from official OHM business. Just talking to others helps so much. The community is small enough to be close-knit. The Kerala Association [the pan-Kerala association in the region], on the other hand, is very large. Around four hundred people show up for each function, so you won't know most of the people there.*
>
> *OHM also helps us in practical matters. We have doctors with different specializations from psychiatrists to cardiologists, engineers, accountants, business people, scientists, and attorneys. So, whatever problem comes up, we have an expert who can help us.*

Earlier he described how he had been informed by his office that his immigration papers were not in order (which turned out not to be true) soon after arriving in the United States. He was pressured by his employer and ran from attorney to attorney, but they just exploited his gullibility and cost him of a lot of money. He repeated several times, "If there had been an organization like OHM, nothing like this would have happened." He went on: "I did not know the American system . . . and we had no one to turn to for advice or help. We were so lonely and depressed—it almost drove us out of our minds at times. We looked through the phone book for Indian-sounding names and called them but many of the Indians we reached were not very friendly. Another time he said, "On the occasions of death, marriage, etc., members are there to help with flowers, consolation, and practical details. For instance, Savithri's father died at 4 A.M. in the morning. By 6 A.M. everyone in the community knew about it, and many of us went over." I have personally witnessed this community support at a function where OHM members helped with the serving and organization.

Several OHM members mentioned that they found the *bhajan* singing to be cleansing and uplifting. During those hours, they could forget all their worries and get some peace of mind. Others talked about how beneficial the group has been for their children, as one women explained: "Earlier they [the children] went through a period when they wanted to have nothing to do with anything Indian. My oldest child (who has a long, traditional name) had Anglicized and shortened his name earlier. Now he insists that his friends call him by his full name. And my other children ask me why I did not give them traditional names!"

The effects of the OHM on the children have sometimes been overstated by the adults, since the teenagers felt that "it was an organization for adults." At the same time, all of the teenagers did say that the group had helped them at least indirectly by putting them in contact with adults and other children from the community. "It made me finally comfortable as an Indian. I realized that there were many other people out there who are like me, who talk like me, and that I am not by myself," elaborated Anand, one of the teenage boys in the group.

Developing Religious Traditions

I had been told that the OHM was the only organization in the United States that held a special pooja for Lord Aiyappa during the time of the annual Aiyappa pilgrimage in India. I could see that Aiyappa worship was also an important part of the monthly OHM *pooja,* so I asked whether this was because Aiyappa was the most popular deity in Kerala. "No," answered Mr. Vellatheri, "we picked Aiyappa since it was the least controversial choice. He is the one deity that everyone in the group could agree on. Aiyappa worship is a unifying factor in the group since there are *Vaishnavaites* and *Shaivaites* [worshipers of Vishnu and Shiva, respectively, reflecting a major division among Hindus][13] and members of different castes." He went on to tell me that Aiyappa was also a "secular" deity since a lot of non-Hindus perform the annual pilgrimage in Kerala. In an OHM booklet Mr. Vellatheri (1992) wrote about Lord Aiyappa and the pilgrimage he undertook with two other OHM members: "What is more important, right in front of the shrine, there is the temple of Vavara, a Muslim, the first lieutenant of the Lord, standing as a permanent monument to the Lord's declaration of the equality of mankind."

I was also curious about how members learned the *bhajans.* Most are in Sanskrit and a few are popular in Kerala, but from my conversations I gathered that many of the others were those that "an average Hindu growing up in Kerala would not know." In fact, often it is only the person leading the *bhajan* who knows it.; the rest just repeat the song, line by line. I asked several of the *bhajan* leaders how they had learned the songs. Mrs. Indira Iyer, wife of the lay priest and the primary *bhajan* leader of the group, said that she made it a point to pick up new *bhajans* from friends, relatives, and tapes. Mrs. Kamala Devi told me that she learned them primarily from an older Tamilian woman. Latha, a teenager who had led a few, including at least one in Hindi, and Mr. Nair had both learned them at their respective singing classes. Another woman sang two that she had just composed the previous day. It was only during my fieldwork that copies of the *bhajans* (handwritten by Mrs. Iyer in English script) were handed out to members before the meeting. Around the middle of my study, Mrs. Iyer also tried to formalize the sequence of the *bhajan* singing according to the deities to whom they are addressed (using the South Indian practices with which she is familiar). Again, as mentioned, the group instituted a Gita discussion period and some youth programs toward the end of my study. Thus, the group was developing and modifying traditions to fit into the American milieu.

The Tamil *Bala Vihar*

"What is the most important thing parents should impart to their children?" Ramachandra Iyer asked R. Stephen Warner rhetorically, as the three of us stood outside the prayer hall before an OHM *pooja*. He then answered his own question by saying: "Values, those are the most important things—ethical principles of living and values. This is what we should impart to our children when they are young, until they complete high school. If we do this properly, they may have some adjustment difficulties for a semester or so in college, but then they will be set for life."

Mr. Iyer was talking about the *bala vihar* that he is part of and helped found fourteen years ago (he is a Tamil Brahmin from a family settled in Kerala, so he is a member of both Malayalee and Tamilian organizations). He credits the *bala vihar* with being vital in imparting a cultural and moral orientation to his two daughters, now twenty-two and fifteen years of age. He told us that it is important for parents to do this while their children are young, since later they are faced with so many temptations. "This way their time and minds are filled with other things instead of 'unwanted thoughts.'" he said.

Through Mr. Iyer and his wife, I was introduced to the Tamil *bala vihar* and have attended several of the monthly meetings. While I am a Malayalee by ancestry, I grew up in Tamil Nadu and studied Tamil in school, and am therefore familiar with the language and culture. However, as a Christian and non-Tamil single woman, my outsider status has been even more conspicuous in this setting. The friendship extended to me by a group member—Mrs. Lakshmi Narayan, a university researcher who could relate to my project—has therefore been crucial in easing my entrance into the group. At the same time that I gave the OHM committee a copy of my draft chapter, I also gave a copy to Mrs. Narayan to be circulated among the *bala vihar* parents and have obtained their approval as well.

I have been extremely impressed with what the group has been able to accomplish through its monthly meetings. Clearly, the meeting was an occasion that the children looked forward to, and they seemed to have formed close friendships within the group. Unlike the OHM meetings, the *bala vihar* provided children with a lot of structured interaction time when they could talk through many of the issues they were confronting in their everyday lives, particularly their struggles in trying to balance their Indian and American identities. The *bala vihar* shows the children how this balance can be successfully achieved. Both adults and children sat down together as an "extended family" to discuss the meaning of Hinduism, to explore the ethical and moral dilemmas of day-to-day living in the United States, and to cultivate an appreciation for the beauty of the Tamil language and culture.

At one of the cultural programs organized by OHM, I spoke to Mr. Ramakrishnan, the person who had initiated the *bala vihar* meetings in the region (including the Tamil *bala vihar*), and his daughter. They are both very involved with the Chinmaya Mission, founded by Swami Chinmayananda (a Hindu 'guru' or religious teacher) and the *bala vihars* that Mr. Ramakrishnan had initiated were organized under its auspices. They told me that they used a book of lectures by Swami Chinmayananda[14] as the *bala vihar* text and that it was full of matters of everyday relevance. Mr. Ramakrishnan gave me the following example: "For instance, it helps deal with anger. It describes how anger develops and why, and gives practical suggestions for dealing with it. It also talks about how meditation and yoga help to cope with the daily problems of life." His daughter, now at the University of California at Berkeley, has started a regular discussion group to study the teachings of Swami Chinmayananda and how they can be used in their lives. Her goal, she said, was to show students of Indian origin "that our heritage is not a hinderance but can be of help."

The effect that the *bala vihars* can have on the youngsters is eloquently described by Hema Narayan, one of the students in the Tamil group, in a school essay on diversity that won a national prize. Initially, she writes, she struggled to "fit in" by trying to be just like her class-mates and rejecting her Indian identity. But over time, as she began to learn more about her heritage and her religion from her parents and the *bala vihar*:

> *I became more confident and sure of myself. With a wealth of knowl-edge by my side, I felt strong. I stood up to my classmates and intro-duced them to my beliefs. To my surprise, they stopped mocking me, and instead, wanted to know more. . . . I felt a sense of belonging, but not sameness, as though I were an individual piece adding color to the complete picture. I could fit in but still be different.*

The adults who attend the *bala vihar* have been able to devise interesting ways to impart this knowledge. As part of a Father's Day surprise, the older children were practicing a skit (written by Mrs. Mallika Badrinath) during their language class. They were enacting the bedlam that exists in a Tamil Brahmin household in India consisting of a busy professional couple, their three irrepressible children, and their disorganized servant. The conversation used was in colloquial Brahmin Tamil, which is very different from "official Tamil." Besides teaching these idiomatic usages, the skit exposed the children to ap-propriate gender and intergenerational behavior as well as her views about the distinctness of the Brahmin language, values and food habits.

The importance of family relationships and obligations were clearly among the most important lessons that the adults in the group wanted to teach the children. Undoubtedly this concern was due to the Amer-ican setting, since the comparison was always implicitly or explicitly between the Indian and the American family. However, here again the aim was to show how Hindu values were important and relevant in the American context. The interpretation given to the tale of the *pativrata,* or "ideal wife," is a good example. The story was about an exemplary wife who, through her devotion to her husband, was able to amass greater spiritual power than a mendicant who had performed severe austerities for many years. The moral was that a woman's earthly duty to her husband was more important and fundamental than her spiri-tual obligation, and that this devotion alone could bring her supernat-ural powers. After concluding, Mrs. Sudha Subramanian, the narrator, triumphantly stated that "women actually have a better deal since men do not have this power," but hastened to add that "this is not because women are seen as dumb or passive but precisely because they are capable." She went on to emphasize that this duty was not one-sided, since men too had the obligation to look after their wives and to take care of their needs. It also did not mean that women should be submissive, giving several examples from the Hindu epics of loving husbands and of assertive women. She concluded: "All these stories were written to show that the family was seen as the fundamental unit of society and to provide rules to keep the family together. If this requires patience and forbearance from the woman, so be it. If the woman is always asking, 'What's in it for me,' the family can never survive." Throughout the narration and explanation, there was much teasing, laughter, and booing along gender lines from the group (both children and adults). In the animated discussion that ensued, several of the older teenage girls seemed to be taking feminist positions, with one questioning some gender-differentiated religious practices, and two others presenting feminist interpretations of the epics.

Although the children graduate from the *bala vihar* when they leave high school, the parents, as Mr. Iyer expressed, hope that they will take with them some valuable lessons that will help them through college and adulthood. In fact the Tamil *bala vihar* was going a step further to ensure that the graduates had a concrete reminder of what they had learned in the classes by giving them tapes of the *bhajans* that "the children can play in their dorms when they feel homesick," as one mother told me.

While the *bala vihar* is meant for the children, it was also very clear that the adults enjoyed it as much as the youngsters. The parents actually mentioned to me and to the others in various contexts that they were learning along with their children. During the *pativrata* story, for instance, I overheard several of the adults discussing its implications among themselves as animatedly as the children. On another occasion, when some ex-*bala vihar* parents (whose children had gone on to college) had been invited to one of the *bala vihar* dinners, they talked about how much they missed the meetings. One of them said, half-jokingly "How about an alumni evening the day before the *bala vihar*?"

While the members of the Tamil *bala vihar* are less comfortable than members of the OHM with being designated as "elite" (they objected to my characterizing them in this manner in this chapter), they are also well-placed professionals. From their discussions of such issues as grades, study strategies, of schools like Harvard, and the writing of scientific papers, it is clear that the group is self-consciously adopting the "model minority" discourse.

An American Hinduism?

Steven Vertovec (1989, 159) has noted that "in virtually every case, Hinduism in diaspora has developed substantial modifications from the traditions originally carried abroad." While this is the case of all religions, modifications are even more likely in Hinduism due to the nature of the religion. The Federation of Hindu Associations (1995) states that, "Hinduism, . . . by not being a rigid revelation of a single prophet, book or event and by not preaching to destroy any existing schools of thought, has become an adaptable system to realize God, to live and let live, and attain Universal peace and brotherhood." Thus, the form that diasporic Hinduism takes depends on the nature of both the Indian community in the host country and the larger context. Vertovec compares the differences between Trinidadian Hinduism and British Hinduism. In Trinidad, the circumstances surrounding the colonial migration of indentured workers resulted in a "cultural blending" of the Indians (Vertovec 1991, 167) and the emergence of a "virtually casteless, 'lowest common denominator' Hindu tradition which catered to the religious needs of a diverse community" (Vertovec 1995, 134). Thus, by the late 1980's Hinduism was put forward into the public space as an ethnic communal ideology in bold and conscious contradistinction to the hegemonic Creole norm" (Vertovec 1995, 141). In Great Britain, however, "a rather fragmented picture" of Hinduism emerges, for "although some attempts are being made to organize Hindus and to formulate Hinduism on a national scale, in local quarters it is mainly segmentary forms of religion reflecting traditions specific to provenance, caste and sect that are practiced and institutionalized" (Vertovec 1995, 146). Vertovec (1995, 147) explains this phenomenon as a result of the "dominant multicultural discourse" in Great Britain. Scholars have noted that in the United States, Hinduism is being transformed into what has been variously called an "American Hinduism" or "Ecumenical Hinduism" (Williams 1988, 238–240). At the same time, as I have pointed out, there is a great deal of segmentation into region, caste, and sect. Thus, Hinduism in the United States appears to combine the features of the religion in both Trinidad and Great Britain. In other words, while there is greater sectarianism, the sectarianism is based largely on language and subcultural differences, and a certain uniformity is developing in the Hinduism practiced by the various subgroups.

The Evolution of Hinduism

As is clear from the 1995 statement by the Federation of Hindu Associations, Hinduism is different from other major world religions in many ways. The term "Hinduism" was introduced around 1830 by the British to refer principally to the culture and practices of the non-Islamic people of the Indian subcontinent. As such, "Hinduism is both a civilization and a congregation of religions; it has neither a beginning or founder, nor a central authority, hierarchy, or organization." ("Hinduism" 1993). Thus, the nature and character of Hinduism have varied greatly by region, caste, and historical period. In fact, there are even those who question whether there is one unitary religion called "Hinduism" at all, arguing instead that "what we call 'Hinduism' is a geographically defined group of distinct but related religions" (Stietencron 1989, 20). However, while scholars like Robert Frykenberg (1989) and Daniel Gold (1991) agree that in precolonial times there was never a "single 'Hinduism' . . . for all of India" (Frykenberg, 1989, 20), they claim that during the colonial period, Hindu revivalist movements developed and in the process created "modern" and "organized" pan-Indian versions of Hinduism. In the late nineteenth century, groups like the Brahmo Samaj, the Arya Samaj, and the RSS (Rashtriya Swayamsevak Sangh) emerged to reformulate the message of Hinduism in reaction to the activities of Christian missionaries and the escalating communal tensions between Muslims and Hindus. (Ironically, in their attempt to counter the Christian threat, such groups ended up developing "Christianized" models of Hinduism.)[15] However, for the most part, these created or recasted generic versions of the "Great Tradition" had little impact on the majority of Hindu Indians. It has been only in the past five years, with the televising of the Hindu epics and the rising Hindutva movement demanding a "Hindu" India, that a pan-Indian Hinduism has gained some degree of mass support, particularly in northern India.

It is one form of the "Great Tradition" that is being recreated in the United States. According to Williams (1992b, 239):

> An ecumenical Hinduism is developing in the United States that unites deities, rituals, sacred texts, and people in temples and programs in ways that would not be found together in India. In temples and centers created on an ecumenical model, emphasis is placed upon all-India Hindu "great tradition," on devotion to major deities, and upon some elements of the Sanskrit tradition. . . . Study and devotional groups use universally accepted Hindu texts, such as the

Bhagavad Gita and the Ramayana. Languages used are Sanskrit for rituals and English for instruction, commentary and business.

In other words, Indian immigrants coming to the United States from their "little traditions" are here socialized into a pan-Indian Hinduism.[16] I have noted how this has taken place in the OHM with the selection of Aiyappa as the central deity, the development of the *pooja* format and the inclusion of a range of *bhajans*. Again, "ethnic" *bala vihars* such as the Tamil meeting are not common. Many of the other *bala vihars* are pan-Indian, and here the children are taught Sanskrit or Hindi. In the *bala vihars* run by the Chinmaya Mission, the children use a textbook published by the mission that leads to some amount of uniformity among them.

One of the characteristics of diasporic Hinduism seems to be the "convergence toward de facto congregationalism" (Warner 1993, 54), that is, the tendency to develop forms of group study or worship. While many Hindu immigrants never join any such groups, the number and proliferation of religious associations are astounding. The 1995 directory of the Federation of Hindu Associations lists over thirty associations for southern California alone. (This does not include *bala vihars,* and not all or even most *satsangs* in this region have become members of this umbrella organization.) Williams (1988) also indicates that religiocultural *satsangs* like the OHM now exist all over the country. As indicated, one reason for this development is a conscious adoption of the Christian model, although another is the immigrants' need for community.

Historically, Hinduism has adapted itself to challenges posed by Jainism and Buddhism, and Western colonial missionaries by incorporating key elements of these traditions. Hinduism has similarly adapted to American society. During the process of "transplanting" Hinduism in the United States, it has also been "translated" so that it can be understood in and relevant to the new cultural context.[17]

The congregational format adopted by the OHM and the recent addition of the Gita discussion period (modeled on Bible study sessions) are examples of this adaptation process. This is even clearer in the case of the *bala vihar* (described as "Sunday school" when members talk to their American friends), where concepts such as "family values" and the "work ethic" have become the focus of the lessons, and where a more egalitarian interpretation is accorded to traditions such as the *pativrata*.

These modifications have also taken place in the many Hindu temples around the country. The regional temple that members of both the OHM and the *bala vihar* visit as individuals or families holds a "graduation-day celebration" for high school and college graduates within the community. Father's Day, Mother's Day and Children's Day, none of which is a traditional Hindu function, are also celebrated. The temple has likewise to some extent become a center of cultural activities; its hall is frequently used for programs by various Indian groups, and music classes are conducted in one of its rooms. Narayanan (1992, 172) refers to how a Hindu temple responded to American popular psychology by sponsoring workshops and lectures that use Indian scriptures to examine topics such as "Living in Freedom," "Stress Management," and "Positive Thinking and Living." She also mentions that "the publications and activities of the temple sometimes reflect concerns that are not seen at . . . temples in India. The [temple's] publications have consistently offered articles which symbolically interpret aspects of the Hindu tradition" (Narayanan 1992, 164). After discussing some examples of such interpretations, she points out that they "seem to owe more to some Western modes of analyses than to traditional Hindu exegesis," and goes on to say that since in the United States, unlike in India, such publications "may be the only regular religious education" people get, the effects of this "controlled diet" on the younger generation remain to be seen (Narayanan 1992, 168–169).

The adaptation of Hindu ideology and practice to "fit in" with American society also accords with Warner's (1993) thesis that religion in the United States operates under "market conditions." The "doxic," or "taken-for-granted," status that Hinduism enjoyed in India does not hold here, and Hindu religious organizations and leaders (like those of other religions) now have to "market" their ideas and show how their "product" can best satisfy the needs of the "consumers" (Warner 1993, 1053–1055). I have referred to some of these needs and to how the lay religious leaders have tried to "market" Hinduism as the best means by which Indian immigrants can achieve psychological well-being, professional success, and harmonious family lives.

Developing an Indian American Community and Identity

It is perhaps not surprising that, like the assimilation theory in the United States, the secularization theory has come under attack (Warner 1993, Swatos 1993). I believe the key to understanding ethnicity and religion in the United States is to realize that they are, as William

Swatos (1993, xv–xvi) points out about religion, "neither 'in decline' nor 'resurgent' as much as changing." He goes on to state that in order to "comprehend these new forms, sociology must change its analytical paradigms." Such modifications come about as people attempt to create new identities in the face of changing conditions that make old ones irrelevant or unsuitable.

Religion has been the most legitimate form of ethnic expression in this country (Warner 1993). It has also been one of the most powerful bases of group formation. Smith (1978, 1168) argues that ethnic organizations in this country "coalesced out of both economic and psychic need and found meanings for personal and communal life in the cultural symbols and the religious ideas that their leaders believed were marks of a shared inheritance and hence, of a common peoplehood." Both the structure and the culture of these emerging ethnoreligious groups helped participants compete more advantageously with members of other groups. As such, it is not surprising that the latest wave of immigrants have formed ethnoreligious organizations in their attempt to adapt to American society.

I have argued that the members of both the OHM and the Tamil *bala vihar* seem to be using these religious organizations as means to forge ethnic communities and to formulate and articulate their identities as Indian Americans. As well-settled, successful professionals, they take pride in being able to maintain a balance between Westernization and Indianness, drawing the best from each tradition. Besides their economic and professional advantages, group members primarily emphasize their fluency with the American culture, their greater liberalism with respect to intergenerational and gender relations, and the greater openness and awareness that their transnational experience brings when they compare themselves with their Indian counterparts (Kurien 1995). However, they use the *satsangs* and *bala vihars,* the close-knit extended families, and the marriages of their children to spouses within the community as evidence that they have done this without losing their inner values or their cultural integrity, which they believe not only distinguishes them from the wider American society but also from many Indians in India whom they characterize as "too Westernized."

As the examples of the OHM and the Tamil *bala vihar* demonstrate, being part of such a community helps members create, celebrate, reinforce, and transmit their status and success. There are direct and indirect mechanisms to restrict membership to those with similar backgrounds and interests. Members of both organizations have told me that they did not go out of their way to recruit new members, since it was important that they should be only families who will "mix well with us" (in the words of Mr. Rajagopalan, director of the *bala vihar*), and who will "fit in with the ethos of the group" (as Mrs. Ramachandran, an OHM committee member, put it). For this reason, new members are carefully selected. Indirect mechanisms such as the professional, upper-class atmosphere, the religious and cultural orientation of the activities, and the discussions regarding children's educational achievements also seem to work to push out those who do not "fit in."[18]

Smith has indicated that membership in ethnoreligious groups confers a "competitive advantage" on its members. I consider the comment made by Krishnan Kutty, the OHM secretary, regarding the benefits of belonging to an organization with such a diverse group of professionals. On another occasion, he and a fellow OHM member were talking about a common acquaintance, a Kerala Hindu who had been laid off, and Mr. Kutty said, "Ask him to join OHM. It will help him." Besides the psychological benefits, Mr. Kutty was referring to the fact that the group, through their professional contacts, might be able to help him obtain a job. Referring to yet another type of "competitive advantage" that groups like the OHM could provide, Mr. Nair, its president, told me that one reason he wanted to have a religiocultural organization for Malayalee Hindus was because "I noticed that Tamil Brahmins here have a tight-knit community and hold on to their traditions. I felt that their discipline is the reason for their doing so well."

Besides the material advantages offered, being part of a successful, professional community also empowers the second generation to avoid "assimilating to the norm" and to chose a trajectory that emphasizes educational achievements over social popularity. Most of the college students in both groups are in top institutions. The University of California at Berkeley seems to be the favorite choice, but others include Stanford, the University of California at Los Angeles, Yale, the University of California at San Diego, and Harvard. Not only is education strongly emphasized by the professional parents and relatives (who are also willing to shoulder most of the expenses involved, thus making it easier for the children to spend longer hours at their books), but being part of a group such as the OHM and *bala vihar* provides both children and parents with the concrete resources and know-how to achieve educational success. Thus, information regarding every step in the process is available within the group and is exchanged over the monthly dinners and the phone. This includes advice about which high schools, summer programs, extracurricular activities, and SAT coaching classes have the best record at placing students in top schools;

which test-preparing and -taking strategies have proved most successful; and what should be emphasized in personal statements on college applications. Once in college, there is a sufficiently large number of co-ethnics and friends available to serve as a support group and to provide further information about success strategies and professional opportunities, all of which increase the youngsters' chances of continuing to do well and ending up in good positions.

The nurturing community environment provided by the OHM and the *bala vihar* also inculcates in the children a strong sense of subcultural affiliation and pride. Most of the teenagers who attended the meetings on a regular basis told me that they would prefer to marry a fellow ethnic, since such a person would best be able to relate to their family and their culture. Since the second generation is still quite young, it is too early to say whether they will stick with their plans. However, of the four marriages that took place during my fieldwork, two were intracaste marriages (the young people were introduced by their parents), and one was between the daughter of an OHM member and a fellow South Asian immigrant of Sri Lankan Buddhist background (described to me by Mrs. Menon, the bride's mother, as someone who had "very similar cultural and religious values"). In the fourth case, the young man married a white American classmate. Whom the second generation marries will be a very crucial factor in shaping the Indian American community of the future, so these patterns bear watching.

Conclusion: Staking out a Place at the Multicultural Table

Joshua Fishman (1985, 344) talks about the "sidestream ethnicity" (or "symbolic ethnicity" [Gans, 1979]) that has become chic in the aftermath of the ethnic revival in the United States, and compares it to the role that religion has traditionally played in American life. Both are, he argues,

> *recognized as being not only natural but humanizing and strengthening in some very general sense. . . . Americans now expect one another to have some sidestream ethnicity [as well as religion]; any sidestream ethnicity will do . . . because their role is no longer to help or hinder "being a success in America" but to provide "roots"— that is, give meaningful cultural depth to individual and family life. Thus, a sidestream ethnicity as part of one's background . . . has become part of an enriched and overarching American experience.*

In other words, according to Fishman, to have religion and sidestream ethnicity is, in the postassimilation era, to be mainstream American. Mary Waters (1990) similarly vouches for the trendiness of "symbolic ethnicity" and its widespread adoption, while providing a more detailed and critical analysis of its content and implications. Thus, paradoxically, while the increase in religiosity and the emphasis on Indianness and/or regional culture are ways of resisting Americanization, they are, as noted, particularly American ways of expressing an "autonomous identity," and, especially for the second generation, acceptable ways for people to demonstrate their individualism and ethnicity and to take their place "at the multicultural table." Although the ethnicity of groups such as first- and second-generation Indian immigrants can hardly be described as "sidestream" or "symbolic," since it shapes most aspects of their everyday life and behavior, the prevalence and acceptance of a multiculturalist discourse (however limited and shallow) allow room for groups like Indian Americans to use it to legitimize their own brand of ethnicity, although different in content and nature from that of most other Americans.

Arvind Rajagopal (1995), in a provocative paper entitled "Better Hindu Than Black?" further argues that the choice of Hinduism to represent "Indian" identity in the United States has been a way for the predominantly uppercaste immigrants to avoid confronting their problematic racial location in this country. Many of the teenagers that I spoke with seemed to corroborate this thesis indirectly as they described the pain they experienced growing up "brown skins" in a predominantly white environment. Like Hema Narayan, the prize-winning essayist, they said that their eagerness to be accepted had initially led them to turn away from their Indianness and to try to be as much like their white friends as possible. This, however, only increased their identity crisis and feeling of alienation. According to them, the crisis was only resolved when they accepted their Indian heritage and began to try to learn more about Hinduism and Indian culture. Over time, they told me, they came to see the beauty and value of their heritage, and also finally started to feel comfortable with themselves as Indian Americans—Americans with Indian roots. In other words, a crisis revolving around racial identity was resolved by turning to ethnicity. Thus, after discussing the psychological well-being she experienced after learning about "the uniqueness of my background," Hema goes on to proclaim, "I am no longer ashamed of my dark skin."

While Fishman applies his "sidestream ethnicity" thesis rather uncritically to the case of Mexican Americans, Waters points to the difference between the symbolic, costless, and voluntarily chosen ethnicity of third- and fourth-generation white ethnics and the ethnicity of immigrants of color such as Indians. As my work has shown, the development, content, and implications of the two are very different. Again, as the experience of the teenagers I interviewed demonstrates, it is difficult for Indian Americans, with or without ethnicity, to be easily accepted as "mainstream Americans." Further, the religion and ethnic culture they have are also less likely to be perceived as "mainstream." Pat Robertson's recent stinging denunciation of Hinduism as "demonaic" and his call that Indian immigrants be prevented from coming into the country[19] are just two examples of the way being Hindu and being Indian are conflated and of the negative light in which Hinduism and India are viewed in this country. Thus, far from being the means of achieving individual feelings of being special and of belonging that they are among white ethnics (Waters 1990, 151), the ethnic organizations of Indian Americans are group efforts to provide support in an alien and frequently hostile environment.

As in the case of the Iranian Jews that Shoshanah Feher studies (Chapter 2), it is Jewish Americans and not white ethnics who provide the model that Indian Americans uphold and wish to emulate. As a highly successful group that is integrated into mainstream American society while maintaining its religious and cultural distinctness, close community ties, and connections with the home country, American Jews represent for Indian immigrants a group that has been able to "fit in" while remaining different. This is the route to success that Indian Americans also want to adopt in their quest to stake a position in American society. A June 1996 news report in *India West,*[20] a regional Indian American newspaper, seems to indicate that this status has been achieved at least by Indians in Britain. According to the item, several British newspapers labeled Indians as the "New Jews" of Britain on the basis of a study analyzing the 1991 British census returns of different groups.

As indicated above, forming religious "congregations" as a means of creating an ethnic community and preserving cultural distinctness comes with its own dilemmas and contradictions. The first and second generation have different needs and concerns, and it is difficult to develop an institution that successfully addresses these differences. Mark Mullins (1987, 320–334) has argued that over time ethnic churches become gradually deethnicized as they adapt to these generational differences, an observation that seems to be corroborated by Karen J. Chai's account of the Korean Protestant church (Chapter 9).

Mullins (1987, 327) further argues that if "ethnic closure and support" continue to be the goals of the ethnic churches, their future "is likely to be one of eventual disappearance" as cultural and structural assimilation proceed.

How much of this analysis is relevant to the survival of groups such as the OHM and the *bala vihars?* It seems fairly clear that Indian languages do not have much chance of surviving beyond the first generation. Particularly because of the English-language fluency of professional Indian immigrants, very little of the ethnic language is retained by their children. Even in the Tamil *bala vihar,* where Tamil is emphasized and taught, the level of spoken and written language fluency of most children is not high. Again, since the rituals and devotional songs are predominantly in Sanskrit, the linguistic distinctiveness of the groups are unlikely to be preserved. For these reasons, together with the development of the "ecumenical Hinduism" noted by Williams, the forging of a pan-Indian American community after a generation or two seems likely. At the same time, however, there is the constant stream of new immigrants from India for whom the support of the linguistic and subcultural community continues to be important. A great deal therefore depends on the future immigration policies of the U.S. government. If the immigration is not drastically curbed, the *satsangs* might become the primary community resource for first-generation immigrants and the *satsangs* and *bala vihars* the socializing agencies for the second, with third and fourth generations continuing to participate at least occasionally in the cultural and religious programs organized by these groups, particularly if they marry other Indians. Youth associations and religious groups in colleges and universities are becoming important venues for second-generation Indian Americans to meet fellow ethnics, celebrate ethnicity, and discuss its meaning and significance. Their importance is likely to increase over time.

In an earlier paper, I argued that one consequence of the fact that Hinduism has become the axis around which community, ethnic pride, and individual identity in the United States revolve is that organizations such as the *satsangs* and the *bala vihars,* while not necessarily directly supporting the call of Hindutva for a "Hindu" India, indirectly provide the receptive soil in which the seeds of the movement can be sown (Kurien 1995). That there is a close relationship between the Hindu renaissance that is currently taking place in India and the development of an American Hinduism has been frequently pointed out.[21] Southern California is now the home of the Federation of Hindu Americans (FHA), an organization formed in 1995 to "specifically pursue Hindu political interests."[22] Despite its short history, FHA leaders have become a highly visible and influential presence at all Hindu functions in southern California. While the OHM leadership and most members emphasize that they are against "Hindu fundamentalism," the OHM is a registered member of the FHA, and FHA officeholders have given speeches pushing the Hindutva agenda at the OHM's function on the occasion of Onam, the most important Kerala Hindu festival. The articles of FHA leaders have also been published in the OHM's annual *Souvenir* for the past two years. The implications of this development for the OHM and for other *satsangs,* and for the construction of a Hindu American identity and politics, remain to be seen.

Because of the distinctiveness and fluidity of Hinduism as a religion and the racial identity of Indian Americans, it seems unlikely that either Hinduism or Hindu Indian communities in the United States will disappear in the near future. Since Hinduism, at least to some extent, seems to be serving as a substitute for an Indian racial identity, its future also depends largely on how race and racial politics evolve in this country. Based on the evidence from countries around the world with long-established Hindu Indian communities, such as Southeast Asia (Mearns 1995), Fiji (Kelly 1991), Africa (Bhachu 1985), and the Caribbean (Vertovec 1992b, 1994), where the communities remain distinct, it does seem as though Hindu Indian ethnicity in the United States will continue to play a substantial role in shaping the lives of its members for a long time to come (although the content of that ethnicity will undoubtedly be much modified).

NOTES

1. I am greatly indebted to R. Stephen Warner for pointing this out to me.

2. This is despite the fact that they may be part of the "neo-Hinduism" of the modern Hindu revivalist movements.

3. A more recent estimate puts the population at 1,300,000. This statistic, provided by Krishna Reddy, president of the local branch of the Federation of Hindu Americans at a recent meeting, is not unreasonable in the light of the 126% growth rate the group experienced in the 1980s.

4. In John Y. Fenton's study (1988, 39), 78% of the Indian respondents indicated that they intended to stay in America.

5. For poignant accounts of the Indian immigrant experience, see Priya Agarwal (1991), Sathi S. Dasgupta (1989), Maxine P. Fisher (1980), Usha R. Jain (1989), Arthur W. Helweg and Usha M. Helweg (1990), and Parmatma Saran (1985).

6. According to Fenton (1988, 50), "92.4% of the Indian survey popula-

tion in Atlanta could be considered at least nominally religious." Again, 71% of the respondents reported carrying out some form of individual worship, prayer, or meditation at least once a week (ibid; 51).

7. Birthday parties and weddings are other such occasions.

8. Many of these second-wave Indians come with a long stay in mind, knowing that there is an established community in the United States and that "everything Indian is available in the country" (from food to kitchen equipment to make Indian dishes to temples to the latest Indian films) that enables them to re-create an "Indian life" at a much higher standard of living than they would have had in India.

9. A particularly good example is the work by Jain (1990), who studied the community in 1963 and 1987, and came to this conclusion.

10. My uncle, who lives in the Chicago suburbs, told me that in their "early days" here, the Malayalees were a small but unified group. As the numbers increased, however, tensions and conflicts emerged, and now the group is split into several religious and sectarian factions.

Similarily, an Indian American student of mine, whose family lives in the Chicago area but does not associate with other members of their community (although they nevertheless expect her to be "completely Indian"), came to me to talk about her problem about feeling so alone in her struggle to straddle the two cultures. She told me that she had asked her one Indian American friend she had (who belonged to another subculture in India) whether she could be part of her Indian American youth organization, but that the friend replied, "You can come for a meeting as my guest if you like, but you can't join since it is only for the 'X-X' Indian youth."

11. In addition to local organizations such as the OHM, many groups also organize annual or biannual conferences—some for the whole family and some just for the youth—where members of a particular denominational religious community living in the United States and Canada meet for "retreats" (e.g., the Marthoma conference).

12. It does appear that the parameters of the "community" seem to be gradually expanding to include larger Indian regional areas. For instance, I have come across a few arranged marriages between Hindu immigrants of roughly comparable caste status from different linguistic regions in South India.

13. Aiyappa is the child resulting from the union of Mohini, who was Vishnu in his female incarnation, and Shiva.

14. He was based in southern California for the last few years of his life and died in 1992 in San Diego.

15. This is particularly the case with the Brahmo Samaj and the Arya Samaj. See Daniel Gold (1991) for a detailed description.

16. For instance, I was told that early members of the Kualamandalam, a Kerala Hindu organization in Chicago, learned many of the Sanskrit *bhajans* that they now sing as part of their worship from their North Indian friends.

17. It is often pointed out that Indian holy men, such as Swami Vivekananda, Ramakrishna, and their more contemporary counterparts such as Swami Chinmayananda change their presentation and message when speaking to a Western audience (see Roy 1993).

18. This statement was challenged by the Narayans (Hema's parents) who asserted that it was not applicable to the Tamil *bala vihar.* Since my fieldwork there was shorter and was confined mainly to participant-observation of the monthly meetings, I do not have direct evidence to support my claim. However, it seemed to me more than a coincidence that all the members seemed to be well placed and to have children in top schools and universities (see my discussion of this later in the chapter). However, there is more evidence of this class selectivity in the case of the OHM. The original group had split into two, and from the information I was given, the division seemed to be largely on class lines. The overwhelming upper-class atmosphere and the constant talk about economic and professional achievements were also alluded to by several members, and two members who had been well placed in the past but had recently experienced some economic misfortunes told me that such talk made them uncomfortable.

19. Reported and discussed extensively in *Hinduism Today* (July 1995) the *India Post* (July 28, 1995).

20. July 19, 1996, B24.

21. All panels on Hindu fundamentalism at the annual meetings of the Association for Asian Studies and the Conference on South Asia over the past few years have had panelists making this point.

22. Statement made on July 22, 1995, in speech given by the president of the FHA, Prithvi Raj Singh, at a banquet organized to raise money for a local temple.

REFERENCES

Agarwal, Priya. 1991. *Passage from India: Post-1965 Indian Immigrants and Their Children.* Palos Verdes, Calif.: Yuvati.

Bhachu, Parminder. 1985. *Twice Migrants: East African Sikh Settlers in Britain.* London: Tavistock Publications.

Bosch, Lorens P. van den. 1991. "The Development of a Hindu Identity Among the Hindustani in Suriname and the Netherlands." Pp. 53–65 in *Religion, Tradition,and Renewal,* edited by Armin W. Geertz and Jeppe Sinding Jensen. Aarhus, Denmark: Aarhus University Press.

Bowen, David. 1987. "The Evolution of Gujarati Hindu Organizations in Bradford." Pp. 15–31 in *Hinduism in Great Britain: The Perpetuation of Religion in an Alien Cultural Milieu,* edited by Richard Burghart. London: Tavistock Publications.

Burghart, Richard. 1987. "The Perpetuation of Hinduism in an Alien Cultural Milieu." Pp. 224–251 in *Hinduism in Great Britain: The Perpetuation of*

Religion in an Alien Cultural Milieu, edited by Richard Burghart. London: Tavistock Publications.

Dasgupta, Sathi S. 1989. *On the Trail of an Uncertain Dream: Indian Immigrant Experience in America.* New York: AMS Press.

Federation of Hindu Associations. 1995. *Directory of Temples and Associations of Southern California and Everything You Wanted to Know About Hinduism.* Artesia, Calif.

Fenton, John Y. 1988. *Transplanting Religious Traditions: Asian Indians in America.* New York: Praeger.

Fisher, Maxine P. 1980. *The Indians of New York City: A Study of Immigrants from India.* Columbia, Mo.: South Asia Books.

Fishman, Joshua. 1985. "The Ethnic Revival in the United States: Implications for the Mexican-American Community." Pp. 309–354 in *Mexican-Americans in Comparative Perspective,* edited by Walker Connor. Washington, D.C.: Urban Institute.

Frykenberg, Robert. 1989. "The Emergence of Modern 'Hinduism' as a Concept and as an Institution: A Reappraisal with Special Reference to South India." Pp. 29–50 in *Hinduism Reconsidered,* edited by Gunther Sontheimer and Hermann Kulke. New Delhi: Manohar Publications.

Gans, Herbert. 1979. "Symbolic Ethnicity: The Future of Ethnic Groups and Cultures in America." *Ethnic and Racial Studies* 2 (January): 1–20.

Gold, Daniel. 1991. "Organized Hinduisms: From Vedic Truth to Hindu Nation." Pp. 531–593 in *Fundamentalisms Observed,* edited by Martin Marty and Scott Appleby. Chicago: University of Chicago Press.

Helweg, Arthur W., and Usha M. Helweg. 1990. *An Immigrant Success Story: East Indians in America.* Philadelphia: University of Pennsylvania Press.

"Hinduism." 1993. Pp. 519 in *Encyclopedia Britannica, Macropaedia.*

Jain, Usha R. 1989. *The Gujaratis of San Francisco.* New York: AMS Press.

Kelly, John D. 1991. *A Politics of Virtue: Hinduism, Sexuality, and Countercolonial Discourse in Fiji.* Chicago: University of Chicago Press.

Knott, Kim. 1987. "Hindu Temple Rituals in Britain: The Reinterpretation of Tradition." Pp. 157–179 in *Hinduism in Great Britain: The Perpetuation of Religion in an Alien Cultural Milieu,* edited by Richard Burghart. London: Tavistock Publications.

Kurien, Prema. 1995. "Hinduism in Diaspora: The Case of the United States." Paper presented at the annual meeting of the American Anthropology Association, Washington, D.C.

Kurien, Prema. 1996. "Gendering Ethnicity: Creating a Hindu Indian Identity in the U.S." Paper presented at the annual South Asia Conference. Madison, Wisc.

Mearns, David James. 1995. *Shiva's Other Children: Religion and Social Identity Amongst Overseas Indians.* New Delhi: Sage Publications.

Michaelson, Maureen. 1987. "Domestic Hinduism in a Gujarati Trading Caste." Pp. 32–49 in *Hinduism in Great Britain: The Perpetuation of Re-*

ligion in an Alien Cultural Milieu, edited by Richard Burghart. London: Tavistock Publications.

Mullins, Mark. 1987. "The Life Cycle of Ethnic Churches in Sociological Perspective." *Japanese Journal of Religious Studies* 14: 320–334.

Narayanan, Vasudha. 1992. "Creating the South Indian 'Hindu' Experience in the United States." Pp. 147–176 in *A Sacred Thread: Modern Transmission of Hindu Traditions in India and Abroad,* edited by Raymond Brady Williams. Chambersburg, Pa.: Anima.

Pocock, D. F. 1976. "Preservation of the Religious Life: Hindu Immigrants in England." *Contributions to Indian Sociology* 10: 341–365.

Rajagopal, Arvind. 1995. "Better Hindu Than Black? Narratives of Asian Indian Identity." Paper presented at the annual meetings of the Society for the Scientific Study of Religion and Religious Research Association, St. Louis.

Roy, Parama. 1993. "As the Master Saw Her: Sexuality, Surrogacy, and Religious Discipleship in Colonial India." Paper presented at the annual South Asia Conference, Madison, Wisc.

Saran, Parmatma. 1985. *The Asian Indian Experience in the United States.* Cambridge, Mass.: Schenkman.

Smith, Timothy. 1978. "Religion and Ethnicity in America." *American Historical Review* 83 (December): 1155–1185.

Stietencron, Heinrich von. 1989. "Hinduism: On the Proper Use of a Deceptive Term." Pp. 11–28 in *Hinduism Reconsidered,* edited by Gunther Sontheimer and Hermann Kulke. New Delhi: Manohar Publications.

Swatos, William. 1993. *A Future for Religion: New Paradigms for Social Analysis.* Newbury Park, Calif.: Sage Publications.

Vellatheri, Ravi. 1992. "From the Secretary's Desk." In *OHM Souvenir.*

Vertovec, Steven. 1989. "Hinduism in Diaspora: The Transformation of Tradition in Trinidad." Pp. 157–186 in *Hinduism Reconsidered,* edited by Gunther Sontheimer and Hermann Kulke. New Delhi: Manohar Publications.

———. 1992a. "Community and Congregation in London Hindu Temples: Divergent Trends." *New Community* 18: 251–264.

———. 1992b. *Hindu Trinidad: Religion, Ethnicity, and Socio-Economic Change.* London: Macmillan.

———. 1994. "'Official' and 'Popular' Hinduism in Diaspora: Historical and Contemporary Trends in Surinam, Trinidad, and Guyana." *Contributions to Indian Sociology* 28: 123–147.

———. 1995. "Hindus in Trinidad and Britain: Ethnic Religion, Reification, and the Politics of Public Space." Pp. 132–156 in *Nation and Migration: The Politics of Space in the South Asian Diaspora,* edited by Peter van der Veer. Philadelphia: University of Pennsylvania Press.

Warner, R. Stephen. 1993. "Work in Progress Toward a New Paradigm for the Sociological Study of Religion in the United States." *American Journal of Sociology* 98 (March): 1044–1193.

Waters, Mary. 1990. *Ethnic Options: Choosing Identities in America*. Berkeley: University of California.

Williams, Raymond Brady. 1988. *Religions of Immigrants from India and Pakistan: New Threads in the American Tapestry*. Cambridge: Cambridge University Press.

———, ed. 1992a. *A Sacred Thread: Modern Transmission of Hindu Traditions in India and Abroad*. Chambersburg, Pa.: Anima.

———. 1992b. "Sacred Threads of Several Textures." Pp. 228–257 in *A Sacred Thread: Modern Transmission of Hindu Traditions in India and Abroad*, edited by Raymond Brady Williams. Chambersburg, Pa.: Anima Press.

2 | # From the Rivers of Babylon to the Valleys of Los Angeles: The Exodus and Adaptation of Iranian Jews

Shoshanah Feher

On June 9, 1995, a group of young Iranians went to see a movie in Los Angeles's San Fernando Valley. As they left the theater, one of the youths, a sixteen-year-old Jewish Iranian, was shot and killed by two African American gang members who were driving past. His friends recognized a few Iranian girls in the car with the gang members. The incident shook the Los Angeles Iranian Jewish community; more than two thousand mourners attended the memorial service.

Ramtin Shaoulian's death was a turning point for Los Angeles's Iranian Jews because it forced the community to come to terms with life in the United States in new and challenging ways. *Chashm Andaaz (Viewpoint),* a magazine published by the International Judea Foundation, devoted an entire issue to Ramtin and the implications of the shooting. The cover of the magazine was stark red; the blackened profile of a young man's upper body reflected the Iranian Jews' somber reaction to the incident.

The initial reaction of the Los Angeles Iranian Jews was that they had failed their young people. What, they asked themselves, were Ramtin and his friends doing at the movie theater on a Friday night? Didn't he have better things to do? Why weren't they at Shabbat dinner at home? Later, concern shifted to the girls in the car. What were they doing with "gangbangers"? How had they managed to influence perpetrators of crimes against their own people?

Throughout the 1980s, Iranian Jews thought they were in the United States temporarily; figuratively their bags were packed and at the front door. In the 1990s, they began to realize that they were staying, and they changed their main goal to creating a balanced life in their host society. Ramtin's shooting awoke them to the fact that they were less successful than they had hoped or thought. With this incident, they had to acknowledge that their youths were no longer Jewish Iranians, but Jewish Iranian-Americans. The seemingly random shooting of a Jewish Iranian youth and the involvement of other Iranian youths in the crime forced the Iranian Jewish community to take a closer look at its young people and to admit to themselves that they are involved in "unsavory" acts and events, to which the community had thought itself immune.[1]

Background

Los Angeles is home to the largest concentration of Iranians outside Iran (Bozorgmehr 1992).[2] This group includes Armenians, Assyrians, Zoroastrians, Kurds, Muslims, Bahais, and Jews. In Iran, Jewish religious expression was largely monolithic. Even after coming to Los Angeles, 90 percent of Iranian Jews maintain their preimmigration levels of religious observance (Bozorgmehr 1992). This finding fits well with Raymond Brady Williams's (1988) assertion that religion is one of the most important identity markers employed by immigrant groups (especially religious minorities) to preserve self-awareness and group cohesion. Like many other immigrant groups, however, Iranian Jews have had to juggle their religious and their national identities.

Iranian Jews have had to find new ways to transmit vital aspects of their culture. How do Iranian Jews adapt to their new social setting? I begin by sketching the community's history and its migration to the new host society. Then I examine how the community has struggled to manage American, Iranian, and Jewish identities simultaneously. Finally, I discuss the strategies employed by the Iranian Jewish community to align itself with American Jewry.

A History of the Iranian Jewish Community

A Jewish community has existed in Persia at least since the destruction of the first Temple by Nebuchadnezzar (586 B.C.E.) and even earlier, according to some scholars (Haddad 1984, Loeb 1979, Papo 1987). After the destruction of the Temple, some Persian Jews returned to Palestine, but most remained in Persia. The Jewish community in the Middle East was established, for the most part, long before Islam, and

Shoshanah Feher

Middle Eastern Jews have always been part of the country in which they lived.[3]

Persian Jewry suffered a blow in 642 C.E. with the advent of Islamic rule. Although legally protected, Jews and other religious minorities were relegated to second-class status. In the sixteenth and seventeenth centuries, after Shiite Islam was adopted as the state religion, the situation deteriorated even further. Jews were subjected to forced conversions, social restrictions, and other indignities. Non-Muslims' status did not begin to improve until 1906, with the new constitution.

Tensions between Muslims and Jews peaked in 1948, when the state of Israel was established; the Arab world united in opposition to the Jewish state, instilling fear and intimidation in Middle Eastern Jewish communities. It is estimated that twenty-eight thousand Iranian Jews left Iran for Israel between 1948 and 1955 (Bozorgmehr 1992). Nonetheless, the secularization policy of the Pahlavi Dynasty, extending from 1925 through 1979, proved to be a positive force for Iranian Jewry (Bozorgmehr 1992, Cohen 1973); it allowed them to participate in nearly every professional aspect of society, including business and higher education (Haddad 1984, Sachar 1985).

The Islamic revolution of 1979 and the consequent fall of Mohammad Reza Shah and the Pahlavi dynasty returned Iranian Jews to second-class citizenship. Many Jewish leaders, accused of supporting Zionism and the deposed Shah, were summarily executed (Haddad 1984). Another wave of Jews left Iran at this time; many flocked to the United States.[4]

Today the Iranian Jewish community numbers roughly thirty thousand in Los Angeles alone (Kelley 1993). Most came to the area to be near family and friends. Together they have established the largest community of its kind in the United States. Most make their home in an area of the city known as the West Side; there 85 percent are self-employed, primarily in the fields of technology, sales, and administrative support (Bozorgmehr 1992).

In many ways the Iranians' experience is unique among Jewish immigrants to the United States. Unlike many other Jewish groups, Iranians did not receive a warm reception, either from their own co-religionists or from the larger American community. The Iranian Jews learned that they had little in common with American Jews (Harris 1982). Because the Jewish paradigm in North America is predominantly the German-based Ashkenazi one (Deshen and Zenner 1982, Harris 1982, Matza 1990), that brand of Judaism has come to be identified as normative in both its ritual and its cultural aspects. But Iranian Jews do not share the Ashkenazi culture common to most American Jews; nor do they share the Iberian experience of the much smaller Sephardic minority.

The Iranian experience is unlike that of the other, largely Ashkenazi groups who emigrated to the United States in the 1970s and 1980s. Russian Jews have been a cause célèbre in the American Jewish community for decades. Many American Jews trace their ancestry back to the former Soviet Union, thus creating a perceptible link between themselves and Soviet Jewry (also see Markowitz 1993, 61). American Jews rallied around Anatoly Scharansky and other prominent *refuseniks*. Thus, when thousands of Soviet Jews began to arrive on American soil, they were received with open arms (and open pocketbooks) by families, synagogues, and Jewish agencies across the country (Gold 1992a, 1992b; Markowitz 1993; also see Kelley 1993). The South African Jewish immigrants were far less numerous and less noted than the Russian Jews, but they brought many cultural traits consistent with American culture, including the English language and Anglo-Saxon values.[5]

The majority of both South Africans and Russians were Caucasian and Ashkenazi;[6] the Iranians are neither. While the South African and Soviet Jews sought ultimate refuge in the United States, and did not expect to return to their homelands, Iranian Jews frequently had one eye on this country and the other on Iran; they sought only temporary refuge from what they regarded as a time-limited resurgence of Islamic fundamentalism. This fact helps to explain why the Iranian Jewish experience in the United States has been characterized by segregation, not integration.

A Case Study

The Iranian Jews I discuss here are affiliated with the International Judea Foundation (IJF)/SIAMAK.[7] I use IJF/SIAMAK as a case study to clarify how a new ethnic and immigrant community reshuffles its ethnic and religious identities in settling into a new host society.

I would like to say that my involvement in IJF/SIAMAK was derived from a theoretical perspective and that I chose them thoughtfully and systematically, but this was not the case. As often happens in ethnographic work, theoretical perspectives change and projects are redirected. My own involvement with the organization began when I met fortuitously an IJF/SIAMAK board member who took an interest in the New Ethnic and Immigrant Congregations Project, sympathized

Shoshanah Feher

with my frustration (described below), and suggested that I use IJF/SIAMAK as a case study to understand ethnic identity. Probably not by chance, the group that was willing to talk with me and allow me to join its activities is also interested in accommodating to the American Jewish community. By studying a cultural organization such as IJF/SIAMAK, one can examine how cultural rules and norms are negotiated and transmitted to individuals through organizations and associated networks (Meyer 1988).

I began this project with the assumption that as a Jew, the daughter of immigrants, and an experienced ethnographer, I would be able to navigate my way into the Iranian Jewish community. I was wrong; I found the Los Angeles Iranian Jewish community very difficult to penetrate. I attended a predominantly Iranian synagogue twice weekly for six months, yet I was never able to engage in conversation with any of the Iranian attendees. I obtained only two interviewees, one of whom was unwilling to meet with me in person. Perhaps my lack of success was due to my being a tall, educated, single, Ashkenazi, North American-born woman, or perhaps there were other reasons that I can only guess at. My frustration increased, as did my irritation with acquaintances saying, "I told you so."

The Iranian community in Los Angeles has a long-standing reputation for being insular. Dr. Behnaz Jalali (1996), a clinical professor of psychiatry at the University of California, Los Angeles, School of Medicine, has spoken of the difficulties of treating this tight-knit community because of the high value placed on keeping difficulties and conflicts "in the family." An Iranian herself, Jalali believes that gaining access to the community is difficult, and even more so for non-Iranians. Ron Kelley (1983, 102), too, describes this phenomenon: "On the whole, Iranian Jews have kept to themselves, preferring the familiarity of their own social networks and Persian cultural traditions."

IJF/SIAMAK is one of approximately fourteen Jewish Iranian organizations in the Los Angeles area. By its own accounts, it is a forward-looking, progressive, and outspoken group, and therefore quite different from the other local Iranian organizations, which range from religious to secular. They deal with issues such as synagogue worship, land for cemeteries, schools, and funds for Israel, and include the Iranian branches of B'nai B'rith, Hadassah, and ORT (Organization for Rehabilitation and Training) as well as Magbit, the Eretz Cultural Center, the Iranian Jewish Federation, Nessach Israel, and Torat Hayim Academy. The members of these organizations are the community's elite; as one respondent told me, the groups are "headed by men from big [well-known] families back home who came in their early to middle fifties and are now in their seventies." Samira,[8] who heads IJF/SIAMAK's Singles Group, mirrored the sentiment of other members when she said that

> organizations like Magbit, like Haddasah, like the Iranian Jewish Federation . . . they collect money and send it to hospitals in Israel. [They] don't do anything for the community here. Not a dime. First of all, Israel is receiving help from all the countries around the world, but for our own society here [in Los Angeles], I think there's a lot to be done. I think we need our own libraries, centers for the youth, to keep our heritage alive. Not only as Jews, but as Iranian Jews.

IJF/SIAMAK is a group of individuals who, as one member said, "know what the problems are and are trying to do something about it." They belong to an "in-limbo" generation (as they describe themselves), those who came to this country as young adults and have spent half their lives here. Therefore they serve as a buffer between those who came to the United States as middle-aged adults and those who arrived as small children or were born here. Most of the members range from their late twenties to their early forties. They make their living as insurance agents, bakery owners, real estate agents, lawyers, and physicians.

Because of their age and their position in society, IJF/SIAMAK members are at the interface with the U.S. community and therefore experience the problems themselves. They speak not only the English language but the cultural language of the United States as well. Perhaps most important, the members respond actively to the problems and work to improve the quality of life of Iranian Jews in Los Angeles.

Most IJF/SIAMAK members maintain some level of religious involvement but are not committed to a weekly worship schedule or to a particular synagogue. As an organization, IJF/SIAMAK sponsors yearly High Holiday services for its members; more than one thousand participants turnout for Rosh Hashanah and Yom Kippur services.

IJF/SIAMAK was founded by Dariush Fakheri, who came to the United States as a university student in the late 1970s. In August 1979, reading a newspaper in his North American home, he came across an article about a retired colonel who had asked the Ayatollah Ruholla Khomeini for permission to start a nationalistic political party.

Fakheri, recalling the rise of Adolf Hitler, likened the situation in Iran to that in Germany and Italy forty years earlier. He and a friend asked the Los Angeles Jewish Community Relations Council (JCRC) to help them find a place for Iranians to meet and devise ways to get Jews out of Iran before it was too late. Fakheri smiles as he remembers those days: "The first reaction of the JCRC was 'What is an Iranian Jew?' They did not know that such a species existed." Fakheri and his friend called every Iranian name in their personal phone books, and 450 persons attended the first meeting.

A few months later, the political situation in Iran became critical. The floodgates opened, and Iranians emigrated to the United States by the thousands. Fakheri and his friend organized SIAMAK to help the émigrés settle. He says,

> People used to come from London and have only one telephone number in their pocket, [that] of SIAMAK. SIAMAK helped them settle into American life, from finding jobs and apartments to telling the newcomers what April 15th is. They didn't know anything; we had to tell them to stop behind the stop sign when you're driving because in Iran we didn't stop at the stop sign. We had to have English classes. We had to do a lot of things.

IJF/SIAMAK credits itself with having helped 80 percent of the Iranian Jews who came to the United States to settle.

After the large influx of immigrants subsided, IJF/SIAMAK lost some of its momentum. Having helped to resettle thousands of Jewish Iranian immigrants, the organization no longer had an active reason for existing. Although it survived, it provided little more than the yearly High Holiday services. Mansour, a co-owner of a printing shop now in his early forties, described IJF/SIAMAK as it was during the 1980s:

> It was the decade of us not knowing where we are. We're so confused and we didn't have an identity. We did the most stupid financial investments that anyone could do. Then with the recession, [we] lost all of it. And we didn't know which school to go to, how to adjust ourselves to the education. We were totally lost to the aspects of American life.

Mitra, the English-language editor of IJF/SIAMAK's magazine, agrees with this perception of the 1980s and attempts an explanation:

> When everybody came here, everybody was assuming we would go back, the next day actually. Then they thought, "OK, next week; OK, next month." Then four or five years passed and they thought, "We'd better unpack and start living." I came here just for vacation; I still have my return ticket. I came to visit my brother and go back.

> *I was going to college. . . . Then my parents called and said that school would be closed, and I knew that I'm not going back because my parents were coming here.*[9]

In 1990 the organization experienced what members call a "rebirth." The 1990s signaled a new era with a new vision and a new mission: trying to form tighter networks with the American Jewish community. David, a young professional in the organization, believes that the new direction taken by IJF/SIAMAK is a positive one:

> *For the first ten years they thought they were here temporarily, so they did not try to get involved and try to get know the society. But now we've come to a point that we've put down our luggage and we've decided that . . . we're going to be here for a long time, so we need to get know the society and the problems that our community faces here.*

According to its members, IJF/SIAMAK is special because it can see the issues involved in assimilating and really "starting to live" in the United States.[10] The main concern of this group has shifted from settling immigrants to balancing identities and ensuring that Judaism is maintained in the community.

Today IJF/SIAMAK provides an array of social services for the Jewish Iranians in Los Angeles. It offers help with immigration status, unemployment, job placement, taxes, and medical-legal referrals, as well as other services. IJF also conducts yearly fund-raising parties, a singles group, and a book club. As for outreach, IJF/SIAMAK sponsors University of Judaism classes, lectures, food for the poor, visits to old-age homes, and other community-oriented activities and events. IJF/SIAMAK also publishes *Chashm Andaaz,* a bimonthly magazine with approximately nine thousand subscribers; among them are thirty universities, including all the Ivy League universities. One of its short-term goals is to expand its subscription list to ten thousand households across the country. *Chashm Andaaz* has the greatest distribution of the five Iranian Jewish magazines published in Los Angeles (the others are *Peyman, Shofar, Jewish World,* and *Matana*) (Fakheri 1996, Naficy 1993).

During my seven months at IJF/SIAMAK, I attended both executive and board meetings, and conducted eight in-depth interviews (lasting two to five hours each) with each of the committee chairs; these included the heads of the Singles Group, Tikkun Olam (Charity), and Fund-Raising, as well as the Farsi- and English-language magazine editors. I also interviewed Fakheri and the vice-president. In my account of these interviews, I have changed the names and identifying details of all the respondents except Fakheri, who is a public and historic figure for IJF/SIAMAK. In addition to attending meetings and conducting interviews, I involved myself by editing articles for the English section of *Chashm Andaaz*.

Tricultural Conflict

Like any immigrant group, Iranian Jews have had to adapt to their new environment. This adaptation has involved balancing three identities—Iranian, Jewish, and American. One respondent refers to this as the "tricultural conflict." According to a 1992 study, 14 percent of Jewish Iranians in Los Angeles consider their ethnic identity primarily Jewish, while two-thirds regard their identity as Jewish Iranian (Bozorgmehr 1992, 164). David explained:

> When you are in Iran, you are a Persian Jew. But here, you have to face the fact that you're a Persian American Jew. So you have to deal with the fact that part of your identity is coming from the Persian society and part of it from the American society.

Living in the United States has allowed the Iranian Jewish community to excel in previously unknown ways. One respondent explained that in this country they can no longer say they don't succeed or advance because "the mullah didn't let us." That is, they can no longer blame the Muslim leadership that stood in their way in Iran. Already, IJF/SIAMAK members point out proudly that the young men and women are moving beyond their parents' educational levels. Mansour said:

> We have a lot of doctors [in Los Angeles]. I think we have between sixty and eighty practicing attorneys, and by the year 2000 we will have more than two hundred practicing attorneys. Some of them will go into the political arena. If you talk to these young people, you see [in them] something strikingly different from their parents: they're not afraid. They're not afraid to challenge this country.

Yet some Iranian Jews are discovering that American society has negative aspects as well. Soheil, part-owner of a Persian kosher bakery, commented:

> We have lots of doctors and lawyers, [but] I see criminals on the other [end of the spectrum]. And this is the beauty of this country, that it gives you the opportunity to be anything you want. [If] you want to be the greatest criminal, you can be. If you want to be the greatest scientist, you can be [that] as well. It's your choice.

Another IJF/SIAMAK respondent agreed that the American experience has given Jewish Iranians a new outlook and a new set of tools from which to choose:

> Since the American society is very open and free, we have the opportunity to interact and get involved with people who don't have the same culture as [ours]. It's going to open you to more opportunities that you didn't have in Iran. . . . Being a Jew helps you to have a very rich culture to pick and choose and get the best out of.

This concept of selecting the useful aspects of a culture is consistent with Joane Nagel's (1994) idea that ethnic culture is composed of the things we put into our "shopping cart." Culture is not handed to us; rather, we construct it by picking and choosing items "from the shelves of the past and the present" (Nagel 1994, 162). As a result, cultures are in a constant state of dynamic flux; they are borrowed, blended, rediscovered, and reinterpreted.

IJF/SIAMAK tries to help with the "picking and choosing" by encouraging the best of all three cultures. They do this, according to one respondent, "with the stories we write, by the heroes that we try to promote (like Elie Wiesel), to tell them that life is not all money. . . . Life is a balance." All of the respondents said they wanted to keep the best of the Iranian and adopt the best of the North American. They all mentioned their admiration for Iranian family values and their hopes of maintaining them in this country. One respondent observed that among Iranians "you respect the old. You stand up when they come in, you don't start [eating] before they start, you have extended family." Shireen, a loan broker and the vice-president of the organization, cited an example of life in Iran:

> There, during the weekend, the whole family would get together, go out for lunch, not just the immediate family. It would be aunts and uncles; we would reserve a big table. After lunch we go to somebody's house. The kids would hang out with each other and the older people would go play cards, do whatever. It was more the family together.

Vacations, she explained, were spent with the extended family. She remembers summer vacations with ten families participating.

Mitra, too, appreciates the family relationships that she experienced while growing up. She admires the love that she sees in Iranian families and feels that this value should be passed on:

Unfortunately, in American families, there [isn't] that much love. Persians have a lot of love to give and they are very family-oriented. This [non-Iranian] guy I used to work with has one brother, and he didn't know where his brother lived, where his mother lived, and they're all in California. I couldn't believe it!

All my respondents expressed a desire to maintain the values they identify as Persian. One respondent remarked that he'd rather lose the food, music, and language if he could keep the "good values" that, he believes, provide the individual with his or her identity. He said, "You have to be distinguished by something because in life, there are setbacks and falls, and this is something that keeps you going." These values, members point out, are especially important because they overlap with traditional Jewish values.

Although family values are prized highly, the family itself is suffering as a result of juggling identities. The tricultural conflict is evident in families: parents no longer know how to talk to young people, and vice versa. IJF/SIAMAK members divide the Jewish Iranian community into three generations: those who came to the United States as middle-aged adults; the "in-betweens," who came as young adults and have spent approximately half their lives here; and those who were born here or came as small children. The older generation has no real need to accommodate to American culture. Because of their large numbers in West Los Angeles—some people refer to Westwood as "Little Teheran," "Teherangeles," or "Persia Town" (also see Bozorgmehr et al. 1993, Jalali 1996)—they can manage daily life without speaking English. In the late 1980s about a dozen Iranian newspapers and magazines were published in Los Angeles alone (Bozogmehr 1992, 179; Naficy 1993, xvii). As Esther said, "Our parents are taken care of. They have Persian TV, stores, radio, they don't [even] need to learn 'yes' or 'no' [in English]."

Mitra, speaking for the "in-between" generation said, "We grew up in a totally Persian environment, with the Persian culture. We came here, went to school, went to work, and . . . [got] caught in the middle. At home, we had to be 100 percent Persian; at work, 100 percent American; and that's where we . . . really got lost." A younger member of the organization, who was raised in the United States, added, "We call them the lost generation. They are lost to both Americans and Persians. They're trapped in both but don't feel well in either." As I have stated, IJF/SIAMAK is made up primarily of this "in-limbo" generation, a group that understands and knows Iran but is a part of the U.S. experience.[11]

The youngest generation is considered totally Americanized. According to Mitra, the most important thing IJF/SIAMAK can do now is "to help the next generation, or my generation [the in-limbo generation] and the generation after me."[12] IJF/SIAMAK members are torn; they feel the pain of what they had but recognize, that for the good of their children, they cannot have it in the future.[13] Their children, they believe, must be comfortable in their new home and learn to integrate into it.

This has proven difficult, however. Mitra believes that second-generation Iranian Jews are picking and choosing their qualities, but she believes that they are acquiring the bad qualities of North American culture at the expense of the good: in the United States "there are so many good qualities we could pick up, but we only pick up what we see on TV—lots of gangs and drugs and all those things." The Los Angeles community is finding that, instead of maintaining the good aspects of American culture, their children are falling prey to the negative American norms. David, a young lawyer, said:

> We can be touched by the society we live in. We are not untouchable and basically everything that goes on in LA can affect us if we want it or don't want it to. We used to say: our kids won't be in gangs, our kids won't do drugs, our kids don't commit crimes. But that [the shooting of Ramtin Shaoulian] basically showed us that our kids are like other kids. It just shows that you can't be isolated from the society that you live in. You can't brush it off.

At one IJF/SIAMAK meeting the director of Torat Hayim, the Iranian Jewish school in Los Angeles, addressed these concerns:

> There are about 3,200 to 4,000 [Iranian Jewish] students in LA. For every hundred American Jews, sixty-four marry out of the religion. Consider the above statistics and the numbers of Iranian Jews in public schools of LA. This is alarming. Take, for example, the Jewish [Iranian] girl in the valley area who is involved in a black gang. When her father found out that she was dating a black guy, he forbade her to go out. She jumped out [of] the second floor, where the guy took her away. She was hurt, and she told the doctors at the emergency room that her father had pushed her out. There are teenage pregnancies, parents who send their children to San Francisco to drug detox programs.

At the same meeting, board members discussed the need for the community to recognize "that there are Iranian Jewish women working as prostitutes on Sunset Boulevard, that teenagers are involved with local gangs, and that there are Persian Jews who have AIDS."[14] Ramesh, a young lawyer, described her personal involvement and frustration with troubled Iranian Jewish youths:

> There are huge numbers of blue-collar crimes in the community. The jails are full of our people, and it makes me sick. I don't know what to do about it. I can't sleep at night. Tonight I bailed out a [Jewish Iranian] kid from jail with my own money. I don't know what to do anymore. I really want to expose this problem, but I don't know how, or how to make people listen.

Someone else asked, "How many young people do we have marrying non-Jews? How many calls do we get from our own who are in prison? How many of us are in AA programs? We are witnessing a holocaust of our young people."

IJF/SIAMAK members believe that the Jewish Iranian community would like to turn a blind eye to these events and pretend that its members are not involved in these aspects of American life. But members do not believe that continuing to try to "save face" will help the youths—or the larger community. They feel that the time has come to open the community's eyes and to respond to the dangerous problems facing its young people. A large part of the community, to IJF/SIAMAK's disappointment, still does not acknowledge that these issues exist. Other segments see them but do not want to discuss them, in keeping with the community's cultural history. Even the members of IJF/SIAMAK, a group committed to helping the youths, are unsure how best to address these concerns. The Ramtin incident, however, served as the "last straw" and increased their determination to find a way. This change was a long time in coming, but it shook the members of the Los Angeles community awake.

A Bicultural Solution?

In the attempt to reduce the tricultural strain on its youths, IJF/SIAMAK is turning increasingly to the American Jewish community for guidance. Members believe that it is primarily their Judaism that has enabled them to make the transition into U.S. life. The new immigrants are willing to identify with their potential co-ethnics because of structural and cultural circumstances both in their homeland and in their host society (Uriely 1995). The "proximal host" model (Mittleberg and Waters 1992) suggests that the identity of recent immigrants in the host country can be determined by the existence of a proximal host group—that is, the group to which the natives of the host country assign them. Immigrant groups might either reject their identification with the proximal host or integrate into American society through assimilation into the proximal host group (also see Orsi 1992, Portes and Rumbaut 1990).

The English-language editor of *Chashm Andaaz* explained how her own Jewish identity helped her entry into the United States:

> *Being Jewish helped me a lot. Because I was Jewish, [the brother of a] friend of mine helped me: Gave me a job, applied for a green card. . . . He helped me immensely. He told me that his mom and dad were Holocaust survivors, and he was told by his mom that whenever you see a human being, especially if he or she is Jewish, and they need a helping hand, you help them.*

She added that her Jewishness also helped her during the Iranian hostage situation in 1979–81: "During the hostage situation, people asked me where I was from. And if I were to say, I'm Persian, people would say, Oh! You bad people, you have our hostages. If I said, Jewish Iranian, it would help me. Even the non-Jews would take it more calmly." Samira brought up this issue as well:

> *The fact that we're Iranian Jews separates us from Iranian Muslims because the first thing people ask is: "Are you from Iran?" "Yes." "Are you a Muslim?" "No. I'm Jewish." And as soon as I say, "Jewish," I'm . . . "better" than a Muslim Iranian. American Jews especially sympathize with our problems because they realize that, as minorities, we went through certain restrictions back home.*

The tricultural strain has made IJF/SIAMAK members think about their priorities regarding identity. Shireen remarked that unlike the Persian side, "the Jewish side, no matter what, stays with you, because no matter where you are, you are first Jewish and then Persian." Another respondent said, "We're *almost* American because of living here, but we're 100 percent Jewish because wherever we go, we take that with us."

This sentiment is reflected in the respondents' talk of marriage. Majid, a single man, has given marriage a great deal of thought:

> *I have no problem marrying an American Jew. As long as the person is Jewish, I have no problem. If I have an option, I would like to marry a Persian Jew first because I think that we have something in common culturally. But if that's not an option . . . marrying an Argentine Jew, an Iraqi Jew, a Syrian Jew . . . [is] no problem.*

Indeed, all respondents mentioned the importance of marrying Jews, regardless of national identity (also see Bozorgmehr 1992). In practice, however, I found that no group members had ever married outside the Iranian community. This dichotomy between word and act can be explained by the fact that many respondents were married in Iran or shortly after coming to the United States, when language was still a barrier.

Strategies for Becoming More American-Jewish

Designated as "Iranian/Middle Eastern/Arab," Iranian Jews strive to identify with the American Jewish community and hope to assimilate into that group as a proximal host.[16] IJF/SIAMAK members discuss the experience of being identified as Iranian in Los Angeles. In a city heavily populated by Iranians of all religious backgrounds, they are easily and quickly identified. One respondent recalled the hostage crisis of 1979:

> The Immigration Service came to our school [Santa Monica College] and they rounded us [Iranians] up. No matter if you were Jewish or Muslim, they took us to the offices and you were being treated exactly as a criminal. They took pictures of us, they took fingerprints. All I was missing was a number, like this [she demonstrates as if in a mug shot]. . . . I felt like, "What did we do? We're just students here."

IJF/SIAMAK members are "pegged" in their businesses by co-workers and clients on the basis of their accents and their physical features. A real-estate agent commented, "In this part of town [in my business, my clients] . . . they ask you where you're from, and when you say, "Iran," you feel the tension. We're just being judged as—I don't know what goes on [in] their minds."

Even on the street, they feel these tensions:

> Every time I do something that makes someone else upset, the first thing they throw at us is, "You foreigners. Go back to where you came from." At that moment, I'm not part of the society. I live here, I pay taxes like everybody else. . . . Small things we're talking about [such as mistakenly taking a parking space]. It has to do with my accent or my features. Sometimes I don't [even] open my mouth and I hear it.

Samira said that all she has to do is speak a few words, and people ask her if she's from Iran. Her answer always has negative consequences:

> Every time you hear the name Iran, there's a negative thing being said about it. There hasn't been anything good said about Iran in the past sixteen years.[17] As soon as you say something about Iran, peo-

*ple automatically think about terrorism, a bunch of barbarians. . . .
Especially what the media shows. They never show what really the
culture is all about. They never show our museums, how . . . people
are much closer in our culture than they are here. But they [Ameri-
cans] have never seen that side. All they see is people who go into
the street and protest, people who start hitting themselves with
chains and all that.*

In the aftermath of the Oklahoma City bombing, IJF/SIAMAK members felt that even more antagonism and tension was directed toward
them. In an environment where Arabs and Middle Easterners are not
warmly welcome, all Iranians (although they are not themselves Arab)
feel this atmosphere.[18]

In his work with Israeli immigrants to the United States, Natan
Uriely (1995) found that a focus on Judaism is a determinant of
immigrants' willingness to be integrated into the Jewish American community and of their adaptation to the wider society. This point supports the idea that the link to the American Jewish community may
be a way for Iranian Jews to legitimize themselves. Newcomer immigrants are more likely to identify and integrate with their proximal
host group when such assimilation facilitates their adaptation in the
host county or when they perceive it as a way to improve their social
status. Becoming a Jewish American means upward status mobility for
these immigrants. In keeping with scholars' observations, forming ethnic solidarity with established Jewish citizens gives Iranian Jews access
to the political institutions at work in the United States, which is a
type of strategic mobilization (Nagel 1986, 1994; Nagel and Olzak
1982; Nagel and Snipp 1993; Okamura 1981).

Most Iranian Jewish groups still keep to themselves, but IJF/
SIAMAK is trying to change this pattern. Currently the organization
is making an effort to become involved in the local Jewish community.
For the first time, it is planning activities that include non-Iranian Jews,
organizing joint events with other Jewish communities (such as other,
new-immigrant Jewish groups and mainstream American Jewish organizations), and inviting non-Iranian Jewish representatives to speak to
members of IJF/SIAMAK. On the one hand, the Iranians believe they
have much to learn from established Jewish groups. On the other, they
feel that it is time for them to contribute back to the community. As
Mansour said, "The American Jewish community could learn from us.
Together we could build a healthier Jewish community." This segment
of the Iranian Jewish community is eager to become part of the American Jewish community. David stated, "We have to get the lines of

communication open so that we don't isolate each community from each other. It's to our community's advantage to do this right now, and to work toward a specific goal."

IJF/SIAMAK's attitude of adaptation to the host society recalls Williams's discussion of Bene Israel (Jews from India). According to Williams (1988, 125), the Indian Jewish institutions are a living museum for liturgy, folklore, and artifacts that, if treasured and properly preserved, will enrich the larger American Jewish community. For Bene Israel, participation in activities outside their own group enables new immigrants to build bridges into the established community. In turn, the American community provides a religious home for the Indian Jews and an established identity for their children.

Organizationally, IJF/SIAMAK is stressing alignment with the American Jewish community in three major ways: by trying to "bring Judaism to the younger generation," by addressing the issues in *Chashm Andaaz*, and by working to build a Jewish community center. The first of these, according to some members, is the ultimate goal of the organization.

Education: IJF/SIAMAK subsidizes Jewish education. In Soheil's words, "Jewish education is the most important thing. Therefore, if they [IJF/SIAMAK] have to pay to get one more person to 'come back to Judaism, to become interested in their religious tradition, it's worth it." Soheil explained that IJF/SIAMAK was willing to subsidize a course it sponsored at the University of Judaism because "if someone is 'in-between' thinking about intermarriage, and [if] they come [to the class] and this changes their mind, it'll have been worth it. Just for that one person." Mansour added, "That's the same reason we subsidize the magazine."

All of the respondents would like their children to attend Jewish schools. The older generation regrets that their children went through the public school system. As one older respondent said, "I was not aware of the importance of sending them to Jewish school. And then I couldn't afford it. But if I [were to] come back to the U.S. right now, with the knowledge that I have, I'd put them in Jewish schools. Not Jewish Iranian schools, Jewish schools."

The Magazine: In the English section of *Chashm Andaaz*, IJF/SIAMAK is addressing critical issues facing teens today, such as pregnancy and sexually transmitted diseases. The English editor feels that these subjects must be broached delicately, saying, "It needs to be done moderately. . . . You need to make these kids feel like it's OK to talk about these things." She grew very heated on this subject: "We need to make it clear to teens that these [topics] are not shameful. They shouldn't be ashamed; they can talk about it." She hopes the magazine will make them start talking.

Dariush Fakheri explains that the English section brings Iranian Jews to the American culture and simultaneously brings the Americanized community members into the Iranian culture:

> It's two together. It's a very gray area. You can't just cut and deal with one part of the organization, of the community. You can't just go deal with the little kids because they have parents, they have brothers, they have family. I cannot chose one part of the community and give them services.

Community Building: IJF/SIAMAK is trying to raise funds for a building of its own. Currently, the group operates out of an office in Santa Monica,[19] and hosts activities at various secular and religious locations. IJF/SIAMAK members would like to have a community center where activities would be offered all the time and where the "kids" could have a "home away from home." Fakheri would like to call it "Second Home." Playing on the theme of familial values, he explained the choice of name:

> You know why? Because we are the extended family. We are the aunts and uncles of our young. For those families where the father works sixteen hours a day and the mother is away at work, the kids come here, and we are their aunts and uncles. Aunts and uncles will take charge for those parents who aren't able to or are not capable. We are their second home.

Conclusion

IJF/SIAMAK regards the Jewish "one-third" as the most important aspect of its American Jewish Iranian identity (also see Ayalon et al. 1985, Uriely 1995). This is the basis of its strategy for moving from tricultural conflict to a bicultural solution. IJF employs Jewish education, the magazine, and the hope of a community center to reach out to its youths and help them with the problems they face in balancing their identities.

The Iranian Jewish community, a new immigrant group, is still learning how to deal with its new surroundings. Majid, a loan broker in his early thirties, is simultaneously hopeful and resigned:

> We are trying to change and learn. . . . It's just going to take a while, but I'm sure in the long run it's going to work out, and hopefully, within the next generation or two, they will be American Jews,

> *like any other Jewish immigrant group, like the Russians, like the Eastern Jews who came to the United States. They tried to keep their own cultural identity, but no matter how hard they tried, they assimilate into the culture and become American Jews. . . . As a matter of fact, maybe it would be easier for them—because they'll just have one identity and they won't have to balance the identities.*

Samira commented:

> *Our kids will not have the same kinds of problems communicating with their kids as their parents had with them. Let's say, my younger sister will have less of a problem with her kids because she was brought up here. She didn't go through the cultural shock. She was brought up here, so she knows how it is—the school system, etc. All these problems are just going to be less and less as time goes by, but part of our heritage is going to die. It doesn't matter what we do; a lot of people are just going to let go. I guess as time goes by, it becomes less and less important.*

Another respondent added that he believes the Persian Jews in Los Angeles are an "endangered species," and that in twenty or thirty years their community will be gone. He pointed out that "Iran for us was a temporary dwelling. It's just like you're a tenant in a country for 2,700 years." Soheil adds:

> *I don't think Persian Jewry is going to last more than twenty more years. The elements of a culture, like language, music . . . once people stop reading and writing that language, that's the end of the story. As I said, German Jews hoped they could keep their children German . . . and you're talking about a hundred years ago when MTV didn't exist, so it was much easier to keep it than [it is] today. So . . . my hope is to keep the Judaism alive by pushing our community into American Jewish system.*

Iranian Jewish ethnicity is fluid and dynamic, in keeping with many researchers' findings (Gold 1992b, Nagel 1986, Nagel 1994, Nagel and Olzak 1982, Nagel and Snipp 1993, Okamura 1981, Portes and Rumbaut 1990). Ultimately, IJF/SIAMAK members believe that their Iranian culture is a thing of the past and that they must look toward the future. Fakheri said:

> *When I swear that I'm an American citizen, I mean it. To me, Iranian culture and Iranian language [are] something that I brought with me. I'm not going to live in it anymore. I enjoy listening to [Iranian] music, but I'm not going to go back to Iran anymore. To me, that country is another country. My kids don't even know it.*

From the Rivers of Babylon

This sentiment may help to explain IJF/SIAMAK's constant looking toward the future. This view is unlike that of other immigrant groups discussed in this volume, whose reference point is still the "old country" (see Nancy J. Wellmeier, Chapter 3, and Elizabeth McAlister, Chapter 4). Jewish Iranians have few ties to their homeland. Indeed, the literature they read and the movies they watch are produced in Los Angeles, (Naficy 1993), and they no longer look toward Iran for cultural production.

Within the Los Angeles Iranian Jewish community, IJF/SIAMAK is at the forefront in concerns relating to ethnicity and religious identity, perhaps because this group has the most to gain by being aligned closely with American Jewish community—or the least to lose in the Iranian Jewish community.[20] In any case, their efforts are not typical of the community. Because IJF/SIAMAK is the most outspoken of the Iranian community groups, its members hope they are creating the way for others to follow. They are looking into the future and paving the way for their young people.

ACKNOWLEDGMENTS

This research would not have been possible without the gracious funding given to the New Ethnic and Immigrant Congregations Project by the Lilly Endowment and the Pew Charitable Trusts. I am also grateful to Judy Wittner and the NEICP participants for their feedback on this chapter and for making the project the wonderful experience it was. In particular, I'd like to thank R. Stephen Warner for making the project happen and for his advice, insight, and support. Thanks, too, to Elsa Feher and Geoffrey Sternlieb for reading early drafts of the chapter. Finally, my heartfelt thanks go to Mehdi Bozorgmehr for his help and to the members of IJF/SIAMAK for their openness and giving of themselves.

NOTES

1. Murders have been catalysts causing other immigrants as well to reexamine their lives in the United States (see Markowitz 1993, 240–246).

2. The size of the Los Angeles Iranian community and of its religious minorities is controversial. Estimates for the community overall range from 53,000 to 300,000 (Bozorgmehr et al. 1993).

3. Indeed, Muslims and Jews apparently shared widespread pre-Islamic beliefs and practices. There was little that outwardly distinguished Jew from Muslim: they spoke the same language, wore the same clothes, and possessed many of the same cultural traits (Kelley 1993, Sharot 1982).

4. Before the 1979 revolution, there were between 62,000 and 90,000 Jews in Iran (according to the Iran Statistics Center; see Bozorgmehr 1992, Kelley 1993). Today only 25,000 remain (World Jewish Congress 1995).

5. This is not to say that Soviet Jewish immigrants have not encountered problems in relation to American Jews. For an excellent ethnography on Soviet Jews and their experience in the United States, see Fran Markowitz (1993).

6. Ten percent of Soviet Jews are not of European descent (Gitelman 1991).

7. SIAMAK is the Farsi acronym for "Organization of Iranian Jews in Southern California." Members use IJF and SIAMAK interchangeably. Also see Nancy J. Wellmeier's essay (Chapter 3) for a discussion of another religiocultural association.

8. Except for Dariush Fakheri, president of IJK/SIAMAK, I have used fictionalized names for members.

9. See Stephen J. Gold (1992a, 13) for similar rhetoric used by Israeli Jews in Los Angeles.

10. Mehrdad Amanat (1993, 28) discusses the Iranians' dawning realization that they would remain in the United States permanently.

11. In contrast, the Koreans studied by Karen J. Chai (Chapter 9) have consensually recognized a "1.5 generation," those who came over at about age 12 to 16 and thus are fully bilingual and bicultural.

12. This problem of intergenerational communication extends beyond generations to interpersonal relationships within generations. All the women I interviewed spoke of the difficulty of evolving gender roles in a new environment. Although the men are finding it more difficult to adapt to women's changing roles, the women feel the brunt. For a more detailed discussion of changing gender expectations among Iranian women, see Arlene Dallalfar (1989), Shideh Hanassab (1993), and Nayereh Tohidi (1993).

13. Similarly, Williams (1988, 125) writes that among the Bene Israel (Jews from India), "the children will not have a sense of being Bene Israel; they will think of themselves as American Jews."

14. The Soviet Jewish community faces similar circumstances, both in New York and in Israel (Gitelman 1995, Markowitz 1993), as does the Israeli community in Los Angeles (Gold 1992a).

15. On November 4, 1979, armed students occupied the U.S. embassy in Teheran and held its staff hostage, demanding to be returned to Iran to stand trial. The Shah died in Egypt in July 1980. The hostages were released on January 20, 1981, the day Ronald Reagan was sworn in as president (Kelley et al. 1993).

16. In contrast, the Soviet Jews' entire program of resettlement is directed toward involving émigrés in the American Jewish community (Gold 1992b, 155).

17. Samira's reference to the "past sixteen years" is the number of years since 1979. This interview was conducted in 1995.

18. The bombing of the Alfred Murrah Federal Building in Oklahoma City occurred on April 19, 1995. Until an American was charged with the

bombing, blame was directed toward those from the Middle East and at Arabs generally.

19. IJF/SIAMAK has moved to the San Fernando Valley where they are able to rent a larger space.

20. The impenetrable synagogue that I attended perhaps represents one of the doomed options that my IJF/SIAMAK informants describe so eloquently.

REFERENCES

Amanat, Mehrdad. 1993. "Nationalism and Social Change in Contemporary Iran." Pp. 5–31 in *Irangeles: Iranians in Los Angeles,* edited by Ron Kelley and Jonathan Friedlander. Berkeley and Los Angeles: University of California Press.

Ayalon, Hannah, Eliezer Ben-Rafael, and Stephen Sharot. 1985. "Variations in Ethnic Identification among Israeli Jews." *Ethnic and Racial Studies* 8 (July): 389–407.

Bozorgmehr, Mehdi. 1992. *Internal Ethnicity: Armenian, Bahai, Jewish, and Muslim Iranians in Los Angeles.* Doctoral dissertation, University of California, Los Angeles.

Bozorgmehr, Mehdi, Georges Sabagh, and Claudia Der-Martirosian. 1993. "Beyond Nationality: Religio-Ethnic Diversity." Pp. 1–54 in *Irangeles: Iranians in Los Angeles,* edited by Ron Kelley and Jonathan Friedlander. Berkeley and Los Angeles: University of California Press.

Cohen, Hayim J. 1973. *The Jews of the Middle East: 1860–1972.* New Brunswick, N.J.: Transaction Books.

Dallalfar, Arlene. 1989. *Iranian Immigrant Women in Los Angeles: The Reconstruction of Work, Ethnicity, and Community.* Doctoral dissertation, University of California, Los Angeles.

Deshen, Shlomo, and Walter Zenner. 1982. "The Historical Ethnology of Middle Eastern Jews." Pp. 1–34 in *Jewish Societies in the Middle East: Community, Culture, and Authority*, edited by Shlomo Deshen and Walter Zenner. Washington, D.C.: University Press of America.

Fakheri, Dariush. 1996. Personal communication, February.

Gitelman, Zvi. 1991. "Ethnic Identity and Ethnic Relations Among the Jews of the Non-European USSR." *Ethnic and RacialStudies* 14 (January): 24–54.

———. 1995. *Migration and Identity: The Resettlement and Impact of Soviet Immigrants on Israeli Politics and Society.* Los Angeles: The Susan and David Wilstein Institute of Jewish Policy Studies.

Gold, Steven J. 1992a. *Israelis in Los Angeles.* Los Angeles: The Susan and David Wilstein Institute of Jewish Policy Studies.

———. 1992b. *Refugee Communities: A Comparative Field Study.* Newbury Park, Calif., London, and New Delhi: Sage Publications.

Haddad, Heskel. 1984. *Jews of Arab and Islamic Countries: History, Problems, Solutions*. New York: Shengold Publishers.

Hanassab, Shideh. 1993. "Premarital Attitudes of Young Iranians Regarding Mate-Selection: Arranged-Marriage vs. Inter-Marriage." Doctoral dissertation, University of California, Los Angeles.

Harris, Tracy. 1982. "Reasons for the Decline of Judeo-Spanish." *International Journal for the Sociology of Language* 37: 71–97.

Jalali, Behnaz. 1996. "Cultural Issues in Assessment and Treatment of Persian Patients." Paper presented at the seminar series in Transcultural and Community Psychiatry, UCLA Division of Social and Community Psychiatry, February 14.

Kelley, Ron. 1993. "Ethnic and Religious Communities from Iran in Los Angeles." Pp. 81–157 in *Irangeles: Iranians in Los Angeles,* edited by Ron Kelley and Jonathan Friedlander. Berkeley and Los Angeles: University of California Press.

Loeb, Laurence. 1979. "Prestige and Piety in the Iranian Synagogue." *Anthropological Quarterly* 52 (2): 155–161.

Markowitz, Fran. 1993. *A Community In Spite of Itself: Soviet Jewish Émigrés in New York*. Washington and London: Smithsonian Institution Press.

Matza, Diane. 1990. "Sephardic Jews Transmitting Culture Across Three Generations." *American Jewish History* 79: 336–354.

Meyer, John. 1988. "Levels of Analysis: The Life Course as a Cultural Construction." Pp. 49–62 in *Social Structures and Human Lives,* edited by Matilda White Riley. Newbury Park, Calif.: Sage Publications.

Mittelberg, David, and Mary Waters. 1992. "The Process of Ethnogenesis Among Haitian and Israeli Immigrants in the United States." *Ethnic and Racial Studies* 15 (July): 412–435.

Naficy, Hamid. 1993. *The Making of Exile Cultures: Iranian Television in Los Angeles*. Minneapolis: University of Minnesota Press.

Nagel, Joane. 1986. "The Political Construction of Ethnicity." Pp. 93–112 in *Competitive Ethnic Relations,* edited by Susan Olzak and Joane Nagel. Orlando, Fla.: Academic Press.

———. 1994. "Constructing Ethnicity: Creating and Re-Creating Ethnic Identity and Culture." *Social Problems* 41 (February): 152–176.

Nagel, Joane, and Susan Olzak. 1982. "Ethnic Mobilization in New and Old States: An Extension of the Competition Model." *Social Problems* 30 (December): 127–143.

Nagel, Joane, and C. Matthew Snipp. 1993. "Ethnic Reorganization: American Indian Social, Economic, Political, and Cultural Strategies for Survival." *Ethnic and Racial Studies* 16 (April): 203–235.

Okamura, Jonathan. 1981."Situational Ethnicity." *Ethnic and Racial Studies* 4 (4): 432–465.

Orsi, Robert. 1992. "The Religious Boundaries of an Inbetween People: Street

Feste and the Problem of the Dark-Skinned Other in Italian Harlem, 1920–1990." *American Quarterly* 44 (3): 313–347.

Papo, Joseph. 1987. *Sephardim in Twentieth-Century America: In Search of Unity*. San Jose, Calif.: Pele Yoetz Books.

Portes, Alejandro, and Rubén G. Rumbaut. 1990. *Immigrant America: A Portrait*. Berkeley and Los Angeles: University of California Press.

Sachar, Howard. 1985. *Diaspora: An Inquiry into the Contemporary Jewish World*. New York: Harper and Row.

Sharot, Stephen. 1982. "Judaism in 'Pre-Modern' Societies." Pp. 49–83 in *Jewish Societies in the Middle East: Community. Culture, and Authority,* edited by Shlomo Deshen and Walter Zenner. Washington, D.C.: University Press of America.

Tohidi, Nayereh. 1993. "Iranian Women and Gender Relations in Los Angeles." Pp. 175–217 in *Irangeles: Iranians in Los Angeles,* edited by Ron Kelley and Jonathon Friedlander. Berkeley and Los Angeles: University of California Press.

Uriely, Natan. 1995. "Patterns of Identification and Integration with Jewish Americans Among Israeli Immigrants in Chicago: Variations Across Status and Generational Groups." *Contemporary Jewry* 15: 27–49.

Williams, Raymond Brady. 1988. *Religions of Immigrants from India and Pakistan: New Threads in the American Tapestry*. Cambridge: Cambridge University Press.

World Jewish Congress. 1995. "Where the World's Jews Live." *Chashm Andaaz* 41: 82.

II

Transnational Migrants and Religious Hosts

3 | Santa Eulalia's People in Exile:
Maya Religion, Culture, and
Identity in Los Angeles

Nancy J. Wellmeier

Lucax Xuxep's[1] home is a typical California-style bungalow. It is also typical of new Central American immigrant households in that it is home to fourteen people, including Lucax's immediate family of six, two brothers-in-law, an adult niece and a nephew, and an unrelated family of three. None of this was likely to surprise me as I began my research by ringing the bell at the front door. But nothing could prepare me for the time-space machine that greeted me as I stepped into the large living room. The entire area was filled with the native Guatemalan instrument known as a marimba. Consisting of three long tables with wooden keyboards and sound boxes, the marimba was being played by seven musicians, each holding four *baquetas,* or rubber-tipped sticks. A drummer, guitarist, and percussionist took up any remaining space. The floorboards vibrated with the sonorous boom of the music.

The auditory illusion was complemented by the visual: one wall of the room was completely covered by a colorful painting of Santa Eulalia, the Guatemalan mountain village that once was home to Lucax, his family, and friends. With the whitewashed colonial church in the center, surrounded by the red-tiled and tin-roofed houses, the scene and the sound had transported the ten men (and me!) back into the Maya highlands. But it wasn't just a sensory illusion: these two focal points, the marimba and the parish church of Santa Eulalia, turned out to be key symbols for my understanding of the religiocultural association known as FEMAQ', the Fraternidad Ewulense Maya Q'anjob'al.

Lucax and the members of the marimba team are refugees from Guatemala, descendants of the Maya people who built the pyramids and temples in Mesoamerica, the creators of one of the world's most advanced prehistoric civilizations. Although many people are surprised to learn that the Maya still exist, they are in fact the majority population in several southern Mexican states and in most of western Guatemala (Garrett 1989, 424–504). The Maya are also present in the United States, particularly in the states of Florida and California, an unrecognized Native American tribe; as their sacred book, the *Popol Vuh,* proclaims: "We are going away, but we have still not died" (Recinos 1977, 53).

In this chapter I describe the FEMAQ' community, one of many saints' associations formed by the Maya in the United States, discuss its trajectory in terms of ethnicity-based religious groupings, deconstruct the notion of Hispanic immigrants, and show how both cultural and religious differences that distinguish the Catholic Maya from other Hispanic Catholics tend to spur the formation of religious associations that are both loyal to and disconnected from the local Catholic parishes in Los Angeles. I argue that indigenous Maya Catholics have an experience of life and of "church" unlike that of mestizo Hispanics, those of mixed European and indigenous ancestry, and that even most U.S. Catholic parishes attentive to their Latino populations have failed to integrate the Maya. Their underlying indigenous spirituality and their life in communities focused on the church have produced a cosmovision[2] unlike that of other Latino immigrants in the United States. Because the rise of self-initiated lay associations based on the hometown parish and emphasizing cultural specificity is one outcome, the marimba and the village church serve as the key symbols. This case study has theoretical implications for exploring immigrant religious practice, particularly in situations of involuntary immigration; for understanding how newcomers find points of insertion into U.S. society; and for refining theory regarding how identity is constructed and reinforced through religious ritual. This chapter documents how the religious practice of one group of new immigrants both adapts to a situation of exile and stimulates changes in the host churches or congregations.

My Project, Myself

As is common in the practice of postmodern anthropology, I want to situate myself in the research picture and clarify my relationship to the Fraternity of Santa Eulalia, or FEMAQ', in Los Angeles.

The research data presented here were gathered by the traditional

Nancy J. Wellmeier

cultural anthropological method of participant observation. As an anthropologist specializing in Maya culture, I had previously researched the religious practice of Maya people in both Guatemala, including Santa Eulalia, and in Florida, home of thousands of Maya exiles. As a woman member of a Catholic religious order, I had been in contact with the FEMAQ' organization in the context of pastoral work with Central American refugees before beginning this project. The members of the FEMAQ' directorate were enthusiastic about having me collaborate with them; they expressed hope that their children would have some documented history of the early years of the exile experience. They also accepted me as a possible bridge to the official Catholic church in the United States, and as a potential service provider for processing of legal documents, translations, and other contact needs. However, they were wary of publicity and wanted to insure that their personal anonymity as well as the good reputation of their group would be safeguarded in published material. Their negotiation of these terms was indeed sophisticated from the first meeting and can perhaps be attributed to the fact that Guatemalan highland communities have been saturated with anthropologists since the 1930s. The Maya resent the fact that they never see the published results of such research. "Libraries are full of books about us, in English, that we are unable to read. The researchers never return to give us the results of their studies. What can we expect from your research that will benefit our community?" was the question posed to me and to R. Stephen Warner, project director, by one leader at that intense first meeting.[3] This desire to control indigenous intellectual property, the cultural capital of each society, together with an effort to conserve the core beliefs and history of each culture, is part of what has been called "an amazing crescendo of indigenous political assertiveness throughout the Western Hemisphere" (Greaver 1995, 3–4). The 1992 Nobel Peace Prize Laureate, Rigoberta Menchú, an indigenous Maya woman and advocate for indigenous rights, symbolizes the Maya participation in this resurgence.

Participant observation means "hanging out" with the members at all group events, attempting to participate as a member would in preparing for religious and social gatherings, which includes decorating, serving food, and collaborating in publicity and technical activities. It also means living for periods of time with the families, eating and conversing with the folks in an informal manner. I also conducted twenty directed interviews with FEMAQ' members and a few nonmembers, as a check on my own perceptions. As a woman, I found that the women members of FEMAQ' were comfortable talking to me, but I also realized during the course of the research that I was being treated as an honorary male by the men, given access to decision-making meetings where FEMAQ' women were not present. This I attribute to my identity as a church representative. The research was conducted between October 1994 and April 1995, with continuing contact with the group through the present.[4]

FEMAQ' Profile

The Fraternidad Ewulense Maya Q'anjob'al, or FEMAQ', is an association of Maya refugee families from Guatemala who live in central Los Angeles. The basis of their association is their common origin in the municipality of Santa Eulalia, a mountainous "county" in the Department of Huehuetenango, in northwestern Guatemala near the border with Mexico. The men and women members speak Q'anjob'al, one of twenty-three Maya languages,[5] and most of the men are bilingual in Spanish. The older members fled the scorched-earth policies of their own government in the early 1980s, and function as a receptive community for those who continue to arrive in the United States, pushed by economic, political, and familial factors.

In 1986 a small group of Roman Catholic men from Santa Eulalia organized themselves in Los Angeles in order to accomplish three goals: to hold their traditional religious service in their own language, to collect and send funds to their home parish to help reconstruct the church building that had been destroyed by fire, and to preserve their Maya culture. This informal association increased in membership during the years, and in 1990 they invited the pastor of their Guatemalan parish, a native Maya priest, to visit the group in Los Angeles. Their pastor helped them at that time to formalize their association by choosing directors and forming committees, modeled on modern Catholic parish organization in Huehuetenango.

By 1992 the membership was at around two hundred, and the financial resources of the group were such that they were able to purchase a marimba, their autochthonous musical instrument, and have it shipped from Guatemala to California. The group had also sent thousands of dollars back to their village for the church reconstruction and for a vehicle to be used as an ambulance, and had begun to help pay the salary of a medical doctor for their town. This group and other Maya associations continue to sponsor yearly visits from their Guatemalan pastor, during which he has attempted, with limited success, to make connections with the Catholic clergy in the local Los Angeles

Nancy J. Wellmeier

parishes where his people attend Sunday mass. Caxín, the prayer leader, explains the group name, FEMAQ', thus: "*Fraternity [Fraternidad]:* we hope to achieve it; *of Santa Eulalia: [Ewulense]* we all have the same root and origin; *Maya:* we are Maya and want to preserve our values; *Q'anjob'al:* our language is part of our culture." Their internal organization includes a *directiva,* or "directorate," with a president, vice-president, secretary, treasurer, and at-large members, a prayer leader, and catechists, or teachers of religious doctrine.

By 1995, the Santa Eulalia Maya in Los Angeles had subdivided into several groups based on different perceptions of their goals. FEMAQ' became the marimba/fiesta/cultural affairs section. The approximately forty adult members, men and women, meet weekly for prayer. The men also accept contracts for marimba performances and plan the annual Fiesta of Santa Eulalia. The members of the larger association, around eight hundred,[6] are organized into other sections or committees that function as small communities. For example, the medical insurance committee collects and remits funds to the Santa Eulalia parish clinic to pay the doctor. The emergency committee collects funds to send to Guatemala the bodies of Maya people who die in the United States and to ransom compatriots from border smugglers who sometimes hold them hostage. Some of these committees also represent groupings according to village origin: the municipality of Santa Eulalia includes over thirty sizeable *aldeas,* or "villages," as well as the *cabecera,* or "municipal seat." All members actively participate both by financial contributions and by their presence at special events, namely, the visits from their pastor, the fiesta, and seasonal devotions. There is also widespread participation in the fiestas of other Maya hometown saint associations in Los Angeles and in the all-Maya soccer league, which is organized in Los Angeles according to municipality of origin and thus by Maya languages.[7] Linguistic diversity among the Maya has presented some of the same problems Fenggang Yang found in his research among the Chinese (Chapter 10), and the small communities are perhaps a parallel to the fellowship groups in the Chinese Christian church.

The members of FEMAQ' are young to middle-aged, and for the most part work in the Los Angeles garment industry. The leadership has been rotated among the men who were the first to arrive in the United States, some of whom were involved in some aspect of modern Catholic organization in their home parish. Many received training there from U.S. Maryknoll missionaries, and worked as catechists, faith animators, or choir members. Eight of twenty interviewees had served on a church committee and thirteen had helped with saints' fiestas in Santa Eulalia. These men are only in their mid-thirties, yet they represent the traditional leadership exercised by elders in Maya society, since they are the oldest "elders" present.[8]

Although the members are poor by U.S. standards, they pay rent, own vehicles, have relatively steady employment and, send their children to public schools. Many of the women work in factories and make significant adaptations to their host society yet proudly wear their traditional and colorful Maya dress at home and for communal gatherings. The group is male-dominated, as is religious practice and leadership in indigenous Guatemala, partly due to the men's greater facility with Spanish. It is also a fact that the Los Angeles Maya community is typical of the Maya population in the United States in general, in that men outnumber women approximately three to one. Yet the men are conscious of the gender imbalance in their organization; recent meetings of the FEMAQ' directorate have included developing strategies to get wives and sisters more actively involved, especially in roles that demand speaking. The women, of course, have traditionally provided the support system for all the group activities: food preparation and serving, decoration of worship space, and representation of the group as "princess" or "Indian Queen" at fiestas. If the number of young women who have finished elementary school in Guatemala (and thus are literate and speak Spanish) grows, their presence in Los Angeles will no doubt shift the balance of decision-making, power, as is happening in Guatemala.

The group has also been successful in incorporating new arrivals, usually younger men who are either relatives or friends of members. There is likewise an oft-stated concern among the founders and leaders about how to insure that the younger men and women will know, respect, and practice the religious traditions of Santa Eulalia. The group has, at this point, few adolescents who are children of the members; their offspring are either very young, having been born in the United States in exile, or have been left behind in Guatemala to support their grandparents.[9]

The Exile Experience

Maya people from Guatemala have come to the United States because they fear for their lives. Even before the outbreak of the worst violence in the early 1980s, long years of government repression targeted labor union and cooperative leaders, catechists, church workers, and any one suspected of informing the indigenous people about their human rights. From 1981 through 1985, government troops systematically massacred entire village populations, "disappeared" numerous church workers, and kidnapped, tortured, and brutally killed hundreds of indigenous leaders. Many residents of the highland villages fled in the night across the border to Mexico in refugee waves that overwhelmed the Mexican state of Chiapas.

During the following years, and up to the present, any person in Guatemala whose neighbors warned him of strangers asking about him or who received written threats made his way quickly to the border. As it became clear that Mexico intended to keep the refugees interned in U.N. camps instead of granting them political asylum, the United States became a more attractive safe haven. Human rights projects in this country worked feverishly during 1982 through 1989 to prepare and file political asylum applications for them on the grounds that Maya Indian people were subject to repression and persecution in their own land because of their race, religion, or perceived political involvement. In many cases, it was simply a case of being Indian in an area where all Indians were suspected of being guerrilla sympathizers.

The road to the United States is long when one has to take local buses, skirt around checkpoints, try to talk like a Mexican, and get off somewhere in the Sonoran desert to walk three days to safety. But thousands of Guatemalans have done this; they arrive in Arizona with their shoes and feet worn out, thirsty and hungry beyond belief, and grateful for the food, clothing, and advice offered by an ecumenical coalition of church volunteers.[10] Many if not most Maya people at first made their way to south Florida or Los Angeles. The presence of one or two forerunners was reason enough for others to follow, since that meant they had a contact who could be counted upon to provide temporary housing, a job lead, and advice about the necessary papers.[11] The magnet effect of social service agencies specializing in Guatemalan asylum applications was another factor. Even though documentable asylum cases are rare now, border enforcement more energetic, and legal immigration all but impossible, people still continue to arrive, the pull to reunite the nuclear family overcoming their fear of both the Border Patrol and the currect wave of xenophobia.

Most FEMAQ' members who arrived in the United States during the 1980s and early 1990s filed for political asylum, and are still awaiting decisions in their cases. Some obtained residency through the agricultural provisions in the 1986 Immigration Reform and Control Act (IRCA). The more recently arrived have no such coveted legal status and have usually purchased counterfeit documents in order to be able to work. Most of the women whose husbands are here legally have family reunification petitions on file in their names, but have come to join their husbands before the visas have been granted. The temporary and potentially dangerous nature of the immigration status of most of the respondents in this study is the reason that their identities have been disguised.[12]

The Maya immigrants in the United States could be characterized as "cross-fire refugees" (Ferris 1987, 5) a term that indicates that although they were in real and proximate danger of death because of the civil war in their country, the United States does not recognize them as having a legitimate claim to political asylum because of its own ambiguous relations to Guatemala and because they cannot prove that they were direct and named targets of either the guerrilla or the army. Many FEMAQ' members as well as members of other Maya associations have lost family members in massacres. The hidden trauma, nightmares, nervousness about the approach of any uniformed person, and reluctance to talk about their political views or their involvement in political life in Guatemala are among the results of their experience. The diffuse, impersonal accounts and "flat" tone of Maya victims of violence noted by other researchers (Burns 1995, Warren 1995) are both an attempt to avoid bringing the conflict into the newly formed community and a way of dispersing blame over a wider number of perpetrators.[13]

None of the members of FEMAQ' is a U.S. citizen, and none is an officially sponsored refugee. As such they do not draw on public assistance except for health care. As in many cases of involuntary migration, however, the patterns established by the pioneers in terms of contacts, jobs, housing, and the desire to reunify the nuclear families have led to further and almost continuous subsequent migration, no longer provoked by crisis but by other motives.[14]

In Florida, the Maya people work directly in flower nurseries, landscaping, golf-course maintenance, and vegetable picking (see Ashanbranner 1986, 4, 7; Burns 1989a, 12; 1989b, 46; 1988, 41–45). In Los Angeles, they labor largely in sweatshops. In central-city factories owned mostly by Koreans, Maya men and now women make jeans, shirts, and underwear for the U.S. market. The hours are never enough to earn a livable wage, since there are more laborers than can be absorbed in an industry that is rapidly moving offshore. The Maya are forced to piece out their income by taking in boarders, cooking for strangers, collecting and selling old cardboard, and engaging in a variety of other microenterprise initiatives.

Nancy J. Wellmeier

Many of the unaccompanied men live in central Los Angeles apartments, two-bedroom units cracked in the 1994 earthquake, renting for $700 a month. This becomes economically feasible only by giving up the dispersed Maya settlement pattern and sharing space among up to fifteen people. Others, like Lucax's family described in the introduction, rent houses. Yet the style of life in these households remains very Maya, with the rhythm only superficially disturbed by the capitalist work schedule. Food, dress, conversation, and priorities are all Maya. Household hierarchy is Maya, with the oldest male somehow responsible for the whole group. Especially Maya are the prayer and devotional life, the cultural celebrations, and the engagement of the household in the network of former citizens of Santa Eulalia who find themselves exiled in the City of Angels.

Lucax, only thirty-five years old, is recognized as one of the elders; his arrival in 1984 gives him the status of wise man. But he is not alone in his leadership role: a growing number of colleagues of about the same age as well as younger men have banded together to re-create their face-to-face village life and especially their cultural and religious life as well as circumstances will allow until their longed-for return.

The Catholic Church in Santa Eulalia

To understand the extent of the adaptation of the Fraternity members' religious practice to the Catholic scene in Los Angeles, it is necessary first to understand a little of how the Catholic church is organized in Santa Eulalia. After initial evangelization and colonization in the early 1500s, the Huehuetenango area was left thinly pastored from the beginning of independence (1820) until 1943, when Maryknoll missionaries from the United States were given charge by the archbishop of Guatemala. Their efforts were designed to prepare the laity to tend to the spiritual needs of the remote villages, to sponsor cooperatives and other social programs, to teach people about their dignity and human rights, and to attempt to root out the still strong practices of the Maya religion. Results were mixed.[15]

The lay leaders who went through the Maryknoll training programs began a tradition of initiative and self-reliance in church matters that is still operative today. Each village has a prayer leader, teachers for adult religious education, and a choir. The Maryknollers also managed to inspire enough young men to enter the priesthood that the diocese has been in the hands of the native clergy for over fifteen years. These Maya Catholic priests have reevaluated their ancestral religious practices and found many of them compatible with Christianity; they are beginning an effort to reindigenize Catholicism, opting to resume the inculturation process interrupted by the American missionaries.

Elements of indigenous Maya religion include a concept of the divine as a duality, called Mother-Father, or Grandmother-Grandfather, together with a strong consciousness of the unity of all creation. Many practices, such as asking permission of the earth to till it, of animals to kill them for food, or of trees to cut them down, are common to other Native American peoples and aborigines throughout the world. The talk circle, or community council that comes to decisions through a process of respectful turn-taking and consensus, is another Maya practice. The burning of pine splits, copal incense, and wax candles before cross shrines is still seen in most highland towns, and some practitioners sacrifice chickens and pour rum for the spirits who live on the mountaintops. One of the most characteristic Maya religious practices is the following of the sacred calendar, the *tzolkin,* which consists of two intertwined cycles of named and numbered days, each with its own patron spirit, assigned prayer intentions, and probable luck.[16] Another is the election or appointment of the *alcalde rezador,* or "prayer leader," and his wife, elders who are chosen to do nothing but pray for the health and prosperity of the community for the period of a year, during which time they are supported by the community.

At this point it is impossible to separate out the Maya religious elements that have been "baptized" or taken over into Catholic practice. Practices such as praying on one's knees in the church while holding a burning candle, consulting the diviners about the proper name to give a new baby, and being aware of the calendar days, the saints' fiestas,[17] and the lay Catholic leadership all have been thoroughly interwoven into a new cloth in the five hundred years since the first evangelization, in spite of the efforts of both the early Spanish and the later U.S. missionaries to eradicate them. This syncretic tapestry, as some would call it, is further embroidered by some of the Maya Catholic priests, who promote prayers to the four directions, initiation ceremonies on significant calendar days, the use of copal incense, and other revived Maya elements. In the parish of Santa Eulalia, the Catholic pastors have been, for the past fifty years, personally involved with the lives of the people, known to all and knowing most, with different degrees of appreciation of Maya customs but generally respectful of local incarnations of Catholicism.

This study is limited to Catholic Maya, but the reader should be aware that there is a widespread, if not strong, evangelical Protestant presence in the Guatemalan highlands. Small fundamentalist sects have established churches there, and during the violent years, they inducted many new members who found it safer to be Protestant at a time when Catholic workers were targeted (see Hagan 1994, 28–29). Evangelical Protestant teaching emphasized the diabolic nature of Maya ancestral religious practices. Huehuetenango is 65 percent Catholic, 17 percent Protestant and 13 percent *costumbre,* or Maya religion. The Q'anjob'al speakers are mostly Catholic (Diócesis de Huehuetenango 1994, 26–30).[18]

The most striking characteristic of Maya-Catholic religious practice is the tradition of visible and sustained self-sacrifice on the part of leaders for the good of the community. To be recognized as a leader among the Maya means to have visibly given one's time, energy, skills, and even funds for the good of the community. This is the result of the self-initiated, production-oriented nature of traditional Mesoamerican religious cargo systems,[19] the functional equivalent of which has been continued in Maya Catholicism by conscious efforts of missionaries to empower lay leaders. The interesting thing is what happens when this production-oriented religious practice comes into contact with the very different, somewhat consumer-oriented style of U.S. Catholic parishes, even those which are sensitive to Latino/Hispanic traditions.

Maya Religious Production in Los Angeles

When Catholic Maya people from Guatemala try to find a Catholic church in Los Angeles, they begin with the nearest one that they can identify as Catholic. In Los Angeles, these central-city, point-of-entry parishes struggle to meet the needs of the multicultural Latino population that fills the scheduled Masses to capacity, but they have no policy or philosophy about trying to distinguish among the distinctive groups, all of whom are lumped together as "Hispanic." This approach, which can be called "super-tribalization,"[20] perhaps does meet the needs of the majority of Mexican, Salvadoran, Nicaraguan, and Honduran immigrants, for the most part from Spanish-speaking urban settings. The U.S. Catholic church has not begun to deconstruct the concept "Hispanic"; only recently has it become normative to provide culturally sensitive services in Spanish. Many Maya, who are rural and speak Spanish only as a second language, are acutely uncomfortable interacting with Latinos, even in the church setting. Their indigenous style is much more reserved, interior, slow, and quiet. The dissonance is complicated by the fact that their proximal hosts are the very kind of folks—mestizos, or mixed-ancestry Hispanics—who are seen as their oppressors in Guatemala.[21] When asked about the differences between their home parish and the one they attend in Los Angeles, FEMAQ' members unanimously mention language as the first difference. They are used to at least some of the Mass being celebrated, preached, and sung in Q'anjob'al Maya. Another difference mentioned is the lack of a personal relationship with the priest in the Los Angeles parishes.

One outcome of this cultural immersion into an unfamiliar style of church is the formation of quasireligious associations, usually based on the parish of origin, in which some attempt is made to satisfy religious and other needs by an "extracurricular" ritual practice. As the Los Angeles Maya have moved out from the downtown area, they have begun to attend Sunday Mass at several Catholic parishes. None of these parishes have welcomed them *qua* Maya. As one informant told me, "We haven't found a home church."[22] The Fraternity of Saint Eulalia is one example of an incipient house-church, but there are many such groups all over the United States. In Los Angeles alone, there are also groups named for the Huehuetenango parishes of San Miguel, San Sebastián, San Pedro, and Santa Cruz.

The practice that has developed revolves around three main activities: a weekly prayer session, the collection and sending of money to the home parish, and an annual fiesta in honor of the patron saint. In all of these activities, FEMAQ' members re-create their face-to-face village society centered on the church and the marimba. The weekly prayer ritual consists of a paraliturgy that closely follows the form of the Mass. A typical example took place in mid-November of 1994.

The community gathered at about 7 P.M. at the home of Cuin Tomín. The living room of the small house had no furniture except for a sofa where the five or six women were invited to sit. The white stone fireplace had been converted into an altar, with four pictures of Jesus on the mantel and a lighted votive candle on the floor. Cuin's wife, Eul, was dressed in her Maya finery. Thirty people filled the room, but the men surrounded Cuin's small marimba until Caxín, the prayer leader, positioned himself near the altar and began the service. A subtle atmosphere of contemplation descended. The prayer was conducted bilingually. The sign of the cross in Spanish was followed by a welcome in Q'anjob'al from the host, Cuin, who asked the community to pray with him to thank God for his job, the health of his family in Los Angeles and in Santa Eulalia, and the unity of the FEMAQ' community.

Matín led the group in a hymn, taken from the Huehuetenango diocesan hymn book. Caxín then invited all to recite the Confiteor, or prayer for forgiveness of sins, and then to listen to the Scripture. Another participant, Palás, read the passage in Spanish and explained it. It told the story of the shepherd who left his ninety-nine sheep to look for one that was lost. He suggested that they all need to forgive those group members who have fallen away and to encourage them to return. Caxín repeated the explanation in Q'anjob'al and retold the story.[23] He then opened the service for sharing, and there were several commentaries that affirmed the theme of forgiveness. He summarized and then began a litany of special requests to God. Many of those present added their petitions, directed to *Mamín* (an affectionate term of address to one's father in Q'anjob'al). Then all recited the Our Father in Spanish, shared handshakes and hugs, contributed to a collection basket, listened to the ending prayer, and sang a final hymn. Caxín ended by asking the group to pardon any errors he may have committed, and requesting a host family for the next week. Simple refreshments— Mountain Dew soda (favored all over the United States by the Maya) and *chek'a* (a typical sweet bread, made in downtown Los Angeles by a Guatemalan bakery)—were served, preserving the fellowship of Holy Communion. During this social time, news from Guatemala and plans were shared, and announcements concerning an approaching religious festival were made.[24]

The effort to collect money for Santa Eulalia is made through monthly assesments of all known townspeople and sent to the parish finance committee in Guatemala by money order. Thousands of dollars have already been sent, accomplishing wonders in terms of rebuilding the church and staffing the parish clinic. One motive behind all this energetic effort seems to be that the exiles wish to retain their membership rights in their home community and insure a place there when they return. They also believe that they can more effectively contribute to the hometown through the church than through civic or political organizations, which are highly mistrusted.

One of the most interesting ways that the Fraternity of Saint Eulalia has invented to garner funds is the formation of a marimba team. The marimba, to many Maya people, embodies the soul of their culture and is regarded as semisacred. The sonorous boom of the *hormigo*-wood keys forcing air through the wooden soundboxes elicites a feeling of sheer joy mixed with painful nostalgia in the hearts of the exiles. In recent years, there have been attempts to prove an autochthonous origin for the instrument, arising from the discovery of a codex picturing the *marinmaya de brazo,* a string of keys fastened to an outstretched arm (Gomes 1993, 8–9; see also Camposeco 1995). In Guatemala it is identified with indigenous music, although in neighboring Chiapas this is not the case (see Kaptain 1992). Although the marimba is capable of lending itself to any musical style and indeed is frequently used for salsa and other Latin rhythms, it is *el son,* the slow and plaintive waltz melody of the highlands, that helps the exiled Maya both to chase away their sorrow and yet to remember it.[26] The marimba is also played cooperatively, usually by seven musicians, and this is sometimes referred to as an example of the cooperative rather than competitive nature of the indigenous community life and organization.

The marimba is an important symbol of indigenous identity and has been used in cultural festivals at the Smithsonian Institution and even at Disney World to represent the Maya culture. The members of FEMAQ' imported their marimba from their own hometown, one of the recognized centers of marimba craft (Camposeco 1995, 12). It requires constant upkeep to repair and replace broken or worn-out *clavijas* (wooden pegs that hold the keys) and the *mux,* or "navel," of the soundboxes, a small orifice covered with a piece of porcine intestine (*tela*) glued on with black beeswax, and to keep the instrument in tune during changes in humidity. It also requires communication with suppliers of these materials in Guatemala, as well as weekly practice sessions that bring together at least ten men. It is entirely appropriate that the members of FEMAQ' have formed their marimba team as a way to announce their identity to others while raising funds through their performances. The role of music in forming and maintaining identity across time and space should be noted; it parallels the findings in the chapters in this volume by Luís León (Chapter 5), Randal L. Hepner (Chapter 6), and Sheba George (Chapter 8).

Two other facts about the marimba merit mention here. One is that the Santa Eulalia Maya are known throughout the Guatemalan highlands as lovers of music; wherever they live in the United States, they soon manage to import a marimba, which then becomes a focal point for gathering the community. There are full-sized marimbas in Colorado, Florida, Arizona, and at least three in Los Angeles, each the prized possession of a group of Santa Eulalia's people. In Los Angeles, material, cultural, and spiritual control of the marimba has been a point of controversy that has led to the subdividing of the larger community. Renting space to store the instrument, finding a place for practice sessions, purchasing community-owned vans to transport the marimba to fiesta sites, and accounting for funds generated by the marimba in live and recorded performances have all become reasons for mistrust among the groups. There is also controversy about how "Latino" a marimba group can become in order to appeal to the general public, without losing its mystical significance as Indian cultural property.

The other fact is that marimba playing is gendered space. Maya women do not, generally speaking, play the marimba anywhere. Informants claim that there is no actual taboo connected with the participation of women, but that no self-respecting father would allow his daughter to be involved in an activity that is frequently associated with drinking.[27] My own "honorary male" status broke down in this space: I was never invited to do anything more than listen to the marimba. It is nonetheless true that learning to play the marimba is a rite of initiation for young men from several highland municipalities, including Santa Eulalia, so much so that young Santa Eulalia men who find themselves in the United States with no marimba accessible have purchased electronic keyboards with a "marimba" setting and have begun to produce tape recordings of their native *sones* (Maya waltzes) in this medium.

The patron saint in highland Guatemala symbolizes not only the holy person him- or herself, but the parish under his or her patronage, as well as the municipality, language group, and particular cultural patterns of that municipality. Thus Santa Eulalia is shorthand for all of these identity configurations—the Roman maiden martyred in Barcelona in the third century, the parish and its church, the governmental unit or division, and the distinctive dress, speech, and customs of the Maya-language group who live in that area. When exiled Maya groups choose to sponsor a fiesta in honor of their saint, ethnic pride is at stake. This is one reason why such an enormous amount of time and energy is expended on these events, both in Guatemala and in the United States. Months of preparation, practice, fund-raising, and other planning takes place in committee meetings. The fiesta and all its corollary events are premier examples of what I term "popular religious production," that is, self-initiated religious activity that is not dependent on official or hierarchical organization. The contrast with the Haitian devotees of Our Lady of Mount Carmel studied in Elizabeth McAlister's research (Chapter 4) is striking. On the other hand, the Hindu *satsangs* and Chinese Christian fellowship groups described respectively in the work of Prema Kurien (Chapter 1) and Fenggang Yang (Chapter 10) are not hierarchically controlled.

For the February 1995 fiesta of Santa Eulalia in Los Angeles, the fifth annual celebration of this event, FEMAQ's most talented artist painted a canvas backdrop for the stage at Saint Vincent's auditorium. It was a colorful and accurate rendition of the town of Santa Eulalia, with the Cuchumatán mountains in the background, the newly rebuilt parish church in the center, and homes, shops, and the evangelical church clustered around it. So realistic was this painting that many of those attending the fiesta were able to identify their own former homes. The hall was also decorated with palm branches in cross-like patterns around the walls and wooden crosses at the entrance. The image of the saint herself was on a throne, decorated with flowers, palm leaves, and woven Maya cloth. Visually, the participants could have easily imagined that they were not in Los Angeles at all but back in Santa Eulalia. The dress of the participants added to the illusion: all of the women wore their typical clothing—*corte* (long colorful woven skirt)and *huipil* (embroidered or tapestry blouse)—while the men wore white cotton trousers, straw hats, and the *capixay,* a thick, black woolen pullover jacket.

The effect of the decorative arts employed in the preparation of the hall was augmented by the marimba music, played by the marimba team dressed in their typical dress, and by the poetic declamations made by the announcers in both Spanish and Q'anjob'al. The religiocultural ceremony was witnessed by an audience of over eight hundred, and included a solemn procession of young FEMAQ' members, men and women in their twenties who were dressed to represent the *icham alkales,* the elderly Maya *alcaldes rezadores.* They came into the hall with bare feet and kerchiefs on their heads, bent over, their staffs decorated with flowers, and carrying gifts of flowers, corn, fruit, and bottles of rum, incense in a clay censer, and yellow and black candles. At each of three wooden cross shrines, they knelt and lifted their gifts to the four directions, while the master of ceremonies explained that this was the custom of the ancestors. One young man blew his blowgun (still used by highland Maya to hunt) to the four points of the Maya cosmos. The procession mounted the auditorium stage and left their offerings at the feet of the image of Santa Eulalia.

Finally, the dance that followed the cultural program alternated Latino rhythms with the *son,* the Maya waltz that is not just a folkloric performance but the actual form of social dance used in the highlands to this day. The new year begins with the patron saint's fiesta, and many older Maya believe that the new cycle of crops and children needs to be danced in. This fiesta was satisfactory, according to comments of some participants, because they were able to fulfill their duty to their town and their saint by dancing the *son*. At the same time, the younger men and women were delighted to dance to the popular music they frequently hear on Spanish-language radio.

The production of the fiesta is thus a cooperative effort, as is most production in the Maya universe, and is done for the good of the whole group, not for individual recognition or fame. As one Huehuetenango priest told me, "The fiesta as a whole is a religious act, even when it seems to be secular, since it is a celebration of life." The music, ceremony, and dance have a religious purpose: to create the proper setting to honor the saint, to renew life, to reaffirm identity even in exile, and to create greater unity among the saint's people.

Problems with the Local Church

Although there are no open conflicts with the Los Angeles parishes that are attended by Maya people, the potential for problems is very real, and the perception on the part of the Maya that the church is not interested in them has already had its effect. When we speak of "the church," it is important to distinguish between the different levels or manifestations of church. The hierarchy of the U.S. Catholic church, through its Office of Pastoral Care of Migrants and Refugees, has been particularly vigorous in encouraging dioceses around the country to initiate ministry projects to tend to the various new immigrant groups. The philosophy at this level is that the local church should attempt to become inculturated, respecting and incorporating the religious culture of each new group. The Archdiocese of Los Angeles has a whole page in its official directory listing the different contact persons for ethnic ministry to various groups, from Argentinians to Zimbabweans. The official position is to provide services that are culturally appropriate to each group and, if possible, in the appropriate language.

On the local parish level, these policies get translated according to the training, sensitivity, and pastoral judgment of the local pastor. In the case of the parishes where Maya people attend Mass, the presence of many cultural groups, albeit all of them describable as Hispanic or Latino, makes for a difficult situation in which the easiest solution is to assume a cultural unity that does not exist or to go with what appears to be the majority culture, in this case Mexican. In this scenario, any group that wishes to emphasize its own peculiar experience of church, or to insist that culture and religion are inseparable for them, is perceived as divisive by local pastors. The extraliturgical religious meetings of Santa Eulalia's people and other Maya saints' organizations are considered to be private efforts not connected to the official church. The saints' organizations are perceived to be siphoning off funds that should be coming to the local parish and that are instead being sent to Guatemala. The visits by the native priest from Santa Eulalia have been coordinated with the local parishes only with difficulty, although about one-third of those attending the 8:30 A.M. Sunday Mass at one downtown parish is visibly Maya. Parish facilities are not available for activities of the group unless they are requested by group members who are active and registered in the parish. This situation is slowly changing as the Maya establish personal relationships with local church leadership.

The lack of official recognition, interest, and insertion into the local Catholic church is one of the spurs for the persistence of FEMAQ'. People who are used to producing their own religious practice without the presence of the clergy, as well as their own food, are not easily satisfied with the more passive religion they find practiced in this country, and their past training as lay leaders gives them the impetus and the know-how to organize their own religious house-churches, not to replace the local parish, but to supplement it. Ethnicity and religion are so intertwined for the Maya that they cannot conceive of remaining identified as Santa Eulalia's people unless they continue to pray in the accustomed way and in the accustomed language, with the accustomed hymns and responses. Like the medieval Christians of Western Europe, who "took for granted the fundamental intuition that Christian faith and the daily lives of those who professed it could not be separated without destroying or compromising both" (Espín 1995,16), the Maya experience life as a unity. They believe that to be Maya, they must relate to their Creator. In this they are like the first humans described in the *Popol Vuh*—people of corn whose first action was to give thanks to their Creator for the gift of life: "Truly we give thanks two and three times. We have been created, we have been given a mouth and a face, we talk, hear, think and walk. We thank you for creating us, for giving us our being, O Creator and Shaper, O our Grandmother, O Our Grandfather" (Recinos 1977,101–102). To be human is to pray; the Creator in fact rejected and destroyed the first three attempts to form humans because they did not thank their "Former and Shaper."

In different settings things turn out differently. The Santa Eulalia Maya people in Alamosa, Colorado, for example, have gained the respect and admiration of the Catholic pastor, the other parishioners, and the ministry staff of that small town. The association of Maya

Nancy J. Wellmeier

people that has formed there has full use of the parish facilities; it is recognized as a legitimate Catholic community. In Indiantown, Florida, another rural place with a small parish, the Maya people are the majority in the town, and their priest attempts to re-create, as nearly as possible, the style of church to which they are accustomed. In Indiantown, the parish *is* the Maya community, and no saints' organizations have formed to supplement religious practice (Wellmeier 1994b: 186–194). In Mesa, Arizona, the outcome of the local parish's attempts to include everyone under the multicultural umbrella has led to the formation of a strong, religiously oriented saint's association that meets weekly for prayer.

In Houston, home to roughly three thousand Maya from El Quiché and Totonicapán departments (Hagan 1994, 49, 149), the immigrants attend two different Protestant churches and one Catholic church. The experience of the Catholic Maya seems to be similar to that in Los Angeles in multicultural parishes, whereas the Maya members of the Protestant *Iglesia de Dios* are the majority in that congregation and center many of their activities around it (Hagan 1994, 30, 68–74). There is an association of soccer teams that supports the annual hometown saint's fiesta in Guatemala, although "the fiesta system has not been reproduced in Houston"(Hagan 1994, 74).

Common elements leading to the formation of saints' associations seem to be critical mass—a sufficiently large group to generate the energy needed for such a sustained effort—and a benign neglect of the ethnic specificity of the Maya by the proximal host. This would tend to strengthen the theory that identity construction takes place in situations of contact and conflict (Gonzalez 1989, 9). The Maya, an oppressed although not minority population in Guatemala, come to the United States with a strong sense of identity, but the experience of being a little-understood minority group here serves to reinforce the identity-defining process. All of these situations are, of course, subject to ongoing change and revision, as the local parish personnel begin to understand the challenges of multicultural sensitivity, and as the Maya themselves become more familiar with the U.S. churches and begin to create their future.

The Future

No one knows what that future may be. In the wake of California Proposition 187, which would deny health care and education to undocumented immigrants, and similar anti-immigrant legislative initiatives all over the country, a very real possibility is that they will return to Guatemala. This may be voluntary, as the danger there is perceived to be a thing of the past, or it may be involuntary, as forced deportation and repatriation may take place. The experience of those who have returned since 1993 is anything but encouraging.[28] However, all of the FEMAQ' members interviewed express the hope of return.

At the same time, at least two members of the community have purchased homes in the United States, giving rise to the speculation that their expressed hope is only that and that they may stay here. Eleven years of exile has meant increasing ties with the local community, including schools and employers, but it has also meant increasing frustration with rental housing among a population accustomed to owning their self-built homes and farms. In the case of definitive settlement, several outcomes seem possible with respect to the religiocultural specificity of the Maya. First, they could take the least line of resistance and meld with or assimilate into the general "Hispanic" category. Those who come knowing how to speak only Maya soon learn Spanish in order to fit into the barrios where they live. Their children speak English. They could become "consumer Catholics," allow themselves to be coopted by the U.S. parish system, forget their lay leadership ideals, and give up their struggle to be recognized as having a different identity. There are Maya individuals and families in Los Angeles who have done this, joining charismatic-style prayer groups, opting to submerge their indigenous identity.

Another possibility is that the U.S. Catholic church may catch up to the challenges of the new immigration, perhaps even grouping newcomers into ethnic subparishes where the ministry would not only be done in an appropriate style and language, but where their experience and ethnicity would be seen as a model for and a contribution to the catholicity of the church. This would strengthen the Maya renaissance now taking place in Guatemala and reaching into the exile community here. It would definitely change the face of the U.S. Catholic church. The experience of the San Miguel Maya in Los Angeles might be an incipient model for this.[29] The formation of a national-level Catholic Maya pressure group to negotiate with the hierarchy is not impossible; such groups exist for Haitian, Korean, Vietnamese, and Filipino Catholics.

The fourth possibility is that Maya Catholics will not wait around for their church to notice them, but will join the evangelical organizations that recognize their cultural and language needs, such as the storefront ministries that have already sprung up in Los Angeles to

Nancy J. Wellmeier

offer services in Q'anjob'al and Kiché to those who came from Guatemala as evangelicals.

One suspects that all four futures will find realization. Some FEMAQ' members will certainly return to Santa Eulalia. Others will find the Catholic parishes of Los Angeles becoming increasingly aware of their gifts and their needs. Still others will decide that to be American means to be assimilated to the generic Latino category or even to become Protestant. The exile experience is still new, and the second generation has not yet given evidence of how they will adapt the age-old Maya religious culture to their new home. What is certain is that the Maya will not relinquish their role as agents of their own adaptation. As John Watanabe (1995) analyzes it, the Maya have survived for the last five hundred years with an largely intact distinctive culture precisely because of their locally inherited cultural forms that enable them to "imagine" their communities and "invent" their traditions within the impinging global system. The continuing process will bear watching.

ACKNOWLEDGMENTS

Grateful acknowledgment is due to the Lilly Endowment and Pew Charitable Trusts, which funded the New Ethnic and Immigrant Congregations Project, of which this study was a part. The encouragement and suggestions of R. Stephen Warner, Judith G. Wittner, and Ana-María Díaz-Stevens are also heartily appreciated.

NOTES

1. "Lucax Xuxep" is the Maya equivalent of "Lucas José"; the *x* is pronounced like the English *sh*.

2. *Cosmosvision*: "A world view that integrates the structure of space and the rhythms of time into a unified whole" (Carrasco 1990, 166).

3. This chapter has been translated into Spanish and made available for FEMAQ' members to honor their request. Translation into Q'anjob'al will have to wait for help from someone more competent than I.

4. I began in 1994 to coordinate a project sponsored by the U.S. Catholic Bishops' Conference, attempting to provide culturally appropriate religious support to Maya Catholics. I also serve as a consultant with the Catholic diocese of Huehuetenango in Guatemala.

5. The Academia de Lenguas Mayas has standardized the orthography and promotes recognition of the Maya languages as part of the Maya cultural renaissance taking place in Guatemala. Languages spoken in Huehuetenango

include, in addition to Q'anjob'al, Mam, Chuj, Poptí (Jakalteko), Kiché, Aguakateko, and Spanish (see Maxwell 1992).

6. This number is based on estimates made by group leaders in November 1995. The number of Maya in the United States is all but impossible to document, since there are no census categories for Native Americans not from North America. Fernando Peñalosa (1995,3) estimates 4,000 Q'anjob'ales in southern California; Jacqueline M. Hagan (1994, 149), 3,000 Maya in Houston; Allan F. Burns (personal communication), 20,000 in south Florida. My own estimate is that Maya people in the United States may number about 100,000.

7. This league has 12 teams and is a year-round activity, as it is in Florida, (see Wellmeier 1994a, 15–16; Peñalosa 1995, 151).

8. Robert Harmon (1995) has researched the role of elders in the diasporic Maya community of Los Angeles.

9. Almost every couple who are together in the U.S. Maya communities have at least one minor child living in Guatemala.

10. See Nancy J. Wellmeier (1994a) for a description of the Arizona transit station for Guatemalan migration.

11. See Elizabeth Ferris (1987, 9) and Sergio Aguayo (1986, 109, 115) for a discussion of the patterns of migration. See also Sarah J. Mahler (1995, 83–104) on why refugees choose one U.S. location over another; south Florida early became a haven for the Maya because of its similarity to the coastal areas of Guatemala, its abundance of agricultural labor, and the relatively thin presence of the Border Patrol, among other reasons.

12. However, Santa Eulalia is a real place (see LaFarge 1947; Comité de Vecinos 1969). Both books have recently been translated and published in Spanish by Fernando Peñalosa of Yax Te' Press, Rancho Palos Verdes, California. The names of the members are also Maya names (see my discussion of this in Wellmeier 1994b).

13. No one is ever named as guilty of atrocities; perpetrators are "the army" or "the guerrilla." Recognizing the long-term psychological effects of this collective amnesia, the Guatemalan Catholic church has initiated a project called *Recuperación de la Memoria Histórica* (Recovery of the Historical Memory), an attempt to interview survivors and document their stories so that a national reconciliation can take place. My conversation (June 1996) with Edgar Hernández, project director in Huehuetenango, proves that the interviews are revealing the extent of the damage to the Guatemalan social fabric (see Unger 1996 for details of the project).

14. A study of the effects of emigration from Santa Eulalia, together with the effects of cash remittances sent from the United States to relatives there, is currently being conducted by Erik Popkin, Department of Sociology, University of California, Los Angeles.

15. For a historical and statistical study, see Diócesis de Huehuetenango (1994, 74). Also enlightening is a recent study of the presence of Maryknoll priests in San Miguel Acatán, Huehuetenango, by Timothy B. Jafek (1996).

16. See Walburga R. Alvarado (1995) for an explanation in Spanish of how this works.

17. There is speculation that Catholic saints may correspond to pre-Columbian Maya deities: San Miguel is connected to K'anil, the patron of lightning, for example, and San Sebastián, a Roman soldier martyred by arrows, may have substituted for Tecún Umán, the Mam leader who was defeated by conquistador Pedro de Alvarado; but Santa Eulalia has not been linked to any Maya gods, as Our Lady of Mount Carmel "stands for" Ezili Dantò in Vodou (see Elizabeth McAlister, Chapter 4). What is curious is that although she is called "the Virgin Santa Eulalia," in popular tales she is the consort of San Miguel, San Sebastián, or San Mateo, all patron saints of neighboring *municipios*.

18. See Hagan (1994) for research among the largely evangelical Protestant Maya in Houston.

19. See John Watanabe (1992) and Wellmeier (1994b, 9–28). The literature on the Mesoamerican cargo systems is extensive (see the bibliography in Watanabe 1992).

20. See Nina Glick-Schiller et al. (1992) for a discussion on transnational migration and the tendency for more and more specific origin-based groups to arise, in order to avoid being lumped together in supercategories such as "Latinos" (see also Olzak 1983, 355–374).

21. The "proximal host" concept can be attributed to David Mittelberg and Mary Waters (1992, 413). As historian Enrique Dussel (1995, 41) says, "There have been few serious dialogues, in Latin American history, between the original inhabitants (ill-named 'Indians') . . . and the mestizos."

22. Dispersed among several Los Angeles Catholic parishes, the Santa Eulalia Maya have no opportunity to present a united front to any pastor and to petition for a Mass in Q'anjob'al, even if there were a priest who could satisfy their request. In an exception, the original Catholic church of Los Angeles, Nuestra Señora de los Angeles, or "Placita," on Olvera Street, has recently recognized the San Miguel Acatán Maya as a parish organization. Special events, Masses with parts in Q'anjob'al, and meeting-room privileges are part of the welcome, although Migueleños continue to hold their weekly prayer service in private homes.

23. There is a Q'anjob'al translation of the New Testament, prepared by the International Biblical Society (1981), but it is not generally used in the Catholic church in the Huehuetenango parishes. Rather the readers do a sight translation, as Caxín did here.

24. One influence of the missionaries has been to teach the Catholic prayers and Mass ritual in Spanish; it thus functions somewhat as a sacred language, since native priests have only recently begun to celebrate rituals in the Maya languages.

25. Camposeco's (1995) explanation of the Te' Son, Chinab' O K'ojom, the Guatemalan marimba, is a history of the instrument in the Maya highlands.

26. See Gaspar Pedro González (1993, 155) for a description of this nostalgic quality of the *son* within an autobiographical novel, the first to be written by a Q'anjob'al Maya.

27. Note the similarities to the gender issues raised in Sheba George's study of Indian immigrants (Chapter 8).

28. See Victor Montejo (1993) for an account of the problematic situation of those who have repatriated from Mexico to Guatemala.

29. See n. 22 above.

REFERENCES

Aguayo, Sergio. 1986. "Refugees: Another Piece in the Central American Quagmire." Pp. 95–176 in *Fleeing the Maelstrom: Central American Refugees,* edited by P. Fagen and S. Aguayo. Baltimore: Johns Hopkins University Press.

Alvarado, Walburga R. 1995. *El Tzolkín Es Màs que un Calendario.* Iximuleuw, Guatemala: Centro de Documentación e Investigación Maya.

Ashanbranner, Brent. 1986. *Children of the Maya: A Guatemalan Indian Odyssey.* New York: Dodd, Mead.

Burns, Allan F. 1988. "Resettlement in the U.S.: K'anjobal Maya in Indiantown, Florida." *Cultural Survival* 12 (4): 41–45.

———. 1989a. *Immigration, Ethnicity, and Work in Indiantown Florida.* Gainsville: University of Florida.

———. 1989b. "Internal and External Identity Among K'anjobal Mayan Refugees in Florida." Pp. 46–59 in *Conflict, Migration, and the Expression of Ethnicity,* edited by Nancie Gonzalez and Carolyn McCommon. Boulder, Colo.: Westview.

———. 1995. "Chains of Communication and Chains of Violence in the Guatemalan Immigrant Community." Paper presented at the annual meeting of the American Anthropological Association, Washington D.C.

Camposeco, José B. 1995. *Te'Son, Chinab' O K'ojam, La Marimba de Guatemala.* Rancho Palos Verdes, Calif.: Yax Te' Press.

Carrasco, David. 1990. *Religions of Mesoamerica: Cosmovision and Ceremonial Centers.* San Francisco: Harper and Row.

Comité de Vecinos. 1969. *Santa Eulalia.* Guatemala: Instituto Nacional Indigenista.

Diócesis de Huehuetenango. 1994. *Así es Huehuetenango II.* Huehuetenango, Guatemala.

Dussel, Enrique. 1995. "Ethical Sense of the 1994 Maya Rebellion in Chíapas." *Journal of Hispanic/Latino Theology.* 2 (3): 41–56.

Espín, Orlando. 1995. "Pentecostalism and Popular Catholicism: The Poor and Traditio." *Journal of Hispanic/Latino Theology* 3 (2): 14–43.

Ferris, Elizabeth. 1987. *The Central American Refugees.* New York: Praeger.

Garrett, Wilbur E. 1989. "La Ruta Maya." *National Geographic*. 176 (4): 424–504.

Glick-Schiller, Nina, Linda Basch, and Cristina Blanc-Szanton. 1992. *Towards a Transnational Perspective on Migration: Race, Class, Ethnicity, and Nationalism Reconsidered*. New York: New York Academy of Sciences.

Gomes, Carlos Ramiro. 1993. "Marínmaya de Brazo." *Guatemala in USA* (Los Angeles), 5 January: 8–9.

González, Gaspar Pedro. 1993. *La Otra Cara*. Guatemala: Ministerio de Cultura.

———. 1995. *A Maya Life: Sb'eyb'al Jun Nag Maya*. Rancho Palos Verdes, Calif. Yax Te' Press.

González, Nancie L. 1989. "Introduction." Pp. 1–10 in *Conflict, Migration, and the Expression of Ethnicity*, edited by Nancie L. González and Carolyn McCommon. Boulder, Colo.: Westview.

Greaver, Thomas. 1995. "Cultural Rights and Ethnography." *General Anthropology* 1 (2): 1–4.

Hagan, Jacqueline M. 1994. *Deciding to Be Legal: A Maya Community in Houston*. Philadelphia: Temple University Press.

Harman, Robert. 1995. "Intergenerational Relations Among Maya in Los Angeles," Pp, 156–73 in *Selected Papers on Refugee Issues IV,* edited by Ann Rynearson and James Phillips. Washington, D.C.: American Anthropological Association.

International Biblical Society. 1981. *Ja'an Nuevo Testamento*. New York: IBS.

Jafek, Timothy B. 1996. "Community and Religion in San Miguel Acatán, Guatemala, 1940–1960." Master's thesis, Department of Anthropology, University of Arizona.

Kaptain, Lawrence. 1992. *The Wood that Sings: The Marimba in Chiapas, Mexico*. Everett, Pa: Honey Rock.

LaFarge, Oliver. 1947 [1974]. *Santa Eulalia: The Religion of a Cuchumatán Town*. Chicago: University of Chicago Press.

Mahler, Sarah J. 1995. *American Dreaming: Immigrant Life on the Margins*. Princeton: Princeton University Press.

Maxwell, Judith. 1992. "Standardization in Kaqchiquel Maya, and the Demise or Reintegration of Spanish Loan Words." Paper presented at the Conference on Rediscovering America, Louisiana State University, Baton Rouge.

Mittelberg, David Baton, and Mary Waters. 1992. "The Process of Ethnogenesis Among Haitian and Israeli Immigrants in the United States." *Ethnic and Racial Studies* 15 (July): 412–35.

Montejo, Victor. 1993. "Realities of Return." Paper presented at the annual meeting of the American Anthropological Association, Washington, D.C.

Olzak, Susan. 1983. "Contemporary Ethnic Mobililzation." *Annual Review of Sociology*. 9: 355–74.

Peñalosa, Fernando. 1995. *Tales and Legends of the Q'anjob'al Maya*. Ranchos Palos Verdes, Calif.: Yax Te' Press.

Recinos, Adrian, trans. 1977. *Popol Vuh: Las Antiquas Historias de Quiché*. San José, Costa Rica: Educa.

Unger, Linda. 1996. "La Palabra que Salva." *Revista Maryknoll* 17 (June): 24–27.

Warren, Kay. 1995. "Intellectual Dialogue and Identity Production in Latin America." Discussion at the annual meeting of the American Anthropological Association, Washington, D.C.

Watanabe, John. 1992. *Maya Saints and Souls in a Changing World*. Austin: University of Texas Press.

———. 1995. "Community and Maya Ethnicity: The Economic and Cultural Consequences of War. Paper presented at the annual meeting of the American Anthropological Association, Washington, D.C.

Wellmeier, Nancy J. 1994a. "Rituals of Resettlement: Identity and Resistance Among Maya Refugees." Pp. 9–28 in *Selected Papers on Refugees Issues III*, edited by A. Zaharlick and J. MacDonald. Washington, D.C.: American Anthropological Association.

———. 1994b. *Rituals of Resettlement: Identity and Resistance Among Maya Refugees in the United States*. Ph.D. dissertation, Arizona State University. Ann Arbor: University Microfilms.

4 | The Madonna of 115th Street Revisited: Vodou and Haitian Catholicism in the Age of Transnationalism

Elizabeth McAlister

Reclaimed by the Virgin

Every year on the fifteenth of July, the tall, wrought-iron gates of the big, brick Church of Our Lady of Mount Carmel in East Harlem swing open to welcome thousands of religious pilgrims. Women and men, children and the elderly, throng to the church for evening Mass, after which they follow a larger-than-life statue of the Virgin Mary through the New York City streets in a long, night-time procession. After a midnight Mass they spend the night in the church, or go home and come back early the next day, dressed in the Madonna's colors of blue and white and carrying flowers, letters, rosaries, and money. In this way, the faithful celebrate the feast day of Our Lady and perform devotions for one of the many appellations of the Blessed Mother.

In 1995, ten-year-old Marie-Carmel wore a puffy, sky-blue satin dress whose many layers and petticoats made her look as though she were the topmost decoration on a multitiered cake. She sat patiently through the Mass, listening to the priest while she wrestled with her squirming baby brother on her lap. Her long, dark hair was carefully oiled and braided, each braid ending in a shiny blue and gold ribbon tied in a bow. As she rose with her family to join the line to receive Holy Communion, she faltered and tripped, and her mother had to catch her by the arm and

---

In this essay, I capitalize the term Black American to refer to the specific national group that is regularly designated as a category separate from other Americans.

help her up. Marie-Carmel looked down in embarrassment and studied her patent-leather Mary Janes as she approached the priest.

When Marie-Carmel lifted her head to receive the Host, her knees buckled and she staggered backward, wheeling into an aunt standing behind her. After she took communion, the family helped Marie-Carmel out of the church for some fresh air in the courtyard. They smiled and waved away the concern of the deacon who approached them about the little girl. "She'll be fine, thank you," said her mother, "it's just that she hasn't eaten today."

She turned to her sister and to me, as I was a friend of the family and had come to join them. Beginning in French, she finished in her mother tongue, Haitian Creole: *"C'est la Vierge. Li vin manifeste nan tèt ti-moun nan"* (It's the Virgin. She manifested herself in the child's head.)" To indicate her continuing protection over the little girl, Notre Dame du Mont Carmel (Our Lady of Mount Carmel) had, briefly, possessed her namesake, Marie-Carmel.

The little girl's fall inside the church yielded two different interpretations, delivered in three languages. The family explained to the deacon, in English, that the girl was simply hungry.[1] But the deeper reality for the family had to do with their long relationship with the Virgin. That meaning was expressed in Haitian Creole, with, as a nod to me, a *blan* (foreigner), a translation in French.[2] This ten-minute drama at the church in East Harlem was only a small part of a much larger story about the involvement of Notre Dame du Mont Carmel in the life of a new immigrant family from the island nation of Haiti. It is a story about migration and religious expression, production, and performance, and like language itself, it contains multiple levels of meaning for various audiences.

Thousands of Haitian people have been making the yearly pilgrimage to the Church of Our Lady of Mount Carmel in East Harlem for the last two decades. It is surely the largest annual religious gathering of Haitians in North America. It takes place at the same moment when thousands in Haiti flock to a mountainside waterfall at a village called Sodo (pronounced "So-DOE"), for the Fèt Vièj Mirak (Feast of the Miracle Virgin). Temporarily relaxing class, color, and political boundaries during the pilgrimage, the feast day of the "Miracle Virgin" also brings Haitian people in New York together for two days to pray, sing, and socialize in a particularly Haitian style. In this sense, Marie-Carmel's small drama in church was also part of an even wider story about Haitian religiosity in the United States.

For several years I have been following that story through the words

Elizabeth McAlister

and actions of the Haitian people who come to visit Our Lady of Mount Carmel. The stories here will not only feature individual women and men expressing their devotion, but will also consider the role of social forces in their religious lives. These social forces extend back to the legacies of French colonization and the lasting effects of slavery, and the ways that Afro-Haitian religion appropriated Roman Catholicism to form what Haitians call "le mélange" (the mixing) and what anthropologists call "religious syncretism." Another shaping factor is the postcolonial or, more properly put, the neocolonial relationship between Haiti and the United States. This relationship has contributed to the creation of the Haitian *djaspora,* or "diaspora," which, since the fall of Jean-Claude Duvalier in 1986, has been increasingly shaped by the phenomenon of transnational migration—the frequent movement back and forth of migrants from home countries to host countries.

What, then, can this pilgrimage tell us about immigrant religiosity? What do Roman Catholic devotions mean in the ritual vocabulary of Afro-Haitian religious culture? What meanings do these same devotions acquire in the United States? This chapter tries to answer these questions by focusing on the Haitian experience of the feast.

I offer four central points. First, religious culture in Haiti is a creolized system, wherein actors have learned to "code-switch" between performances of Catholicism and Vodou. Second, it is in Vodou that the feminine divine spiritually enfranchises Haitian women. Third, in the United States, Catholic codes themselves become part of a strategy of Haitian disaffiliation from African Americans, in an attempt to contest and renegotiate United States systems of racialization.

Fourth and finally, West Indians and Latin Americans actively use religion to articulate American identities, and in so doing they continue a long-standing strategy used by previous immigrant groups. Unlike older immigrants from Europe, however, Haitian religious articulations are bound up with the realities of transnational movement. Religious sites in the United States become added to the American landscape; they multiply, rather than replace, spiritual centers of the home country.

Revisiting 115th Street: Religious Borderlands

The story of the Haitian devotion at the Church of Our Lady of Mount Carmel in East Harlem is only the latest chapter in the ongoing history of that feast. Although the annual July feast at 115th Street now attracts thousands of Haitians, the church was built in 1884 by the Roman Catholic Pallottine order as a mission church to minister to the Italian immigrant population of that era. Italian Harlem nourished itself with the love and protection of La Madonna del Carmine, continuing a tradition they had known back in Italy. Robert Anthony Orsi's book *The Madonna of 115th Street: Faith and Community in Italian Harlem, 1880-1950,* paints a lyrical and sensitive portrait of the ways the *festa* for the Madonna shaped people's lives—especially the mothers, wives, daughters, and sisters in the community for whom the Blessed Virgin was mother, goddess, protector, and role model. Her feast day, July 16, grew to be a major ritual marker in Italian New York, helping Italians forge an American identity based largely on their Catholicism (Orsi 1985). Although the mission of the church officially remains the same—to minister to Italian immigrants—now only 750 Italian Americans are left in its neighborhood (Laurino 1995).[3]

The ethnic flavor of the area began to change when Puerto Ricans started migrating into East Harlem just before World War II. By 1963, eleven public housing projects were built in the vicinity of the Church of Our Lady of Mount Carmel for twelve thousand low-income black and Latino families (Orsi 1992, 326; Bourgois 1995, 51). The neighborhood transformed into Spanish Harlem, the strong "Nuyorican" community affectionately known as "El Barrio" that now shares its territory with Mexicans, Dominicans, and West Africans.

The Italian immigrant families that moved to East Harlem between the 1880s and the 1920s had prospered by the 1950s, and as the Puerto Rican families moved in, the Italians emigrated to middle-class suburban communities with lawns and fences. Many of them still come back to the church to organize the feast, to attend the novena still prayed in Italian beforehand, to celebrate a special Mass for the dead, or to bless a bride or groom the day before their wedding. But these days, the majority of the pilgrims form a sea of coffee-, mahogany-, and cinnamon-colored bodies, clad in sky blue and white, praying and singing in French and Haitian Creole. The Haitians' presence at the feast is actually part of a larger social drama that is playing itself out among the Virgin, the Pallottine order, the Italian Americans who organize the event, their Puerto Rican (and other Latino) neighbors, and the Haitian pilgrims. Haitians have become actors on a multiethnic social stage that is vastly more diverse than their relatively homogeneous home ground.[4]

This Catholic church and its surrounding neighborhood have become a religious borderland of sorts. During the feast for Our Lady, Masses are said every hour in Latin, Italian, Spanish, English, French, or Haitian Creole. There are a very few Latino pilgrims in attendance, and only a handful of Irish Americans who search out the Tridentine

Mass still said there. But this feast, which is sponsored and produced by Italian Americans, has come to be peopled by new immigrants, who turn the space of the large church into a site of Haitian religious activity.

Haitians at East 115th Street

Most Haitians in New York know where the Church of Our Lady of Mount Carmel is and have visited it—or know someone who has. By attending what they call the "Fête du Notre Dame du Mont Carmel" by the thousands, the New York Haitian population has collectively placed the church on an invisible community map. Stepping onto the public stage of this Catholic feast, they orient themselves within the shifting "ethnoscape" of New York City (Appadurai 1990). They make sense of the confusing complexity of this ethnic landscape by locating the church as a center of spiritual power where they will be welcome.

Haitians come in pilgrimage to East Harlem from diverse places in Haitian New York—Queens, Brooklyn, Manhattan, Long Island—and New Jersey, and from as far away as Atlanta, Chicago, and Montreal. Although they could attend feasts at other churches for Our Lady of Mount Carmel, like the one in Brooklyn's Williamsburg, thousands choose instead to cross the East River to Harlem.

Some say the Haitians come en masse to 115th Street because the church is a shrine, an official sanctuary for the Blessed Mother. It received this special status in 1903 from Pope Leo XIII, who thereupon donated two emeralds from the Vatican to adorn the golden crown of the parish's statue of the Madonna.[5] Others say that the statue's hair—real human hair—makes her the most powerful Virgin in the area. Some Haitians are attracted to 115th Street because of the French Mass said there on the first Saturday of every month in support of the canonization of Pierre Toussaint, a Haitian slave who emigrated to colonial New York with his master. There may be another factor as well: as *teledjol* (word of mouth) began to bring Haitians to the shrine, others came to be able to worship La Vierge (the Virgin) in the presence of their countrymen and -women. While they cannot possibly re-create the busy, celebratory atmosphere of the Sodo pilgrimage in the Haitian mountains, they can nevertheless find friends, reunite with long-lost neighbors, speak and sing in Creole and French, and perform spiritual work for the Vièj Mirak.

The Haitian community, as did (and do) the Italians, begins to celebrate the feast nine days before July 16 with a novena—a series of daily prayers to the Virgin at the 115th Street church. Their numbers increase until the two days the feast is celebrated, the fifteenth and sixteenth of July. The activity at the church begins to build throughout the day of the fifteenth. The Italian American ladies who form the religious articles committee unpack the goods they sell on behalf of the church: statues, medallions, scapulars, prayer cards, crosses, and crucifixes. Soon pilgrims pull up in cars, step down from buses, and climb the stairs leading from the subway. For the two days of the feast the sidewalks leading from the Lexington Avenue IRT trains become rivers of people wearing "Sunday best" outfits of the light blue associated with the Blessed Mother (and with ritual begging in Vodou), or white, a color of ritual purity for Catholic and Vodouist alike. They stroll on the arms of husbands, children, old people, and friends. Boys dressed in little suits and ties gallop ahead, racing little girls wearing dresses of satin tiers of sugary-looking cloth.

Notre Dame du Mont Carmel is especially known for the miracles she bestows on her followers, particularly those related to marriage and childbirth. I stop to talk to one young family and learn that their little girl—another Marie-Carmel—has ritually dressed in blue all of her life. She is *an ve* (in French, *en voeu,* or "in the condition of wishing"). At birth her mother dedicated her to Mont Carmel because she was born with an illness. To repay the Vièj Mirak for her recovery and continued protection, she will wear only blue or white clothing until the day of her First Holy Communion.

Pilgrims arrive throughout the day, and by nine o'clock that evening the huge church is filled to capacity for the Latin Mass; more than two thousand are in attendance. Hundreds more gather together in the courtyard and spill out into the sidewalk for the candlelight procession behind the larger-than-life statue of Our Lady of Mount Carmel.

Soon a great popping can be heard; this is the fireworks that announce and salute the Virgin at various places on the procession route. The smell of gunpowder fills the air, and the Haitian ladies, candles in their hands, lift their hands upward in a posture learned from Charismatic Catholicism.[6] The noise and smell of the firecrackers "heat up" the prayers, as each pilgrim hopes that the fireworks will carry his or her message to the Virgin. But the sound of bursting gunpowder is also an aural semiotic sign for Ezili Dantò, the goddess who "walks behind" the Vièj Mirak. In Vodou services for Dantò and the rest of the spirits in the Petwo rite to which she belongs, whips are cracked and gunpowder is lit to create the slaps and pops that Petwo spirits like. When the fireworks go off in front of the Madonna on 115th Street, not a few women falter and clutch at those around them, fighting off spirit possession.

Each July fifteenth, the statue of Our Lady is brought out thus, and she is paraded along a route designated by the church priests. Past Second Avenue after a left to Saint Ann's Church on 110th Street, more fireworks are lit, and more prayers launched heavenward. Some pilgrims take the opportunity to go inside and visit Saint Ann. Just as she is the mother of Mary in Roman Catholicism, in Vodou cosmology she is Grann Ezili, an older form of Ezili. A few Haitian pilgrims have come to East Harlem specifically to see her. "The power starts with the mother," confided one woman. "Me, I come to the *fèt* to *pran woulib* [take a ride] on the procession." She uses the mystical power of the feast day to strengthen her request to the older feminine powers, Grann Ezili/Saint Ann.

The procession winds down Second Avenue from Saint Ann's back up First Avenue, past 116th to 118th Street, pausing at various points along the way to light firecrackers. Many of these stopping places are homes of the Italian American families still in the neighborhood, who contribute time and money to the feast. They have decorated their brownstones, some in the old style of hanging linens from the windows, others by placing blue candles and statues along their steps. The fireworks are a sort of salute to patronage that the Haitian community understands from their own Carnival and Rara celebrations, where music is played for the contributions of local *gwo nèg,* or "big men" (McAlister 1995a).

During the procession some families walk together and sing hymns like "Ave Maria,""Louange a Toi," and "Chez Nous Soyez Reine," or the Lord's Prayer in French. Others crowd toward the float bearing the Madonna, touching the blue and white plastic fringe as they walk. Candles in hand, the pilgrims wear the brown scapulars of Our Lady of Mount Carmel. Bearing a brown scapular when she originally appeared, the Blessed Virgin promised that whosoever wore her scapular at the moment of death would escape the fires of eternal damnation.

When the procession reaches the church, every seat is filled for the midnight Mass. The courtyard is a scene of another sort, one closer in mood to the mountain celebrations at Sodo. Each year several women bring food, which they ritually distribute among the pilgrims. Standing in the vicinity you may be handed delicious *soup joumou,* (pumpkin soup), rice and beans, *griyo* (fried pork, the ritual food of Ezili Dantò), soda, and black, sugary Haitian coffee. The women who bring the food explain that they are continuing a tradition they kept at Sodo, inherited from their mothers, a form of ritual feeding of the poor. In late-night New York there are no homeless or needy people around this church, so other Haitian pilgrims stand in for the poor and consume the food with gusto. The menfolk stand around drinking rum or whiskey, talking politics among themselves. Manbo Miracia, a priestess of Vodou who is a pilgrim here, nudges me and nods to a knot of middle-aged gentlemen. "The majority of them are married to Ezili Dantò," she said. "I know because I performed the services."[7]

On the day of the sixteenth, the feast day proper, a 9:00 A.M. Mass is followed by another procession. Throughout the day, a quick Mass is said every half-hour in a different language, as hundreds of people arrive at the church, hand flowers to the workers in the sacristy, light candles, pray to the saints, attend Mass, and receive communion. Pilgrims pass in front of the various statues, praying out loud in the Haitian style, asking for the intercession of the Blessed Mother.

Some pilgrims bring a practical orientation born out of their Afro-Creole religious culture. "Never come into the church through the back door from the courtyard," one woman instructs me. "You should not approach the saint from her back—she has to see you walking in." Other pilgrims come to perform spiritual work that is meaningful in the ritual logic of Vodou. They leave money near the statues, either dollar bills or ritual amounts of coins. A few leave candles or sprinkle Florida Water, the cologne commonly used in Vodou for its sweet, spiced scent. Occasionally the priests have found plates of food as offerings to the *lwa*, the spirits of Vodou. Many leave notes and letters stuffed in Jesus' hands, on Saint Lucy's plate of eyes, and in the folds of the gowns of Saint Damien and Cosmos. The priests walk the length of the church from time to time, collecting the money and sweeping up the letters into piles (which they later throw away). Some of the letters are written to the Virgin for help in a specific problem, related to good health, jobs, or love. Other letters are formulas for spiritual work with *lwa*. One, with name written seven times with three *X*s and the word *Jistis,* is asking Ezili Dantò for justice. Another name, written repeatedly on one side of a scrap of paper, is echoed by a name listed on its reverse. Here Ezili is asked to reconcile two enemies, or two lovers.

Every once in a while at the shrine in East Harlem, I have seen newly born *ounsi,* or "initiate," arrive with their godmother or godfather in Vodou. A *ounsi* must dress in white for a period of time designated by the *lwa,* usually forty-two days. In the first week after the week-long *kouche kanzo,* or "formal initiation," each *ounsi* must go to a new church each day and speak to the saints and the *zanj,* or "angels," of Vodou that "walk with them." For anyone initiated around July sixteenth, a trip to the Fèt Vièj Mirak is a special opportunity. These pilgrims arrive dressed entirely in the whitest white from head to toe, with white head ties and straw hats. By performing the spiritual work of Vodou in a Catholic sacred space, they illustrate how Afro-Haitian religion uses and incorporates Catholicism.

The new *ounsi* is a rare sight in East Harlem, but not because people are not initiated in the summer. On the contrary, the summer season is the best time for those who are *reklame* (reclaimed) by the spirits to undergo the long religious ordeal of ritual worldly death and the joy of spiritual rebirth, instruction, and fortification. But just as churches are sites of spiritual power, physical space is very important in Vodou. Whenever possible Haitians will return to Haiti for initiation at the place of their *demambre,* or "ancestral spiritual homes." If these places in the countryside have been sold or stolen by the *tonton makout,* (destroyed), then people will be initiated into the formal temple system in Port-au-Prince. After the fall of Duvalier in 1986 allowed the Haitian population abroad to return home, the geography of spiritual work changed. As a result, the United States has become chiefly a place to perform healings and interventions in crisis. Sickness, work-related problems, and love are the most pressing issues brought to *oungan* (priest) and *manbo* (priestess) here. The more serious works—initiations, funerary rituals, or becoming a priest or priestess—are all carefully planned for trips back to Haiti (Brown 1991, McAlister 1992–93).

Religious Culture, Diaspora, and Transnational Migration

In many ways, Haitians' experience of the Mount Carmel feast is similar to that of their Italian predecessors at the church. In fact, their general positions as immigrant populations run parallel. Like Italians fleeing from *la miseria* (poverty) at the end of the last century, Haitians have come to the United States to escape the structural violence of *la mizè,* the poverty of the poorest country in the Western Hemisphere. Both agricultural peoples, arriving Italians and Haitians were (and are) similarly independent, family-centered, and devoted to local religious forms. The Italian emphasis on *rispetto* (respect) and dependence on *padroni* (patrons) (Orsi 1985) is similar to the Haitians' social hierarchies, articulated through patronage and loyalty to a *patron,* or *gwo nèg.*

There are, however, major differences between the experiences of these two communities that visit this shrine for the Madonna. For example, compared to the Haitians, Italian immigrants fit better the classic pattern of nineteenth-century migration. "Uprooting" themselves from the home country, they were "transplanted" to the United States and gradually created a new, Italian American national identity (Handlin 1951, Orsi 1992, 316). In contrast, many Haitians in the contemporary United States perceive themselves to be living *nan djaspora,* "in the diaspora," defined against Haiti as an essential location of its own, regardless of whether they live in Miami, Montreal, Paris, or Senegal. Haiti itself is real, tangible, and, in fact, often a place of partial residence. From local points "in the diaspora," Haitians live transnational lives. That is, they live embedded in international networks, sustaining social relations that link their societies of origin with their new settlement (Basch et al. 1994). Haitian transmigrants typically work jobs in New York to support homes in Haiti, keeping their children in Haitian schools until they are young teens. They return to Haiti during periods of illness or unemployment; for vacations; for important family events like baptisms, marriages, or funerals; and sometimes for national celebrations like the inauguration of a president, the yearly Carnival or Rara, or the pilgrimage to Sodo for Fèt Vièj Mirak. After decades in the United States, the elderly may return to spend their last years at home. Family roles shift between the two countries, so that children come of age and migrate north, and old folks retire and return southward to home. Both opportunity and tragedy can be the occasion to *janbe dlo,* or "cross over the water."[8]

It is the U.S. Immigration Act of 1965 and its liberalizing entrance policies that allowed for the legal immigration of large numbers of non-European peoples. We can look to this moment as a pivotal occasion that heralds the vast increase in migrants from developing countries, many of whom have brought new religious traditions—Hinduism, Buddhism, Islam, and numerous local, "traditional" spiritualities—to the United States. But this legislation cannot be the sole explanation for the increase of Caribbean (and other) immigrants. It does not explain, for one thing, why so many thousands of people would want to leave their homelands and cultures and come live in the *djaspora* in cold and hostile environments.

Such drastic movement of people is linked to economic conditions. The past several decades can be characterized in terms of new levels of capital penetrations into "Third World" economies, the development of export processing, and the increased migration of people from the peripheries to the centers (Wallerstein 1974, 229–231; Nash 1983, 3–69; Sassen-Koob 1982). Individual actors who maintain lives in two nation-states at once are engaging in a creative strategy that maximizes their position in the present configuration of global capital. It is more

Elizabeth McAlister

practical, for example, for many women to work as nurses in New York and send remittances back to Haiti to raise small children so that they will become *kretyen vivan* (good people, or literally "living Christians") and not *gate* (ruined) by the harshness of New York life. In this way we can see that economic conditions are affecting both the flows of transmigrant activities and "the manner in which they come to understand who they are and what they are doing" (Basch et al 1994, 12).

It is increasingly true that in order to understand religious life for some new immigrants, we must also understand their continued relationship with the religious world of their home countries (Levitt in press). Unlike the earlier Italian immigrants of East Harlem, who shifted their religious focus from the churches of the old country to East 115th Street, Haitians join congregations and undertake pilgrimages *nan djaspora,* and also continue religious activities when they go to Haiti. They often plan business or vacation trips to coincide with opportunities to perform religious work at one of the many important spiritual sites at home. When they arrive, they are labeled *djaspora* by the townspeople who could not afford to leave.

As spaces where other Haitians congregate, religious sites in diasporic locations become inflected with meanings that span both home and host nations. Working with Cubans at a shrine church in Miami, Thomas Tweed (1997) suggests that we can usefully understand diasporic religious communities as translocative (moving symbolically between the homeland and the new land) and transtemporal (relating to a constructed past and an imagined future). In Latin America the saints, with their feast days on the calendar and their churches in different villages, already have both temporal and territorialized identities, and become an organizational principle in the countryside. Each saint governs a day of the week, and the market days correspond to the saints' days. In Capotille, Haiti, for example, the church is dedicated to Notre Dame du Mont Carmel, and Tuesday is her day. Tuesday is also market day in Capotille.

The pilgrimage to Our Lady of Mount Carmel in East Harlem expands the saint's influence in the Haitian world. Rather than substituting the New York feast for the ones they left behind in Haiti, they add the Harlem location as another site of spiritual work. In this way East Harlem is opened up as one more place in the expanding "religioscape" of transnational Haitian religious culture.[9] During the pilgrimage to the Vièj Mirak in New York, the Haitian population reterritorializes spiritual practice, reinscribing sacred, translocative space onto their new landscape of settlement.[10] Haitians in diaspora reach out to Mont Carmel and Ezili Dantò, powerful nationalist symbols, extending prayers for family and friends throughout the *djaspora* and in Haiti. Temporally they include concern for the dead and departed in Haiti as well as the hoped-for children of the future. Insofar as the Haitian population is able to return to Haiti—unlike the Cuban community at the time of this writing—the activities at the shrine are those of an actively transnational religious culture.

In 1993, commercial air travel was suspended during the U.S. embargo against Haiti after the 1991 coup d'état that had ousted Haitian president Jean-Bertrand Aristide. Many Haitians who had come to New York for brief visits were delayed in the United States for months, and some who came to the feast that year told me they regretted not being back in Haiti. Their prayers on behalf of their beleaguered home nation were especially poignant. They were praying not for a remote ancestral homeland but for an embattled place of (partial) residence. Thus the feast in New York is not an isolated enclave of Haitian festivity focused solely on life in the United States. The movements, religious practices and ideologies of pilgrim actors mirror the realities of Haitian transnational migrants.

Vièj Mirak: Mont Carmel in Haiti

Many of the pilgrims at the New York Church of Our Lady of Mount Carmel, if they are in Haiti in July, would go to one of the pilgrimage sites for the Vièj Mirak back home. The biggest one, at Sodo in Ville Bonheur, attracts thousands of pilgrims who come for summer vacation and stay for weeks around the time of the July sixteenth feast. This small village is located high in the mountain range between Mirebalais and Saint Marc, with a population that is probably under three thousand (Laguerre 1989, 84). During the month of the feast, the town swells with pilgrims and vacationers, who rent rooms and houses from the villagers.

It is for the Fèt Vièj Mirak that many *djaspora* are willing to plan their international travel, don the light blue clothing of the ritual beggar pilgrim or the burlap sacks of penitence, and ride for seven hours on a *bourik* (donkey) into the mountainous Haitian countryside. Although Notre Dame du Perpetuel Secours (Our Lady of Perpetual Help) is the official patron saint of Haiti, the chapel for Notre Dame du Mont Carmel at Sodo is the most popular pilgrimage of the country.

"Sodo" is the Creole spelling of "Saut d'Eau," which in French means "waterfall." The great waterfall of Sodo was created during an earthquake on May 7, 1842 (Rouzier 1891, 262; cited in Laguerre 1989, 86). Farmers in the region understood "sodo" to be a natural dwelling place of various water spirits in Afro-Haitian cosmology: the serpent Danbala Wèdo and his rainbow wife Ayida Wèdo, Simbi Dlo (Simbi of the water), and others. It is indeed a beautiful place. White, frothy mineral water falls hundreds of feet, bounces off boulders, and runs through twisting tree roots into pools below. As the cool spray splashes off the rocks, tiny rainbows glisten in the air. Pilgrims, hot from the seven-hour ride through the mountains, step under the falls and are sometimes possessed by the spirits. Their faltering steps and wide-eyed expressions become the visual currency of the ubiquitous foreign photographers who ring the falls, fighting for the best spots for their tripods in the undergrowth.[11]

In July 1849, some time after the creation of the waterfall, rumors began to circulate that a peasant farmer had sighted the Virgin Mary in a nearby palm tree. President Faustin Soulouque, Haiti's ruler from 1847 to 1859, appointed members of his legislative cabinet to study the apparition. After satisfying himself with their report, he ordered the (now) lemon-yellow chapel built in honor of Notre Dame du Mont Carmel (Laguerre 1989, 87).[12]

Since the apparition, the pilgrimage at Sodo has been not only a center of spiritual power but also a place of celebration. Haitians of all classes travel to Sodo in July with their families. Struggling entrepreneurs arrive early to set up food stalls, market stands, and gambling houses. Rich vacationers build or rent houses and arrive in private cars with the family to spend a few weeks enjoying the festivities. Among these, the *djaspora* from the United States are easily recognizable. They arrive wearing the latest fashions from Brooklyn or Miami, the women in shorts and halter tops with blonde streaks in their permed hair and long acrylic nails painted with designs. Young men likewise adopt the styles of Black American popular culture, often crossed with a Jamaican sensibility they learn through their contact with the Jamaican youth in their own West Indian neighborhoods. They wear athletic shoes, baseball hats, and the red, green, and gold belts of the Rastafari looped through their baggy jeans.[13] This small mountain village turns into a crossroads of the global Haitian diaspora each July, as returning pilgrims also come from Zaire, Martinique, Guadeloupe, the Bahamas, Boston, and Montreal.

Nights in Ville Bonheur before and after the feast are a series of ongoing parties by all the classes that come together in the village. The town is without electricity, like the rest of the Haitian countryside. The wealthy sit on their porches, enjoying whiskey, telling jokes, listening to Haitian *konpa* dance music on portable radios they power with batteries. Young sons may go out into the night in search of the many *bouzen* (prostitutes) who come into the town especially for the feast.

The less well-to-do stroll through the streets, tend their businesses, or stop in at one of the many Vodou ceremonies that enliven the village during the month of July. Traveling Vodou societies may bring their entire personnel, who set up their drums and call out the songs of the *lwa,* who are sometimes called *zanj* (angels) of Vodou. Street life is full and lively. By the light of the *tèt gridap* (kerosene lamps) or the burning torches set around the town, people recognize old friends, acquire new ones, make economic transactions, and perform the spiritual work they need to do in order to effect change in their lives.

The Haitian Religious Continuum

The chapel and the waterfall at Sodo are both important and impressive. However, *manbo* and *oungan* who serve the spirits of Vodou insist that the most powerful spot is the actual place where the Madonna appeared. Called Nan Palm (In the Palm Grove), this site stands near the entrance to the village. It is here that the Virgin dwells with her counterpart Ezili Dantò, the powerful Afro-Haitian goddess. Dantò's co-existence with the Vièj Mirak is an example of the great mystery of le mélange, or the syncretism of African and Catholic symbolisms. Like Mexico's Virgin of Guadalupe, who appeared to an Indian man at the shrine of an Aztec goddess, Notre Dame du Mont Carmel at Sodo is a powerful national figure resonant with multiple layers of meaning. When pilgrims make the trip through the mountains to Sodo, they visit the church, the waterfall, and the palm grove—a three-fold spiritual site.[14]

The *manbo* I have worked with tell me that Notre Dame du Mont Carmel "walks a path" with Ezili Dantò, a *lwa* or *mistè* "mystery" who has become one of the most important divinities in the culture.[15] While she can be represented by Mont Carmel, Ezili Dantò is most often represented in popular Haitian iconography as Notre Dame du Czestochowa, the Black Virgin of Poland, whose face bears two scars running down her cheek. Like both Czestochowa and Mont Carmel, Ezili Dantò carries a baby in her arms. Dantò's baby is not the infant Jesus but, interestingly, a daughter. Some call her "Anayiz," others "Ti-Gungun." Dantò is known as single mother, a hard-working black woman, and a powerful warrior and fighter. A symbol of nationalist pride, she is said to have been a leader in the slaves' victorious war of independence against Napoleon's army, when she earned the scars she carries (Brown 1991, 229).

Sometimes Dantò is described as a lesbian, and she is thought to choose which men will live as effeminate homosexuals. When she possesses people (for she can "ride" both women and men), she drinks *kleren* cane liquor and demands to eat pork, often the ears and feet of the roasted pig. In her incarnation as Ezili Ge Wouj (Red Eyed Ezili), she speaks without the use of the front of her tongue, saying only "ke ke ke ke," and pantomiming her meanings. Some say her tongue was cut out during the Haitian revolution so she would not betray her side's secrets (Brown 1991, 229).

When pilgrims go to the East Harlem shrine or to *Nan Palm* at Sodo and light a candle, sing to the Virgin, and *fè demann* (make requests), they are addressing Notre Dame du Mont Carmel and Ezili Dantò *at the same time*. This overlapping, simultaneous practice of Catholicism and Vodou has puzzled outsiders—both Haitian intellectuals and foreigners—for generations. Within anthropology, "syncretism" was the theoretical concept developed by Melville Herskovits (1941) and then Roger Bastide (1960) to understand the processes of change that arose with culture contact. Syncretism came to describe an "impure" religious tradition, saturated with local, unorthodox strains. Recent terms used to describe cultural mixings have included "creolization," "symbiosis," and "inter-culture" (Stewart and Shaw 1994, Desmangles 1992).

The received way of thinking about Vodou and Catholicism is to imagine them as a pair of binary opposites. It is true that Haitian Catholics have affirmed their own status by stressing their apartness from Vodou. A Catholic who is not at all involved in serving the *lwa* identifies as a *fran katolik* (straight Catholic), and there are some in the Haitian upper classes who know nothing of Afro-Haitian religion. The upper classes were (and are) generally literate, French-speaking, politically enfranchised, light-skinned, and emphatically Catholic. On the stage of cultural politics, Vodou was (and is) held up as the pagan, Satanic superstition of the poor, dark, nonliterate, and disenfranchised majority. Politically, then, Catholicism has always positioned itself in opposition to Vodou.[16]

In practice, it may be more helpful to imagine these two traditions occupying either end of a continuum, with Roman Catholicism on one end and Vodou on the other.[17] Any given actor in Haiti falls somewhere along the continuum, some as Catholics, some as Vodouists, and the vast majority living their lives in the middle, going through the rites of passage of the Catholic church while simultaneously maintaining contact with Vodou healers and the *lwa,* especially in times of crisis.

Even this continuum model must be complicated with further qualifications. Elsewhere, I have written that both the Afro-Haitian religion and the Catholicism that evolved in Haiti were constructed in dialectical relation to the other in a process of creolization. In this sense there is simply no "pure Catholicism" or "pure Vodou" in Haiti. To a degree that some advocates in each tradition might not like to admit, each has incorporated the other into its philosophies and practices. Each tradition is therefore constitutive and revealing of the other (McAlister 1995a, 179).[18]

While one tradition may be bound up in the other, the Haitian cultural politics that divides the enfranchised from the disenfranchised insists on seeing each as a separate religion. This same politics governs the behavior of actors in public space. It can be useful to understand the Haitian majority as being "bicultural" or "bireligious," a population able to speak both of the religious languages operating within the culture (Murphy 1988, 124). People strategically employ "religious code-switching" to translate the logics of Catholicism and Vodou back and forth to suit the social situation at hand. For this reason it may make sense to view the religious worldview of the vast majority as "Haitian religious culture," a term that "reflects a religion in two-way communication with the structures of authority around it" (Davis 1982). It is a religious culture that contains within it shifting sets of possible elements, complicated yet bounded by the theologies and practices of both Roman Catholicism and Vodou.

Catholics throughout Latin America make *promesas* (promises) to the saints, in which they ask for a favor and in return make a sacrificial promise. Some promise to return to a church on its feast day each year, others make pilgrimages barefoot, and still others donate family treasures to the saint's shrine. In Haiti, people will also make a request (*fè demann*) and tell the saint what they will give in return. Often the requests to the saints are governed by the logic of Vodou.

Madame Luc, an older woman who grew up in a small village in northern Haiti and who now goes to the East Harlem pilgrimage each year, explained to me that her family was Catholic and did not serve the spirits. But although she considers herself Catholic, she "thinks in Vodou" (Murphy 1988, 124). In keeping with a worldview focused on the family, she maintains that the Virgins of Mont Carmel, Altagrace, and La Merci are sisters.

For Catholics, the Virgin Mary and the saints are intercessors; they

Elizabeth McAlister

carry our prayers to God. If they grace us with our wish, we are blessed, but if they do not, we must accept things as they are as God's will. For Vodouist Catholics, things are slightly different. If one saint does not give us what we want, we may berate it, argue with it, and ultimately turn to a different saint with the same wish. Just as we can punish them by turning away, they can punish us if we do not live up to our promise. Madame Luc told me that making promises to the saints is tricky: "Watch out, because if you promise something to them and then you forget, you're in trouble." She told me that if you promise to give the saint a cow, for example, you had better make good on your word. "How do you bring a cow to the church?" I asked her. "No, you don't give it to the church; the church isn't involved in that sort of thing," she said. "You make your request at the church. But you are dealing with the spirit behind the saint." She explained that if you promise a cow to the saint and your request is granted, you must give the cow to "the people who serve the *zanj* [angels]," a Vodou society. Madame Luc therefore places herself in an intermediary space where her actions are performed in the Catholic church, but her dealings are with the *zanj* of Vodou. Thus it is possible to situate her toward the Catholic end of a continuum between Catholicism and Vodou, themselves intertwined in Haitian culture.

The fact that people do the spiritual work of Afro-Haitian religion in church settings does not mean that they are not also fully participating Catholics. For the Haitians, the pilgrimage at 115th Street is very much respected as a Catholic event, and any spiritual work that is done explicitly for the *lwa* is done discreetly. Vodou remains an unspoken presence at the feast in New York, and each sign that carries meaning within Vodou can also be read as a form of Catholic devotion. Wearing light blue clothing, saying prayers during fireworks, distributing pork in the churchyard, writing letters to the Virgin—all these things have a place in the ritual vocabulary of Catholicism, even if they are seen by the priests at the church as the quaint expressions of the "folk."

The spiritual works of Vodouist Catholics are achieved in a process of religious code-switching through the subtle use of language, the nuanced use of color, and discreet offerings of spiritual significance. It is possible, then, to communicate with Ezili Dantò through Mont Carmel on the public stage without detection, even by fellow community-members standing at one's side. Devotions to Our Lady that are also spiritual work for Ezili Dantò are masked with a discretion that has come from generations of experience with colonial and postcolonial repression from France and Rome. Because of the historical circumstances involving the church's repression of Vodou, then, it is quite possible to serve Ezili Dantò through the coded performance of Catholicism.

Anthropologist Initiate–Outsider Insider: A Word on Position and Method

The first time I went to Haiti, I traveled with a group of friends "back" to that country with a master drummer of Vodou music. We went as musical apprentices, and not as anthropologists. Rather than choosing a site for field research and then going to it, my trip mirrored patterns of transmigration, as I went "home" with an immigrant who had settled in my area.

Because we were traveling in July, our host insisted that we go to Sodo for the Fèt Vièj Mirak to receive good luck from the spirits. The trip was 1984, two years before the fall of Jean-Claude Duvalier. Since then much has happened between us as a result of that trip, which was launched under the auspices of Notre Dame du Mont Carmel. The stories are too long and too complex to tell here. Some of us married Haitians. Five children have been born, and two doctoral dissertations on Haitian culture were written (Wilcken 1991; McAlister 1995a, 1995b). Three of us were initiated together as *marasa* (twins) in the Afro-Haitian spiritual system.

Anthropologists are supposed to go off to the field by themselves (or with a spouse, who is briefly mentioned in the final academic work), and to conduct fieldwork and interviews alone. This has rarely been the case for me working in Haiti or in Haitian New York. Starting with that first visit to Haiti with a group of friends, I have always seemed to work with others, be they friends, family, photographers, assistants, or colleagues.

By the same token, I have never been to the pilgrimage to Mont Carmel in Haiti or in New York by myself. To arrive somewhere by oneself in the Haitian context is to signal unimportance, or worse, unconnectedness; it implies that *ou pa gen moun,* "you have no people." I have visited the site with other scholars, with Haitian friends, and with a group of women in a Brooklyn Vodou society. This is not to say that because I am with companions I am not doing field research, not taking notes, not making audio recordings, and not acutely observing the ritual around me. In a sense I am in my own mental universe, while others are in theirs.

The methodologies I have used in this study have ranged from the casual visit to Haiti with friends in 1984 to the formal interviewing of pilgrims in New York in the early 1990s. Much of my knowledge of Afro-Haitian spirituality comes from being a partial "insider" as a Vodou initiate, although I recognize myself fundamentally as an "outsider" to Haitian culture. My own research and writing have been ongoing, and the period of my doctoral fieldwork let me taste the experience of transnational migration as I went back and forth to Haiti seven times in five years. (McAlister 1992–93, McAlister 1995a.)

To research and articulate the inherent realities of new migrants means following the movements of immigrants and retracing circuits of transnational migration. It entails working in immigrant enclaves in American cities and returning to home countries with recent immigrants. As one becomes embedded in these networks, field research involves working in proximity with others in new ways. This may well become the predominant field model in sociology and anthropology as scholars increasingly understand their own neighborhoods as places of globalizing cultural contact and cultural change.

A Household Reception for the Vièj Mirak

One evening in New York, as the candlelight procession for the Blessed Mother returned to the church courtyard, I noticed a ring of ladies in Creole dresses of the dark blue colors associated with Ezili Dantò. They were sitting in a semicircle atop bags of dresses and spices they had come to sell at the feast. I recognized them as *manbo* of Vodou. They were, in fact, the core initiates of a small Vodou society in Brooklyn. They would sleep in the church and after Mass in the morning set up their wares in a makeshift market on the church sidewalk.

Karen McCarthy Brown's 1991 book *Mama Lola: A Vodou Priestess in Brooklyn* recounts the spiritual biography of a Brooklyn *manbo* with great insight and sensitivity, showing the many relationships Mama Lola maintains with the spirits of Vodou. Like Mama Lola, Manbo Miracia, the spiritual mother of the society I encountered, has had a long-standing relationship with Notre Dame du Mont Carmel. Her own mother was born on July sixteenth, the Virgin's feast day. Miracia was born a twin, and her mother named her "Miracia" to tie her to the "miracle Virgin." To her sister she gave the name "Lamèsi," for "Notre Dame de la Merci," another Virgin represented by a statue in the Ville Bonheur chapel. "Ever since we were in the womb, my mother brought us to Sodo each year," said Miracia proudly with an emphatic nod. "And my daughter Carmel went with me in *my* belly."

Manbo Miracia grew up to fall in love with a man also born on

July sixteenth, dedicated to Mont Carmel by virtue of his birth. When she was pregnant with their daughter, she had a vision of a dark-skinned woman with two scars running down her cheek. It was the same face as the Polish Virgin of Czestochowa, the image Haitians know also to be Ezili Dantò. "The lady was carrying my daughter in her arms," she confided. When her daughter was born on the feast day for Czestochowa, September 2, she dedicated her to Ezili Dantò and the Virgins of Czestochowa and Mont Carmel, naming her "Marie-Carmel." Thus Miracia is linked to Notre Dame du Mont Carmel in various ways through the significant dates in her family.

Manbo Miracia invited me to a reception in her home for the Virgin. Every year she holds this event to honor their special relationship. The reception would not be a Vodou ceremony where drums, antiphonal singing, and dancers would call the spirits. Rather, it would be a series of Catholic prayers said in honor of the Vièj Mirak in the presence of family and friends. By sponsoring the service in her own home, Miracia positioned herself as a producer of her own religious work, sustaining a direct relationship with the saints and the spirits, outside of the direction of male, possibly non-Haitian, Catholic priests.

Manbo Miracia lives in a small apartment in the Crown Heights section of Brooklyn with her daughter Carmel and Carmel's two children. She had rearranged her house for the prayer service by pushing her furniture to the walls and setting up chairs in the living room. A simple altar table was set up under a large poster depicting Notre Dame du Mont Carmel. Flowers fashioned from blue crepe paper framed the image to create a baroque effect. On the lace-covered table sat a homemade oil lamp used on altars in Haiti, made of a metal star supporting a cotton wick suspended in oil by four corks. Two deep-blue, seven-day candles flanked the lamp, near a bouquet of flowers.

A number of people were assembled, dressed nicely and sitting on chairs against the three walls not taken up with the altar. I recognized in their number one of Brooklyn's busiest and most popular *oungan* (priest of Vodou), dressed in a white dashiki and surrounded by his entourage. But it was not he who would lead the service. That honor was reserved for the *prèt savann* (bush priest).

A *prèt savann* holds a distinct rank in Vodou. Specialists in the Catholic rites of baptism, marriage, and last rites, these officials are always men proficient in Latin. A number of *prèt savann* make the main cemetery in Port-au-Prince their daily place of business, singing in Latin and French the memorial masses that Vodouists perform a year and a week after death.

As I fell into a conversation with the priest, I learned that he had joined an order of brothers in his youth, intending to be a monk. On the eve of the fourth and final vow, he was rejected for candidacy. The *zanj* in his family appeared to him in a dream and told him that they had adopted him; he was *reklame,* or "reclaimed," by the spirits (see also McAlister 1992-93). Three years later he underwent the *kouche kanzo,* or initiation into a Vodou society. On his finger he wore both gold and silver wedding rings; he confided to me that he was married to both Ezili Dantò and Ezili Freda, her light-skinned counterpart. Many Haitian men accept marriage to these two powerful goddesses; they must both be "served" to achieve the correct balance.

Formally schooled in the Latin and French texts of the church, he now lends his services to say novenas in the home, to officiate over marriages between people and the *zanj* during a Vodou ceremony, or to preside at the sort of reception that Manbo Miracia had decided to hold. He had brought a black leather bag with him, out of which he extracted several prayer books, a chalice, a brass censer, and a small bucket of holy water. When the proper time came, he selected a white lace chasuble and donned it, adding to it a necklace bearing a large wooden cross.

Like many Catholic events requested by the *lwa,* the event was full of coded signs meaningful in the logic of Vodou. The priest began, for example, by purifying the room, scattering the four cardinal directions with Florida Water. Then he lit a bundle of charcoal topped with frankincense in the incense burner and moved through the congregation for all to be touched by rich, pungent fingers of smoke. He disappeared into the kitchen and returned for a dramatic entrance, singing loudly and formally in Latin. Taking up his small bucket and sprinkler, he scattered holy water on all of us. He motioned to Miracia to light the two big, blue candles on the altar.

The priest moved to a *ti chèz ba* (little low chair), the kind of small wooden chair used by Vodou priests for the long series of Catholic prayers sung in French before a Vodou ceremony. He proceeded to lead the small congregation in a Mass drawn from photocopied pages and prayer books he had brought. The assembled guests knew most of the songs and prayers. After a while he stopped the prayers and introduced himself by name, saying that we were saying our Hail Marys for Miracia's family, for the homeless, for the children who live in the streets, and for Haiti.

The service featured none of the songs or invocations for the *lwa,* and none appeared in possession. But as in the end of a Vodou ceremony for Ezili Dantò, Manbo Miracia distributed plates filled with rice and beans and fried pork. We bit gratefully into the meat, deliciously greasy and spiced with garlic and *piman,* the hot scotchbonnet pepper of Caribbean cuisine. She set aside the remainder of the enormous pot of meat. This dish would "sleep" on the floor under the altar table, a practice called "feeding the spirits" that would nourish Ezili Dantò with Miracia's symbolic sacrifice. On the altar itself would "sleep" a big cake with blue frosting, a sweet dessert for Ezili to consume. We returned the next day to enjoy a slice of the cake after it had slept. By then Manbo Miracia had put her apartment back in its usual state, with the altar table replaced by television and stereo. She was tired but pleased to have received the saints into her home with her family and friends.

Domestic prayer services like this one are not uncommon in the Haitian context. The home is transformed into sacred space by rearranging furniture, constructing an altar, and assembling a familial community in prayer. Susana Gallardo (1994) illustrates the ways in which the institutional ritual of the church is not central to Catholicism as it is practiced in many Chicano/a communities. Like the Chicana/o case, the Haitian home altar can be seen as an alternative sacred space controlled primarily by women. Prayer is offered according to the codes of Haitian religious culture, and dedicated to the spiritual work necessary to maintain relationships with the spiritual energy of both the saints *and* the *lwa.*

The Roman Catholic Church and the Haitian Community in New York

The current population of an estimated four hundred thousand Haitians in the New York area has brought an increase in Catholics to the region. The Catholic church's response to this Haitian migration has followed the pattern it established with other ethnic groups of encouraging the creation of separate ethnic congregations within the local parish. In this way the church has joined other institutions in promoting ethnic group formation and the maintenance of ethnic identity (Glick-Schiller 1975, Buchanan 1980).[19]

The head of the Haitian Apostolate for Brooklyn and Queens, Father Guy Sansariqc, is effectively the leader of the Haitian Catholic church in the New York metropolitan area. He leads a thriving Haitian congregation at the church of Saint Jerome in Brooklyn, which he estimates one thousand four hundred parishioners attend each Sunday.

As the coordinator of the National Office of Haitian American Catholics, he is also a national and transnational figure. He travels to Haiti frequently for conferences, always looking for Creole-speaking priests who might be able to serve the New York community. He also organizes pilgrimages to Our Lady of Perpetual Help in Bay Ridge, Brooklyn, and to Our Lady of Fatima in New Jersey. He terms the pilgrimage in East Harlem "without guidance," since it was not initiated by the church but rather by the pilgrims themselves.

Besides Saint Jerome's, there are various other Catholic churches serving the Haitian community. A French Mass for Haitians in New York was said by a Haitian priest as early as 1966, and by 1970 eight hundred people regularly attended. In the early 1970s ten other parishes instituted French Masses, and the Brooklyn diocese created the Haitian Apostolate of Brooklyn (Glick-Schiller 1975, Buchanan 1980).

Today, there are fourteen churches with French or Creole Masses to serve the Haitian community in Brooklyn and Queens, and another four or five in Manhattan and Rockland County.[20] The Haitian Apostolate struggles to maintain service centers for Haitian refugees and immigrants, many of whom are traumatized in various ways from their experiences of military repression and flight from Haiti.[21] Father Sansariqc identifies other issues to be more critical for the Haitian population in the New York area than the question of syncretism. The legal issues that revolve around immigration status are his most pressing concerns.

The Haitian presence at the shrine for Our Lady of Mount Carmel began as a spontaneous devotion; no church institution initiated or invited the Haitian participation. Not even the sponsoring Pallottine order ministers to the Haitians as a group, except for holding a monthly Mass in French. Part of this has to do with diocesan politics and the territorial jurisdictions of the church. The Haitian leadership is located in Brooklyn and Queens, in the Brooklyn diocese. The feast in East Harlem falls into the New York archdiocese, covering Manhattan, Rockland, and Westchester. With only thirty-five priests of Haitian descent living and serving in the United States, there is a shortage of priests with Haitian cultural fluency. Yet the pilgrims at Mount Carmel do not seem to be concerned.

A small, informal group of committed Haitians prints the text of the Mass in French and distributes it during the feast. The priests at Mount Carmel explain that they offer two Masses in French out of the eight that are said that day "as a courtesy." They have also appointed a Haitian man quasideacon, endowing him with some, but not all, of the responsibilities of that position. Yet the pilgrims who come to the feast have not played a great role in organizing it. The pilgrimage is, for the Haitians, a matter apart from their regular church activities. It is an affair between themselves and the Virgin.

The community of Haitians at the Church for Our Lady of Mount Carmel is what makes this site a translocative one—symbolically engaged with both home and host countries. The image of the festivities back in Haiti at Sodo is a quietly spoken reference. Ezili Dantò, the powerful feminine divinity who fought for Haitian independence, forms the backdrop for prayers and conversation about the various transmutations of Haitian national politics—the fall of Duvalier, the election of Aristide, the coup d'état, and the U.S. military "intervasion"—as well as U.S. elections and immigration legislation. People can see old friends, be seen by new friends, and ritually distribute their Haitian foods to enthusiastic recipients. By sharing this important date with one another, actors build a religious community of sorts, maintaining the nostalgia for Haiti and reaffirming the dream of eventual return. As they would at Sodo, they can stay up late to *bay blag* (tell jokes) and sleep in groups in the church on the night before the feast. They can pray the rosary together in French and relax into the common codes of their culture. In one of the few times of liminal community solidarity, they can enjoy the deeply satisfying company of their sisters and brothers from Haiti around them as they pray, sing, and speak to their common mother, the Vièj Mirak.

Catholicism and the Haitian Strategy of Alterity

bell hooks (1989) has noted that scholars may be more comfortable focusing on international or postcolonial issues than addressing race and class differences at home. She points out that language that diasporizes and internationalizes U.S. minorities can obscure understandings of structured inequalities of class and race in the national arena. While they are dubbed *"djaspora"* when they return to Haiti, in the United States the Haitian population is engaged in a struggle over questions of identity and definition that are inseparable from American processes of racialization.

Immigrants who establish themselves in the United States enter an increasingly plural society, where ethnic identity is structured through various processes that include race, class, religion, language, and gender as well as the politics of nationalism. Recent scholarship by David Mittelberg and Mary C. Waters (1992) suggests that immigrants' identities in the United States will be formed out of a dialectic of sorts. Identity will be made up of the category into which the receiving society assigns them on one hand and the "cognitive map" of the immigrants themselves on the other. Mittelberg and Waters offer the hypothetical case of a Polish immigrant. Americans, familiar with other Polish Americans, assign him or her to the category "Polish." The Polish American population becomes what is referred to as the "proximal host," the group to which the receiving society would assign the immigrant. The newly arrived Pole is different, of course from Polish Americans, but most likely perceives a series of historical similarities and begins to develop a Polish American self-understanding and identity (ibid., 416).

But what if the receiving society assigns the new immigrant to a proximal host that the immigrant does not recognize? Afro-Caribbean immigrants are caught in this problematic position. As black immigrants they are offered the label "African American." But here the proximal host to which the dominant society assigns them is not the identity that they understand themselves to have. They understand themselves to be historically and culturally distinct from Black Americans. Yet social scientists have shown that groups defined through race will have the least amount of choice in self-identification. Groups of black African descent will inevitably be labeled "black." In contrast, "white ethnics" like Irish Americans or Italian Americans have a considerable amount of choice in the ways they may cast their identity (ibid.).

Scholars of race have demonstrated that there is no such thing, really, as "race," but rather that racializations and racisms are processes in historical evolution, changing through time and across space (Hall 1978). We can see the ways in which the former slaveholding societies of Latin America, the West Indies, and the United States have all developed differently racialized configurations. When Haitians arrive in the United States, they carry cognitive maps charting a complex sense of Caribbean racialization in which people are located along a color continuum, mitigated by class and family lineage. Race in the United States has been constructed along a color line, making people either black or white. Haitian Americans' identity and subjective positions of racialization must be seen as being superimposed onto their new experience of United States constructions of race. Part of the challenge people of color face when they emigrate is in assessing and renegotiating a newly found racial status in North America.

Unpacking the complexities of Haitian American identity, Carolle Charles (1990) argues that the categories of race, class, and ethnicity by which Haitians identify themselves are expressions of their social consciousness, and are part of a process of rejection and redefinition of categories of race and ethnicity ascribed in the United States. Charles's work reveals Haitians' tendency to disaffiliate with African Americans. Haitians are acutely aware that Black Americans have been assigned again and again to the lowest status position in the United States. Haitian immigrants see that meanings of blackness in the United States are subordinated, that blacks represent the bottom of United States society. Haitians reject this placement and tend to dismiss U.S. meanings of blackness, while affirming their own race and culture.

Although Haitians self-identify as black, they link their blackness through Haitian history to Africa and not via the United States. Haitian racial identity is closely connected to pride in the Haitian revolution of 1791–1804, which created the first black-ruled nation in the Americas. The revolution was fought by slaves said to be inspired by Vodou and fortified by magical weapons. Blackness and militarism became key tropes of Haitian nationalism, along with allusions to Afro-Creole spiritual power. Citizens of the black nation that defeated Napoleon's army, Haitians carry a deep sense of national pride that is linked to blackness and independence (Charles 1990; see also McAlister 1995a).

The paths that they chart reveal Haitians in the United States to be actors constructing their own identity as a population. Two important performative elements they have available to use in carving out their own identities are language and religion. A common Haitian American tactic is to display, use, and value their Francophone (and Creolophone) abilities. By referring to themselves as "Frenchies" and speaking French in public, Haitians display a foreign-born status that is at once an upper-class marker in Haitian society (Charles 1990, Mittelberg and Waters 1992). By continuing to participate in Catholic congregations and public feasts, Haitian Americans distinguish themselves further from African Americans, whom they generally view as members of the black Protestant church establishment.[22]

It is thus possible to view the Haitian devotion at the Church of Our Lady of Mount Carmel and at other pilgrimages to the Blessed Mother in the United States as a partial strategy in the Haitian American struggle to create an American identity, "a self-constitution through the strategy of alterity within the broader context of American racial semiotics" (Orsi 1992, 321). By maintaining Frenchness, Creoleness, and Catholicism, and by dressing in conservative, French-influenced fashions and hair styles, Haitians broadcast their difference from African Americans. By displaying and practicing their Catholic culture with its Latin and French linguistic attributes, Haitians can underscore to themselves, their children, and the larger society that they are fully Haitian, Afro-Caribbean, Catholic, immigrant—and not African American. In a sense, Haitian Americans can be said to be struggling to create a new black ethnicity in the United States.

While this conservative Francophile strategy is a long-standing one for Haitians throughout the diaspora, it is worth noting that this is not the only stance possible for Haitian American identity. Since the fall of Duvalier in 1986, the *racine* (roots) movement has created an alternative Haitianized identity. This politically progressive movement cultivates a peasant, "folksy" style and an explicitly pro-Vodou ethos. There are also many important political and social alliances between African American and Haitian American groups, each working out of a pro-black consciousness (McAlister 1995a).

Nevertheless, while the pilgrimage is a place to perform spiritual work, it is also an occasion to perform Catholicism on the public stage, regardless of where each person stands on the Catholic-Vodou continuum in Haitian religious culture. Catholicism becomes one ritual performance among others in the larger cultural repertoire. This performance is a continuation of a stance developed in slavery and throughout the postcolonial history of Haiti in the face of church repression of African-based spirituality. In the U.S. context, the performance becomes one element in the Haitian strategy to redefine American categories of race and ethnicity.

Italians and Haitians: Race and Religious Symbiosis

The arrival of both Italians and Puerto Ricans into the United States has been racially charged, each in a specific way. Robert Orsi (1985, 160) writes of the "racial inbetweenness" of late-nineteenth-century Italian immigrants, arguing that Italians were initially viewed as unassimilable "African racial stock." Tallulah, Louisiana, became the bloody scene of race hatred when five Sicilian men (targets of a terrorism historically reserved for African Americans) were lynched "because they had violated the protocols of racial interaction." Italian Americans created an identity in reaction to early racism against them and, in turn, larger issues about their position with respect to other dark-skinned peoples. Immigrants from Italy learned that "achievement in their new environment meant successfully differentiating themselves from the dark-skinned other" (Orsi 1992, 314–317).

In New York Puerto Rican people have also been met with a racialized hatred (Orsi 1992, Díaz-Stevens 1993, Bourgois 1995). When

Puerto Rican migrants moved into Italian Harlem in the pre–World War II period, the Italians reacted with hostility to this "other dark-skinned other," and three-way violence broke out between African Americans, Italian Americans, and Puerto Ricans. Insofar as organized crime syndicates held sway in the Italian community, they forced local landlords to maintain white-only segregated buildings (Bourgois 1995, 60).[23] They could not, however, stop the public housing projects being built in the neighborhood, which were replacing Italian families with black and Latino ones. "We had to leave when the 'goombas' moved in," an Italian American pilgrim returning to Our Lady of Mount Carmel told me. Italians spoke with disdain of the "so-called Puerto Ricans" who as Latins were culturally and linguistically similar, yet whose arrival threatened Italian control of East Harlem and soon turned *cara Harlem* into *el barrio* (Orsi 1992, 326).

Despite the important place reserved for Our Lady of Mount Carmel in their devotions, Puerto Ricans quickly sensed that they would find no welcome at the feast on 115th Street. "Puerto Ricans knew to stay away, because on these days and nights Italian Americans were in the grip of a profound experience of their own power and identity (conflicted and polysemous as this was) and would not tolerate the appearance of 'outsiders' among them, especially those 'outsiders' who lived in the neighborhood" (ibid., 330). The Italians were determined to maintain the Italian ethnic flavor of the feast, ensuring that the *festa* not become a *fiesta*. Even at the present writing, few Puerto Rican pilgrims attend the July sixteenth festivities.

By the time Haitian immigrants began to attend the feast in large numbers in the 1970s, the Italian battle for territory was over. Most Italian American families had moved out of East Harlem, and for them the July feast had become another sort of pilgrimage—a nostalgic visit to the old neighborhood where their parents' American journey began (ibid.). Today Italian American families return to the feast with video cameras; after Mass they line the sidewalks to film the old neighborhood for posterity. The feast is still produced and controlled by the Pallottine order, and the Italian American old guard organizes the feast committees. But the fact is that without hundreds of Haitian bodies at the processions and thousands of Haitians who come to Mass, the feast of Our Lady would not be possible.

The Italians producing the feast receive the Haitians very differently from the way they did the Puerto Ricans a generation ago. The Haitians' arrival from outside the neighborhood and their departure afterward makes their yearly "invasion" less threatening than that of the Puerto Ricans who overtook East Harlem as residents (see also McGreevy 1996). The Italians make gestures welcoming the Haitians, adding a French Mass "as a courtesy," and flying the Haitian flag next to the Italian one in the parade. They comment on how prayerful and devoted the Haitians are. "Look how they pray, the beautiful way they dress, they come from all over, they are so devoted to the Blessed Mother," said one lay worker approvingly. They sense *rispetto* (respect) for the Blessed Mother in the little suits and "wedding-cake dresses" that make up the Haitian "Sunday best."

The Italians express hostility toward Puerto Rican *santeros* (priests in the Yoruba-based religion called *La Regla de Ocha*) when they come to do spiritual work at the church. They describe *Ocha* as "satanism" while at the same time denying that the Haitians are involved in Vodou. Florida Water, candles, and fried pork set near the altars are left only by "a few crazy ones" (Orsi 1992, 334). The elderly Italian American women are nevertheless anxious about the new influx and express fears to one another about the statue's safety in the midst of the newest pilgrims. Some advocate restricting Haitian access to the nave of the church (Bourgois 1995, 347).

Despite Italian anxieties, the Haitians are accommodated and even respected at the church. Language has been an important marker shaping the respect the Italians have for the Haitians. Well versed in the Tridentine Mass, the Haitians chant the prayers in Latin along with the priests, which impresses the Italians. In the respect and prayerfulness of the Haitians, the Italian Americans recognize a conservative, pre–Vatican II religiosity, and identify them as "traditional Catholics" (Orsi 1992, 333). The Haitians' Creole impresses the Italians, on whom the difference between French and Creole is lost. The Italian Americans recognize the Haitian strategies of racial alterity and emphatically assert that "Haitians are not considered as black people" (Orsi 1992, 334). In a sense, the two communities find sympathetic reflection in one another.

For the days of the feast, Haitians and Italians form a sort of symbiosis, each allowing the other to extend once again a cherished event from their past into the future. Italians and Haitians engage in a kind of pact, and each community fills the needs of the other. While the Italian Americans produce the feast, they maintain control over their old neighborhood and the shrine church, one of the three most important Marian sites in all the Americas. Meanwhile, the Haitians are consumers at the shrine. They arrive with flowers, make donations, and buy religious articles—scapulars, statues, and prayer cards. They sing the Mass in Latin and French, and their presence fills the streets in the procession. Without having to organize and produce it, they use the feast as a public stage upon which to serve the Virgin and perform their ethnicity. When it is all over the Haitians retreat, leaving the Italian community to itself. In the often racially tense landscape of New York, this week represents a smooth collaboration that suits everybody involved. For one week each year, the Italian American community of East Harlem becomes a sort of "religious host," welcoming Haitians from near and far. Each community allows the other to preserve their myths, their hopes, and their own deep sense of identity.

Conclusions

Let us return for a moment to little Marie-Carmel, who was touched by the Virgin at the opening of the chapter. This ten-year-old Haitian American girl had never seen Haiti, yet her life story was intimately tied to both the symbols of Haitian religious culture and to social networks of migrants moving back and forth to the island. Her mother, years earlier, was diagnosed with cancer just after she migrated to New York. Like many immigrants of little means in her position, she gathered her things to return to Haiti to die. When she arrived, as she tells it, she dreamed her own mother came to her with a message. "Nothing is wrong. You're just pregnant. When you deliver your baby, call her Marie-Carmel." Convinced that the Vièj Mirak removed her cancer and gave her a child, she attends her *fèt*—whether in Haiti or in the *djaspora*—each year in gratitude.

When little Marie-Carmel fainted at the communion rail, she experienced a profound religious crisis, common in narratives about the spirits in Afro-Haitian culture. Marie-Carmel's mother saw clearly that the Vièj Mirak, with Ezili Dantò next to her, had reclaimed (*reklame*) the little girl. Usually beginning in adolescence as a series of fits, faintings spells, or full-fledged spirit possessions, the process of learning to serve the spirits is initiated when the spirits themselves choose and adopt the children who will become mediums and healer-priests. Having once made Marie-Carmel's life possible, the Vièj Mirak was continuing to bestow her grace on the family through this "reclaiming" spirit possession (McAlister 1992–93).

The fact that this important moment of spiritual contact came to pass at a Catholic church is not out of the ordinary in Haitian religious culture, nor is it uncommon for people to discreetly conceal such events. Catholics who also serve the spirits of Vodou have learned to practice a form of religious code-switching by performing one ritual practice through the codes of another when socially appropriate. One story is switched for another, and both become true. Language here reveals levels of intimacy: to respond to the concern of the priest, the family used English to report that Marie-Carmel fainted for lack of food. For insiders—family and others in Vodou societies—an interpretation emerged in French and then Creole that Marie-Carmel had been "touched," briefly, by the Virgin, and thus "reclaimed" by Ezili.

The deft and quick response of Marie-Carmel's mother to the priest comes out of an historical tradition of religious code-switching developed in Haiti in the face of dominant Catholic pressures. I have argued in this chapter that Vodou and Haitian Catholicism are at once opposed politically and intertwined historically, two religions on either end of a continuum of Haitian religious culture that contains within it multiple and shifting symbols and practices. Individual actors live their lives at various points on the continuum, here going through Catholic sacraments, and there making contact with the spirit world of the angels. It is possible to be a fully practicing Catholic who, through Catholicism, also receives the spiritual calls and blessings of the Vodou spirits. In church spaces, work for the spirits is switched into subtly coded Catholic ritual language.

The New York pilgrimage, I have argued, becomes the site for a second kind of code-switching, where Haitian actors respond to a new cultural politics of race. Haitians are assigned by the dominant society to the African American proximal host niche, yet they do not understand themselves to be African American. Haitian Americans' identities are in tension as the immigrant population struggles to define itself on its own terms. One tactic (among others) of the Haitian American community is to develop French-inflected identities, stressing their French and Creole language, French style of dress, and Roman Catholicism. By attending Roman Catholic churches, schools, and pilgrimages, Haitians broadcast their distinctive language, culture, and religion. Through this "strategy of alterity," Haitians broadcast cultural difference from African Americans and contest U.S. systems of racialization.

Roman Catholicism is, for Haitians, one ritual performance among others in a larger cultural repertoire. It is a religious "code" that in the United States can stand in public for all of Haitian religious culture, Vodou and Catholicism alike. Catholic churches are familiar spaces that host the saints intimately known to many Haitian Catholics. And whether one is praying to Ezili or to the Virgin Mary, stepping into a Catholic church is also stepping into a legitimate modern American identity. In a process quite similar to that undergone by the Italian American community before them, Haitians find an aspect of their public face in the church. Perhaps the Italian Americans who host the feast for the Blessed Mother at 115th Street recognize themselves in the new immigrants praying before them.

In this chapter I set out to illustrate that in order to understand religious life for some new immigrants, we must understand their continuing relationships with the religious cultures of their home countries. The Haitian diaspora represents an actively transnational population, embedded in social, political, and financial networks that span home and host countries. The Fèt Vièj Mirak on East 115th Street is a religious event whose meaning also spans New York and Haiti. But rather than substituting the New York feast for the one they left behind at Sodo, Haitians add the Harlem location as another possible site of spiritual work. In this way East 115th Street is opened up as one more site in the expanding "religioscape" of transnational Haitian religious culture. During the pilgrimage for Notre Dame du Mont Carmel in New York, the Haitian population reterritorializes spiritual practice, reinscribing sacred space onto their new landscape of settlement.

The pilgrimage to Mont Carmel in East Harlem expands the saint's influence in the Haitian world. Haitians in diaspora reach out to Mont Carmel and Ezili Dantò, both nationalist divinities, extending prayers for family and friends throughout the *djaspora* and in Haiti. By attending the feast by the thousands, the New York Haitian population has collectively placed the Church of Our Lady of Mount Carmel on an invisible community map. In stepping onto the public stage of the Catholic feast, they orient themselves within the shifting "ethnoscape" of New York City. They make sense of the confusing complexity of this ethnic landscape by locating the church as a center of spiritual power where they will be welcome.

Most Latin American countries have national shrines that use religion to connect tropes about the nation to other symbolisms about gender and sexuality.[24] Mexicans make pilgrimages to the shrine of Nuestra Señora de Guadalupe, Puerto Ricans to Nuestra Señora de la Monserrate, Cubans to Nuestra Señora de Caridad del Cobre, Colombians to La Virgen de Las Lajas, Brazilians to Bom Jesus da Lapa, and Dominicans to Nuestra Señora de Altagracia del Higuey (Laguerre 1989, 83; Diaz-Stevens 1993, 47). When national populations spread through migration to new localities, they bring their divinities with them, re-territorializing their religious practices. The supernatural world assents, and comes to bear up communities in transition.

ACKNOWLEDGMENTS

This project is indebted to the helpful comments of David H. Brown, Karen McCarthy Brown, Father Gerald P. Cohen, Ana-María Díaz-Stevens, Tom F. Driver, Paul Uhry Newman, R. Stephen Warner, Anna Wexler, and my colleagues in the New Ethnic and Immigrant Congregations Project, as well as the Pallottine Fathers, the East Harlem Italian American community members, Manbo Miracia, Madame Luc, Manbo Jaklinc, Holly Nicolas, Father Guy Sansariqc, and the many Haitian pilgrims who shared their views with me. The chapter was funded by the Lilly Endowment and the Pew Charitable Trusts and was written at The Writer's Room in New York City.

NOTES

1. Before the Second Vatican Council of the 1960s, it was customary to fast until taking communion. While this particular family no longer observed that tradition, it did serve as an implicit, legitimating explanation for Marie-Carmel's fainting.

2. Although I speak Creole fluently, older Haitians often address me in French, as they might any non-Haitian, for French is more widely spoken worldwide and is also a marker of prestige. In Haitian Creole, foreigners are always called *blan,* implying "whiteness." An Anglo-American woman like me is a *fanm blan,* while an African American woman would be a *nègès blan,* a "black white/foreigner." In Creole, blackness is normative, hence the word for "man" is *nèg,* connoting "black man." A Haitian man is always a *nèg,* even if he is of European descent, in which case he is a *nèg blan,* a "white black man," or a *nèg milat,* a "mulatto black man." Much has been written on Haitian codes of racialization, which are different from those in both the United States and other parts of Latin America and the Caribbean (see Nicholls 1979, Dupuy 1989).

3. Robert Orsi (personal communication, New York, July 1992) notes that the last Italian religious supply shop closed in 1990.

4. The vast majority of Haitians are black people of African descent. There is also a small minority of *Ayisyen blanc,* or "European Haitians," *milat,* or "mulatto Haitians," and a tiny but economically significant sector of *Siryen,* a gloss for the Lebanese, Palestinian, Syrian, and Israeli diaspora merchant community in Port-au-Prince.

5. Only a few hundred other statues of the Virgin share this special shrine status worldwide, and of these, the church at 115th Street was only the third in all the Americas. The two others were designated by the same pope. Our Lady of Perpetual Help in the Ursuline Convent in New Orleans was erected in 1727. Our Lady of Guadalupe, now in the Basilica in Mexico City, was erected on an Aztec site in 1532 (Orsi 1985, 60; Pistella 1954, 76–88).

6. Interview, Father Guy Sansariqc, head of the Haitian Apostolate, Brooklyn, June 1996.

7. Spiritual marriage to the spirits, or *lwa,* of Vodou is common in Haitian religious culture (see Brown 1991).

8. Tragedy can include forced deportation, for example. Increasingly the United States and weaker nations are collaborating in an institutionalized transnational policy whereby persons convicted of crimes are deported to their home country after serving their sentences in U.S. jails. This policy was made possible by Title 3 of the Illegal Immigration Reform and Immigrant Responsibility Act of 1996, and represents a new era in international relations.

9. Arjun Appadurai (1990, 6) writes of the disjoined flows that are set in motion with increased globalization: "ethnoscapes, mediascapes, technoscapes, financescapes and ideoscapes." It is possible here to think of "religioscapes" as the subjective religious maps (and attendant theologies) of diasporic communities who are also in global flow and flux.

10. Important religious sites dot the New York landscape, and include intersections where offerings can be made to Papa Legba, *lwa* of the crossroads; public parks where trees and rocks are used for their spiritual power; cemeteries where the recently dead can be honored; and churches housing the saints, where Creole Mass is spoken. Other pilgrimages are also mapped onto the metropolitan area as well: for example, thousands of Haitians take chartered buses to the Church of Czestochowa in Pennsylvania for the Feast of the Assumption. For a treatment of sacred urban lanscape in Afro-Cuban tradition, see David Hilary Brown (1989, 353–357).

11. See, for example, Carole Divillers, (1985) and the Winter 1992 issue of *Aperture* (vol. 126) that focused on Haiti.

12. He was subsequently crowned emperor of the Haitian Republic and the de facto head of its Roman Catholic church (see n. 18 below). Sodo is still a site of political manipulations. During the period after the fall of Jean-Claude Duvalier, the ruling junta members built cinder-block vacation houses among the wooden and straw houses right next to the falls in order to maintain a visible public presence at the site.

13. For the only ethnographic work to date on Rastafari in New York City, see the essay by Randal L. Hepner in this volume (Chapter 6).

14. Another spot, called Fey Sen Jan, was the site of a ritual the night before the Mont Carmel feast in Ville Bonheur, but it has virtually disappeared (Laguerre 1989, 84; interview with Manbo Gislene, New York City, July 1994).

15. In French her name was written "Erzulie Dantor," and it appears that way often in Vodou flags, songs, and other works of art, as well as in priests' notebooks and other sacred writings. The etymological history of her name merits future research.

16. Throughout Haitian history, the Catholic church has launched waves of repression against Vodou practitioners in "anti-superstition campaigns" (see Desmangles 1992).

17. This understanding applies to religion the theories on Creole linguistics worked out by Lee Drummond (1980).

18. Although the history is too lengthy to elaborate here, it is important to note that with Haitian Independence in 1804, ties were officially cut to the Vatican, and a Catholicism in Haiti evolved with its own national flavor. In 1860 a concordat was signed reopening the relationship with Rome. By that time, Afro-Haitian spirituality had established itself as the worldview of the vast majority of Haitians.

19. Although Haiti has historically been a Catholic country, evangelical Protestantism is now enjoying enormous success. On the Haitian American membership in the Southern Baptist Convention, see Carolle Charles (1990, 262–280).

20. Interview, Father Guy Sansariqc, Brooklyn, June 1996.

21. In the three devastating years after the coup d'état against Aristide, the Haitian military run by General Raoul Cedras embarked on a terrorist campaign of rape unprecedented in Haitian history. Many people who fled the country by sea ended up in the U.S. naval base in Cuba, Guantánamo, to be further traumatized by human rights abuses there (see Americas Watch et al. 1991).

22. Haitians also tend to send their children to Catholic schools in relatively high numbers (see Lawrence 1997).

23. In his ethnography *In Search of Respect: Selling Crack in El Barrio,* Philippe Bourgois (1995, 48–76) chronicles the largely Puerto Rican–controlled drug trade that ravaged the neighborhood around the Church of Our Lady in the 1980s. He argues that this area of Manhattan has long been a site of "crime, violence and substance abuse," from the early Dutch tobacco farms to the heroin and cocaine trades of Italian crime families to the Latino crack dealers. While it is dangerous to attempt to describe drug-dealing networks because of the potential for stereotyping, it is important to be conscious of the realities of both legal and extralegal economic spheres and subcultures and their influence on wider communities.

24. See Andrew Parker et al. (1992).

REFERENCES

Americas Watch, Physicians for Human Rights, and National Coalition for Haitian Refugees. 1991. *Return to the Darkest Days: Human Rights in Haiti Since the Coup.* New York: Americas Watch.

Aperture. 1992. 126 (Winter): 40–47.

Appadurai, Arjun. 1990. "Disjuncture and Difference in the Global Cultural Economy." *Public Culture* 2 (2): 1–24.

Basch, Linda, Nina Glick-Schiller, and Cristina Szanton Blanc. 1994. *Nations Unbound: Transnational Projects, Postcolonial Predicaments, and Deterritorialized Nation-States.* Langhorne, Pa.: Gordon and Breach.

Bastide, Roger. 1960. *The African Religions of Brazil: Towards a Sociology of the Interpenetration of Civilizations.* Baltimore: Johns Hopkins University Press.

Bourgois, Philippe. 1995. *In Search of Respect: Selling Crack in El Barrio.* New York and Cambridge: Cambridge University Press.

Brown, David Hilary. 1989. "Garden in the Machine: Afro-Cuban Sacred Art and Performance in New Jersey and New York." Ph.D. dissertation, Yale University.

Brown, Karen McCarthy. 1991. *Mama Lola: A Vodou Priestess in Brooklyn.* Berkeley: University of California Press.

Buchanan, Susan. 1980. "Scattered Seeds: The Meaning of the Migration for Haitians in New York City." Ph.D. dissertation, New York University.

Cabon, Adolphe. 1933. *Notes sur l'Histoire Religieuse d'Haiti: De la Révolution au Concordad (1789-1860).* Port-au-Prince: Petit Seminaire College Saint-Martial.

Charles, Carolle. 1990. "Distinct Meanings of Blackness: Haitian Migrants in New York City." *Cimarron* 2 (3): 129-138.

―――. 1991. "A Transnational Dialectic of Race, Class, and Ethnicity: Patterns of Identities and Forms of Consciousness Among Haitian Migrants in New York City." Ph.D. dissertation, SUNY Binghamton.

Clifford, James. 1994. "Diasporas." *Cultural Anthropology* 9 (3): 302-338.

Davis, Nathalie Z. 1982. "From 'Popular Religion' to Religious Cultures." Pp. 312-343 in *Reformation Europe: A Guide to Research,* edited by Steven Ozment. St. Louis: Center for Reformation Research.

Desmangles, Leslie G. 1992. *The Faces of the Gods: Vodou and Roman Catholicism in Haiti.* Chapel Hill: University of North Carolina Press.

Devillers, Carole. 1985. "Haiti's Voodoo Pilgrimages of Spirits and Saints." *National Geographic* 167 (March): 394-408.

Díaz-Stevens, Ana-María. 1993. *Oxcart Catholicism on Fifth Avenue: The Impact of the Puerto Rican Migration upon the Archdiocese of New York.* Notre Dame, Ind.: University of Notre Dame Press.

Dolan, Jay. 1985. *The American Catholic Experience: A History from Colonial Times to the Present.* New York: Doubleday and Company.

Drummond, Lee. 1980. "The Cultural Continuum: A Theory of Intersystems." *Man* 15: 352-374.

Dupuy, Alex. 1989. *Haiti in the World Economy: Class, Race, and Underdevelopment Since 1700.* Boulder, Colo.: Westview Press.

Gallardo, Susana. 1994. Proposal to the New Ethnic and Immigrant Congregations Project. Unpublished manuscript, Stanford University.

Glick-Schiller, Nina. 1975. "The Formation of an Haitian Ethnic Group." Ph.D. dissertation, Columbia University.

Hall, Stuart, ed. 1978. *Policing the Crisis: Mugging, the State, and Law and Order.* New York: Holmes and Meier.

Handlin, Oscar. 1951. *The Uprooted.* New York: Grosset and Dunlap.

Herskovits, Melville. 1941. *The Myth of the Negro Past.* Boston: Beacon, 1958.

hooks, bell. 1989. "Critical Interrogation: Talking Race, Resisting Racism." *Inscriptions* 5: 159-164.

Jolibois, Gerard. 1970. "Notre Principal Pelerinage Marial." *Le Nouveau Monde*, no. 1299, July 30.

Laguerre, Michel. 1989. *Voodoo and Politics in Haiti*. New York: St. Martin's Press.

Laurino, Maria. 1995. "Sharing a Saint: The Two Worlds of Our Lady of Mount Carmel." *New York Times*, July 23, sect. 13, p. 5, col. 3.

Lawrence, Stewart. 1997. "U.S. Immigrants in the Catholic Schools: A Preliminary Assessment." Unpublished paper, Catholic University of America, Washington, D.C.

Levitt, Peggy. In press. "Local-Level Global Religion: The Case of U.S.-Dominican Migration." *Journal for the Scientific Study of Religion*.

McAlister, Elizabeth. 1992–93. "Sacred Stories from the Haitian Diaspora: A Collective Biography of Seven Vodou Priestesses in New York City." *Journal of Caribbean Studies*, 9 (1–2, Winter 1992–Spring 1993): 10–27.

———. 1995a. "'Men Moun Yo; Here Are the People: Rara Festivals and Transnational Popular Culture in New York City." Ph.D. dissertation, Yale University.

———. 1995b. "A Sorcerer's Bottle: The Art of Magic in Haiti." Pp. 304–321 in *The Sacred Arts of Haitian Vodou*, edited by Donald J. Cosentino. Los Angeles: Fowler Museum of Cultural History.

McGreevy, John. 1996. *Parish Boundaries: The Catholic Encounter with Race in the Twentieth-Century Urban North*. Chicago: University of Chicago Press.

Mittelberg, David and Mary C. Waters. 1992. "The Process of Ethnogenesis Among Haitian and Israeli Immigrants in the United States." *Ethnic and Racial Studies* 15 (3): 412–435.

Murphy, Joseph. 1988. *Santeria: An African Religion in America*. Boston: Beacon Press.

Nash, June. 1983. "The Impact of the Changing International Division of Labor on Different Sectors of the Labor Force." Pp. 3–69. In *Women, Men, and the International Division of Labor*, edited by June Nash and Patricia Fernandez-Kelly. Albany: SUNY Press.

Nicholls, David. 1979. *From Dessalines to Duvalier: Race, Color, and National Independence in Haiti*. New York: Cambridge University Press.

Orsi, Robert Anthony. 1985. *The Madonna of 115th Street: Faith and Community in Italian Harlem, 1880–1950*. New Haven: Yale University Press.

———. 1992. "The Religious Boundaries of an Inbetween People: Street Feste and the Problem of the Dark-Skinned Other in Italian Harlem, 1920–1990." *American Quarterly* 44 (3): 313–341.

Parker, Andrew, Mary Russo, Doris Sommer, and Patricia Yaeger, eds. 1992. *Nationalisms and Sexualities*. New York: Routledge.

Pistella, Domenico. 1954. *The Crowning of a Queen*, translated by Peter Rofrano. New York: Shrine of Our Lady of Mount Carmel.

Price-Mars, Jean. 1983. *So Spoke the Uncle*, translated by Magdaline W. Shannon. Originally published 1928. Washington, D.C.: Three Continents Press.

Rouzier, Sémexan. 1891. *Dictionnaire Géographique d'Haiti*. Paris: Charles Blot.

Sassen-Koob, Saskia. 1982. "Recomposition and Peripherialization at the Core." *Contemporary Marxism* 5: 88–100.

Stewart, Charles, and Rosalind Shaw. 1994. *Syncretism/Anti-Syncretism: The Politics of Religious Synthesis*. New York: Routledge.

Tweed, Thomas A. 1997. *Our Lady of the Exile: Diasporic Religion at a Cuban Catholic Shrine in Miami*. New York and Oxford: Oxford University Press.

Wallerstein, Emmanuel. 1974. *The Modern World System*. New York: Academic Press.

Wilcken, Lois. 1991. "Music, Folklore, and Haitians in New York: Stage Representations and the Negotiation of Identity." Ph.D. dissertation, Columbia University.

III

Institutional
Adaptations

5 | Born Again in East LA: The Congregation as Border Space

Luís León

Currently, Los Angeles International Airport welcomes more immigrants than any other port of entry in American history. Public mythology, however, still reveres Ellis Island and the Statue of Liberty and looks toward Europe. Historical writing on immigration in the United States surely suffers from this severe regional imbalance; most studies still focus on the Northeast and selected cities of the Old Northwest. The fact that the American Southwest has been the locus of one of the most profound and complex interactions between variant cultures in American history is repeatedly overlooked. —George J. Sánchez, *Becoming Mexican American* (1993)

Los Angeles is a veritable Jerusalem. Just the place for a mighty work of God to begin. —Frank Bartleman, *Azusa Street* (August 1, 1906)

East Los Angeles was our Jerusalem and the birthplace for Victory Outreach. Spiritually speaking, California is our Judea and the United States is our Samaria. The "uttermost parts" is the rest of the world. —The Victory Outreach Mission Statement

Over the past ten years, the movement of Latino Catholics to forms of evangelical/pentecostal or "born-again" religion has captured the attention of scholars and journalists who are interested in the configuration and active reconfiguration of religion in the Americas (Deck 1994, León 1994, Stoll 1990, Stoll and Garrard-Burnett 1993, Suro 1989). Over the past thirty years, the once impenetrable walls of Catholicism in Central and South America have been shaken by waves of evangelical conversion, and now "nearly ten percent or more of the

163

Latin American population identifies itself as *evangelico,* with the percentage substantially higher in Brazil, Chile, and most of Central America" (Stoll and Garrard-Burnett 1993, 2). Scholarly interest in Latin American "born-again" conversion has been buttressed by the debate on the "failure" of the Catholic church to serve the needs of the Latino masses and more particularly the actual impact of liberation theology. That the Latin American Catholic church has functioned historically, in effect, as a bulwark of the landed elites by mystifying class inequities is now axiomatic (Stoll 1990). In spite of promising and well-intentioned post–Vatican II discursive and practical attempts at reforms in Latin American Catholicism engineered by the bishops and made manifest as liberation theology, some argue that theologies of liberation in Latin America have been "better at filling faculties, bookshelves, and graves than churches" (Stoll 1990, 310).

At the moment, academic research on Latino pentecostalism is disproportionately focused on Latin America. In its assessments of motivations for evangelical conversion, this literature falls into two broad interpretive categories, which I have named *Marxist social determinism* and *rational-choice humanism.* Both are commonly applied to explain Chicano/United States Latino evangelical conversion as well (Deck 1994).[1] Hence, they are worth pursuing here.

What I call rational-choice humanism is an intellectualist position that implies that the Latino religious "consumer" is endowed with all the necessary information and the requisite freedom and privilege to choose, based on *reason,* one religion over another and make that religion best fit his or her particular needs—in short, empowerment (Espinosa, forthcoming, Stoll and Garrard-Burnett 1993). This position rarely takes into account the often limited and degrading choices available to working-class Latinos.

On the other hand, the Marxists proclaim that evangelical religion provides a mechanism for social disengagement by channeling people's repressed energies, anxieties, and general social dissatisfaction into a spiritual obsession and attendant eschatological hope that preclude critical political thought and revolutionary practice (Anderson 1979, D'Epinay 1969). In the words of one pentecostal historian, the pentecostal movement teaches us "something about the way in which movements of the 'disinherited' that arise out of protest against the social order are transformed into religious forces that serve to perpetuate that order" (Anderson 1979, 8). While some have separated the positions, I see as closely related David Martin's (1990) argument that Latin America has been religiously, socially, and politically latent, and that it is therefore only now experiencing its Protestant Reformation. Evangelicalism, in this narrative of modernity, creates docile and complacent workers who are focused on the afterlife.

Although not unproblematic, Martin's theory is helpful for identifying the social space opened by pentecostalism where power, group loyalties, identity, and resistance can be reimagined and expressed. This space has been widened to include Latina feminist concerns. Some have recently argued that pentecostalism provides Latin American women with a sacred mallet for pounding the cultural beast of a peculiarly Latin American machismo into submission (Brusco 1995, Martin 1995). In this view, clever women choose pentecostalism as a mechanism of empowerment to restrain their husband's "machista" habits. In other words, the rational-choice humanism model posits a free—indeed *transcendent* subject—who, in spite of social limitations, can choose at will, whereas the Marxist social determinism model posits the opposite—a submissive pawn who is duped into submission by the elites for political and economic exploitation.

Neither of these binary paradigms explains fully the complex phenomenon of Mexican American or Chicano pentecostalism. Nonetheless, both are illuminating. Certainly there are escapist elements in pentecostalism, just as there are modes of empowerment. No human agent, however, is free from social context, and Chicanos face many social, political, symbolic, and economic forces that limit not only their choices but also their ability to choose. Hence, I attempt in this essay to determine the conditions of possibility under which the choice for Alcance Victoria, a group of about two dozen Spanish-language churches that are part of the mainly English-language evangelical church movement known as Victory Outreach, headquartered east of Los Angeles in La Puente, is made possible. My thesis is that Alcance Victoria at once enables the reproduction of both modes of empowerment and modes of docility or domination. In what follows, I attempt to illuminate ethnographically how these modes are enabled in one particular context: the Alcance Victoria congregation in the Boyle Heights district of East Los Angeles.[2]

Given its institutional affiliation, the story of Alcance Victoria is a story within a story, a tale of an elaborate religious organization located strategically within a larger, highly articulated network of religious and social organizations. In the local congregation, Alcance Victorians negotiate and rework their identities in the context of often overwhelming social conditions by spinning understandings of time and place, together with self and society, into webs of religious-meaning systems. What follows attempts to unravel the Alcance Victoria web to tell the stories of the individual lives that together constitute what I call the "congregational narrative."

Victory Outreach/Alcance Victoria Ministries: Possess the Land

Victory Outreach was founded by Sonny Arguinzoni in Boyle Heights in 1967 as a ministry to Chicano gangs. From its humble beginnings in the Pico Aliso public housing projects during the late 1960s, Victory Outreach has become a vast and highly organized movement spanning the globe and touching and improving the lives of many. Recounted in a number of autobiographical books and on video- and audiotapes, Arguinzoni's story (or "testimony," in pentecostal vernacular) has become a foundational myth for the Victory Outreach cosmos (Arguinzoni and Arguinzoni 1991; Arguinzoni 1995). Arguinzoni's testimonial narrative functions as a template for believers concerning matters of doctrine—as well as gender relations and expectations of women. (It is required reading at many of the Victory Outreach women's retreats.)

A Puerto Rican (or better, "Newyorican"), Arguinzoni began using heroin as a youth in Brooklyn. His parents were both active pentecostals and prayed for their son's "salvation." During the late 1950s, after he had spent time in jail and after an increasing heroin addiction further alienated him from his parents, Arguinzoni became "saved" one afternoon through the intervention of evangelist Nicky Cruz, a notorious ex-gang leader. Arguinzoni's interest in pentecostalism was aroused by the dapper appearance of a former heroin-addicted associate of his who had been "born again." Arguinzoni followed his former associate to the para-church organization Teen Challenge, founded by David Wilkerson, author of *The Cross and the Switchblade*. There Arguinzoni encountered Cruz, the former president of the infamous Puerto Rican "Mau Mau" gang who earned fame in the Bronx for waging war on the police. Arguinzoni met his match in Cruz, who physically prevented him from leaving the Teen Challenge Center until he was able to kick drugs. In his personal narrative, Arguinzoni describes how he beat his addition and enrolled in La Puente Bible College located east of Los Angeles. While there, he met Julie Rivera, a Chicana from East Los Angeles.

Julie Rivera came from a Catholic home. Her entire family had converted to pentecostalism, however, after they came to believe that her brother had been revived from the dead after a drug overdose. The family attributed the brother's second chance at life to the prayerful intercession of Julie's aunt, a pentecostal. Julie and Sonny were married shortly after graduation in the early 1960s.

The Arguinzonis' first home was a rented unit in the Pico Aliso housing projects in Boyle Heights. There Sonny began preaching to the drug addicts, gang members, and ex-convicts who populated the tenements; he often sheltered them in his own tiny apartment for rehabilitation. Eventually he rented a church located within the city blocks that comprise the giant housing complex. Even after the church was rented, he and Julie sheltered a number of needy Chicanos in their home, helping them to kick the drug habit. It was in this way that the idea for Victory Outreach, a drug rehabilitation and rescue ministry, was born.

After its beginning in the 1960s, Victory Outreach moved to a number of rented locations to hold church services, including a discotheque that had to be sanitized early every Sunday morning. In the late 1980s, Victory Outreach acquired fourteen acres in a former school property in La Puente for $1.7 million. This property now houses the "mother church" (pastored by Arguinzoni), the Victory Outreach School of Ministry, and a bookstore. Each Sunday morning at 8:30 and 10:30, services are held at the mother church sanctuary, which seats one thousand people. Currently Victory Outreach is in the process of building a larger temple on that site that will seat between three and four thousand.

Today Victory Outreach is a sophisticated organization with over two hundred churches and twice that number of drug rehabilitation homes throughout the world. Not all congregations look alike; each assumes an identity that largely depends on its own geography and class. Most churches are made up of working-class members. The expressed goal of Victory Outreach, together with Alcance Victoria, is to have one thousand churches by the year 2000. In addition to the La Puente headquarters, Victory Outreach also rents two thousand feet of office space in West Covina, California, where the business offices of Arguinzoni and his staff are housed. Victory Outreach sponsors a number of programs designed especially for women, United Women in Ministry, and a television ministry that broadcasts infrequently on the Trinity Broadcasting Network.

One of the organization's most successful programs is a youth ministry called God's Anointed Now Generation (GANG). GANG creates a Christian image that mimics a Los Angeles Chicano youth gang aesthetic, encoding it within a Christian vernacular. Victory Outreach has its own rap groups that sample rhythms and riffs of popular songs but inscribe Christian lyrics over them. Many members of GANG continue to sport the hairstyles, makeup, and baggy clothes of Los Angeles youth culture, but they espouse Christian teachings.

When a convert feels a "burden" to open a church in a particular place, he is "launched out," or given one year of support from the organization for that ministry. The first church was "launched out" eastward from Boyle Heights to Pico Rivera, California. It is expected that such a church will become self-supporting within a year, although some exceptions are made and cutoff dates extended. Hence, the impressive growth of Victory Outreach can be explained largely by the individual initiative of its male members. Women are not able to become pastors to or head churches themselves, but they can become evangelists and work as leaders among other women.

As the Spanish-language branch of Victory Outreach, Alcance Victoria now has over twenty-five churches in Mexico, Spain, and the United States. Alcance Victoria began in 1983, in an abandoned synagogue on Bridge Street in Boyle Heights. This first congregation was taken over by Eliodoro Contreras, known as "Pastor Lolo," in 1989, after the original pastor became ill. Pastor Lolo had been "born again" in Victory Outreach ministries, and he felt a "burden" for Mexico. Although he spoke very little Spanish, armed with his Bible and $500, Lolo, along with his wife, Catty, and their infant son, made the pilgrimage to the sacred heart of Mexico: Mexico City. From that vantage point they planned to win Mexico for Jesus. Upon returning to the States several years later, Lolo assumed the leadership of the Spanish congregation, which had moved from the synagogue on Bridge Street to a storefront on McDonald Street. Soon the group grew too large, and in 1992 Lolo moved them into a former painters' union hall on Soto Street in the heart of Boyle Heights, which they rented monthly. In 1994, Pastor Lolo resigned his post after the stress of the job took its toll on his marriage and family life. The congregation was given over to one of Pastor Lolo's "generals," Jesus Figueroa, who goes by the nickname "Chuy." At the time Chuy was twenty-two-years-old, which made him the youngest pastor in the Victory Outreach organization.

Pentecostalism in the Borderlands

In 1994, Alcance Victoria Este de Los Angeles (East Los Angeles) moved from the painters' union hall to a defunct movie theater in Boyle Heights, where they still meet today. Although they rent the edifice, they have made substantial permanent changes to it and intend to buy it eventually; in the words of the pastor, they are "trusting God" for its purchase. The building's facade is dominated by a marquee, which in times past announced films starring Cantinflas and other Mexican legends. It now sports a hand-painted cloth sign announcing Alcance Victoria's presence and the order of their services, and welcoming all passersby. On the exterior wall that Alcance Victoria shares with another building an advertisement reads, "You can change your eye color." When passing, I never fail to reflect on the appropriateness of this statement as a welcoming sign for Alcance Victoria, whose message is of personal transformation and the omnipotence of God: "You too can be changed—spiritually, morally, *physically*."

Inside, the building is big but spare, with high ceilings and a plain decor. A banner behind the pulpit proclaims: "Alcance Victoria E.L.A. Posseer La Tierra" (Possess the Land). Eight flags of various nations, fresh flowers, a Plexiglas podium, and red carpeting complete the furnishings of the platform. At the very top center of the ceiling hang two flags, one Mexican, the other American. The auditorium is brightly lighted.

Men make up over half of this Alcance Victoria congregation, which is generally young. About 75 percent of the membership is under the age of fifty, and most are in their twenties, thirties, and forties. The average Sunday morning and evening attendance is three hundred, of which, according to the pastor's estimates, about one-half are recently arrived Mexican immigrants, and the other half Mexican Americans or Mexicans living permanently in the United States.

While East Los Angeles (not unlike its inhabitants) is officially "unincorporated" into the city, it is nonetheless Los Angeles, and this ambiguous fact is evident in the built environment, from the growing downtown skyline that, when not obscured by smog, is visible from most areas in this part of town. This section of Los Angeles is densely built for a western city; the buildings are two and three stories high with no side yards. The blocks are long, and the streets teem with humanity. During my typical one-block walk from where I park my car to the church on the corner of the block, I pass one Mexican grocery store, one general grocery store owned by immigrants from India, a large basketball gymnasium that is usually open (operated by the Hollenbeck Division of the Los Angeles Police Department, located opposite the Alcance Victoria edifice), and a pet store with its cages of birds and rabbits lining the broad sidewalk, making their presence known with their exotic sounds and odors.

During the dry, hot summer months, while making the trek from my car to the church (usually an adventure in itself), I have encountered young Chicanas and Chicanos loitering in front of the general grocery store drinking beer out of bottles wrapped in brown paper bags; Alcance Victoria members are usually in their midst, ministering to them passionately. Their evangelistic narratives resonate with the *consejo* in Mexican culture—proverbial words of wisdom gained from life experience imparted to the youth by elders. The youth outside the liquor store, suffering from the shortsightedness that plagues most young generations, endure this exchange with the Alcance Victoria members respectfully: they try to restrain giggles with smiles, and they nod quietly and patiently, all the while appearing generally appreciative of the elders' concern. This is the reaction of most gang members to whom Alcance Victorians preach on their weekly pilgrimages into the depths of the gang-infested neighborhoods of East Los Angeles—patient, respectful, even grateful.

That Boyle Heights is ridden with gangs might come as a surprise to the uninformed visitor. Indeed, there is a feeling of community here, of being among family; the maxim that "we are all in this together" seems to define the sentiments of the collectivity. Strangers initiate Spanish conversations in stores, in restaurants, and on the streets. Just a few blocks away from the church, where Cesar Chavez Avenue meets Soto Street, any warm summer night will find hundreds of people passing the time together. Under the mesmerizing Los Angeles moon, they eat together and barter with the vendors whose pottery and leather wares cover colorful blankets on the sidewalks in neat rows; on sizzling and steaming carts, Mexican pastries and tacos are prepared to be sold fresh. I often stop there before making the ninety-minute drive back to my home in pristine Santa Barbara. If this scene were taking place outside a massive park instead of in parking lots, it could easily be mistaken for Mexico City or Guadalajara. East Los Angeles's public culture is largely organized around food, and its effervescence is reflected in Alcance Victoria (León 1994, 79).

In the center of the Alcance Victoria church vestibule stands a small island where food is prepared and served by the women members. Eating takes place at each service, and without question commensalism is the ritual practice definitive of Chicano culture. On one level, the relegation of women to food preparation and service is easily understood to be an extension and actualization of cultural norms that contribute to the marginalization of women. On the other hand, women too are agents in the production of religion, and their control of food provides them an arena of power. (The full exploration of this topic goes beyond the scope of this study.)

The gendered division of religious and cultural labor is further evident in the assignment of worship leaders. Ushers who stand at the entranceways and distribute worship programs are more often men, although women do sometimes serve as ushers. Sunday morning and evening services are led by a man who holds a title in the church hierarchy. The songs are projected onto a screen with an overhead projector. The music is provided by a band made up entirely of men. Electric keyboards, guitar, and bass play to the rhythm of acoustic drums. Perhaps the main attraction at the pulpit are three teenage and young adult female singers, who often wear slinky dresses or other colorful outfits and stand stage left of the male song leader. These women alternate song-leading responsibilities with other women, but one is always the pastor's wife. It is impossible to overlook the allure of the women's chorus for the typically single male audience member. This is indeed part of the appeal for the men: the likelihood of finding the idealized "virgin" woman to marry. It seems that in spite of the pentecostal iconoclastic rejection of the Virgin of Guadalupe, the realm of women's possibilities she symbolizes and circumscribes still dominates the Chicano imagination.[3]

The order of the Sunday morning and evening services is roughly the same. An opening prayer is followed by lively singing and even some dancing, interspersed with more prayers. Here, instead of the rock and roll and soulful beats borrowed from black churches and inscribed with the Spanish lyrics once characteristic of Latino pentecostal churches, the most popular songs in this congregation are taken from the Psalms of David, sung in minor keys with Hebrew lyrics. During the faster numbers, young children rush to the front of the church and jump around, forming a mosh pit of sorts, while several men spill into the aisles and begin twirling on one leg and lifting their arms above their heads.

After the congregation sings and prays for fifteen or twenty minutes, the pastor makes a dramatic entrance, walking stoically yet briskly from the rear of the church with two or more of his church officials, all sporting dark suits, ties, and short hair shaven on the sides. They assume the places reserved for them in the first row of the sanctuary and do not stop to greet anyone. In this way, they symbolically command the respect and authority of an intensely committed religious group; everyone knows who is in charge here. Several announcements are then made, and the offering prayed for and collected. A brief round of special songs follows, during which individuals who are prepared beforehand are asked to mount the pulpit and sing a solo. Others from the audience are asked to deliver special *tesimonios,* or "testimonies." Finally, the pastor assumes the pulpit about one hour to ninety minutes after the service begins. He leads the congregation in choruses of rousing songs while swaying a tight fist up and down to form a U-shape. Next, he allows the congregation to be seated and announces a passage from the Bible that will serve as the text of his sermon. While waiting for the congregation to locate the Scripture and follow along, he asks how many love Jesus or some other rhetorical question. As he reads the text, the congregation is perfectly silent.

Pastor Chuy's sermons are animated and compelling. He begins by reading a passage from the Bible, and then illustrates (most often indirectly) how it is relevant to the congregation's life. His preaching has a folksy quality about it, and his topics vary. However, he always emphasizes personal responsibility and the transformative power of God. He typically exhorts congregation members to maintain their faith, to work hard for Jesus, to continue coming to church, and to love and help one another, for Jesus' return is near. His sermons average between forty-five minutes to an hour. On Father's Day of 1995, he preached about how to be a good and responsible father, and urged fathers to spend time with their children. He related a deeply moving story about his own father, who had abandoned his family when Chuy was very young. Pastor Chuy told the congregation about the time he contacted his father, whom he barely knew, to invite him to his high school graduation. His father declined. Pastor Chuy responded by telling him that all he wanted was for his father to be his friend. The point of the message was forgiveness: Pastor Chuy was admonishing his congregants to behave in kind and to forgive their fathers.

On Mother's Day of 1996, two women preached. This surprised me, for I had not seen women preach to the congregation previously. The first woman, probably in her fifties, had been in the United States most of her life. She gave a *consejo* about the power of a mother's love and the witness of a Christian mother to her children. She analogized a mother's love to God's claiming that just as mothers love their children in spite of their flaws, so too God does love his children in spite of their mistakes. She spoke for about twenty minutes before leaving the pulpit to the next speaker.

The woman following was in her late twenties; she had arrived in the United States from Mexico within the last five years. Her message was very stern. She opened by asking, "What kind of influence are you on your husband?" She cited Jezebel as an example of a negative influence, because Jezebel was always speaking her mind and giving her kingly husband advice. This woman claimed that a woman's divinely stipulated role was to be a supportive helpmate, enabling her husband to work for God. The main task of women was to be a "positive" influence. However, she argued, women should not try to influence their husband's decisions. She assured the crowd that to "live the Bible" is "not nice: to live the Bible you have got to suffer." She ended her sermon by confessing that she realized that her message was going to anger some parishioners, but that it was the message that God had given her, and she had to please God, not the parishioners. She spoke for approximately thirty minutes.

Slow, emotional singing and an altar call follow the preaching; this is the climactic moment of collective effervescence. Most parishioners make their way up to the altar, resulting in heated crowding and sensual body contact. The music, the contact, the emotion, the groans, the passion—all intensify the sensuality of the moment. Indeed, men make much physical, emotional, and spiritual contact with other men during the periods of intense prayer. Worshipers embrace one another, hold hands, place their arms around one another, kneel down together, and hold each other tightly while cathartically weeping and praying together. During this time, congregants speak in tongues and experience mystical trances as their bodies are repossessed anew by the Holy Ghost. This period of charismatic worship lasts up to a half-hour and is followed by more slow, emotional singing before the service ends. The whole service is about two hours long.

Pentecostal Mariachis and Other Cultural Oxymorons

Generally, congregational singing at Alcance Victoria Este de Los Angeles is regularly accompanied by two or three trumpeters, which gives the rhythms and choruses a distinctively Mexican sound. The trumpet players are brothers, and together with their father and mother they form a mariachi band called "Mariachi Genesis." During special services they are summoned to the pulpit—either all together, the father and mother together, or the father or mother alone. On very special occasions, the brothers and father will be accompanied by musicians playing an acoustic bass and acoustic guitars, with all band members wearing the tight-fitting red and black slacks, coats with gold trim, and big sombreros that define mariachi style. All the songs in their extensive repertoire are done in the classic mariachi fashion, but their lyrics express evangelical theology. At times, the band performs traditional

Mexican songs that have no explicit religious message but convey instead a strong spiritual yearning for Mexico, a melancholy acquired during the long and difficult years spent in exile. One of Mariachi Genesis's most popular songs mixes secular and Christian themes. Entitled "Mexico para Cristo" (Mexico for Christ), the song's chorus goes as follows (the translation is my own): "I love my Mexico, I love the Lord, I love my people/race [*raza*] with all of my heart; I'm not ashamed of the Gospel, because it is power and salvation."

The first time I heard Mariachi Genesis perform a secular Mexican song without Christian references during a worship service I was stunned. I was at the same time overwhelmed by the wildly enthusiastic reaction of the crowd. The performance of a secular song might be disallowed in a pentecostal church with more severe fundamentalist underpinnings, for such a song belies the "holiness" interpretation of the biblical mandate calling for strict separation from the secular world.[4]

It was this willingness to address the needs of the people by appealing to cultural narratives that provided my first major piece in the complex puzzle of Alcance Victoria's success. Alcance Victoria is a pragmatic group, relying on contextual truth—within scriptural parameters. As mystics, they interpret truth in trance (Cox 1995). This pragmatic philosophy and praxis unfold to the pulse of everyday life in the heart of East Los Angeles, and is revealed in the creation and utilization of religious symbols and discourses that emerge to satisfy physical need, spiritual desire, and lust of memory. Mariachi Genesis is but one product of this cultural strategy that throws mysticism in the mix with pragmatism and arranges it around Mexican symbolism to produce a new cultural matrix that can sustain what at one time may have been a cultural oxymoron: pentecostal mariachis. When asked how a church that preaches a new life in Christ can support songs during worship services that are not explicitly Christian, Pastor Chuy explained that the churches must become "culturally relevant."

Often on Wednesday evenings members of the church meet in smaller groups called "cell units." These *grupos familiares,* or "family-style groups," assemble for prayer and reflection on the Bible. Church members invite friends and family to join them, so the group is intended to grow; once it reaches fifteen, however, it is divided into another group, with all members attending church.[5]

The congregation sponsors four drug rehabilitation homes. One of them is located directly across the street from the church, and the others are in surrounding areas. Three of the shelters house men, and one is for women. On average, the "rehabs" are home to fifteen people each, although turnover rates are high, and most of the members do not stay in the homes for the nine-month duration of the program. One home director, Kiko, who looks much older than his eighteen years, recounts to me his daily tasks dealing with gang members: "I get in their face and tell them who we are and what we are about. They respect us." Recently, he nearly evicted someone for speaking badly about him. Kiko, a tough young warrior, was reduced to tears by vicious gossip.

Alcance Victoria in East Los Angeles has experienced marked growth in the two years that Pastor Chuy has been at the helm. Chuy was attending Alcance Victoria as a member before Pastor Lolo brought him into the ministry full-time. Pastor Lolo made Chuy an attractive offer to work as his assistant for $6 an hour. At the time, however, Chuy was working for a Los Angeles high school earning $12 an hour, and the school was paying for Chuy to pursue a bachelor's degree in business administration at California State University, Los Angeles. Hence, Chuy told Pastor Lolo that he would "pray about it." His conversion experience precipitated the decision for full-time ministry, or what he calls his "Road to Damascus" experience.

> When my brother first started coming here to this church, I thought it was good for him because it changed him. Then he started preaching to me. But I wasn't in any trouble, everything was going fine for me, I didn't need church. But deep inside of me something was missing. I was getting good grades, but in my heart I was wondering what was the purpose of this life. Why are we here? I use to lie awake at night meditating about this. It was the Lord speaking to me. So I accepted Jesus into my life. I began to feel a burden for the full-time ministry. I didn't want to. I thought God had blessed me with my job and school, and I knew that God was not an Indian-giver. But shortly after that, I was witnessing to a sister and her husband at her home, and, when I left, the sister gave me the pentecostal [hand]shake—she slipped a bill into my hand while shaking it. Usually this is about $10 or $20. But, later, driving in my car, I took out the bill, thinking it might be enough to get some tacos or a hamburger, and it was actually four-$20 bills all folded up! I began to cry in my car. I cried and knew at that point that God would take care of me in ministry. It was the Holy Spirit who spoke to me (May 22, 1995, Boyle Heights).

When Chuy was tapped for the Alcance Victoria pastorship in 1995, he was newly married and planning on "launching" a Victory Outreach church in Brazil. He claims, however, that God had other plans for him.

Pastor Chuy's "Road to Damascus" experience has proven to be a harbinger of the blessings he was destined to receive in ministry. In 1995 a member of the church arranged for him to buy a new condo in the Monterey Park hills. At the Father's Day morning service in 1995, much to Pastor Chuy's surprise, the congregation ceremoniously handed him a check for an amount they had collected among themselves that he was instructed to use as a down payment on a new car. Later that day, at the El Sereno drug rehabilitation home, an enthusiastic Pastor Chuy was busily walking around giving orders, supervising the making of the *carne asada* (roasted meat), greeting people, choosing the tapes that were being played on the huge boom box, and counseling members. There were to be baptisms in the aboveground pool that sits on the property. He stopped briefly to chat with me. "We baptize before we eat," Pastor Chuy explained, "or else everyone will leave before the baptisms" (May 22, 1995, Boyle Heights). Pastor Chuy is a *guerito,* or a "light-skinned Latino." He stands about five feet, ten inches, tall and wears a thick mustache. For this occasion he was wearing long athletic shorts, basketball shoes, and an oversized T-shirt with a picture of the Tasmanian devil that read "Houston Rockets." (He had recently returned from Houston, where he supervised the opening of a church.)

"I'm the youngest pastor here in Victory Outreach," Pastor Chuy told me. Hence, his biggest challenge, he feels, is to get the older men to respect him. For that reason, he tries to look older. In the two years that Pastor Chuy has led Alcance Victoria, he has met that challenge and has risen to deal with an even greater dilemma: with the variety of interests and problems represented in this congregation, how can it be managed cohesively? A turn now to the stories of Alcance Victoria parishioners, what I call the "congregational narrative," will address this question.

Constituents of the Church

One Victory Outreach preacher has called the movement's adherents the "Lazarus Generation," meant as an allegory for those who have been raised, metaphorically, from the dead, like Lazarus in the Christian Scriptures. In this context, the "dead" refers to the gang members, drug addicts, prostitutes, and the like who were "dead in sin" in Victory Outreach language. While the Lazarus element is certainly present in the Alcance Victoria congregation, they are not the only constituency. Indeed, Alcance Victoria welcomes newly arrived Mexican immigrants and their young families in addition to widows and widowers, divorcees, and young single men and women, some of whom are college and high school students. Many of the young congregants have never been on drugs and have other motivations for joining this rescue ministry. I identified several life situations of individuals in the Alcance Victoria collective. Below, I weave their stories together into the congregational narrative.

The former drug addicts, gang members, and prostitutes are in many respects the cornerstone of the congregation, for they are the foot soldiers that march and fight most loyally in the Victory Outreach army. Collectively the Lazarus Generation has done more to shape the congregational narrative than any other group, for they are the ushers, deacons, musicians, rehabilitation home leaders, and church administrators. More than any other, this group stressed the notion of "the change." Twenty-seven-year-old Manny Martinez, a former gang member who works as an usher in the church, spoke for them:

> *The change, the change is the most important thing. I was a drug addict before [I came here]. I went to jail and everything, but now God has changed my life. Twenty-five years ago Pastor Sonny [Arguinzoni] got the burden, and that's why he opened the first church. So when people come here they can see with their own eyes, people can see the results. People are always happy here! It's knowing God. It's knowing who he really is. I know God is love, peace, happiness; God is like air—you don't see it, but you feel it (April 30, 1995, Boyle Heights).*

"The change" enables former gang members to take control of their lives, and to imagine and live in a coherent world.

As Martinez notes, there is a sensual, corporeal quality to Alcance Victoria worship. It is experienced as electric charges and ecstatic trancelike states that assure the believer that God is real and that believers have tapped the power of God—directly. Martinez also notes the centrality of Arguinzoni to the Victory Outreach cosmogony. Arguinzoni enjoys a virtual apotheosis in the minds of the Victory Outreach believers. He is the living embodiment of the power of God, the capacity for the quick change, the election, and material success. Arguinzoni lives in a large house in a fashionable Los Angeles suburb, drives a new BMW, and travels extensively. In his rise from gang member and drug addict on the streets of Brooklyn to successful religious entrepreneur, Sonny Arguinzoni is a living, breathing, preaching symbol of the American success story—from rags to riches.

The Victory Outreach empire was built by preaching that other men can do the same: become born again, marry a "nice girl," pastor a church, and become part of what the Victory Outreach collective refers to informally as the "corporation." Here, the rhythms and cycles of life are marked by renewal and progress: spiritual, symbolic, and material. All involved in the leadership of Victory Outreach will vehemently insist that the motivation to pastor a church is entirely spiritual. Nonetheless, they will in the same breath concede that many of the men come to church looking for a wife and that Alcance Victoria encourages the men to realize their individual calling as pastors and to open their own churches. This is the path taken by hundreds of men in Victory Outreach/Alcance Victoria. Certainly Manny is following this path. Less than a year before our interview he married a young woman he had met in the church; he had been active in the church leadership and was planning eventually to pastor his own church. Meanwhile he was, like the majority of the Chicanos in the congregation, working seasonally in construction.

Kiko, the former director of the men's transition home, is actively working in the Alcance Victoria offices, running errands for Pastor Chuy. He explains that he does not receive a regular salary for this work but that the pastor "blesses" him often. This means that the pastor will spontaneously hand Kiko some cash. The pastor of each church controls the financial resources. While becoming a pastor is the most common goal, it is not the sole upward path open to Alcance Victoria's men. Kiko plays keyboards in the church, and would like eventually to earn a living as an Alcance Victoria evangelist and marry an Alcance Victoria woman. In the mythology of the Victory Outreach movement, all these things were shown to be possible through the example of Arguinzoni, which is particularly meaningful for the men of the Lazarus Generation who have few other role models.

Women too are part of the Lazarus Generation. One such woman has been in the United States for four years and a member of Alcance Victoria for three of those years; she is now forty-two-years-old and a director of an Alcance Victoria women's home. I call her Magdalena. Her "change," as in the case of others who appear at the doorstep of Victory Outreach, took place at a dramatically low point in her life. "I was going crazy," she recounts. "I was looking for answers, but only Jesus is the answer" (July 9, 1996, Boyle Heights, interview conducted in Spanish). The answer to Magdalena's existential crisis came first in the form of witchcraft (*echiseria*) and lesbianism, which she now attributes to her witchcraft practices—all while she was a confirmed Catholic living in Mexico City. Her change occurred while she was confined to a bed in a mental hospital. It was Magdalena's sister who preached the evangelical Gospel to her, as refracted through the Alcance Victoria prism. She freely employs military metaphors in explaining that only God can help her to "fight that battle" with temptation, against the enemy. In her maneuvers on the battle lines, she leads six other women who live in the home. One is a former gang member, a twenty-two-year-old Chicana who has a baby with her in the home. Four others are Mexican immigrants who have nowhere else to go. A pregnant woman from Guatemala also lives there with her baby; she came to the States to earn money to support her husband back home.

Magdalena claims that the mission of the home is to restore women's "dignity" and to teach them to be "blessings in their homes and with their children." Some women have had their children taken away from them by the county, Magdalena explains. Therefore, the home helps to rehabilitate them and to have their children returned to them. In these efforts, the women are hired out to help support the basic needs of the home.

I asked Victory Outreach members what they imagine themselves doing in five or ten years. Magdalena wants to return to Mexico City to work with the children of the streets: "This country [the United States] is blessed; this God will bless us [Mexicans too], not with money but with faith in God." Like the Mexican and Chicano myth of "La Llorona" (a myth of infanticide), Magdalena says she knows Mexican mothers who have killed their children because they cannot feed them. She believes that her work in the Alcance Victoria women's home is "preparation" for the work she feels called to do in Mexico City.

When this same question about life ten years hence was posed to the Lazarus men, most seemed puzzled and had to meditate solemnly before responding. One twenty-nine-year-old Chicano spoke to me in Spanish; he had been in the home for eight weeks and just wanted to stay there for three months without "messing up." If he could make it for that long, he was almost certain that he could go the full nine months. Ultimately, he said, he would like to be married with a family and "have a regular life." I asked him if he would like to work in the ministry, and like all the others in the Lazarus category, he said he definitely would. At the moment, however, his energies were focused on overcoming a five-balloon-a-day heroin habit. He could not think much further than tomorrow or the next week.

Beyond the Lazarus Generation:
The First Second Generation

Another group of Alcance Victorians is distinct from the Lazarus Generation, for they have clear goals and time lines for achieving them. Most of these people I name the "First Second Generation" (FSG): they are the first group of Chicanos to be second-generation pentecostals, unlike many of the Lazarus Generation. All of them have pentecostal parents—they did not convert from Catholicism, as did the rest of the church—but their lives have followed two distinct patterns. Some in the FSG were involved in drugs and gang warfare; others were not. Of those who were not, many are pursuing an education and have ambitious career goals. Those formerly involved in gangs and drugs have career ambitions directly related to the church. A number of these folks are simply trying to make it in the intensity of turn-of-the-century Los Angeles while waiting to start their own Alcance Victoria church. Both types of FSG individuals seem keenly aware of the elasticity of social boundaries.

An example of a member of the group who is just getting by is an eighteen-year-old woman named Catalina. Both her mother and father were "saved" in the English-speaking Victory Outreach ministries, and Catalina was reared in the rehab homes that her parents directed. Catalina married a Victory Outreach minister, Brother Saul, who directed a home where they lived for nearly two years after their marriage. Like many in the FSG, although she was raised in church, she marks the exact age of her conversion: "I was thirteen," Catalina reflects, "when I felt the Lord pulling at my heartstrings. I was partying and rebellious; I would run away and come back. I didn't want to surrender [to God]" (June 29, 1996, Boyle Heights). She remembers the critical moment when she hit bottom: "I got into a fistfight with my mom. My stepdad had fallen—he was using heroin again. But he's saved [again] now. After that, we just felt led to the Spanish ministry." Nearly every FSG member I interviewed had a story of religious devotional lapse that ended with a return and a stronger commitment to the church.

I asked Catalina about her views on women and men in the church. She said that she believes that if you don't count the fifty or so men who live in the homes, there are more women in the church than men. Most women who come are *solteras,* or free or single women who "come and refuge themselves in the Lord. A lot [of women] come here because they are lonely; some get married. My mom came with one kid, me, and had another one here after she was married again." The

Luís León

church has no official teaching on divorce and remarriage. Catalina believes that women and men share responsibility in working with people and spreading the Gospel. According to her, men take responsibility in ministry, and women help them; this conviction was echoed in the vast majority of my interviews with the Alcance Victoria women.

This is also the teaching expressed by the co-founder of Victory Outreach, Julie Arguinzoni. In "Preparing Women for the Vision 2000," a sermon she delivered and recorded on June 25, 1996, at a Victory Outreach women's retreat, Julie Arguinzoni told the women what they must do and what they could expect from ministry. She recounted that women approach her all the time and tell her that they "want ministry." In response, she tells them that they don't really know what they want, because to be a woman in ministry, "you must suffer." (When Julie referred to "women in ministry," she meant women married to a pastor.) She explains that while in ministry will mean dressing "real pretty" and "sitting in the front of the church," women must also be prepared to do "whatever it takes" to help the ministry grow. But, overall, they must "love the Lord."

While waiting for "ministry," Catalina has been looking for a job that will pay her enough money to support herself and her husband, thus enabling him to devote himself to full-time work in the local church ministry and eventually become the pastor of an Alcance Victoria church, perhaps in Mexico. She related a story about a job in West Los Angeles, where she worked as a secretary in a copy shop until she quit because the manager was "verbally abusing" her. Apparently, he was calling her "stupid" and telling her that she was "good for nothing." In spite of this, she hastens to add that she is "smart" and "skilled," and has had many good jobs in the past; she nearly finished high school but ultimately "didn't make it." She expressed the desire for her children to "finish school."

I asked Catalina about her political views. She believed that abortion in all cases is murder, for even if a woman is raped, "sometimes God permits things for a purpose." She voiced support for affirmative action, claiming that "everyone deserves a chance." When asked about California's anti-immigration measures, her answer resounded with ambivalence. She hesitated for a long time before replying. She said that to be in the United States without "papers" (legal immigration documents or status) was "lying," but that it was "not really a sin." Still, living here without documents "will trouble you for a long time, because you are not right with the law." Ultimately, Catalina concluded, it was a matter of personal responsibility and moral choice—a matter of conscience. Her attitude was the same regarding individuals and families who receive welfare or other types of government assistance. She thought that what really mattered were the intentions and actions of the individual or family: "Some people are trying to better their lives by being here without papers or getting welfare, and that is a good thing. Other people are just messing up."

Catalina's thoughtful opinions were echoed in the narratives of other FSG members I interviewed, most of whom expressed ambivalence on issues of political commitment. However, there seemed to be uniform opposition to the anti-immigration and anti-affirmative action ballot initiatives.

Lulu, a thirty-year-old homemaker, volunteers several hours each week in the business office of Alcance Victoria. Born in Mexico, she came to the United States as a young girl and dropped out of school when she was fourteen to help at home with her family. Although her parents were pentecostal, she marks her own conversion to pentecostalism at age fifteen. While Sister Lulu was not involved in gangs, she explains that she was "looking for love," and found it in Jesus and the "love of God" located in the Alcance Victoria congregation. She shared with me a little about her experiences growing up in East Los Angeles and her very informed views on the California ballot initiatives concerning immigration:

> All my friends were either killed or overdosed on drugs. If it wasn't for Jesus I wouldn't be here right now! Fourteen of my friends from school have died! But my family was different: we were the only pentecostals on our block, and we are the only ones left. The most important thing he [God] has done for me is the change, that love he gave to me. If I didn't have love I couldn't be going out to another person, a stranger, and telling them about God. The laws they want to pass against immigration are totally unfair. If a baby is born in the U.S., then that baby is an American, a citizen. That's the way it's always been. It shouldn't matter if the parents are Mexicans— that's racist (April 30, 1994)!

These views were echoed by Lupe, a twenty-one-year-old woman who moved to the United States from Mexico at age thirteen and joined Alcance Victoria soon thereafter. Her parents were pentecostal. Following high school graduation, she attended East Los Angeles City College and worked in a children's store for a year before marrying. I asked her what she believed was the most attractive or important element of Alcance Victoria. She said, "Love!" "What does love mean?" I asked. She replied:

Well, the love we share here is a very special kind of love. Anyone
can love their family, but we show people, strangers, we love them
the way they are! No matter if they are drug addicts, prostitutes,
whatever—we accept them just like that. Sometimes we take them
into our own homes. Now, that is the kind of love that attracted me
to this church (April 11, 1994, Boyle Heights, interview conducted in
Spanish).

In response to my queries regarding the immigration laws, she was
adamant: "I think that the new law they are proposing is wrong—that
your baby born here won't be a citizen! I thought that this was supposed to be America! America is different from any other country—
that's why we came here!" When asked about abortion, she paused
thoughtfully to formulate her response: "Abortion is wrong because
you are killing a baby, right? But you don't have the right to take
another person's rights away."

Lupe delineated the Alcance Victoria teaching on women's and
men's roles in church, claiming that "women can preach only amongst
themselves to other women if there is a special reunion or something.
Women can also be missionaries and evangelists. Women have come
here to our church to preach to everyone. Women cannot become
pastors, but all the pastors have wives."

Another FSG man, Noé, had similar responses. At the time of our
interview, he was twenty-one years old. He was born in Guadalajara,
Mexico, and has been in the United States since age five. He plays the
trumpet in the church with his brothers and is part of Mariachi Genesis. He has never been involved in gangs or drugs. He graduated from
high school, attended East Los Angeles City College for one semester,
and worked delivering phone books around East Los Angeles until he
was injured on the job in a car accident. At the time of our interview,
he was settling this claim and looking for a job. His narrative typifies
many of the FSG in its political outlook as well as in its focus on a
faith crisis that was resolved in an epiphany resulting in a renewed and
deeper commitment to the church:

I never really experienced the streets. But at one point a few years
ago I just got real cold in the Lord. I was addicted to sports. That's
all I wanted to do—watch sports on TV, play basketball, and read
about sports. If you would ask me anything about sports I would
know. I put that first before God. Sports is not a sin, but it shouldn't
be your number one priority. For a Christian the number-one prior-
ity is God. I realize that now, (June 18, 1995, East Los Angeles).

Noé has strong feelings about the Catholic church and the problems in East LA. He carefully distinguishes the Catholic religion from experiential religion and commitment, explaining that Alcance Victoria is not "religion"; instead it is "a relationship with God—this must be the most important thing in your life. The Catholics are a religion. They don't have the Holy Spirit, they have the Virgin [of Guadalupe] and saints—but no God. This [lack] is the biggest problem in East Los Angeles today: gangs, drugs, taggers [spray-paint graffiti artists], and violence." When I asked about justice or injustice for the undocumented, he observed, "One of the things people don't see, economically, is that people don't have the income to live in Boyle Heights; they live in poverty. Lots of people come here, but they don't have what it takes to make it here, so they live in poverty—lots of people living in poverty." Hence, Noé suggests that economic success is intimately related to justice in immigration.

I asked him what Alcance Victoria could do to work for economic justice and empowerment. His response was representative of the Victory Outreach philosophy on these issues: "There is not really a place for the church to confront poverty, except for in rehab homes," he explained. "We get blessed with God at church; the favor of God is there. You can't point out in our church a need. We offer something solid to help out the community; whatever we can do, we do it." Ministry, as Sonny Arguinzoni teaches, must always come before spending energies on social justice "causes:"

> It is not our job to propose legislation resolving immigration conflicts. The bigger and more visible a ministry becomes, the more people are going to come with their agendas. They will want you to get involved with this movement or that cause. It is not uncommon for people to want for us to join a worthwhile project, and then want us to promote it. Unless we are clear as to the vision of our church, the temptation may draw us off track. The enemy has a way of diverting us, getting us involved in so many things that we are unable to accomplish anything. James Chapter 1:8 tells us that the life of a man with divided loyalty will reveal instability in every turn. You simply ask, "What will this program do to help fulfill our vision?" (Arguinzoni 1995, 140).

In spite of Arguinzoni's official teaching, defined by a singular and uniform vision and purpose, Alcance Victorians do formulate individual opinions and support various causes. Individuals become masterfully adept at weaving social and political discourses into their own understandings of the Gospel and of the Alcance Victoria message. They arrive at a particular vision of the world that responds to their own crises and issues, yet this peculiar stance is based on their communion with a community of biblical interpretation.

Alcance Victoria has been nicknamed the "Junkie Church" because the majority of its constituents since the beginning had once been drug addicts. However, as Victory Outreach continues to grow in numbers and in fame, the church has simultaneously increased its respectability. Hence, it has found appeal among sections of Chicano youth previously untapped.

I interviewed a group of eight second-generation Americans, four women and four men, ranging in ages from fifteen to twenty (June 5, 1996, Boyle Heights). Each interviewee had parents involved in born-again religion, and all had attended church regularly since they were children. Seven of the eight had "rebelled" briefly, experimenting with the "things of this world," before returning to the church with a deeper commitment. All participants were serious about their education, whether they were in high school, heading to college, or in a local state or community college. All in this group were single, and none had children. One sixteen-year-old woman had a straight-A record in her college prep courses, and because of this she had assumed the identity bestowed by her peers as someone heading for Harvard. "I'm going to apply there," she tells me when I ask if she is indeed Harvard bound. "We'll see what happens." Most in the group were introduced to the church through their parents, or they were invited by a family member or friend close to their own age. Interestingly, many of their parents had ceased regular church attendance themselves.

The men dominated the conversation, but the women expressed nonverbally their dissatisfaction with the men's manipulation of the interview. Three of the men took the opportunity to relate long, detailed narratives about their lives, while the women were very aware of the project as a group effort and kept their responses short. One twenty-year-old man, Cyrus, took the lead of the group. Cyrus is currently president of the student body at his California State University campus. He is emotionally torn between pursuing a career in public service or in ministry. At the time of our interview he was working in the offices of his local state assemblyman, who is also Mexican American.

I asked why they attended Alcance Victoria in particular; their answers varied, but all turned on matters of personal choice. Two of the women explained that they had been attending another Protestant church, but that it did not have the active youth programs they found in Alcance Victoria. The meaningful participation of the youth in the life of the congregation was the attraction for these women. Another woman had been attending an all-white Protestant church in Burbank where she did not feel entirely at home. At Alcance Victoria the music combined with the general enthusiasm put her at ease, reminding her of the church she had attended with her parents as a child, whereas in the Anglo church she felt isolated by the cold conservatism. Most members in this group were connected to each other through bonds of kinship, or in the case of the men, by "homeboy" bonds. They invited one another to church. One of the men, Ramón, spoke of the inspiration he finds in church:

> The thing that keeps me motivated in coming to church is that whenever I'm feeling down, or whenever I need help with whatever part of my life, with anything at school or here at church, my social life or my family, the thing that keeps me motivated is that I can bend my knees and just look up to heaven and ask God for that extra help and that extra push that I need in my life, and that just keeps me motivated and keeps me going on. So I thank God for that.

Another twenty-year-old man, Eddie, echoed Ramón's testimony, claiming that the key to understanding God and having a rewarding life is obedience to church doctrine. He contended that God must be the priority in one's life, and all other goals will follow. His aphorism was greeted with cheerful agreement: "If you just listen to his word and everything, make God first, everything will go all right."

The youngest woman, Flora, fifteen years old, said that she liked Alcance Victoria because all her cousins attended, and there were many teenagers in the congregation. Gabby, age sixteen, claimed that she too came to Alcance Victoria because her cousins were there, and because she found what she "needed" in Alcance Victoria. Like the others, she then broke into a rehearsed testimony: "That emptiness. I don't have it anymore. I don't need anything because here I found what I needed. I know that God will supply the things that I need. Because he is there for us, to do for us."

I asked them to compare themselves to their parents. The women said that they differ from their mothers because their mothers are "traditional" homemakers. The men said that they differ from their fathers because their fathers work in factories. All agreed that the critical difference is that they now have the opportunity to get an education and "to have a better life" that their parents were denied, as Cyrus and others explained. They recognized that their parents' lives were much harder than their own. When asked what they imagine themselves to be doing in ten years, none identified the ministry as an

Luís León

option. All said they wanted to finish their education. One wanted to become a sociologist, another a doctor, another a teacher, another a child psychologist, and another a police officer. All claimed that they "of course" wanted to be doing "big things for God" and to have families.

All members of this group identified themselves as Chicano or Chicana, with clear and forceful conviction. However, they were conflicted about political issues. All hesitated to express favor for either the Democratic or Republican parties, but claimed instead to vote on particular issues and identified themseves as nonpartisan. Cyrus confessed that he was a registered Democrat, although some of his "moral values are with Republicans." All supported affirmative-action programs and felt that anti-immigration laws were racist and ungodly. They claimed that the laws were "unjust" because they discriminated against Mexicans. Cyrus expressed the views of the group when he attempted to navigate through the complexity of social and political issues: "I'm antiwar but the Republicans are prowar; I'm anti-abortion but the Democrats are pro-abortion." All members of this group were against abortion and all, led by Cyrus, claimed that the Bible provides the definitive template for gender relations—women are to be subordinate to men in the home and in ministry. The women led the response in affirming equal political rights for women, but all agreed that men should be the leaders in church; for that, they claimed with certainty, is what the Bible teaches.

Lapsed Catholics

Finally, I identified a group I describe simply as "lapsed Catholics." Many of the members of the church had not maintained strong ties to Catholicism before conversion and started attending Alcance Victoria because they were actively pursued. The people in this category were not battling drug problems or involved with gangs. They were simply widows and widowers, mostly older, or families with children who had immigrated recently. They tend to be drawn by the dynamic social life Alcance Victoria offers, and many take a while to learn a distrust for Catholicism. In their view, Pentecostalism and Catholicism are both Christianity. Señora Carmela, a fifty-one-year-old unemployed widow, has been a member of Alcance Victoria since coming to the United States from Mexico seven years ago. She serves as an usher, showing people to their seats, collecting the offerings, and preventing people from entering the sanctuary during prayer. She explained her "testimony" as follows: "I've never had any real vices. I maintain myself there in my house—I live close by here. Between my house and my church, that's all I do. And occasionally I go to the store, but that's all, really. I came to Alcance Victoria because they invited me " (May 16, 1994, Boyle Heights, interview conducted in Spanish). Another woman, Modesta, in her thirties, an immigrant from Mexico and mother of four, summarized the feelings of most of the parents by voicing a troubled concern for her children: "There are so many gangs around here. And Alcance Victoria is really doing something to help stop the violence" (June 6, 1996, Boyle Heights, interview conducted in Spanish).

Most of the "lapsed Catholics" came to Alcance Victoria because they enjoyed the company of others, the feeling of belonging, the music, the message of security and control over life—at least symbolically. In the congregation they find emotional security, friendship, and intimacy. For immigrants and Mexican Americans who lack social skills, the congregation functions as a mechanism of cultural brokerage. Symbolically and physically secluded from so many other centers in Los Angeles, they find in Alcance Victoria vibrant fellowship where they remake self, community, and the nation.

In an utterly pragmatic and pithy statement, Pastor Chuy powerfully explained the reason for the success of their church: "Alcance Victoria is successful because we are meeting the needs of the people!"

Recasting the American Dream Through Religious Performance

"Meeting the needs of the people" is no easy task, especially given the diversity of interests and multiple foci of the members. Pragmatism is the pivot on which each judgment turns. This pragmatic turn is most evident in the teaching regarding immigration. Many in the congregation are undocumented workers. The condition of being in the United States without legal sanction is, in effect, living a lie. Pastor Chuy overlooks this fact, and will pray for the successful illegal border crossings of his congregants and their families when asked. He explains that this issue is a matter of personal conscience.

Central to this pragmatic course of meeting needs is endowing each participant with a sense of individual election, calling, and an "inner-worldly asceticism." At the same time each believer is imparted with a sense for the importance of and membership in the collective representation, where success does not exist outside of the collective ability to imagine and represent it, to legitimate and authorize it. Thus, understanding the religious drive of Alcance Victoria pentecostalism requires a mapping of the paradoxical space constituted at the intersection between the imperatives of the collective representation and the demand for individual achievement: between Mexico and the United States—especially between the collective drama and tragedy of Mexican Catholicism and the American Protestant myth of prosperity and success, with its individual orientation and enshrinement of personal responsibility. The borderland provides the cultural stage on which these dynamics are effectively performed.

Victory Outreach is known throughout California for its elaborate stage plays that dramatize the Chicano gang lifestyle and ultimately end with the protagonist's conversion to born-again Christianity through the efforts of Victory Outreach evangelism. These plays are in English, normally portraying a Mexican American experience as opposed to an immigrant's narrative. They are performed at churches, schools, and other meeting halls. Recently, however, the Spanish churches have produced their own play, *Sueño Americano* (American Dream), which represents an immigrant experience. Written and produced by an Alcance Victoria congregation, the play, at once social critique and soteriology, is a native, organic dramatization of the Alcance Victoria congregational narrative. It tells the story of one Mexican Catholic family—a mother, father, and three small children—who immigrate (illegally) to Los Angeles. Their "American dream" is for the children to have a better life in the United States.

The theme song, originally in English, is called "Just a Dream," and its chorus expresses in lyrical melody the message of the play: "Just a dream, just a dream, all our hopes and all our schemes." That is, the social aspirations of Mexican immigrants into the United States are "just a dream," nothing else. Before the family leaves Mexico, a close friend, a *compadre,* pleads for them not to go to Los Angeles, for there, he claims, they will find only "perdition." While being ejected from their home for preaching the evangelical Gospel, the *compadre* exhorts the father to remember in time of trouble that Christ loves him and that Christ is the answer to all his problems. The rest of the story is predictable. In Los Angeles the father becomes an alcoholic, and the children end up in gangs. Ultimately, the family converts to pentecostalism through the efforts of an evangelizer who tells them that even though all their dreams were lost on the streets, Jesus Christ can give them new dreams. The evangelizer tells the audience that they may have come to the United States with dreams that have not come true, yet Jesus Christ can make all of their dreams come true: Christ can give them hope and change them.

The play may hold the key to unlocking the mystery of one aspect of Latino born-again conversion. In the play, evangelical salvation is presented as a panacea, an antidote to social ills. Through evangelical conversion, one can be changed and then rechannel frustrated energies in constructive directions. In his journalistic writing on Victory Outreach, Richard Rodriguez (1986) has emphasized the importance of this sudden and dramatic change. "To immigrants who came to the American city expecting new beginnings, and who found instead the city corrupt," he writes, "the evangelical missionary offers the possibility of refreshment, of cleansing. To the children of immigrants, trapped by inherited failures, the evangelical offers the assurance of power over life. The promise of the quick change" (Rodriguez 1986). This notion of change was stressed by the majority of people interviewed for this study. Key to the experience of pentecostalism, metanoia is the initiatory event that registers membership in a powerful community of God.

Alcance Victoria is continually being reinvented, situationally, in response to particular contexts; this is possible because of the group's approach to Scripture. While based in a literalist reading of the Bible, pentecostal theology is malleable enough so that doctrine can be pragmatically molded to fit the needs of very different constituencies. Thus pentecostalism, in effect, has something for just about everyone. So what does it offer to Alcance Victorians? How do these people change?

Pentecostalism has been described as the *Vision of the Disinherited* (Anderson 1979). Alcance Victorians are disinherited in particular ways. As immigrants, as people with great ambition who moved thousands of miles and jumped many hurdles in the hopes of improving their lives, many found instead the corruption, racism, structural inequality, and xenophobia that plagues much of contemporary Los Angeles.

But what about the individuals who are part of the FSG and the "lapsed Catholics" who are not suffering in the same way as the Lazarus Generation? Perhaps the key to understanding the attraction of pentecostalism to all of these groups is in understanding their belief and practice. Catholics who convert to pentecostalism are not asked to discard Christian theology outright. Rather, they are expected to refuse *mediation* of the sacraments from priests; to discard, in a sense, the priesthood, or "religious specialists." Rejection of sacramental mediation allows pentecostalists to become agents in their salvation and more. To eschew the religious specialists enables the group to authorize by consensus the terms and symbols of the religious life. These are decided upon collectively; Scriptures are interpreted through mystical experiences with the congregation working together as a cohesive unit. Like true Protestants, however, each religious agent must be authorized individually, and success and election are proven through the "bearing [of] religious fruit," and, implicitly, through economic achievement.

To "bear fruit," men become active in the ministry. In contrast to Catholicism, Alcance Victoria allows married men without education to have active and rewarding careers in ministry. In the congregation men discover their entrepreneurial potential (Warner 1993). Through ministerial work in the congregation, they can improve their lot in life and live comfortably. The congregation expects their ministers to live well, because ministers symbolize the aspirations of the group. A man can come to church, marry the woman he has dreamed about, become active in ministry, and move up through the Alcance Victoria/Victory Outreach chain of command. Like Sonny Arguinzoni himself, many of his staff drive BMWs—symbols of prosperity. Thus, included in the gospel of rescue and salvation are narratives of prosperity and well-being. For immigrants with broken dreams, these promises are made to willing listeners.

For the FSG, the message of prosperity is one of possibility. Undergirded by the Alcance Victoria message of power, those in the FSG are enabled to achieve the things in life they have come to desire, so that going to Harvard or holding public office is possible, following from the simple premise that "all things are possible with God." This message for many of the FSG is also one of prevention and maintenance. As Eddie indicated, "If you just listen to his word and everything, make God first, everything will go all right." These bright, ambitious young women and men have much at stake, and they do not want to lose it. They look to God not as an antidote for failed social dreams, and to the congregation not as a way to redirect failed ambitions, but to both as vehicles for fulfilling their dreams—things that remain unimaginable to many of their Chicano peers.

The Alcance Victorians whom I refer to as "lapsed Catholics" come with their own needs and hopes of salvation. The Catholic church, for whatever reason, was simply not able to hold their attention and loyalty, and Alcance Victoria does. This may in part be so because Alcance Victoria is in a sense a total institution that captivates the interests and desires of its membership, keeping them busy and making them feel part of a global movement. This American Protestant voluntarism is nothing new; it has defined American religion since the beginning of the republic. However, Alcance Victoria also offers dignity to each believer. Through Alcance Victoria, those without much economic success, the disinherited, become instated in the American myth: their lives matter; they are special, chosen, given a divine commission direct from God himself. By stressing individual election and achievement, the discursive and ritual community of Alcance Victoria confers self-worth, ultimate meaning, purpose, and a way to make sense of a harsh world.

Additionally, Alcance Victoria does not ask believers to eschew their ethnic heritage. Rather, it spins its message in such a way that it becomes blended with the thinly veiled Protestant symbolism that permeates the American consciousness and ethos. In this sense, Alcance Victoria is a border phenomenon, one that combines Mexican, American, and Christian evangelical archetypes and mythologies into a fresh identity, one that can support such seeming contradictions as pentecostal mariachis.

All of these observations suggest, then, that by taking control of the religious field, by becoming the religious specialists themselves, Alcance Victorians have tapped a new mechanism of empowerment. (The control that the hierarchy within Alcance Victoria exerts over the laity remains to be studied.) I am willing to conclude that insofar as Alcance Victorians are able to achieve the things they desire, through religious discourse and practice—performance—Alcance Victoria is an empowering phenomenon. However, the choices of many of these folks have been so deeply determined by their social conditions that the ability to imagine choices is itself limited. That is, years of oppression have limited not only choices but the ability to choose. Alcance Victoria enables people to work happily and productively within their social limitations, but its members for the most part are not unlimited bourgeois subjects endowed with privilege and the ability to make rational choices. Rather, most are people who pick and choose from within their social limitations; and the choices available to them are often exploitative and degrading. The exception would be those in the FSG who can imagine beyond common boundaries.

This research does not suggest, however, that Alcance Victoria members have been duped into becoming passive citizens and thus more productive workers. Undoubtably, pentecostalism helps them to deal with overwhelming circumstances immediately, sensually, and experientially. There is also no question that Alcance Victoria quiets potential uprisings and social protest. Still, if there is resistance and protest in Alcance Victoria, they lie in the cultivation of ecstasy and in the critique of American society. These aspects of Alcance Victoria, along with others, warrant further exploration.

The roles of women, gender dynamics, and the construction of masculinity in Victory Outreach/Alcance Victoria are areas of research that need to be pursued further. My access to the intricacies of the Alcance Victoria women's world was limited by my male gender; I was not privy to intimate conversation and was unable to spend much time alone with the women. This limitation notwithstanding, my sense from this research is that in Alcance Victoria women attain status as authorized religious/social agents by means of a personal and intensely symbolic relationship to God. Some women use this authority to challenge social and cultural arrangements that confer status and privilege to men, claiming status and privilege for themselves in ways that are often subtle and concealed from public view. Others reiterate narratives of women's submission to God and men. In either case, women here are afforded the space to create their own symbolic worlds, and to live in them in ways authorized by someone even more authoritative than their husbands, fathers, brothers, and ministers: God. What is done with this newly discovered authority varies from case to case.

Still more, the relationship between the local congregation and the Victory Outreach headquarters in La Puente is a topic that deserves further research. Sonny Arguinzoni operates a program called "United We Can," which asks members to donate $1 a day to support Victory Outreach global ministries. In spite of the wide support that Arguinzoni enjoys, only a handful of Alcance Victorians pay membership dues—it is nowhere near the 20 percent of the congregation that the headquarters in La Puente would like, and probably under 5 percent. A study of Sonny Arguinzoni himself would make an interesting report. It will also be interesting to watch the emergence of a new class of religious specialists. What type of congregational control will operate as the hierarchy becomes even more elaborate, powerful, and distinct from the laity? A chart of the lives of individual believers, determining how many remain in the congregation and how many fall back into their old ways or move into another religion, would also be valuable. Recidivism is a problem that characterizes "revolving-door" pentecostalism and is yet to be mapped.

By way of conclusion, I want to repeat that in Alcance Victoria there is hegemony as well as liberation: it is not a question of domination *or* empowerment but rather *modes* of domination *and modes* of empowerment. These two binaries should be seen as markers, as ends of a continuum on which the Alcance Victorians fluctuate. Overall, Alcance Victoria provides a fresh and expansive locus from which to invent an evolving Chicano cultural form. It is the continual reinvention of Mexican American identity by drawing from a number of symbolic reserves that defines the borderlands thesis. L. Vicki Ruiz (1993, 246) has described this process of creation as "cultural coalescence":

> *There is not a single hermetic Mexican or Mexican-American culture, but rather permeable cultures rooted in generation, gender, region, class, and personal experience. Immigrants and their children pick, borrow, retain, and create distinctive cultural forms. People navigate across cultural boundaries as well as make conscious decisions in the production of culture.*

The discourse of Alcance Victoria functions most cogently in the arena of the production and reproduction of consciousness; that is, in the active construction of social expectations and the socialization of desire. "But, bear in mind," cautions Ruiz, "people of color have not had unlimited choice. Racism, sexism, imperialism, persecution, and social, political, and economic segmentation have constrained aspirations, expectations, and decision making" (Ruiz 1993, 246).

For some, the discourse of divine election and rebirth functioning within a community of believers places within reach possibilities that were at one time unimaginable. For others, biblical narratives contract worlds and expectations—including gender roles—and thus limit social intercourse and achievement: symbolic and social boundaries can be narrowed in Alcance Victoria. There is diversity among believers and thus in the congregational narrative.

In this study I have sought to demonstrate the great variety that exists among pentecostal believers. Perhaps the need to respect difference among pentecostals was impressed upon my consciousness because of my own experience growing up in my father's small Spanish pentecostal church in East Oakland, a very traditional church comprised mostly of families who had not been in trouble with drugs or the law. The spectrum of Latino pentecostal churches ranges from traditional and stoic to the emotional rescue ministry of Victory Outreach. For this reason, it was important for me and for the New Ethnic and Immigrant Congregations Project to attach human faces to an otherwise faceless academic discourse on Latino pentecostalism.

Alcance Victoria is a *place* filled with extraordinary people, most of whom have been dealt a bad hand in life but remain happy and optimistic in spite of it. Pentecostal practice equips them with the discursive, ritual, and other symbolic tools to negotiate deftly the precarious social terrain of postmodern Los Angeles. When I entered their lives four years ago, I did so with a bit of fear and trembling, for it was a return, in a sense, to my own cultural memory. To my great fortune, they welcomed me with open arms. Very few of them understood exactly what I was doing there, but still they trusted me and cooperated fully. They made me a part of their family. Without doubt, I learned as much from them as I did about them, and in this, I am enriched.

NOTES

1. I use the term "Chicano" descriptively and interchangeably with "Mexican American" to refer to people of Mexican descent living permanently in the United States, whether born in the United States or in Mexico. Most of those in this study either refer to themselves as Chicano, or do not object to being referred to as such. While I recognize the problems inherent in this descriptive definition, I find these problems the least objectionable among the array of problems other descriptive terms of Mexican Americans engender. I use the term "Latino" to designate people of Latin American heritage, including but not limited to Mexican Americans.

2. The population of Boyle Heights is estimated at 89,000. Unless otherwise noted, interviews were conducted in English. Where the note "interview conducted in Spanish" appears, the translation from English to Spanish is my own.

3. For a discussion of female religious symbols and the ways they have circumscribed Mexican and Chicana female roles, see Norma Alarcon (1989).

4. Many fundamentalists and pentecostals base this teaching on the Christian Scriptures, especially the passage found in 2 Corinthians 6:17 (see Dayton 1987).

5. This is a strategy Victory Outreach borrowed from Dr. David Yonggi Cho, whose 800,000-member Korean pentecostal congregation is said to be the largest in the world (Cox 1995).

REFERENCES

Alarcon, Norma. 1989. "Traddutora, Traditora: A Paradigmatic Figure of Chicana Feminism." *Cultural Critique* 13 (Fall): 57–87.

Anderson, Robert Mapes. 1979. *Vision of the Disinherited*. New York: Oxford University Press.

Arguinzoni, Sonny. 1989. "The Testimony of Sonny Arguinzoni." Video- and audiocassettes. Distributed by Victory Outreach Publications, La Puente, Calif.

———. 1995. *Internalizing the Vision*. La Puente, Calif.: Victory Outreach Publications.

Arguinzoni, Sonny, and Julie Arguinzoni. 1991. *Treasures Out of Darkness.* Green Forest, Ark.: New Leaf Press.

Bartleman, Frank. 1980. *Azusa Street.* Originally published 1925. Plainfield, N.J.: Logos International.

Brusco, Elizabeth E. 1995. *The Reformation of Machismo: Evangelical Conversion and Gender in Colombia.* Austin: University of Texas Press.

Cox, Harvey. 1995. *Fire from Heaven: The Rise of Pentecostal Spirituality and the Reshaping of American Religion in the Twenty-First Century.* Boston: Addison.

Dayton, Donald W. 1987. *The Theological Roots of Pentecostalism.* Metuchen, N.J.: Scarecrow.

Deck, Allan Figueroa. 1994. "The Challenge of Evangelical/Pentecostal Christianity to Hispanic Catholicism." Pp. 409–439 in *Hispanic Catholic Culture in the U.S.,* edited by Jay Dolan and Allan Figueroa Deck. Notre Dame, Ind.: University of Notre Dame Press.

D' Epinay, Lalive. 1969. *Haven of the Masses.* London: Lutterworth Press.

Espinosa, Gaston. Forthcoming. *Borderland Religion: The Origins of Latino Pentecostalism.* Ph.D. dissertation, Department of History, University of California, Santa Barbara.

León, Luís. 1994. "Somos un Cuerpo en Cristo: Notes on Power and the Body in an East Los Angeles Chicano/Mexicano Pentecostal Community." *Latino Studies Journal* 5 (September): 60–86.

Martin, Bernice. 1995. "New Mutations of the Protestant Ethic Among Latin American Pentecostals." *Religion* 25: 101–117.

Martin, David. 1990. *Tongues of Fire: The Explosion of Protestantism in Latin America.* Oxford: Basil Blackwell.

Rodriguez, Richard. 1986. "Evangelicos: Changes of Habit, Changes of Heart: The Crusade for the Soul of the Mission." *Image Magazine,* October 26.

Ruiz, L. Vicki. 1993. "'It's the People Who Drive the Book': A View from the West." *American Quarterly* 45 (June): 243–248.

Sánchez, George J. 1993. *Becoming Mexican American: Ethnicity, Class, and Identity in Chicano Los Angeles, 1900–1945.* New York: Oxford University Press.

Stoll, David. 1990. *Is Latin America Turning Protestant? The Politics of Evangelical Growth.* Berkeley: University of California Press.

Stoll, David, and Virginia Garrard-Burnett, eds. 1993. *Rethinking Protestantism in Latin America.* Philadelphia: Temple University Press.

Suro, Robert. 1989. "Switch by Hispanic Catholics Changes Face of U.S. Religion." *New York Times,* May 14, pp. 1, 22.

Swidler, Ann. 1986. "Culture in Action: Symbols and Strategies." *American Sociological Review* 51 (April): 273–286.

Warner, R. Stephen. 1993. "Work in Progress Toward a New Paradigm for the Sociological Study of Religion in the United States." *American Journal of Sociology* 98 (March): 1044–1093.

6 | # The House That Rasta Built: Church-Building and Fundamentalism Among New York Rastafarians

Randal L. Hepner

The Church of Haile Selassie I (CHSI) is one of a dozen or more formally organized Rastafari "Mansions"[1] active in New York City. It is a small but growing congregation composed predominantly of first-generation Jamaican immigrants and their children together with immigrants from other Anglophone countries of the West Indies as well as a smaller number of African American members and white sympathizers. In size it is dwarfed by the larger Rastafari churches such as the Twelve Tribes of Israel (Queens), the Nyabinghi Order of Divine Theocracy (Brooklyn), and the Ethiopian Orthodox Church (Bronx). However, what it lacks in size it makes up for in a broad array of church-sponsored activities and through the zealous commitment and sacrifice of its members. More than any of the other Mansions, the CHSI most closely approximates traditional models of "sectarian" religious practice and organization, especially in relationship to the broader Rastafari movement, which to this day remains organizationally diffuse and doctrinally heterogeneous. Only a sizable minority of Rastas are affiliated with the organized Mansions; nonetheless, these groups and individuals form the most active and involved enthusiasts within the movement. Moreover, their development in the direction of congregationalism represents both a renegotiation of the movement's millenarian and institutionally anarchic past and a likely trajectory of its further development.

While the CHSI is part of this general trend toward congregational formation, it brings some unique features to the process. Perhaps most importantly its institutionalization in New York and elsewhere portends the possible emergence of what, for lack of a better term, might be called "Rasta fundamentalism"—a new, militant, and modernist reconfiguration of traditional Rastafari.

In this paper I will provide an historical, ideological, and ethnographic account of the development of this particular Rastafari congregation. Beginning with a general introduction to the Rastafari movement in Jamaica, I will proceed to examine the role of the charismatic leader and founder of the Church of Haile Selassie I, Abuna Asento Foxe, a pioneer of Rastafari in England and a central contemporary leader of the movement in North America. Special attention will be paid to Foxe's reworking of traditional Rastafarian themes, the centrality of the CHSI's church-building projects, and the appeal of its fundamentalist "Rastology" to sectors of the larger movement.[2]

The Origins and Development of Rastafari

The Rastafari movement, religion, or worldview, as it has variously been described, was born in the squalid slums of colonial Jamaica during the height of the worldwide depression of the 1930s. Yet it reflected several centuries of indigenous religious practices and ideologies ranging from Myalism and Revivalism to Pan-Africanism and Ethiopianism.[3] Its first preachers appeared in Kingston armed with a new doctrine that proclaimed the divinity or messianic character of the newly crowned emperor of Ethiopia, Ras Tafari Makonnen, who took as his official coronation name and title "His Imperial Majesty, Haile Selassie I [Might of the Trinity], King of Kings, Lord of Lords, Conquering Lion of the Tribe of Judah, Elect of God, and Light of this World."[4] These titles, traditionally associated with Christ in the New Testament, were interpreted by early Rasta leaders such as Leonard Howell, Joseph Nathaniel Hibbert, Archibald Dunkley, and Robert Hinds to mean that Selassie was the returned "Black Christ," that the end of days was at hand, and that Selassie would effect the great redemption and restoration of the black race to its ancient glory. These same preachers announced that Ethiopia was Zion, the true promised land spoken of in the Bible, that black people in the diaspora were living in Babylon, a hopeless hell, and that the emancipation, liberation, and salvation of African peoples everywhere could only be achieved by a collective "exodus" from Babylon and repatriation to the motherland.[5]

Consistent with the message they preached, early Rastafari leaders organized their urban followers into highly decentralized, polycephalous, and grassroots organizations with names such as the "King of Kings Mission," the "Ethiopian Coptic Faith," and the "Ethiopian Salvation Society." Membership was drawn from the poorest strata of Jamaican society, especially among those who had been inspired by the Back-to-Africa preaching and organizing of Marcus Garvey and the Universal Negro Improvement Association (UNIA) during the 1920s.[6] It was Garvey's alleged prophecy "Look to Africa, when a black king shall be crowned, for the day of deliverance is near," that many observers claim provided the inspiration for Selassie's messianic apotheosis by the early Rastafari.[7]

Like the Garveyites before them, Rasta preachers took to the streets to proclaim publicly their new-found faith, arguing that black people owed their allegiance not to a monarch in Buckingham Palace but to the newly crowned Black King in Addis Ababa, Ethiopia. Moreover, they argued that Selassie himself was preparing the coming exodus, and that only repatriation to Ethiopia could solve the plight of oppressed black people and usher in a millennial kingdom of universal peace and cooperation among nations. This stress upon the imminence of repatriation gave the early movement an eschatological and millenarian character. The expressed desire of Rastafarians to "return" to Africa has remained perhaps the most consistent theme in the history of the movement.

Almost immediately British colonial authorities became alarmed at the success of the Rastafari preachers, recognizing in their religious discourse a not-so-disguised call to anticolonial struggle. Howell, Hibbert, Dunkley, and Hinds were subjected to frequent arrests for seditious speech and treason. Although the movement began as an urban phenomenon, police surveillance and suppression forced the nascent Rastafarians into rural camps where, during the late 1930s and 1940s, a collective pattern of communal work and living evolved. It was here that many of today's distinctive Rasta practices and ideology, such as the cultivation of dreadlocks; the ritual smoking of "ganja," or the "holy weed" (marijuana); Nyabinghi drumming and chanting; the proud display of the red, gold, and green colors of the Ethiopian flag; a close identification with nature; and an antipathy to Eurocentric values, capitalism, and modernity; first developed.

In the 1950s, as Jamaican society moved cautiously toward constitutional independence, massive social transformations were underway as North American capital stepped in to replace waning British influence and control. In the space of twenty years more than a half-million rural Jamaicans were uprooted from their land to make way for the expansion of the multinational controlled bauxite-alumina industry. These now landless peasants streamed into the burgeoning slums and shantytowns around Kingston and other urban concentrations, and Rastafarians, who were part of this rural-urban migration, quickly began evangelizing among the displaced peasants (Campbell 1987, 86).

The 1950s and early 1960s witnessed an escalation of tension between the Rastafari and the emerging Jamaican state as the movement spread and began to take on the character of a mass resistance movement among the most alienated sectors of society. As Jamaican authorities attempted to address the crisis of chronic unemployment by exporting ever-larger numbers of its laboring classes to England, Rastas responded with the slogan "Africa, Yes; England, No! Let my people go!" Street preaching, marches, and rallies were met by violent police response. Intensified ganja laws were deployed against cultivators and users of the "holy weed." The state launched programs to drive Rastas from squatted land and razed several of their urban camps and housing projects. Riots broke out, and Rastas were indiscriminately rounded up and forcibly shaved and trimmed. One group, led by the enigmatic Rasta preacher Claudius Henry (and inspired by the recent Cuban revolution), took up arms in 1960 in a futile attempt to press their demands upon the colonial state. Panic ensued as colonial authorities declared a national state of emergency, and sent the combined police and military to contain the rebellious Rastafarians. Henry was arrested and convicted of treasonous felony, while those who took up arms directly, including Henry's son Ronald, were executed (Chevannes 1976).

At the same time, state officials commissioned the first study of the movement by researchers at the University of the West Indies. The results, published as *The Rastafari Movement in Kingston, Jamaica* (Smith et al., 1960), provided the Jamaican public with the first historical and doctrinal overview of the movement and made several policy recommendations favorable to Rastafarians. Most importantly, the study pleaded that the general public recognize the majority of Rastafarians as peaceful citizens; that the government undertake an ambitious array of housing, job training, and other social service projects to meet the legitimate needs of movement participants; and that the police cease persecution of law-abiding Rastafarians. With these findings, along with the state visit of Selassie to Jamaica in 1966, began a process of partial accommodation of the movement. Leonard Barrett

(1977, 146–162) has referred to the period between the mid-1960s and 1970s as a time of "ambivalent routinization" for the movement, meaning a general relaxation of its millennial expectations, a willingness of Rastafarians to participate and contribute creatively to Jamaican culture, and a growing public respect for the movement as the "avant garde who are carrying on the fight for freedom, justice and a better Jamaica."

As the 1960s unfolded, Rastafarians were at the forefront of various new cultural and political developments, including the black nationalist, Black Power, and progressive grassroots movements. Alliances were formed with student groups and with movements of the unemployed. By the end of the decade, Rastas were intimately involved in the evolution of Jamaican popular music, and with the rise of Bob Marley, Peter Tosh, Burning Spear, and other reggae artists to international prominence in the 1970s, Rastafarian themes, images, and symbolic practices were carried worldwide.[8]

It was at this time that the image of the Rasta as a dreadlocked warrior fighting for equal rights, economic justice, and racial pride first emerged in popular consciousness and West Indian literature. The enormous contributions of Rastafarians not simply to Jamaican popular music, but to the visual and plastic arts, traditional ceramics, wood carving, and poetry, made them the primary aesthetic producers within the newly independent nation. Many of those attracted to the movement at this time were drawn in by its countercultural and aesthetic appeal. For the first time it became possible to distinguish between "religious" and more "secular," "political," or "cultural Rastas"—a distinction that is very much present in the heterogeneous movement today. The close identification of Rastafarians with the "sufferahs," those located at the bottom of Jamaica's rigid system of racial and class stratification, legitimated their newly found role as moral witness and prophetic embodiment of the grievances shared by many popular class actors. In less than a decade Rastas had seemingly gone from despised pariahs, criminal outcasts, and lunatic fringe to what the noted Caribbean commentator Rex Nettleford (1970) claimed was the forefront of Jamaican national identity.

By 1972 the movement was prepared to make its new-found respectability count in the national elections. Tens of thousands of Rastafarians mobilized from their ghettos and rural camps to participate in the larger movement that led Michael Manley and his democratic socialist Peoples National Party (PNP) to the largest parliamentary victory in Jamaican history, displacing the conservative and elite-backed Jamaican Labor Party (JLP). For the first time political elites would have to take the "Rasta vote" seriously. Manley himself donned a number of Rasta ritual symbols and incorporated popular Rasta slogans in his electoral speeches. Bob Marley and other prominent Rasta reggae artists wrote the campaign songs and participated in the national mobilization drives that brought Manley's government to office (Waters 1985). The close identification of many Rastas with the early Manley regime and its left-populist program suggested to Barrett (1977, 152) and other contemporary commentators that the Rastafarians "must be seen as the forerunners of the ideology of democratic socialism" that swept Jamaica in the 1970s.

Throughout the 1970s and 1980s the Rastafari movement experienced enormous growth as its Afrocentric themes of black pride and social justice took hold in Jamaica and were carried throughout the African diaspora. Reggae music was the principal vehicle for the international spread of Rasta practices and ideology, and the dance hall the principal location where many middle-class youth in Jamaica, England, and the United States first came into contact with Rastafarians. The spectacular growth of one organization, the Twelve Tribes of Israel, founded in 1968, was largely due to the influx of middle-class youth attracted by the colorful dance parties regularly sponsored by the Twelve Tribes and by the large number of reggae musicians committed to the organization (Barrett 1977, van Dijk 1988).

However, Rastafari is much more than reggae, and as important as the "King's music" has been to Rastafari's global dissemination, the music alone was incapable of meeting the needs of new, immigrant, and highly active Rastafari communities. For the most deeply committed activists, new congregational forms have emerged in recent years, old organizations have been revitalized, and Rastafari ideology and practice have undergone significant modification. The increasingly multiethnic and international character of contemporary Rastafari owes much to its experience in England and North America. A key figure in the history of English Rastafari and a contemporary leader in North America is Asento Foxe. His story parallels the early spread of Rastafari outside of Jamaica and speaks to the changing character of contemporary Rastafari in North America.

Asento Foxe, Rasta Pioneer

In many ways the Church of Haile Selassie I (CHSI) and its political wing, the Imperial Ethiopian World Federation (IEWF), are products of the vision and indefatigable labor of its founding Elder and charismatic High Priest, Abuna (Father) Asento Foxe (also known in Rastafarian circles as "Pinto" and "Emmanuel" Foxe). Born in Depression-era Kingston, Foxe was raised in an Anglican family that was fiercely attracted to Garveyite nationalism. As a child Foxe was an enthusiastic "Scout" in the youth wing of Garvey's UNIA and attended the Ebeneezer Secondary School in Kingston's infamous "Back-O-Wall" ghetto, a Rasta stronghold until it was razed by a fleet of government bulldozers in 1966.[9] At the close of World War II he came under the influence of a Rastafarian uncle and began "sighting [learning about] Rasta." In the early 1950s Foxe participated in Kingston's "rude boy" subculture[10] while attending Jamaica's Technical College, but finally began "manifesting Rasta" before emigrating to England in 1955.

In the late 1950s Foxe emerged as an important early leader of Rastas in West London's working-class and West Indian residential concentrations, organizing the first Rasta meetings in Landbroke Grove after the 1958 Notting Hill race riots. Writing of the nascent Rastafarians in England during the early 1960s, Ernest Cashmore (1979, 54) reports that "Foxe [was] regarded by many as the most formidable and energetic personality in the movement." In 1967 Foxe and others founded the Universal Black Improvement Organization (UBIO) with a political wing called the Peoples Democratic Party (PDP)—dual organizations modeled after Garvey's UNIA and People's Political Party (PPP). Cashmore (1979, 51) writes that the UBIO "sought to incorporate Rastafarian themes into a basically black consciousness-raising vehicle as a way of creating interest and enthusiasm among blacks in Britain and possibly provoking them into collective action." Similarly, Jah Bones (1985, 39–40), himself an important leader amongst Rastafarians in England, reports that Foxe was widely regarded as the "pioneer" and "leading elder" of the movement in London:

> His [Foxe's] vision was to organize Rastas around a conception that embraced a political consciousness. This he felt was needed since it is natural for Rastas to demand social and cultural recognition and other rights according to the principles of democracy. For Foxe, Rastas cannot fight for and seek to obtain cultural rights if Rastas are not politically educated; that means knowing the affairs of politics.

What is unusual about Foxe, according to Cashmore and Bones, is his open and early advocacy of political involvement. Prior to Manley's

1972 election campaign, traditional Rastafarians typically rejected po-
litico-electoral involvement in favor of prophetic critique. Most had
little interest in reforming what they denounced as corrupt and deca-
dent Babylonian societies. The vast majority of Rastas to this day
regard politics as "polytricks," a manipulative attempt by society's
elites to divide and conquer the poor and oppressed. As we shall see,
Foxe has always conceived of Rasta as a social, political, cultural, and
religious movement for black liberation, and his organizational attempts and rather apocalyptic theology have consistently incorporated
these elements. However, Foxe's early political forays were almost entirely within the progressive Black Power and New Left discursive
arenas. As a self-defined "radical, grassroots democrat," in the 1960s
Foxe enthusiastically supported the Cuban revolution and denounced
U.S. imperialism in Vietnam. It would take another decade and a failed
revolution in Ethiopia before Foxe began moving ideologically in another very different direction.

As part of a fact-finding delegation of Anglo-Jamaican Rastas to
Jamaica in 1972, Foxe was converted to the Ethiopian Orthodox
Church (EOC)[11] and baptized by Archimandrite Abba Laike Mariam
Mandefro, now known as Archbishop Abba Yesehaq, head of the EOC
in the Western Hemisphere. At the same time, Foxe was won over to
the Ethiopian World Federation (EWF)[12] and issued a charter to found
a local branch in London. He was also encouraged by Abuna
Mandefro to prepare to found the EOC in England. In 1972 the UBIO
was reorganized as EWF Local 33 with Foxe as president. A few
months later, the first EOC congregation began meeting. Thus, Foxe
had succeeded in reproducing his dual organizations: the EWF would
attend to the political, or "stateical," needs of his followers, while the
EOC would attend to the spiritual, or "churchical," needs. Although
Foxe was a central player in establishing the EOC in England, he was
never able to control the church effectively, as its clerical leadership
was always dependent upon its overseas hierarchy. Nonetheless, newly
converted and seasoned Rastafarians alike enthusiastically flocked to
the new church.

Within a few years, however, many Rastas became disillusioned
with the EOC because of its refusal to accommodate their worship of
Haile Selassie and because the church, for a time, demanded the cutting
of dreadlocks. Foxe and his followers were among those who departed
from the church but carried with them particular aspects of EOC
polity and liturgy. For more than a decade, the EWF had to serve as
the "churchical" and "stateical" institution of Foxe's community, dis-

rupting the dual organizational pattern he favored. Despite competition from other Rasta groups, Foxe's community enjoyed tremendous growth throughout the 1970s. By the end of the decade the London-based EWF grew sufficiently to found locals in Birmingham and Leicester. Soon thereafter, however, internal dissent and disagreements led to the splintering of the EWF and the formation of rival camps.

Much of the dispute centered on questions regarding the proper attitude to take toward the Ethiopian revolution and its provisional military government, the Dergue. Many Rasta groups in Jamaica and England initially supported the revolutionary process, mistakenly arguing that Selassie had approved and was directing the revolution (McPherson 1991, 87). However, the coup that overthrew and allegedly executed Selassie in 1974, combined with the increasingly violent and repressive measures deployed by the Dergue in its war against internal dissent and national secessionist movements, disillusioned some Rastas toward socialism and leftist politics generally. From the moment of Selassie's arrest, Foxe set his followers in motion, organizing the first demonstration against the Dergue at the Ethiopian Embassy in London (McPherson 1991, 66–69). This began a long process of ideological reflection and rethinking on Foxe's part. In the 1980s several Rasta groups began developing an extreme anticommunist ideology. Foxe was in the center of this new development.

At the time of the 1974 coup that overthrew Selassie and imprisoned dozens of members of his family, Selassie's son and heir-apparent, H.I.H. Merd Azmatch Asfa Wossen, was in England recovering from a stroke. In the 1980s a portion of the Ethiopian expatriate community in England and North America rallied around Wossen and began agitating for the restoration of a constitutional monarchy in Ethiopia. Asfa Wossen was elevated from crown prince to king, and became known among his Ethiopian supporters and a minority of Rastafarians as "King Amha Selassie I."[13]

In 1983 Foxe approached the royal family in exile to mediate the dispute in the EWF. Subsequently, Foxe secured a royal charter from Asfa Wossen and an open letter addressed to the "Rastafari Community Worldwide" in which Wossen called upon the movement to "rally under the Imperial banner with a structured body and unified leadership." Once again Foxe reorganized his forces as the Imperial Ethiopian World Federation (IEWF) with himself as international president. This marked the first direct intervention of the royal family into Rastafarian matters and signaled the beginning of a new relationship between Foxe, the royal family, and the Rastafari movement. Armed with the new charter, Foxe and the IEWF declared all other EWF locals defunct and began building their own confederation. All Rastas who refused to join the new "Royalist" and "Imperial" (promonarchial restorationist) camp were labeled "apostate," "socialist," and "devil-inspired traitors to His Majesty" ("A Brief History" 1987).

After securing the new charter, Foxe returned to Jamaica to begin recruiting for his new organization. Headquarters were set up in a Jamaican Labor Party (JLP) enclave on Oxford Street in the heart of West Kingston's infamous ghettoes.[14] There Foxe developed into a prolific composer of Rasta diatribes published as letters to the editor in Jamaica's leading newspapers. With this new forum he launched attacks on nearly every other Rasta Mansion, accusing them of complicity in the overthrow of Selassie's government and of "aiding and abetting the satanic socialist regime in Addis Ababa." In the early 1980s, as Prime Minister Edward Seaga and the JLP began imposing World Bank and International Monetary Fund austerity measures, dismantling the popular institutions and social programs of the Manley-PNP era, Jamaica's leading newspapers welcomed a Rasta voice crying out against the menace of socialism, communism, labor unions, welfare, and the minimum wage.

It is important to recall that throughout the 1970s, as Michael Manley led Jamaica through its experiment in democratic socialism and international solidarity with independence and nonallied movements throughout the developing world, Rastas mobilized popular (but not uncritical) support for Manley and were broadly associated with the PNP's militant left. The association between Rastas and radicalism had been cemented in the popular imagination since the early years of the Cuban revolution, with which many Rastas positively identified (cf. Smith et al. 1960, Chevannes 1976). This association was solidified during the 1979 Grenadian revolution when more than four hundred Grenadian Rastas took up arms and participated in Maurice Bishop's New Jewel Movement and People's Liberation Army that overthrew the despised Eric Gairy dictatorship (Campbell 1987, Tafari 1989). A major Rasta leader and his community breaking with the movement's progressive ideological past was considered something of a coup by those forces in Jamaica intent upon carrying out privatization and other neoliberal capitalist policies of "structural adjustment."

Throughout the 1980s Foxe simultaneously deepened his critique of other left-leaning Rasta forces and boldly declared his political ambitions. In 1985, he, along with Abuna Blackheart of the Royal Ethiopian Judah Coptic Church and a few other Kingston-based Rasta groups in JLP "garrison" strongholds, founded the African Comprehensive Party (ACP) to press for constitutional reform and legal recognition of their respective churches. At the same time, the ACP projected fielding independent candidates in local and national elections.[15] For the first time Foxe announced his intention to establish a "Rasta government" in Jamaica and began referring to the IEWF as "a government-in-exile" (McPherson 1991, 206).

Founding the Church

However, some of this activity seemed to be taking Foxe far afield from more "spiritual" matters. It had been more than ten years since he and his followers had abandoned the Ethiopian Orthodox Church, and now Foxe wanted to redeploy the IEWF as an umbrella organization to centralize the royalist camp into a united front capable of concerted political action. This meant that the IEWF needed to be purged of its dual role as church and political association. Consequently, in 1987 Foxe founded the Church of Haile Selassie I in Kingston. In 1990 he emigrated to New York to prepare for the founding of a North American branch of his church. His intentions were threefold, as he explained to me in New York in 1994:

> I-n-I[16] bredren [brethren] reason and say, for real I-n-I need a
> church to provide Rastafari people worldwide with a documented
> way of worship; a church that would legitimize I-n-I belief and give
> I-n-I offspring and elders security and religious status in the work-
> place, community, and at school. I-n-I need a church to rise up the
> youth dem, to big up [strengthen] the family so I-n-I youths not go
> lick [smoke] crack, buy gun, shot and dead. I-n-I youths need to
> know I-n-I faith so them can defend His Majesty at school and
> know why them carry locks upon them head. At the same time, it
> was I-n-I intention that by the twenty-first century His Majesty, Em-
> peror Haile Selassie I, would be praised in temples all over the
> world. This means Selassie I must be proclaimed and worshiped
> among all nations and incense burned intinually [continually] in His
> name. For His Majesty is the God-of-this-Age, Jah [the Creator]
> come in the flesh. I-n-I must worship HIM [the] same way as the In-
> dian man worship him own Krishma [sic], Rama, Brahma. For this
> I-n-I create the church in the divine name, the new name, and it terri-
> ble and dreadful, 'cause heathen no like Jah name.

According to Foxe the church was needed in order to accomplish several goals: to provide a routinized ritual association in a highly active community, to socialize the new generation and to create strong Rasta families, and to carry out Rasta evangelization in all countries. While these needs may appear to be relatively standard features of North American religious communities, they represent a significant departure from traditional forms of Rastafari practice and organization.

While it may seem odd to talk about "traditional Rastafari" in a movement that is scarcely sixty-five years in the making, I argue that the character of contemporary change within the global movement makes it possible to distinguish an older, "traditional" form of Jamaican Rastafari from the newer, congregational-oriented and transplanted varieties of North America.

Traditionally, Rastas were less concerned with church and institution-building than they were with personal identity and movement formation. To this day the Rastafari movement lacks central organizational structures, has "no formal creeds, few written texts, and no seminaries" or other bodies "to enforce orthodoxy" (Glazier 1986, 432). The customary ritual practices of drumming, chanting, and communal ganja smoking under the leadership of Elders did not require rigorous organizational structure. Formal gatherings were periodic. Informal "reasonings"—highly charged discursive rituals carried out in small, decentralized, egalitarian settings under the influence of sacramental ganja smoking—provided the primary form of socialization in the organizationally diffuse rural camps and urban yards. Moreover, traditional Rastas placed little emphasis upon educating their women and female children; it was enough if their sons began "manifesting Rasta" by the time they came of age. Finally, traditional Rastas knew nothing about preaching Rastafari to all nations as it was a message and movement directed to the sons and, to a lesser extent, the daughters of Africa—the true lost tribes of Israel. Babylon was falling, and it was the duty of Rastafarians simply to prepare themselves individually for the coming exodus, when they would flee Babylon and return to Zion.

While Foxe's community was not the first to elaborate a standard liturgical practice and begin the construction of distinct congregational formations, the CHSI has gone further in this direction than any of the other Mansions. This does not mean, however, that Foxe has given up his struggle to organize Rastas around political issues and demands for "black liberation." On the contrary, the IEWF remains the central institution of his community and its "royal charter" his legitimating authority as an "Imperial Rasta leader." As always, the dual organizations are intended to complement each other as different facets of the same movement, what most Rastas refer to as "churchical" and "stateical" objectives.

Subsequent to the founding of the CHSI in Jamaica, daughter churches were established in London and Paris (1989), Holland, St. Lucia, and New York City (1990). Currently, Brother Foxe and the CHSI in New York are training a number of brothers and sisters from Trinidad, Guyana, Barbados, Haiti, Dominica, and other Caribbean countries to return to their island homes and found branch churches there. The very concept of "training" Rasta leaders is new to a movement that traditionally scorned professional Christian ministers and the very concept of a "learned clergy." The polycephalous and egalitarian character of Rastafari typically required a more organic process of leadership selection. In the absence of formal organizational structures, it was through participation in "reasonings" that certain individuals emerged as leaders and Elders capable of expounding on matters of doctrine and "livity" (practice) (cf. Homiak 1987, 224–225).

Building the Church in North America

For its first four years in North America, the CHSI was located in Harlem, first on Adam Clayton Powell Boulevard and then on 116th Street. In 1994, the church moved to its present location in Bedford-Stuyvesant, a teeming West Indian residential and commercial concentration located in the heart of black Brooklyn. Within the immediate vicinity the CHSI competes with seven or eight other small storefront churches of Afro-Baptist and various pentecostal, apostolic, and Church of God in Christ denominations. Another half-dozen or so larger, mainline black congregations, such as the African Methodist Episcopal Church, can be found within a four-block radius. And just a few miles south in Crown Heights and East Flatbush, the CHSI contends with its main Rasta competitors, the Nyabinghi and EWF.

At present the CHSI is attempting to raise capital funds to purchase and remodel the building in which the storefront church is housed. The additional space will be used to expand the considerable array of programs and activities sponsored by the congregation, including the anticipated establishment of a Rasta day-care center and health clinic. At the same time, the church is sponsoring missions in New Jersey and Florida, where it hopes to found churches in the coming year.

The CHSI holds weekly worship services on Sunday afternoons, preceded by a Sunday School program for children and young teenagers. Weekday auxiliary meetings and services include the Friday night IEWF meeting (education and politics), Rastological counseling, the Daughters of Zion meetings for women, social events, and other programs for children and young people. The church is also heavily involved in, and contributes significant time and resources to, the first Rastafarian prison ministry in New York, where some three to four thousand international Rastafarians are behind bars on any given day—mostly due to this country's failed war on drugs. Asento Foxe is an official, paid chaplain within the New York State Correctional System, and, along with four ordained Priests and fourteen Levites,[17] carries out an ambitious program of Rasta evangelization, education, and edification behind prison bars.

The storefront church itself is modest in size and can comfortably sit only perhaps sixty. Its rectangular meeting hall is lined with an assortment of Rasta ritual iconography: red, gold, and green framed pictures of Haile Selassie, Asfa Wossen, and other members of the Ethiopian royal family; various lion images;[18] the IEWF charter; and a map of Africa. A chalkboard at the front lists the biblical readings for the day's service, which typically favors passages from Hebrew scripture regarding the exodus and future prophecies of Israel's restoration and redemption. Behind a makeshift frame and red curtain emblazoned with the Conquering Lion of Judah symbol are the ark and altar used in the worship service proper. Thirty chairs line the left side of the hall where the men and boys sit, with a dozen pews on the right side for "the sistren and dawtas." Beyond the meeting hall is a kitchen, an office, and an outdoor courtyard used almost exclusively by the "bredren" for ganja smoking and reasoning. The front entrance to the church is usually guarded by Brother Charles, the sergeant at arms, an impressively bearded, tall, and charming individual with a mane of dreadlocks that fall below his waist. He escorts visitors and latecomers into the service, passes out Bibles (The King James Version), and insures that all congregants are properly attired: women and girls in headdress and modest attire, men and boys with heads uncovered. Notices of various church-related activities and pictures of congregational outings and events line the entryway.

In the absence of formal church records, it is difficult to determine the exact size of the congregation. Typical weekly attendance, which hovers around sixty–eighty persons, is not a reliable estimation of the church's actual membership since few congregants attend all meetings. The physical size of the storefront restricts the number of occasions when all members can come together. Moreover, the church counts all baptized prison inmates as part of its New York membership. Thus, in personal communications Brother Foxe has reported a variable membership of some six hundred to seven hundred, many of whom live outside of New York City. It is very possible that Foxe's figures represent the actual number of all persons who have joined or passed through the church since its founding in 1990. Membership appears somewhat transient, and it is not uncommon to hear complaints about backsliding members and "apostates."

What is more remarkable than the size of the membership is the tremendous ethnic diversity in the congregation. While a majority are first-generation Jamaican immigrants and their children, there are also prominent members from Trinidad, Barbados, Grenada, Guyana, Haiti, and St. Lucia. At present there is even a dreadlocked Puerto Rican brother who is being trained as a Levite. A smaller number of African American members and white sympathizers add to the congregational mix. Economically, the congregation has a strong working-class base, although a number of members complain about job prospects in New York's changing economy, and unemployment runs high among new immigrants and young people, many of whom claim discrimination because of their dreadlocks. Reported occupations include painters, construction workers, plumbers, electricians, day-care employees, and nurses. There are a few small-business owners, elementary school teachers, and slightly more artists and musicians. And, as with any large gathering of Rastafarians, a *small* number make a periodic but precarious living in the ganja trade.[19]

Negotiating a common identity given the ethnic diversity within the community is no simple matter. The history of the Afro-Caribbean region is replete with failed attempts at creating a Pan–West Indian identity. However, as Constance R. Sutton and Susan Makiesky-Barrow (1987, 105) report, "New York offers opportunities to build common understandings among West Indians not available in the Caribbean." Certainly the immigration reforms of 1965 contributed to this process, as did the subsequent emergence of distinct West Indian ethnic neighborhoods and institutions in Brooklyn and Queens. Perhaps more importantly, the experience of racial stratification and discrimination forced Afro-Caribbean immigrants to renegotiate issues of race and ethnicity. During the 1980s many immigrants began to think in ethnic terms as a self-conscious strategy to cope with racializing conditions in their host society and to situate themselves better in the competition for housing, jobs, and other resources. More recently, Phillip Kasinitz (1992, 11) has argued that "this sense of Pan–West Indian identity is fast becoming a cultural and political force, both in New York and in the Caribbean as well."

Rastafari has been one of the influences that has helped forge this new sense of identity, providing a common set of symbolic references and practices that simultaneously allow individuals to transcend and preserve their particular national identities. As Brother Raymond, a Trinidadian member of the CHSI and a former Nyabinghi supporter who has been in this country for a decade, explained:

> I-man [I] no check where a man come from, but what him deal with. That means a man can come from Trinidad, Barbados, Jamaica, or wherever, it makes no difference as long as the man [is] sighting His Majesty and doing the works of Rastafari. 'Cause all-o-we is originally African and [it] is to Africa [that] I-n-I must return one day. So I-n-I in the Church of Haile Selassie I don't deal with the tension thing you find among Trinidadians and Jamaicans here. Too much fussing and fighting. I-n-I say, "perfect love, brother, perfect trust, sister." And I-n-I go about the business our Father has called us to, to prepare the coming Kingdom. I-n-I is here at this time to build the Rasta nation.

Aside from Rastafari ideology, which deliberately cultivates a Pan-Africanist identity among its followers, the physical commingling of diverse Caribbean immigrants assists in the creation of new, transcending identities. That these identities are transnational in scope is evident from the concern and attention paid to home societies and the desire of many members to extend the work of the church to their place of origination. To add to the complexity, most Rastafarians regard themselves as "Ethiopian nationals." Even if this identity claim is imaginary or largely symbolic, many struggle to learn the rudiments of Amharic or other Ethiopian languages and to keep abreast of political developments in Ethiopia and throughout the African continent. Brother Jeruel, a twenty-eight-year-old member of the church baptized in June of 1994, embodies the complex identity negotiation of many. As he explained in an interview in 1996:

> I'm an Ethiopian national born and raised in New York. Both of my parents are from Haiti, which is why I was raised in the Catholic church and why I want to go to Haiti to spread the work of this church, the divine Church of Haile Selassie I, the only church where I-n-I can find the truth. That's why I'm trying to learn all I can about Haiti now. But ultimately it's Ethiopia I want to go, 'cause things are bad in the world and you can't be really free in Babylon.

Raised in East Flatbush, Brooklyn, Jeruel began moving in Rasta circles as part of his "search for truth, personal development, and community." He recognizes that his early attraction to Rasta, inspired by a love for reggae, was part of an attempt to re-create links with his Caribbean ancestry. But he also insists that upon joining the church he was "mystically incorporated into the ancient Ethiopian polity." Hence, his desire to go to Ethiopia one day. In the meantime, the church is a kind of "iniversity" [university] where he can learn and grow and enjoy the "fruits of Caribbean diversity."

In New York City Rastafari churches and political associations provide opportunities for individuals to develop organizational and public-speaking skills, and to deepen their knowledge of politics, history, and world affairs. Here too they are able to channel their considerable energy and enthusiasm into collective action to achieve common goals. However, these same institutions also function as community centers where members engage in an array of nonreligious and nonpolitical activities. Whether it is in gathering to play dominoes, to celebrate the birth of children, to assist new immigrant members, or to organize Rasta participation in the annual West Indian Food and Craft Fair in Prospect Park, Rasta churches have become organizations through which Caribbeans purposefully reproduce aspects of their ethnic heritage that have frequently been denigrated and resist stereotypical redefinition in a racializing North America.

The unique linguistic practices of Rastafarians, sometimes referred to as "Iyaric," "Dread Talk," or "Nation Language," contribute to the process of common identity construction and group cohesion. Through a creative lexical and grammatical expansion on Jamaican Creole, Rastafarians have developed linguistic practices and codes that assist in establishing in-group solidarity and in maximizing detachment from their larger environment (Cassidy 1961, Devonish 1986, Pollard 1994). Reggae music, whose lyrical content is composed almost exclusively in Dread Talk, carried the Rastafarian speech code throughout the Caribbean, where it was quickly adopted by young people. Consequently, many immigrants from the eastern Caribbean and elsewhere were already familiar with the distinctive language practices before becoming Rasta. The fact that the speech codes of Rastafarians builds upon English while also subverting it is important to a largely Anglophone community that aims at destabilizing Eurocentric cultural and political supremacy. The popular and poetic appeal of the language is evident as African American and Hispanic Caribbean immigrants within the congregation adopt its usage.

Dietary practices also contribute to the sense of uniqueness and community within the CHSI. Like other Rastas, many CHSI members practice the "Ital" diet, which emphasizes detachment from the Eurocentric dietary habits imposed on Caribbean slaves and their descendants. In place of meat and foreign food imports, Rastas emphasize a locally grown and organic vegetarian diet free from salt and processed additives. Most Rastafarians eschew all hard drugs, tobacco, and alcohol, and prefer natural herbal and homeopathic remedies to modern Western medicine. In the CHSI the sharing of meals is an important community event. Most ritual services are long and sometimes physically demanding. The sharing of a communal meal following the service extends the period of fellowship and fulfills an important practical need, including providing material assistance to the unemployed members.

Perhaps more than anything else, however, Dread Talk, table fellowship, and the Ital diet help set church members apart from those outside the ritual community. For a long time the cultivation of dreadlocks and the uncut beard ("covenant and precept") served as the most universally recognized markers of Rastafarian identity. However, in the last decade or so dreadlocks have become fashionable not only as an Afrocentric statement within the larger black community but among layers of various white youth subcultures as well. In places like New York disentangling genuine Rastafarians from their dreadlocked imitators requires ethnographic research. Conscious of the ambiguity and the blurred boundaries between Rastas and others, groups like the CHSI emphasize linguistic, dietary, and other practices that formerly were quite optional or voluntary within the larger movement but that today serve to differentiate genuine believers from outsiders. Moreover, the insistence on the punctilious observance of particular practices serves other vital functions for the CHSI, for it simultaneously helps to distinguish their "strict version" of Rastafari from competing Rasta conceptualizations, and insures high rates of participant conformity, commitment, and in-group solidarity.[20]

Although women are excluded from officiating in the liturgical or priestly functions of the church, they are far from absent in the life of the community. On the contrary, women play an important and visible role in the CHSI and the IEWF. They are permitted and encouraged to hold office as teachers and spokespersons for the church, and to participate in the economic life of the family and larger community. Currently, Sister Bernadette, an articulate and forceful Guyanese immigrant and mother of six, is president of the New York IEWF local and presides over the Friday night political meetings. Along with Sister

Sonia, Sister Sharon, and a half-dozen other women, she organizes most of the activities for the children and youth as well as social events for the entire congregation. In comparison with older Rasta organizations and the mass of unaffiliated Rastas, women play an active and central role in the CHSI.

As a result of this activity, a new discourse has emerged among CHSI women in relationship to themselves and other Rastafarian sisters. Whereas among more traditional Rastafari it is frequently said that "a woman can only come into the movement through her kingman," meaning her husband or another "Rastaman," thereby becoming a "Rastawoman," the sisters of the CHSI emphasize the necessity of women taking responsibility for their own spiritual and educational development. Moreover, they actively reject the label of "Rastawoman" in favor of "Daughter of Zion," a term that is perceived to be both ennobling and founded in Scripture. In an official church newsletter addressed to the broader Rastafari movement, Sister Sonia, a Jamaican immigrant and mother of five, writes:

> *Rastawoman: the time is now to stop calling yourself a Rastawoman, a word that represents a colonial name given to the woman of a Rastaman. We the Daughters of Zion realize that this name represents a domicile conception which has undermined the socio-religious development of the daughters, and has subjected them to medieval practices which distract from our rightful name and calling. . . . As a Rastawoman you cannot identify yourself in the scriptures except by accepting your true name, Daughter of Zion (Isaiah 37: 22), which is your ancient name. . . . Today we the Daughters of Zion need to take an active part in the development of the Rastafarian community. We should follow the footsteps of our women ancestors, like the Queen of Sheba, Empress Menen of Ethiopia, Sarah and the others. . . . We need to put the colonial behavior behind us and educate ourselves to take part in the future development of our community. Let us not be afraid to question the fundamentals of our belief, either in relationship to our Kingman or the wider society, which our predecessors failed to do. We must remember that the family is the cornerstone of civilization and we the daughters of Zion have to bring up the family. . . . We cannot fail in our responsibilities to the future generation of daughters (Church of Haile Selassie I Document 1994).*

Three themes emerge from this text that are important for the CHSI's church-building project and its reconfiguration of Rastafari ideology. First, there is the rejection of a label that is widely used within the broader movement, "Rastawoman," that seems to suggest a woman's subordination to her husband or another man. This term is associated with a biblically unfounded, "colonial," "domiciled," and "medieval" conception of Rastafari still current within the broader movement. Second, there is a search for empowering female images, both in the Bible and in Ethiopian history and myth, to inspire women's active participation within the CHSI community. A picture of Empress Menen, Selassie's wife, adorned in her coronation attire, is prominently displayed at the front of the church alongside that of Selassie himself, and together they are referred to as "King Alpha and Queen Omega." Perhaps not surprisingly, the brothers of the CHSI refer to their Rastafarian wives as "Queens."

Finally, the text highlights a new emphasis upon the Rasta family that makes central women's role in the transmission of Rasta culture. If we are to trust previous observers' accounts that "Rasta dogma is male-centered and mother-denying" (Kitzinger 1969, 260), and that "women are, indeed, peripheral to the movement as a whole" (Kitzinger 1966, 35), then the CHSI represents something of a dramatic departure from more traditional Rastafari. The women of the CHSI have found a form of empowerment in motherhood and have made it central to the church's goals. Socializing a new generation of Rastafarian children cannot be accomplished without Rastafarian mothers, as many brothers new to the church with non-Rastafarian wives or girlfriends can testify.[21]

What is perhaps most unusual about this congregation in relationship to the broader movement is that fact that the CHSI performs baptisms, weddings, and burials—rites of passage that traditional Rastafarians largely scorn to this day. Aside from the EOC, no other Rastafarian group practices infant or adult baptism. Neither marriage nor monogamy is held in high regard by large sectors of the movement. Many Rasta bredren have children by multiple "baby mothers" but choose to live single or with other men. Even those brothers who do choose to cohabit with one woman and their children typically avoid "legal marriage," as that is perceived as giving over one's autonomy to the Babylonian state. And the concept of "Rasta burials" is virtually oxymoronic in that many traditional Rastafarians reject the very idea of death in favor of "ever-living life." Death is understood as the "wages of sin." But ever-living life is a gift of Jah promised to those who live in the last days and keep themselves clean and free from the circumambient influences of Babylon. In addition, the biblical vows of the Nazarite, by which Rastas justify the cultivation of dreadlocks ("All the days of the vow of his separation there shall no razor come upon his head: . . . he shall be holy, and shall let the locks of the hair of his head grow"), forbid coming into contact with corpses (Numbers 6: 1–8). Finally, most Rastas read the New Testament saying "let the dead bury their dead" (Matthew 8: 22) quite literally and leave the burying of other Rastas to the "spiritually dead," meaning non-Rastafarians.

The Church of Haile Selassie I has broken with the traditional proscriptions on baptisms, marriages, and burials and has developed its own unique rituals to sacralize these events. Baptism is the ticket to formal membership within the CHSI. Moreover, marriage, monogamy, and intra-Rasta relationships are vigorously preached in the church, and the insistence on their practice is a source of some discontent and even alienation by a small number of brothers. One former member, Brother Nyah, justified his departure from the congregation by chronicling Brother Foxe's continued opposition over the years to his involving "all my children and baby mothers in the church." The CHSI places great emphasis on the nuclear family, and the involvement of women and children in the congregation is taken quite seriously. Foxe and the leadership of the church draw the line at polygamous unions and forbid brothers to bring their "extra wives and girlfriends" to services—an injunction, I might add, whose real authors may well be the sisters of the church.

Temple Worship in Babylon

The worship service in the CHSI, which church members refer to as "Temple Worship," draws upon liturgical elements gleaned from Brother Foxe's days in the Ethiopian Orthodox Church but refracted by "Rastological" needs and interests. Four male Priests and Levites officiate at ritual services. A standardized liturgy guides the congregation through various prayers, supplications, and hymns.

As the service begins, a thick cloud of incense engulfs the meeting hall, bells are sounded, and the red curtain is drawn exposing an altar with a gold-framed coronation picture of Haile Selassie at the center, a menorah or seven-pronged candelabra, an incense burner, and other ritual paraphernalia. The Priests and Levites circle the altar four times, bowing respectfully each time they pass the picture of Selassie, and repeating the chant: "Let us worship, let us worship. . . . O'L'abb Woweld wemenfus Kidus Haile Selassie I . . . " (In the name of the Father, the Son, and the Holy Spirit, One God, Might of the Trinity.) Those officiating at the altar then form a procession throughout the congregation, pausing and individually blessing all in attendance. Each carries a different ritual object held up during the blessings: a large, silver Star of David mounted on a prayer staff with Selassie's image in the middle; a leather-bound Bible opened to the passage "His foundation is in Holy Mount Zion" (Psalms 87: 1), which is recited in each blessing; a scroll held with one hand atop the head symbolizing the law of Moses; and an ornamented incense burner dangling from a long gold chain that mixes and sends the pungent fragrances of ganja, frankincense, and myrrh throughout the congregation.

The service revolves around readings, prayers, and hymns (sung without instrumental accompaniment and taken from a mimeographed liturgy) and the recitation of various anaphora (atonal creedal chants). Although the main liturgical action is conducted by the Priests and Levites, a call-and-response structure keeps the congregation involved throughout the service. A typical example is the "Anaphora of Emperor Haile Selassie I":

Rasta Priest: *The Lord Haile Selassie I is with you my people.*

People: *This makes us glad.*

Rasta Priest: *Let us glorify our God and King.*

People: *It is right and holy.*

Rasta Priest: *Lift up your heads, lift up your hearts.*

People: *We have lifted them up to our God and King Haile Selassie I forever.*

Rasta Priest: *Before the world and everything was created Jah is in his Trinity. Jah is in his Holy Mountain. Before the heaven and the stars, before the face of the earth was created, Jah was in his kingdom. Before Jah created man in his image, Jah was in his Kingdom. Let the Priest and the faithful listen and the foundation of the earth shake and be afraid.*

Levites: *Ye that are sitting stand up.*

Rasta Priest: *The Lord "Tafari" [Haile Selassie I] came down through the will of his father, sojourned in Wayzora Yashimabet, was born in the year of John 1892.*

Levites: *Faithful, look to the East.*

Rasta Priest: *He walked openly with the people of his community and was baptized as the Ethiopian Eunuch (Acts 8: 34).*

Randal L. Hepner

Levites:	*Let us pray for mercy.*
Rasta Priest:	*He was tempted by the Devil Mussolini, but as Gideon and his bands of warriors, he won and degraded the rulers of darkness, Rome and Mussolini, through the power of his divinity.*
People:	*Holy, holy, holy, Haile Selassie I, the heavens and the earth is [sic] full of the holiness of thy glory.*
Rasta Priest:	*Thou art the staff of the righteous, the hope of the Race and the persecuted, the refuge of the sufferers. O light of the world, son of the living God, shine upon us with thine unfailing grace, granting us health, faithfulness, wisdom, the power of Rasta faith which is immovable.*
People:	*We thank thee and glorify thee, O Haile Selassie I.*
Rasta Priest:	*Yea, Lord of Host, we thank thee and bless and always pray thee, Jah the Father of the exalted ones, visit Ethiopia from Zion, O Lord of all creation, and have mercy on the people and save those who always fulfill thy holy will. Visit the widows and orphans, accept those who have gone to their rest in Faith. Grant us, Lord Haile Selassie I, a portion with all thy Saints. Grant us knowledge to please thee. . . . For great is thy name amongst all nations, and in every place incense is offered unto thy holy name. For thou art far above every name that is named. holy, holy, Holy Lord Sabbaoth, the heavens and the earth are full of thy glory.*
People:	*As it was, and is, and shall be from generation to generation, world without end. Amen.*

All prayers and supplications are delivered to Selassie, as this anaphora, adapted from the Ethiopian Coptic tradition, exemplifies. The church even has its own unique version of the Lord's Prayer:

Our Father which art in Zion, Hallowed be thy name. Thy Kingdom come. Thy will be done in earth as it is in Zion. Give us this day our daily bread, and forgive us our sins. Lead us not into temptation, but deliver us from evil: through the Divine name, Haile Selassie I, to whom be Glory and Dominion both now and forever, world without end. Amen.

"Heaven" is changed to "Zion" to reflect the movement's rejection of otherworldly Christianity. Rastas ridicule the notion of spirit existence and its attendant "ghost god," and the concept of salvation in an afterlife ("pie in the sky") is scornfully rejected. Heaven is here understood as both a place, Ethiopia, and a state of being, Zion. Both, however, are located on this earth and experienced in historical time. Jah, the divine creator of heaven and earth, is a "living man" revealed and most fully manifest in this dispensation in the personality of Haile Selassie; however, Rastas also insist that the divine is located in every person, and that all can participate in the divine life. This concept is verbally expressed in the pronominal usage of the linguistic construction "I-n-I," which Rastafarians use both as a singular (I, me, mine, my) and collective pronoun (we, us, our) to indicate the unity of humanity as well as the oneness of Rastas with Jah.[22]

Not surprisingly, there is no reference in the Rasta version of the Lord's Prayer to "forgiving those who have trespassed against us." Nor is much attention paid to biblical passages that require "turning the other cheek" in the face of adversity. Whatever else Rastas are, they are those militant sons and daughters ("souljahs") of Africa who will never relinquish their African identity, nor will they forget or forgive the days of slavery. On the contrary, slavery remains for this people an ever-living reality in Babylon. And in typical Rasta fashion they refuse to accept that slavery has ever been fully abolished in Western capitalist societies. Instead, Rastas argue that "the slave chains were melted down and made into money, for money chains you if you don't have it!" (Yawney 1976, 250)

Highly conscious of the oppressive elements of North American culture, the continued racist denigration of persons of African descent, the class divisions and exploitation of working people, and the difficulty of making one's way as an immigrant during a period of xenophobic backlash, Abuna Foxe leads the congregation in prayer. As he bows his head he pronounces the words of many Rastafari faithful:

> *that the hungry be fed, the naked clothed, the sick nourished, the imprisoned visited, the aged protected and the infant cared for; that His Imperial Majesty, Jah Rastafari, be praised in every land; that Ethiopia soon stretch forth her hands unto Jah; that I-n-I African people and all the downpressed of this world be liberated, emancipated, and restored to their own vine and fig tree; that justice flow like water and righteousness cover the earth.*

Following the prayers and anaphora recitation there is a series of biblical readings taken from both Old and New Testaments but typically favoring those passages deemed relevant to the "last days" and the "gathering of Israel." Biblical references to Ethiopia are frequently invoked, such as Psalms 68: 31—"Princes shall come out of Egypt; Ethiopia shall soon stretch out her hands unto God"—which is read as a prophecy foretelling Ethiopia's imminent redemption. The fact that Ethiopia is the first country mentioned in the King James Version of the Bible (Genesis 2: 13) is of significance to a community that takes literally the saying "as it was in the beginning, so shall it be in the end."

Many Rastas work with a tripartite philosophy of history: in the beginning each nation was in the original land Jah bequeathed it, living in harmony with nature and self. Each developed its own appropriate culture, its ancient "roots." However, this ordained pattern of social interaction was disrupted by the rise of European power and the enslavement of Africa, creating a "middle passage of history" that was a catastrophe for indigenous peoples everywhere. Selassie, the Conquering Lion, came to put an end to this "medieval" barbarity by opening up a new dispensation in human history, an epoch in which all things will be restored to their primordial perfection. The conviction that humanity stands on the threshold of this "restoration" lends an apocalyptic character to the discourse of many contemporary Rasta groups, an apocalyptism that is nourished in the CHSI by an intensified attention to personal Bible reading and study. This in turn has stimulated a more literal and fundamentalistic interpretation of Scripture, yet another departure from an older, eclectic, metaphorical hermeneutic practiced by traditional Rastafarians.[23]

Following the biblical readings a sermon or exhortation delivered by one of the officiating brothers draws out the unique Rastafarian interpretation and reappropriation of Scripture. All references to Zion and the "promised land" are reconfigured to refer to Ethiopia and Africa. Biblical promises of liberation and restoration are understood to apply, first and foremost, to Ethiopia's scattered children; however, contemporary Rastas insist that the liberation of African peoples is but a prelude to universal peace and reconciliation. Brother Zacharias, a founding member of the New York church and the leading Priest next to Abuna Foxe, provided a fairly representative example of the CHSI's exegetical method in a public exhortation in 1993:

> As I-n-I read today in Isaiah 48:20, Jah commands the children of
> Israel: "Go ye forth out of Babylon, flee ye from the Chaldeans,
> with a voice of singing declare ye, tell this, utter it even to the end
> of the earth; say ye, The LORD JAH hath redeemed his servant
> Jacob." Bredren and Sistren, a responsibility is delegated to all of us

> *in this earthly dispensation to implement the necessary measures to achieve a society of righteousness which reveals itself in Ethiopia in her full glory. Our Empire should truly extend from Cape to Cairo, as the saying goes, and it is our duty and great honor to cultivate the historical and divine culture of our African heritage while we rally around the imperial flag to consolidate the Ethiopian Royal Solomonic Dynasty and its ancient order. The restoration of our kingdom will usher in a new era for all humanity, one in which all people will be restored to their own vine and fig tree.*

As with other Rastafarians, the CHSI draws upon traditional Ethiopian legends, preserved in the *Kebra Negast,* that link Ethiopia's royal family lineage to the union of King Solomon and the Queen of Sheba (or Axum, the oldest Ethiopian kingdom). According to legend, the first emperor over the whole of Ethiopia was Solomon and Sheba's son, Menelik. As a young man Menelik was supposed to have traveled to Jerusalem, where he was greeted by his father and later stole the Ark of the Covenant, bringing it to the famed city of Axum, where to this day Ethiopians insist it remains. Haile Selassie is understood to be the 225th direct descendant of this sacred union, thus representing the Solomonic dynasty and the only true "divine kingdom" on earth today.

"Modern Ethiopianism" and Rasta Fundamentalism

Like other Rastafarians, the CHSI longs for the anticipated day when Rastas in the diaspora will be repatriated to Ethiopia. They perceive themselves as sojourners, strangers in a foreign land, who will one day be swept up in a great exodus of Israel to the promised land. However, Foxe and his followers argue that "the call for repatriation has been suspended since 1974," and that Rastas must "organize and centralize" around the demand for the "liberation of Ethiopia from Marxist rule" and the "restoration of the Solomonic Dynasty." "Liberation before repatriation" is one of the slogans around which the CHSI participates in a complex process of simultaneous distancing from other Rasta communities and partial accommodation to its host society.

In its original formulation, attributed to Selassie at the time of his 1966 state visit to Jamaica, "liberation before repatriation" was intended to signal the necessity of Rastas coming together to participate in broader movements for social change within Jamaica. Only after Jamaica had been liberated from her "Babylonian captivity," the legacy of slavery, colonialism, and capitalism, could the repatriation of Rastas to Ethiopia be effected (Barrett 1977, 172). However, Foxe has redeployed the slogan to refer more narrowly to Ethiopia as seen through the prism of his own theocratic and monarchical politics. The liberation required to effect the larger goal of repatriation is no longer the liberation of diaspora blacks in Jamaica and other parts of Plantation America, but the liberation of Ethiopia itself. Foxe argues that only after Amha Selassie is restored to power in Addis Ababa can Rastafarians legitimately work toward repatriation. Foxe refuses to support Rastafarians already in Ethiopia, including the famed Rasta community in Shashamane, and has banned his followers from traveling there. In colorful annual demonstrations outside of the United Nations in Manhattan, Foxe's followers have raised their banners calling on the world community to recognize "Equal Rights and Justice for Rastas Universal!" and demanding "We Want King Amha Selassie Back in Ethiopia!" Recalling the League of Nations' failure to come to Ethiopia's aid during the bloody Italian invasion in 1935, Foxe's followers demand: "U.N.: Don't Betray Ethiopia in 1995!"

Foxe has branded his own Rastology "Modern Ethiopianism," which he derives from a variety of sources including the Bible, selective speeches and writings of Haile Selassie, and his own long experience in the movement. Foxe deliberately contrasts Modern Ethiopianism with "sentimentalist" or more traditional versions of Rastafari. Given that the Nyabinghi Order is widely perceived as the most traditional and orthodox wing of the movement (Homiak 1985), and that a large number of Foxe's followers come out of this tradition, it is little wonder that Foxe expends much time and energy denouncing the Nyabinghi as "backward," "reactionary," and "apostate." Indeed, the denunciation of other Rasta groups and leaders forms a major part of the discursive activities of this community and contributes to its sectarian propensities. In New York as in Jamaica, the Nyabinghi are Foxe's principal competitors for the allegiance of the larger but divided movement. Much of the CHSI's congregational structure and liturgical practice contrast sharply with the Nyabinghi, which to this day remains organizationally diffuse and consists largely of outdoor gatherings centered around drumming, chanting, communal ganja smoking, and reasoning. Membership in the Nyabinghi Order is ill defined and its central animating slogan—"Death to all black and white oppressors"—seems, in the eyes of the CHSI, strangely out of place to a movement trying to make its way in a foreign land. The physical decorum and orderliness of the CHSI's worship service, the dedication and discipline of its membership, along with the many services the congregation provides, are a source of pride among church members. "Temple worship" is the phrase proudly employed by CHSI enthusiasts to distinguish their Sunday ritual gatherings from the midweek, sometimes chaotic, gatherings of the Nyabinghi. As Sister Bernadette of the CHSI once argued:

> *You can tell the true Israel from temple worship. Wherever Israel is gathered, Israelites are in the temple at worship, which is no ganja smoking and drumming kind of thing. True temple worship requires order and authority. Only the priest can officiate. Temple worship is a must if I-n-I are to carry this movement into the twenty-first century. And no Nyabinghi, Twelve Tribes, Federation [EWF], or Orthodox [EOC] can do that. Only the Church of Haile Selassie I and the Imperial Ethiopian World Federation can lead Rasta in this crucial time!*

Temple worship and the ideological claims of the IEWF are the central elements of Modern Ethiopianism. Combined with Foxe's own visions and revelations, his organizational aims and objectives, and the strategies he deploys to carry them out, the CHSI approximates contemporary models of global fundamentalism. As José Casanova (1994, 102) has recently outlined:

> *Fundamentalism is, first of all, distinct from traditionalism, conservatism, or orthodoxy in its militancy, radicalness, and highly selective attitude toward tradition. Further, fundamentalism lives in antagonistic symbiosis with modernity insofar as it defines itself against modernity while borrowing selectively also from modernity some of its ideological, technological, and mobilizational means. Finally, fundamentalism is mobilizational and, while it proclaims pristine restoration as its goal, the outcome is likely to be innovative adaptation to modern social conditions if not outright revolution.*

Foxe enthusiastically embraces the term "fundamentalist" and employs it when railing against other Rasta groups and individuals. He frequently compares his struggle with other Rasta Mansions to the tensions between Hamas and the PLO, favorably commending Hamas for their militancy and dedication. However, he tempers his critique of the West, acknowledging a debt he owes to modernity. At a church-sponsored conference on the importance of education in May 1994, Foxe reported:

> *I-man is a fundamentalist, a fanatic for His Majesty, a Rastaman who never sells out. But I-n-I must be modern, I-n-I must arm ourselves with modern education and technology. I-n-I can't be like the old sentimental Nyabinghi who don't send their youth to school and*

live up in the hills. I-n-I must learn all we can from Babylon before I-n-I can return to build the promised land. It is not enough to play drum and smoke spliff [a large, conical ganja cigarette]. I-n-I must become acquainted with the work of nations, politics, and engineering. For this reason Jah send I-n-I into this country at this time. I-n-I must take advantage of opportunities presented here in Babylon if I-n-I is to rule and reign in Zion.

The fundamentalist character of Foxe's enterprise is revealed most clearly in his collapsing of religious and political spheres. As a young "radical, grassroots democrat" in England, Foxe advocated political action on the part of Rastas as a vehicle for achieving social and cultural rights "according to the principles of democracy" (Jah Bones 1985, 39–40). However, in the 1980s Foxe's evolving monarchical position undermined his democratic commitments. Politics was no longer a profane sphere where groups competed for resources and recognition, but increasingly a sacred activity intimately connected with theological goals. The "stateical" objectives of the movement had now become fused with the "churchical." Today Foxe defines his own political theology as "divine theocracy," by which he means the rule of Rastafarian priests and elders under the guidance of the royal monarchy. Foxe prophetically envisions establishing a Rasta government in Jamaica that, after the restoration of the monarchy in Addis Ababa, would become "the fifteenth province of Ethiopia." Foxe claims that "I-n-I government would remain capitalistic, but nonexploitative, and would pull Jamaica out of the clutches of the Western world and into the orbit of the OAU [Organization of African Unity]." Resources from the Caribbean would then be put to work to assist in the rebuilding of Ethiopia and other African nations. Repatriation will be worked out through "government-to-government negotiations" rather than through supernatural intervention. But even after the expected mass repatriation of Rastas to Ethiopia, a Rasta government in Jamaica will still be necessary as "a mission outpost, to bring the saving message of Rastafari to Africa's scattered children, those still living in the darkness of the Western world."

Since the beginnings of the Rastafari movement, its apocalyptic and millenarian character has frequently frustrated attempts at organization building and contributed to its anarchic propensity. Since repatriation was considered imminent and was to be supernaturally effected, little emphasis was placed upon the need to organize the movement. Building churches and congregations in Babylon was considered unnecessary to a movement that both rejected Eurocentric Christianity and sought to flee the Western world. However, the exigencies of life in a foreign country, the delay of repatriation, and the influx of new members of varying ethnic and religious backgrounds have created new conditions and needs, which the CHSI's congregational strategy attempts to address. No doubt, the emergence of Rasta churches also represents a convergence toward or an assimilation of the deep-seated North American religious tradition of church-building and congregational involvement, as R. Stephen Warner (1994) has recently argued. Similar developments can be observed in other immigrant religious communities that have recently made their home in the United States.

Likewise, the conservative or even fundamentalist character of Foxe's congregation probably reflects forces at work not simply in North America but throughout the world today. Religious fundamentalism is a global phenomenon, and while internal variations exist among fundamentalist movements, each in its own way attempts to respond to the crisis of late modernity, the crisis of a posttraditional social order undergoing massive change and dislocation. As Nancy Ammerman (1987, 192) contends, "fundamentalism provides a coping strategy for those who find themselves adrift in a world that seems untrustworthy and unforgiving." Rastas in North America have good reasons to distrust their host environment. Few religious communities in this country have known the rates of prison incarceration that Rastafarians currently face. Few have been subjected to the barrage of negative media and law enforcement reports that have plagued the movement since its emergence in New York in the early 1960s.[24] Far from home and frequently disfranchised from the core institutions of the surrounding culture, Rastafarians are increasingly finding solace and companionship in their local churches. As Warner (1994, 71–72) again points out, "congregations can function as protected enclaves in a hostile world" and provide "one of the few places in our society where the oppressed can predictably expect to find encouragement."

Paradoxically, however, Foxe seems rather sanguine about conditions in North America. The CHSI represents the first and only officially recognized, tax-exempt Rasta church in the United States. Moreover, Foxe enjoys a very different relationship with the New York State Correctional System than do the thousands of brothers incarcerated there—namely, he is a paid employee. For these and other reasons, Foxe refuses to allow his membership to become involved in U.S. politics, instead focusing their political energies on Jamaica and on a distant, mythologized Ethiopia. While other New York Rastas vigorously protested the U.S. Gulf War in 1989–90, Foxe and his followers quietly approved the deployment of U.S. troops, arguing that the restoration of the Kuwait monarchy could portend a viable model for restoring the monarchy in Ethiopia. Closer to home, Foxe has refused to allow his congregation to participate in the broad mobilizations and demonstrations on behalf of the popular, dreadlocked black journalist, activist, and death-row inmate Mumia Abu Jamal. In the summer of 1995 Foxe argued that "Jamal is a socialist, of the variety that turned against His Majesty, and the Church of Haile Selassie I can take no part in his defense." Perhaps more tellingly, Foxe added, "Besides, if the church should do something on behalf of Jamal it could cause a backlash, wiping out the good-will and respect shown to I-n-I church here in New York."

In the end Foxe's attitude toward life in the United States is probably rooted in an instrumental approach: New York is home to the largest body of Afro-Caribbean immigrants anywhere in the world, creating a field that is "ripe for harvest"; it is also presently the center of Foxe's international network of churches and political associations, and an important venue for the mobilization of scarce resources. To become involved in oppositional politics in the United States could, as Foxe recently confided, "Threaten all that I-n-I have accomplished." And so the church's political gaze is turned elsewhere. Instead of attacking U.S. racism, imperialism, the lack of job opportunities, or police harassment, Foxe and his "souljahs" prefer, in typical sectarian fashion, to vent their frustrations on other Rasta Mansions. The failure of the movement to achieve its most ambitious and enduring objective—repatriation to Ethiopia—can be attributed by Foxe and his disciples to the treacherous activity of apostates and not, as in traditional Rastafarian apologetics, to the unwillingness of the Western powers to emancipate their African slaves and laboring classes fully.

Conclusion

The story of Asento Foxe and the Church of Haile Selassie I speaks to the changing character of contemporary Rastafari and contributes to the rich tapestry of new ethnic and immigrant religious communities in the United States today. Although the CHSI's version of Rastafari is considerably different from that presented in much of the scholarly literature on Rastafarians, and, while Foxe and the CHSI represent a minority tendency within the larger movement, it is a version and tendency that is growing. The transformation of an ideologically progressive, liberation-oriented religious movement into zealous fundamentalism probably reflects the conditions of possibility available to popular religious movements in the modern world (dis)order. The prevailing religious economy in the United States seems structurally predisposed to reward its conservative churches and ministers.

However, fundamentalism is not synonymous with congregationalism. And there can be little doubt that part of Foxe's and the CHSI's success in North America has much to do with their deft deployment of the congregational strategy. Indeed, the broader Rastafari community seems to be awakening to the need for more structured, routinized, face-to-face forms of worship and association. At the Nyabinghi- and EWF-sponsored Second Annual Rastafari Meritorious Awards Banquet, held on November 12, 1995, at the Caribe Club in New York City, the Haile Selassie I Meritorious Award was bestowed upon Asento Foxe for "leadership in establishing the first recognized Rastafari Church in this country." Ironically, for all of Foxe's venomous denunciations of their betrayal, many Nyabinghi and EWF followers express admiration and respect for him and his church-building projects. More recently at a "Unity in Diversity" conference organized by Foxe's church in May of 1996, the Nyabinghi and EWF representatives struck a conciliatory note, acknowledging the achievements of the CHSI and resolving to implement similar congregational programs within their respective Mansions.

And so Foxe and the CHSI dig in, laying deeper roots in this country than possibly any other Rasta group, still nourishing dreams of a distant Ethiopia but reconciling themselves to life in a strange land. This is the House that Rasta built, but more than likely it will not be the last.

ACKNOWLEDGMENTS

This essay derives from a larger dissertation project entitled "'Movement of Jah People'—Race, Class, and Religion Among the Rastafari of Jamaica New York City" (New School for Social Research, 1997). I would like to thank José Casanova for guidance and inspiration and the New Ethnic and Immigrant Congregations Project and the Research Institute for the Study of Man for research grants that made possible fieldwork in both Jamaica and New York City.

NOTES

1. The Rastafarian practice of referring to their larger churches, political associations, and community centers as "Mansions" and "Houses" is proof-

texted in John 14:2 "In my Father's house are many mansions." Less formal and typically smaller associations are referred to as "camps" and "yards." It should be noted that few, if any, Rastafarian churches resemble anything like a real mansion.

2. Research for this essay took the combined form of historical and archival investigation at the National Library of Jamaica and the Afro-Caribbean Institute in Kingston, and through long-term participant observation of the movement in New York. I first came into contact with Asento Foxe and the CHSI/IEWF while conducting research in Kingston, Jamaica, in 1992. Subsequently, I began attending services and following the development of the CHSI in New York. Brother Foxe and the core leadership of the CHSI extended a welcoming hand to my research, confident that it would lead to my conversion and membership in their church. Although their expectations have been frustrated, I retain a friendly and respectful relationship with Foxe and other church members. All quotes from Foxe and other church members come from author interviews unless otherwise indicated.

3. For a sampling of the growing literature on the history of Rastafari see Leonard Barrett (1977); Horace Campbell (1987); Ernest Cashmore (1979); Barry Chevannes (1994); Robert Hill (1983); Jack A. Johnson-Hill (1995); Joseph Owens (1976); and Neil Savishinsky (1993).

4. Haile Selassie's coronation occurred on November 2, 1930, in Addis Ababa. Newsreels, newspapers, and magazines carried colorful pictures of the coronation and inspired blacks throughout the diaspora (see Barrett 1977, 81–83; Hill 1983, 25–27).

5. For a treatment of early Rastafari beliefs and doctrines see George E. Simpson (1954, 1955).

6. For representative works on Garvey and the UNIA, see John Henry Clarke (1974); E. D. Cronen (1968); Rupert Lewis (1987, 1988); and Tony Martin (1987).

7. As Hill (1983, 25) has pointed out, "no evidence has so far been found or cited to show that Garvey ever made the assertion attributed to him."

8. The role of reggae in the international spread and dissemination of Rastafari is well documented (for representative works see Bilby and Leib 1986; Davis 1985; Davis and Simon 1977, 1983; Johnson 1976; White 1983).

9. For a first-hand account of the destruction of Back-O-Wall, see Barrett 1977, 156–158.

10. "Rude boys," or "rudies," were a distinct youth culture in Jamaica in the 1950s and 1960s, and were associated in the media and public imagination with ganja smoking, drug trafficking, and violence. Many rudies in the 1970s made the transition to Rasta, shedding their participation in the increasingly violent youth and gun cultures that would give rise to the notorious Jamaican crack "posses" of the 1980s and 1990s (cf. Gunst 1995, Brake 1980, Chevannes 1981).

11. The EOC, historically one of the oldest branches of Christianity, is not itself a Rastafarian church; however, many Rastafarians in London, Jamaica,

and New York City either formally belong to the church or participate as sympathizers. These brothers and sisters constitute something of a distinct community within the larger EOC. Since 1992 the church has been divided in its loyalty to competing leaderships in Addis Ababa and New York City, and separate church formation is occurring. It is still perhaps too early to project whether the schism is permanent.

12. The EWF was founded in New York in 1937 as a lobbying organization to assist Ethiopia in its struggle against the Italian fascist invasion. Its broader goal was "to unify, solidify, liberate, and free the Black people of the world in order to achieve self-determination." A branch of the EWF was established in Jamaica in 1938, and Rastas quickly overtook the organization and put it to work for their own purposes. Today the EWF is exclusively a Rasta organization and draws its membership from the EOC, Nyabinghi, and unaffiliated sectors of the movement (cf. Barrett 1977, 89–96).

13. It is important to point out that only a minority of Rastafarians in Jamaica and North America recognize Wossen's succession claims. Amongst all Rastas, Haile Selassie is referred to as "King Alpha and Omega, the first and the last," and the vast majority refuse to recognize any other claimants to the throne.

14. The JLP is one of the twin parties that dominate national political life. It is closely allied with propertied and multinational corporate interests and, along with the Peoples National Party (PNP), practices a form of political clientelism and favoritism that radically polarizes Jamaica's popular classes. Both parties are implicated in the political tribalism and gang warfare that plague Jamaica's ghettos. During the "democratic socialist" years of Michael Manley, the JLP was the opposition party in government and developed an extreme anticommunist ideology. The JLP enjoyed covert support from Washington and the CIA during the turbulent 1980 elections that took the lives of more than 900 "sufferahs" in Kingston's slums (Gunst 1995, Grey 1991).

15. For media coverage on the founding of the ACP, see the Kingston *Daily Gleaner,* June 29, 1988, and January 1, 1989.

16. For the usage of this linguistic construction, see the text discussion below and n. 22.

17. Levites are "priests-in-training" and function as assistants to the officiating Priest in CHSI liturgical gatherings. According to Brother Foxe the typical training period lasts three to four years.

18. The lion is a significant symbol for Rastafarians for a variety of reasons: It is one of Haile Selassie's official titles, "Conquering Lion of the Tribe of Judah"; it is found on the Ethiopian flag; and it is said that dreadlocks resemble the mane of the lion. The regal character of the lion and its association with royalty also makes this an apt symbol for a movement that aims to restore African peoples to their ancient glory. Among Foxe's followers, however, there is another distinct meaning associated with LION as an acro-

nym for "Liberty in Our Nation"—referring to the necessity of liberating Ethiopia and Jamaica from Babylonian captivity.

19. It is important to note that I have not found any evidence to suggest that genuine Rastafarians in New York are involved in the trafficking of crack, cocaine, or other more harmful illicit substances. The propensity of some Rastafarians to use ganja for ritual, medicinal, and casual (recreational) purposes does not typically extend to other substance use. On the contrary, Rastas are adamantly opposed to substance abuse, whether alcoholic or narcotic. Some New York Rastafarians have even recently begun speaking out against the abuse of ganja by young people (cf. Ferguson 1993; see also Rubin and Comitas 1976).

20. On the role of strictness in promoting congregational solidarity and preventing the "free rider" problem, see Laurence R. Iannaccone (1994).

21. For a recent discussion of the changing role of women within the Rastafari movement see Tricia M. Redeker (1996).

22. Rastas are fascinated with word sounds and language, and have a near cabalistic attitude toward the oral and written word. As many like to say, word sounds have power. Of all the important sounds in Rasta spoken speech, none carry more power or weight than the emphatic "I." Rastas refer to Haile Selassie I not as "the first" but as "Selassie-I [eye]." They also point out that Selassie's precoronation name, Ras Tafari (Makonnen), from which the movement gets its name, ends in a strong, emphatic "I" sound. As Owens (1976, 66–67) points out, "In a further use of this favorite and significant sound, the Rasta takes many key words and replaces their first syllable by the vowel I." Thus, important words like ancient become "I-cient," assembly "I-ssembly" praises "I-ses," continually "I-tinually," Ethiopia "I-thiopia," and so on.

23. For a discussion of the role of the Bible in Jamaican Rastafari, see Laurence A. Breiner (1985–86).

24. For a review of some of the print, electronic media, and law enforcement reports on Rasta in North America, see Randal L. Hepner (1998).

REFERENCES

Ammerman, Nancy. 1987. *Bible Believers: Fundamentalists in the Modern World.* New Brunswick, N.J.: Rutgers University Press.

Barrett, Leonard. 1977. *The Rastafarians: Sounds of Cultural Dissonance.* Boston: Beacon Press.

Bilby, Kenneth, and Elliot Leib. 1986. "Kumina, the Howellite Church, and the Emergence of Rastafarian Traditional Music in Jamaica." *Jamaica Journal* 19 (August–October): 22–28.

Brake, Mike. 1980. *The Sociology of Youth Culture and Youth Subcultures.* London: Routledge & Kegan Paul.

Breiner, Laurence A. 1985–86. "The English Bible in Jamaican Rastafarianism." *The Journal of Religious Thought* 43 (2): 30–43.

"A Brief History of the Imperial Ethiopian World Federation, Inc." 1987. *Imperial Chronicle.* 1 (1): 6–7.

Campbell, Horace. 1987. *Rasta and Resistance: From Marcus Garvey to Walter Rodney.* Trenton, N.J.: Africa World Press.

Casanova, José. 1994. "Protestant Fundamentalism—Catholic Traditionalism and Conservatism." *Catholic HistoricalReview* 80 (1): 102–110.

Cashmore, Ernest. 1979. *Rastaman: The Rastafarian Movement in England.* London: George Allen & Unwin.

Cassidy, Frederic G. 1961. *Jamaica Talk: Three Hundred Years of the English Language in Jamaica.* London: Macmillan.

Chevannes, Barry. 1976. "The Repairer of the Breach: Reverend Claudius Henry and Jamaican Society." Pp. 262–289 in *Ethnicity in the Americas,* edited by Frances Henry. The Hauge: Mouton.

————. 1981. "The Rastafari and the Urban Youth." Pp. 392–422 in *Perspectives on Jamaica in the Seventies,* edited by Carl Stone and Affrey Brown. Kingston: Jamaica Publishing House.

————. 1994. *Rastafari: Roots and Ideology.* Syracuse: Syracuse University Press.

"Church of Haile Selassie I [CHSI] Document." 1994. No. 1, August 10. Pamphlet.

Clarke, John Henry. 1974. *Marcus Garvey and the Vision of Africa.* New York: Vintage Books, Random House.

Cronen, E. D. 1968. *Black Moses: The Story of Marcus Garvey and the Universal Negro Improvement Association.* Madison: University of Wisconsin Press.

Davis, Stephan. 1985. *Bob Marley.* Garden City, N.Y.: Doubleday.

Davis, Stephan, and Peter Simon. 1977. *Reggae Bloodlines: In Search of the Music and Culture of Jamaica.* Garden City, N.Y.: Anchor Books.

Devonish, Hubert. 1986. *Language and Liberation: Creole Politics in the Caribbean.* London: Karia Press.

Ferguson, Isaac. 1993. "Blunt Posse: Why the Hip Hop Nation Is Getting High on 'The Chronic.'" *Village Voice,* June 22, 1993, pp. 34ff.

Glazier, Stephen D. 1986. "Prophecy and Ecstasy: Religion and Politics in the Caribbean." Pp. 430–448 in *Prophetic Religions and Politics,* edited by Jeffrey Hadden and Anson Shupe. New York: Paragon House.

Grey, Obika. 1991. *Radicalism and Social Change in Jamaica, 1960–1972.* Knoxville: The University of Tennessee Press.

Gunst, Laurie. 1995. *Born fi Dead: A Journey Through the Jamaican Posse Underworld.* New York: Henry Holt and Company.

Hepner, Randal L. 1998. "Chanting Down Babylon in the Belly of the Beast: The Rastafari Movement in the Metropolitan United States." In *Chanting*

Down Babylon: A Rastafari Reader, edited by Samuel Murrell et al. Philadelphia: Temple University Press.

Hill, Robert. 1983. "Leonard P. Howell and Millenarian Visions in Early Rastafari." *Jamaica Journal* 16 (1): 24–39.

Homiak, John. 1985. *The "Ancient of Days"—Seated Black Eldership, Oral Tradition, and Ritual in Rastafari Culture.* Ph.D. dissertation, Brandeis University.

———. 1987. "The Mystic Revelation of Rasta-Far-Eye: Visionary Communication in a Prophetic Movement." Pp. 220–245 in *Dreaming; Anthropological and Psychological Interpretations,* edited by Barabara Tedlock. Cambridge: Cambridge University Press.

Iannaccone, Laurence R. 1994. "Why Strict Churches Are Strong." *American Journal of Sociology* 99 (March): 1180–1211.

Jah Bones. 1985. *One Love, Rastafari: History, Doctrine, and Livity.* London: Voice of Rasta Publishing House.

Johnson, Linton Kwesi. 1976. "Jamaican Rebel Music." *Race and Class* 17 (Spring): 397–412.

Johnson-Hill, Jack A. 1995. *I-Sight: The World of Rastafari: An Interpretive Sociological Account of Rastafarian Ethics.* Metuchen, N.J.: The American Theological Library Association.

Kasinitz, Phillip. 1992. *Caribbean New York: Black Immigrants and the Politics of Race.* Ithaca: Cornell University Press.

Kitzinger, Sheila. 1966. "The Rastafari Bretheren of Jamaica." *Comparative Studies in Society and History* 9 (October): 33–39.

———. 1969. "Protest and Mysticism: The Rastafari Cult of Jamaica." *Journal for the Scientific Study of Religion* 8 (Fall): 240–262.

Lewis, Rupert. 1987. "Garvey's Significance in Jamaica's Historical Evolution." *Jamaica Journal* 20 (3): 56–65.

———. 1988. *Marcus Garvey: Anti-Colonial Champion.* Trenton, N.J.: Africa World Press.

Martin, Tony. 1987. "International Aspects of the Garvey Movement." *Jamaica Journal* 20 (30): 11–18.

McPherson, Everton. 1991. *Rastafari and Politics: Sixty Years of a Developing Cultural Ideology.* Fairfield, Jamaica: Black International Iyahbinghi Press.

Nettleford, Rex. 1970. *Mirror Mirror: Identity, Race, and Protest in Jamaica.* Kingston, Jamaica: William Collins & Sangster.

Owens, Joseph. 1976. *Dread: The Rastafarians of Jamaica.* Kingston, Jamaica: Sangster Books.

Pollard, Velma. 1994. *Dread Talk: The Language of Rastafari.* Kingston, Jamaica: Canoe Press.

Redeker, Tricia M. 1996. "Fighting Against Ism and Schism: Changing Gender Relations in the Rastafari Movement." Senior thesis, Barnard College, Columbia University.

Rubin, Vera, and Lambros Comitas. 1976. *Ganja in Jamaica: The Effects of Marijuana Use*. New York: Anchor Books.

Savishinsky, Neil. 1993. *Rastafari in the Promised Land: The Spread of a Jamaican Socio-Religious Movement and Its Music and Culture Among the Youth of Ghana and Senegambia*. Ph.D. dissertation, Columbia University.

Simpson, George E. 1954. "The Rastafari Movement in Jamaica: A Study of Race and Class Conflict." *Social Forces* 34 (October): 161–171.

———. 1955. "Political Cultism in West Kingston, Jamaica." *Social and Economic Studies* 4 (June): 133–149.

Smith, M. G., Roy Augier, and Rex Nettleford. 1960. *The Rastafari Movement in Kingston, Jamaica*. Kingston, Jamaica: Institute of Social and Economic Research.

Sutton, Constance R., and Susan Makiesky-Barrow. 1987. "Migration and West Indian Racial and Ethnic Consciousness." Pp. 92–116 in *Caribbean Life in New York City*, edited by Constance R. Sutton and Elsa Chaney. New York: Center for Migration Studies of New York.

Tafari, Ikael. 1989. "Rastafari in Transition: Cultural Confrontation and Political Change in Ethiopia and the Caribbean (1966–1986)." *Bulletin of Eastern Caribbean Affairs* 15 (March–April): 1–14.

Van Dyk, Frank Jan. 1988. "The Twelve Tribes of Israel: Rasta and the Middle Class," *West Indian Review* 62 (1–2): 1–26.

Warner, R. Stephen. 1994. "The Place of the Congregation in the Contemporary American Religious Configuration." Pp. 54–99 in *American Congregations*, vol. 2, edited by James P. Wind and James W. Lewis. Chicago: University of Chicago Press.

Waters, Anita M. 1985. *Race, Class, and Political Symbols*. New Brunswick, N.J.: Transaction Publishers.

White, Timothy. 1983. *Catch a Fire: The Life of Bob Marley*. New York: Henry Holt and Company.

Yawney, Carol. 1976. "Remnants of All Nations: Rastafarian Attitudes to Race and Nationality." Pp. 231–262 in *Ethnicity in the Americas,* edited by Frances Henry. The Hague: Mouton.

7 | Structural Adaptations in an Immigrant Muslim Congregation in New York

Rogaia Mustafa Abusharaf

The notion that religions change seems in itself almost a heresy. For what is faith but a clinging to the eternal, worship but a celebration of the permanent? Has there ever been a religion, from the Australian to the Anglican, that took its concerns as transient, its truth as perishable, its demands as conditional? Yet of course religions do change, and anyone religious or not, with any knowledge of history or sense for the ways of the world knows that they have and expects that they will. For the believer this paradox presents a range of problems not properly my concern as such. But for the student of religion it presents one, too: how comes it that an institution inherently dedicated to what is fixed in life has been such a splendid example of all that is changeful in it? Nothing, apparently, alters like the unalterable.—Clifford Geertz 1971, 56

How have immigrant Muslim peoples carried on their religious faith and traditions in the context of a predominantly Christian America? What structural changes accompany an immigrant mosque's adaptation to this doubly alien environment? This chapter explores these questions through the examination of an immigrant Muslim mosque that I call the Islamic Mission in Brooklyn, New York. The Mission, one of the oldest immigrant mosques in the United States, has experienced significant changes in its ethnic membership as well as in its organizational structure, and thus offers a unique opportunity to study how Islamic religious practices are institutionalized through a dynamic process of "selective adaptation" to the North American context. In this chapter, therefore, I focus on two significant issues: (1) ethnicization, through which the Mission has undergone a transition from a philanthropic enterprise founded by a wealthy Moroccan immigrant into a Yemeni ethnic religious institution; and (2) organizational adaptation, through which the Mission has become a congregation, having membership, a formal governance structure, a hired clergyman, and regular ethnic activities.

Since the congregation's founding in 1928, its character has been significantly transformed as a result of changing ethnic membership. Sheik Daoud Ahmed Faisal, a Moroccan immigrant, founded the Mission and opened it to Muslims of any background. Recently, though, Yemenis have become the predominant ethnic community in the congregation, and this ethnicization process has had important implications for patterns of participation and worship, notably for women, that I shall examine.

I shall also explore how a religious institution that is not typified by a "congregational" polity in its homeland has adapted itself to the United States by adopting this organizational form. The most significant structural changes in the inner workings of the Mission have been the formalization of the governance structure (the concept of membership in the mosque and the election of a board of directors) and the professionalization of the clergy. These changes, I argue, are partly adaptive changes made in response to forces in the host society.

Yet while the Muslim immigrants have adapted their religious institution to new challenges in North America, they maintain continuity with their traditional culture. This congregation has been and continues to be a vehicle through which immigrants reconstruct their communal identity in the diaspora, thus preserving and safeguarding their ethnoreligious and cultural landscapes. For all its congregants throughout the years, it has been the paradigmatic religious and cultural "home away from home."

Methodology

I first encountered the congregation in 1991 while researching the social history of Sudanese migration to the United States and Canada, but I did not focus on the Mission as a specific ethnographic site until joining the New Ethnic and Immigrant Congregations Project (NEICP) in 1994. The bulk of my fieldwork was done between the fall of 1994 and the spring of 1996. I used traditional ethnographic methods of life-history collection, participant observation, and extensive review of textual material. I also found it necessary to do multisite research in order to establish the distinctiveness and cultural particularity of the Islamic Mission. Most of my visits took place on Fridays, when the *jumaa* (congregational prayer) is held. I paid other visits on Sundays and weekdays and at different times of the day to enable me to observe additional events as well as regular weekday activities. As a result, I witnessed conversion ceremonies with five people during an evening prayer, and I was present at a funeral service.

Several long-time Sudanese members of the congregation (Babikir, Osman, and Eissa) were my initial key contacts. I had established rapport with them during my earlier research. Thus, I experienced little of the initial mistrust, hostility, and suspicion that is so common in ethnographic research. My interviewees introduced me to other influential figures in the body of the congregation, notably the imam, Haj Mukhtar Al Tantawi,[1] and a Yemeni business owner, Haj Ali, who serves on the Mission's board of directors as its treasurer. To protect the privacy of these individuals, I have changed all personal names (except that of the founder, Sheik Daoud, a public figure), drawing from a pool of common Arabic Muslim names. All quotations from interviewees represent my translations from Arabic.

I informed the imam about my plans to study the history of the Mission as part of the NEICP, and from then on he (and other members) referred to me as the *dactora* (doctor), indicating their appreciation of my position and my task. I made it clear that my role was to construct a history of the Mission as well as to explore what the Mission has meant for its members throughout the years. Most of my encounters with Mission members were supportive and helpful.

One member expressed his admiration for the project in these words: "God has given you an excellent opportunity to do good work on the masjid [mosque]. I think it is very important that you do this, and we will be very interested in your work." The imam spared no effort to provide much needed information during the nearly two years of my frequent and lengthy visits to the congregation. He also made it possible for me to interview members for whom my female gender could have caused considerable discomfort in a predominantly male congregation.

My identity as an immigrant Sudanese Muslim female provided multiple avenues for ethnographic insight. As a Muslim, I was able to participate in ways that a non-Muslim obviously could not (for example, attending prayer). However, as a female researcher, I realized that there were limitations to my ability to gather data in a male-dominated congregation. For example, I could not gather data from the main sanctuary when the men were present. I was able to listen to the sermon (*khutba*) as well as to any announcements or commentaries originating in the main male-occupied sanctuary, but only from a remote-speaker-equipped study room on the third floor, and I was aware that listening is only one part of observing. In this respect the imam and my informants were especially helpful in dealing with my gender-related data-gathering difficulties. The absence of other women in the mosque's service prompted me to explore patterns of gender participation. I interviewed several women—three Yemenis (Thahaba, Naseera, and Um Saeed), a Sudanese (Nafisa), and an Afro-Caribbean (Kulthoom). Ultimately, the Mission proved to be a rich and useful site for the exploration of the meaning of congregational experience for Muslims in North America. The Mission today remains a vital cultural expression of the migrants' difficult mix of a desire to achieve legitimacy in their new location while maintaining the cultural and religious principles from their societies of origin.

The Congregation in Islamic Theology

Before considering the evolution of the Mission as an ethnic religious institution, I begin by discussing the place of the congregation in Islamic theology. The first Muslim congregation was found in the Kaaba (sacred tabernacle) in the city of Mecca in Saudi Arabia known as *Elharam Elsherief* (The Sanctified Tabernacle). The centerpiece of the Kaaba is a place for retreat, an embodiment of universalistic Muslim ideals reinforcing communal existence and solidarity among Muslims, especially during the annual pilgrimage rites.[2] Thus, congregations in Islamic tradition appear to serve multiple roles that include both spiritual as well as communal dimensions. These roles, as well as the universalistic claims of Islam, are apparent in the following Qur'anic verse (Sura 2: 125):

> *Remember We made the House, a place of assembly for humankind, and a Refuge of Safety: [So] take the Station of Abraham as a place of Prayer: We covenanted with Abraham and Ismail: that they should sanctify My House for those who compass it round, or use it as a retreat, or bow in prostration therein.*

Throughout Islamic history the *jami* (congregation) has assumed considerable significance for Muslims' religious practice as well as their social worlds. Mosques are established by believers who wish not only to worship the One God but also to seek the warmth, exhilaration, and gratification of the community of fellow Muslims with similar persuasions and worldviews. According to Mona Abul Fadl (1991, 27), "for Muslims communal prayer, *salat el jumaa,* remains more than an act of devotion in a formal place of worshiping, but it is an act that transcends the individual to the community and crosses the bounds of space and time, thus nourishing and fortifying the sense of community and identity."

Gathering in a congregational setting also corresponds to the highly valued Islamic universalistic ideals of the *Ummah,* "the community of faith." The *Ummah* denotes that "purposeful entity, composed of a group or a *jamma* whose members, by virtue of a common faith, way of life and a sense of destiny, have been forged in a common historical consciousness. Thus they are endowed with the awareness of a common identity, allegiance and purpose" (Abul Fadl 1991, 58).

The neighborhood mosque is the religious institution where the five daily prayers are said: *salat elsubh* (morning prayer), *salat elthuhr* (noon prayer), *salat alasr* (afternoon prayer), *salat el maghrib* (sunset prayer), and *salat elishaa* (evening prayer).[3] The main congregational service is held on Friday at noontime, preceded by a *khutba* (sermon). Mosques in Muslim societies derive most of their support from their local community, although most of them are built and maintained structurally by the national government. Mosques have neither a professional ministry nor an official membership; Muslims can worship at any *masjid* they choose. In fact, in Muslim ecclesiology one is not a member of the mosque but rather a "serviteur" of God (see Murphy 1994, 19). Membership in a congregation is exemplified by one's service to God regardless of one's ethnicity, gender, or class, for in the mosque "all marks of distinction that imply a sense of exclusivity or an ascribed privilege are dissolved" (Abul Fadl 1991, 59). With this understanding of the multiple roles the congregation plays in Islamic theology and Muslim social life, I turn now to explore the social history of the Mission.

From Multiethnic Mission to Ethnic Congregation

The Islamic Mission is situated in a residential Brooklyn neighborhood near the street where the bulk of Muslim immigrant-owned businesses are located. Its founder, Sheik Daoud Ahmed Faisal, was born in 1891 in Morocco, was educated in Grenada, and in 1913 immigrated to the United States, where he founded the *masjid* in 1928 (Farrant 1965). From its original location at 128th Street and Lenox Avenue in Harlem, the *masjid* moved to Brooklyn Heights in 1935. Sheik Daoud was a member of a wealthy family who owned gold mines in Morocco, and so he enjoyed an income that allowed him to carry out the duties of his *masjid*. An excerpt from a letter he wrote to the American Consul General in Aden on September 23, 1952, to sponsor a Yemeni Arab who wished to immigrate to the United States, testifies to his financial status:

> *Your Excellency; . . . I am Sheik Daoud Ahmed Faisal, spiritual head of the Islamic Mission of America for the propagation of Islam in the United States. . . . I have property value over $75000.00 dollars [sic] in the United States of America from which my income derives and said income is spent exclusively for the benefit of my Muslim brothers and sisters whom I serve by the leave of Allah, my Lord. I have just completed the extension to our mission house at a cost of over $23000.00 dollars [sic] especially for the accommodation of our ever growing Muslim community.*

The Mission was thus Sheik Daoud's philanthropic offering to the Muslims of New York.

The founding of the Islamic Mission marked the birth of an African Muslim religious body in North America. It also signified Sheik Daoud's efforts to consolidate the Islamic faith in diaspora by keeping alive the community's understanding of the practices of the Sunni branch of Islam upon which his congregation was based. For Sheik Daoud, the Mission not only represented a means of reinventing the homeland but also proved instrumental in legitimizing Islam in the American context. Geertz (1971, 3) argues that "religion may be a stone thrown into the world; but it must be a palpable stone and someone must throw it"; this mosque clearly represented such a "palpable stone."

Mosques in Muslim societies reinforce not only religiosity, or God consciousness, but also community consciousness. Thus, the founding of the Mission was an effective way for Sheik Daoud to reimagine the communal life of the homeland. As Conrad Arensberg argues:

> *To reconstitute a communal life, to live together as an ethnic group, the immigrants have built in exact and revealing terms the key institutions of their native land and its ancestral but ever-changing social order. Culture is a way of life, a way of thinking and feeling, a way grounded in highly specific institutions of distinctive social pattern, articulation, and relationships. To reconstitute one's way of life is to build, reinvent such specific institutions. (quoted in Klass 1961, xiii)*

Indisputably, Sheik Daoud was the central figure in this congregation. He was benefactor, spiritual leader, imam, and zealous missionary. As the mosque's imam, he had an expanded role from that of imams at home. This in itself represented an adaptation to the new challenges of the American context. For example, besides leading the congregation in prayer (as an imam in a Muslim country would have done), he presided at every worship service, wrote marriage contracts and gave divorce certificates, conducted funeral services, and participated in conversions.

The conversion process is a window into the cultural significance of the Mission in its founding period. According to a Brooklyn newspaper account (Farrant 1965), a new birth certificate was issued for each convert, who in turn had "to petition the mosque for 'reclamation' of the names of his slave ancestors, as they were known before enslavement." Because his congregation was initially founded in Harlem, Daoud enjoyed the benefits of reaching out to a sizable African American and Afro-Caribbean population whose memory of Islam was revived in North America after the advent of missionaries from the Islamic Ahmadiyyah sect (Turner 1986).[4] For people of African descent, Daoud's mosque represented an "African space" where commemoration of "authentic" Islamic practices was celebrated. For those many former slaves with Muslim roots, the congregation told "a powerful story about continuities between the present and a past" of African peoples in the Americas (Scott 1991, 267).

In his discussion of religions of the African peoples in the Americas, Joseph Murphy (1994, 186) introduces the concept of "diasporan spirituality" to show their orientation to Africa. He also discusses how in the context of the religious experience of people of African descent,

> the boundaries of space and time constructed by the ceremony [of worship] condense the experience of the community into a limited number of symbols so that the people can show themselves their part in the cosmic drama of the African people. In the construction of the space of the ceremony and in the limited time bounded by the ceremony's opening and closing, the people may enter an African space and time.

In this context Islam is indeed a "diasporan spirituality" that allows African Americans to experience a connection between Islam and the African continent. Murphy's concept of diasporan spirituality helps us understand the meaning of the mosque for African and African American people.

It is worth reiterating that Sheik Daoud was a zealous missionary. His efforts included tours to the Caribbean at a time when many Caribbean nations were under colonial occupation. After one such tour, he wrote to Sheik Hamff Aziz of Princetown, Trinidad, on May 7, 1951, expressing his satisfaction: "I am quite pleased that my humble effort in propagating the faith of Islam to humanity has found favor with such noble minds as yours and those who found satisfaction and guidance in it."

Beside the significant Afro-Caribbean and African American constituency in the Mission, many Arabs and African immigrants had also found "welcome in Boro [Brooklyn]," as was reported in the *Brooklyn Eagle* (Toomey 1951, 10). According to this account, "when Arabic sailors dock in Brooklyn, many of them head immediately for the Islamic Mission of America, 143 State Street." Among those sailors were Sudanese merchant marines known as the "Bahara," who joined the Mission in the 1940s. (*Bahara* is the Arabic word for "seamen," and it is often used by my Sudanese contacts in the Mission to refer to themselves.) The Bahara worked in various international naval companies (for example, the British War Ministry), arriving in American ports during World War II, when they were recruited to join the U.S. Navy, which was greatly in need of their services. Because of this service, they were quickly granted American citizenship, and many settled in New York after the war.

The Bahara, who have been worshiping at the Mission for decades, represent a most unusual immigrant community. Not only are they pioneers of Sudanese migration to North America, they moved at a time when any sort of Sudanese out-migration was relatively unknown. Also, because of their ethnolinguistic makeup as Dongulawis (from Dongula in the Sudan), they managed to reproduce in revealing ways the community they left behind. Within Daoud's mosque, they represented a distinct community by virtue of their ethnicity, their historical experience as World War II servicemen, and their place of origin. Because of their quick access to the benefits of citizenship, as well as their relatively high incomes, the Bahara encountered fewer social problems than other immigrants to the United States. However, in their state of diaspora, they did experience a sociocultural and religious isolation that prompted them to congregate with each other and with other Muslims.

Oscar Handlin (1973, 105–106) has suggested that "the more thorough the separation from the other aspects of the old life, the greater was the hold of the religion that alone survived the transfer. Struggling against heavy odds to save something of the old ways, the immigrants directed into their faith the whole weight of their longing to be connected with the past." However, as did the majority of immigrants in

North America, the Bahara worked to remake their past in an unfamiliar surrounding. They found the ritual observance an appropriate place to start regaining the life they had once extolled back home, as Osman and other members have indicated to me. Indeed, as Earle H. Waugh (1991, xiii) argues, "religious ritual has an important role in strengthening this sociocultural identity; conversely, shared identity is a nurturing soil for the cultivation of religious observances." Even from the outset, however, the varied interplay between the Bahara and the larger North American host society influenced their congregational experience.

Both Eissa and Osman explained that the Mission consolidated their social relations with other Muslims in New York. They agree with the newspaper accounts that report that, since its founding until the mid-1980s, the Mission attracted a diverse Muslim constituency for *jumaa* as well as during *Eid elfitr* (small Ramadan feast) and *Eid eladha* (the big feast following the pilgrimage to Mecca). It does not come as a surprise that many Muslims with marked ethnolinguistic differentiations would find refuge in the Mission, given Sheik Daoud's leadership, effective organization, and generosity.

Babikir, another long-time member, explained the attraction of the mosque for the Bahara in this way:

> When we came to Brooklyn we were young men, we did not have families yet. Only a couple of us were married, and they brought their wives years after our settlement. We had excellent relations with each other because all of us are Dongulawis. We lived in the same apartment building, we ate, prayed, and socialized with each other. But life was not as it used to be, and we missed our extended families, friends, and neighbors in the Sudan. We belonged to a Navy Servicemen's Union here in the United States. Through some black American friends, we were introduced to Haj Daoud. Haj Daoud was extremely fond of Sudanese because he knew Satti Majid, a Sudanese marine who came before us. These blacks told us about Majid's efforts with the black community in Harlem. He converted many people, and he was highly respected by many people. We did not have a formal place to pray and to meet with other Muslims. Very few Muslims were in New York then. The mosque helped us in the ghorba [the state of being away from home] and helped us get to know other Muslim people.

The symbolism attached to the Mission and the fact that it provided a space where Islamic ideals were reinforced are also clear from Eissa's account:

> *Black Americans as well as Caribbeans were always very enthusiastic about worshiping in it. Blacks who told us about Satti Majid's role in converting many black people told us that he emphasized Islamic ideals of equality and that there is no color line in Islam, that everybody is equal in the eyes of God. This was very appealing to black people, and that is why they felt very comfortable in coming with us to the Mission.*

I was told that, in addition to African Americans and other Muslims in Brooklyn, women also used to worship at the Mission. As Kulthoom, an Afro-Caribbean member, indicated:

> *We used to go to the Mission everyday for the* ishaa *[evening] prayer and on Fridays. Mother Khadija, Haj Daoud's wife, was also there all the time. A lot of women—Sudanese, Caribbean, and black Americans—all came here. We used to have also a religious discussion group. We were very happy to be part of the Mission. But now, there is not enough room for women. We go to other mosques now.*

Under Sheik Daoud, the Mission provided its male and female constituency with a means for seeking legitimacy by normalizing Muslim religious practices in the United States. As Osman explains:

> *When the Mission was founded very few Arab Muslims lived in Brooklyn. There were some Pakistanis and Indians, but American people were not familiar with Islam because of the small number. But when the mosque was built, people started to notice. Neighbors became aware of our practices especially during the* jumaa. *Little by little, they became used to the idea of a mosque in their neighborhood. Now there are even more mosques established by both immigrants and nonimmigrants. I think that people in Brooklyn now do not look at these mosques as alien institutions anymore.*

As Osman's account makes clear, the Mission has played a significant role in "reducing the distance" between immigrants and their hosts. This narrative corroborates Thomas Sowell's (1996, 48) argument that "not all cultural interaction resulting from migrations are one way. Just as the larger society surrounding the immigrants may influence their culture, so can the immigrant culture affect the larger society."

In its early years the Mission was a philanthropic offering of a wealthy, religiously gifted Moroccan, Sheik Daoud, who conducted affairs at the Mission in accordance with the Islamic principles that he recognized. In a spirit of noblesse oblige, he made it available to all the Muslims of Brooklyn, an originally small number that came to include African Americans, Afro-Caribbeans, and Sudanese. For years after its founding, the Mission constituency was thus largely multiethnic, both male and female, but since the 1980s, there has been a marked decline in this character. Some previous constituencies have left, and they have been replaced by others.

Many Sudanese Bahara who worshiped in the mosque for four decades have moved away. Some repatriated to Sudan, and some relocated to other, warmer regions of the United States. Currently only three Bahara still live in Brooklyn and pray at the Mission. The African American constituency has also declined. Lawrence Mamiya (1995) indicates that many left to establish the Darul Islam movement (the House of Islam) and their own mosque. In a personal communication in 1996, Mamiya elaborated:

> In regards to the split by the Darul Islam movement, some of the African Americans who were members of the mosque felt that Sheik Daoud and the masjid as a whole were not doing enough outreach work with the black community, who constituted the majority population in that part of Brooklyn. This was in the late 1960s and early 1970s, when the black power and black consciousness movement was in full swing in the United States. So the African American members were affected by those ideas, and they decided that they could form their own masjid (the Yasin Masjid) and do their work in the black community.

Although the decline of the African American constituency did occur when Sheik Daoud was alive, several contacts indicated that some of those who continued to worship at the Mission now go also to Masjid el Taqwa in Brooklyn under the leadership of Imam Siraj Wahaj, an African American. (Daoud died in the mid-1980s. The exact date is unknown.)

Yemenis now constitute the Mission's predominant ethnic group, with nearly two hundred members, according to the chair of the board of directors. Haj Ali observes:

> Many people in this neighborhood know that the Mission is jami Yemeni [a Yemeni congregation]. Apart from Friday service, the mosque is constantly attended by Yemenis. Now we have idara [administration] run by Yemenis. They work very hard to make sure that everything here is taken care of.

Another member indicates:

> It is true that a lot of people come to worship at the Mission, but the majority are Yemenis. Brooklyn is a main area of concentration for Yemeni people. Usually these people do everything together. Be-

cause there is a very large number [of Yemenis] in Brooklyn now, al-
most all of them come to the Mission. . . . They are also in the
board of directors who run the mosque.

The death of Sheik Daoud, the out-migration of Sudanese Bahara,
and the departure of African Americans, as well as the influx of Yemenis into Brooklyn over the last twenty years, have all combined to
change the character of the mosque dramatically in patterns of worship, organizational structure, and gender and ethnic participation.
The Mission has become a Yemeni congregation, governed and regu-
lated by the Yemeni ethos, codes of behavior, and cultural sensibilities.
Of course, as a mosque, the Mission is officially open to the Muslim
public, and this matters for Friday *jumaa,* when Muslim men from all
backgrounds come to prayer. But the rest of the week—most visibly
in the predominance of Yemenis during daily evening prayer—and for
the determination of its future, the Mission now is an ethnic,
specifically a Yemeni, cultural space.

Adherence to a common religion does not guarantee unity. Indeed,
as Richard Weekes (1984, xxvii) argues, "nowhere is the division within
Muslim society more apparent than in the understanding and practice
of religion." Similarly, Geertz (1971, 14) writes that:

> *religious faith, even when it is fed from a common source, is as much
> a particularizing force as a generalizing one and indeed whatever uni-
> versality a given religious tradition manages to attain arises from its
> ability to engage a widening set of individual, even idiosyncratic con-
> ceptions of life, and yet somehow sustain and elaborate them all.*

And Wade Clark Roof (1993, 204), reflecting more on Christians than
on Muslims, writes about local religious communities:

> *Every congregation has its own culture—a set of symbols, values
> and meanings that distinguishes it from others. Aside from the more
> obvious factors that have a bearing, such as religious background,
> polity, and social context, congregations differ in the stories they tell
> about life. They are "thick gatherings," each with its own rich idiom
> and narrative combining elements of world view, ethos, plot, and
> identity. Mood, atmosphere, tone, sight, tastes, and smell are all in-
> volved as is a sense of life's unfolding drama—from where and to
> where does time march. Each congregation has its own "style," its
> own sets of encoded meanings about sacred realities.*

The current congregational membership of the Mission relies on ethnic
affiliation, and in the process it therefore reinforces the majority of its
members' self-awareness as Yemenis.

The Mission as a Yemeni Congregation, 1985 to the Present

Most Yemeni immigrants were sailors who decided to stay permanently in port cities like Detroit and New York and who secured employment in Arab-owned businesses in Brooklyn and elsewhere. They have become a closely knit ethnolinguistic community that has found a cultural and religious home in the Mission. Since the mid-1980s they have become the majority in the congregation and have assumed the leadership of the Mission. This resulted in replacing many of the practices prevalent during the life of Sheik Daoud. The transition from a multiethnic congregation to one with Yemeni predominance heightened the awareness among worshipers of ethnic and gender boundaries within the congregation.

Several factors account for the transformations that took place in the Mission as a result of the changing ethnic fellowship. First, Yemenis are racially and ethnically homogeneous (Held 1989). This ethnic homogeneity has enabled the Yemenis in diaspora to preserve their identity as an ethnic community rather than a religious one. This is understandable, since ethnolinguistic differentiations that characterize other communities do not exist among Yemenis. In fact Yemenis have little interaction with non-Yemenis, and as Carla Makhlouf (1979, 14) points out, "for political, economic and religious reasons, Yemen has been historically a most isolated society." Second, although it is true that Yemenis share the fundamental beliefs of other Sunni Muslims, including the same commemorations related to their faith and the same body of duties that they should perform, they practice them differently and give them different emphasis.

The Islamic Mission now largely reflects Yemeni religious traditions and conceptions of the world, traditions and conceptions that differ from the former practices of Sheik Daoud and his congregation. As Yemenis assumed the leadership of the Mission, they reconfigured the congregation as a more ethnically homogeneous body and, in particular, discouraged the participation of women in worship.

Women and the Mission

According to long-time members of the congregation, women used to worship in the Mission just as men did. In the "old days," women and men prayed in the main area, which was divided by a partition of "thick draperies" (Farrant 1965), similar to the arrangement found in other mosques. Women were active participants in Halaqa, a religious study group run by Mother Khadija, Sheik Daoud's wife.

This has changed in recent times: the very few women who do come to Friday prayer are accommodated in the small study room in the imam's suite. Interviews with my five women contacts, all of whose spouses are members of the Mission, indicate that women do not participate in the congregation. A similar pattern is reported in Barbara Aswad's (1991) study of Yemeni women in Dearborn, Michigan; at the mosque there, considered by women and men alike to be a male congregation, women are excluded.

Therefore, while Yemenis have chosen to adapt in certain ways to American patterns, the position of Yemeni women in the United States with respect to the strict sexual segregation remains the same as in their society of origin. Thus Yemeni cultural and religious ideals are embedded in their practices in the Mission. Elements of Yemeni traditional culture have been well identified by Makhlouf (1979, 21) in her study *Changing Veils: Women and Modernization in North Yemen,* where she observes that "all women [in North Yemen] led similar lives, characterized by a domestic orientation and a strict segregation of male and female spheres of action." Thus, socially constructed boundaries are not necessarily revisited as a result of migration, and in the case of the Yemenis, immigration tends to reorient individuals—especially many older women—toward their traditional culture and lifestyle. Umm Saeed, a fifty-year-old Yemeni woman, stated the following:

> You see, Yemeni women in general will never go to a mosque. They think that only men should go to mosques even during the jumaa and the Eid. They prefer to say their prayers at home. Most of Yemeni women also do not work outside the home. Just like at home [Yemen], very few women work. It is the same thing here: they only take care of khidmat elmanzil [household work].

Thahaba and Naseera (both Yemeni women over the age of sixty) described the Mission as a "men's mosque." Both women indicated that they do not usually attend the Mission, but their husbands and sons are members. Naseera emphasized that

> most Yemeni women pray at home. They never go to the mosque—especially the Mission—because they know that the praying area is filled with men. Even during Eid celebration we don't go. Especially for young Yemeni women who have families, it is difficult. But we know that in other mosques women—Egyptians, Palestinians, and Indians—they all like to go.

To corroborate this perception that the exclusion of women is attributable more to Yemeni culture than to Muslim religion, I conducted supplementary interviews with a member of the Islamic Center of Connecticut (known as Masjid el Madina) as well as with another woman in El Takwa mosque in Brooklyn. In both mosques women not only come to worship and socialize but are seen as important custodians of traditions. They are recognized as transmitters of cultural knowledge to the future generations because of their service as teachers of language and religion. For example, at the Islamic Center of Connecticut the majority of teachers are women. Women also assume responsibilities on the board of directors. Some contacts even claimed that women are trying to influence the process that will result in the appointment of the next imam. The population of this mosque contains a diversity of ethnic groups. The largest are Somalis and Indo-Pakistanis, but smaller numbers of Egyptians, Palestinians, Afghans, and African Americans belong. Sumaya, an Egyptian pharmacist, explained the significant role of women in the Connecticut mosque:

> Women play a very important role in the masjid and assume a lot of responsibilities. I would like to emphasize that 80 percent of the mosque activities are carried out by women. Also most of the Sunday religious classes are taught by women. We conduct workshops and seminars to discuss Islamic feminist issues. We have women's Friday halaqa [religious discussion], and we sponsor community monthly dinners. Women are also responsible for finances, fund-raising activities, and the lunch program for Sunday school. Nowadays we are trying to raise funds to expand the parking lot. Our fund-raising events and workshops are very well attended despite the fact that most of us work full-time elsewhere. Right now we are working on revising the mosque's constitution to formalize the role of women, and so far members of the board are very receptive, because they are aware of the vital role that women play in the functioning of the masjid.

A similar situation exists in El Takwa, an African American congregation in Brooklyn. Women are active in the mosque, which in turn plays a pivotal role in their social as well as religious lives.

The differences in gender participation between these mosques and the Islamic Mission appears to be due to Yemeni cultural practices rather than to a religious mandate. In comparison, Sheik Daoud and his African American and Sudanese congregants originated from societies in which "social segregation of males and females is not nearly so rigorously practiced as in many traditional Arab settings" (see Fernea 1961, 154). Women in Islamic countries have participated in the shaping of their faith, as Saddeka Arebi (1994, 12) notes:

> *Historical developments of Islam testify to the actual participation of women in shaping religion through their leadership of major political revolts, such as the one led by Aisha, the wife of the Prophet in the year 656 A.C., which shaped Islam's political and spiritual future in the most fundamental ways.*

Moreover, Mecca has been the host for women and men during *hajj* and *omra*[5] rituals for centuries. The Mission was clearly a more gender-inclusive place during the long leadership of Sheik Daoud.

It should be noted that, while Yemeni women are aware that other congregations in New York have active female members, they do not associate their own absence with a subordinated or inferior position. Indeed, as Makhlouf (1979, 25) has argued, "in this case where there exists a large amount of sex segregation, women are given a separate sphere over which men have little control and which may constitute a source of support and even power." Makhlouf (1979, 22) describes one of the important female rituals that seems to empower women, the *tafrita,* or "afternoon visit," in which they visit each others' homes to chat, listen to music, and chew *qat* (a substance similar to tobacco). It is not surprising to find similar wide-ranging networks of Yemeni women in New York, through which women develop and consolidate their own alternative congregations. These networks not only give Yemeni women in diaspora an opportunity to congregate with each other but indeed have helped eliminate any form of cultural isolation that faces migrant peoples.

Organizational Adaptation

Examination of the Mission congregation's adaptation to its sociopolitical context provides an understanding of how religious beliefs can be "prismatic"—acting like lenses that generate and reflect influences in both the migrants' and hosts' contexts. The Mission has adapted Islam to its North American environment, but it has not been assimilated into it. The distinction is important. Anthony Richmond (1974, 194) defines adaptation as "the mutual interaction of individuals and collectivities and their responses to particular social and physical environments," whereas assimilation is characterized by "the linear progression of immigrant cultures toward a dominant American national character" (McLaughlin 1992, 6). Indeed, regardless of religious affiliation, immigrants from many places have had to adopt already established organizational forms that have helped them negotiate the transition from their socially marginal position as newcomers to a position of full inclusion in their new country while retaining important cultural practices from their old ones. One way immigrants manage this transition from a position of insularity to one of participation is by selectively adapting structural elements of local religious organizations to fit the needs of their immigrant religious institutions.

Adaptive strategies are effective mechanisms for gaining legitimacy in the host society. They may also be necessary. In fact, transplanting key institutions of the homeland into a new society without making necessary modifications has proved to be an exasperatingly arduous task (Handlin 1973). Muslims' realization of this predicament reinforced their capacity to respond to the new challenges and influences of the religious "open market system" in the United States (see Warner 1993b, 1050). My ethnographic data on the Islamic Mission experience demonstrate that Islamic religious institutions are structurally flexible and internally adaptive. The remaking of the Mission congregation testifies to its adaptation to the new demands of the host environment.

The Mission has made significant changes to common mosque practices in order to adapt to the North American environment. By far the most significant of these has been to accept a professionalized clergy in the form of a hired imam. Other changes include developing a sense of membership in the mosque, creating Sunday events such as Sunday school, and adopting nonprofit organizational structure in order to have a body to own and govern the mosque.

Both internal flexibility and external pressures influence the Mission's structural adaptation. The integrative, accommodative, and adaptive potential of Islam is neither a foreign nor a novel phenomenon. A common Arabic expression often emphasized by the laity is *al Islam salih likul zaman wa makan* (Islam is flexible in time and space). Muslim social scientists argue that Islam can adapt both in its theories and in its practice. Abul Fadl (1988, 172–173) has argued that

> the only paradigm of "knowing" compatible with the requisites of all "being" would appear to be one that could accommodate the elements of the intellect with those of the rational and the empirical modes of knowing. Historically, the Islamic paradigm of knowledge has proven congenial to the different modes of knowing. The legacy of the Birunis, Ibn al Haythams, al Ghazzalis, Ibn Rushds, Rhazis, and Suhrawardis [Muslim theologians] is a monument to this capacity to integrate and accommodate the diverse modes or traditions within what is more of a synthetic rather than a syncretist whole.

In his account of the adaptation experience of Muslims in the United States and Canada, Waugh (1991, 72–73) has maintained that three interconnected factors help Muslims adapt their traditions in a Judeo-Christian environment. First, North Americans rate high in religiosity. Thus, "Muslims do not confront the prospects of an environment hostile to matters of faith." Second, Islam shares an Abrahamic origin with the Christian and Jewish faiths, which helps familiarize Muslims with North American religious ideologies. Finally, the emphasis on individual achievement in the North American society does not depend on religious affiliation. Muslims can seek to succeed socially and financially and thus conform to important social mores without abandoning or even mentioning their faith.

Immigrants appear to have altered the organizational structure of the Mission in several significant ways. Immigrants view these changes not only as indispensable measures but also as a necessary precondition for the establishment of an Islamic foothold in the United States.

The Islamic Mission today has a very different governance structure from the one it had at its founding in 1928. From its founding until his death, Sheik Daoud essentially *was* the organization as the owner of the mosque and the director of its operations. That has changed. General elections for an eight-member board of directors take place every three years, and the board of directors is in charge of all decisions pertaining to Mission affairs, including finances, religious instruction, and the hiring of the imam. The election of the board of directors demonstrates how membership is now defined in the Mission. Haj Ali described it as follows:

> Only contributing members to the masjid are permitted to vote on who will be elected for the board of directors, who in turn are nominated and seconded for a final vote. Records are kept with the names of those contributing members, who are usually contacted for the general elections of the board.

Although the concept of membership is alien to *masjids* in Muslim countries, this immigrant mosque has had to adapt some notion of membership in order to conduct its affairs, and the notion they have adopted is defined by financial contribution.

The mission's most conspicuous adaptive strategy has been the creation of a professional Muslim ministry. Mosques in Muslim societies are led in a fundamentally different way from those in the United States, as Waugh (1994, 572) explains:

> Traditionally, Muslims have placed less stress on the local religious institution as a mechanism of identity than have their Christian counterparts. In Muslim countries, the local mosque might well be no

more than a convenient place to pray with one's neighbors; one certainly never becomes a member *of that mosque. One of the most crucial reasons for this is doctrinal: Islam accepts no mediating or authoritative role for a religious institution between Allah and the believer. Thus* there is no role for an official priesthood in Islam, no need for an institutional body within which those officials may act on behalf of the believers, and no need for membership. *[emphasis added]*

In Islamic countries, then, there is no professional minister in each mosque. Muslims instead choose their leadership from among themselves. This organizational practice originates in Islamic theology, which not only does not recognize the role of intercessors between God and the believer but also emphasizes that an individual or a group should neither stand above others nor claim the privilege of special mission not open to others (Abul Fadl 1991). Therefore, in prayers—the supreme act of worship in the congregation—one prays directly to God without intermediaries, and there is no need for an officially recognized cleric (Weekes 1984). Imams therefore are not a professional class of religious leaders, but are instead local leaders recognized for their extensive knowledge of the holy book, the Qur'an, and the *Hadith* (sayings of the Prophet). The imam's duties are usually confined to leading congregational prayers, which is done on a strictly voluntary, unpaid basis. For those who consider themselves fortunate enough to earn the trust of their community by serving as imams, the role is a source of honor, gratitude, and veneration.

Haj Hassan, a Sudanese national who has served as imam in a neighborhood mosque in Khartoum, Sudan, explains the traditional position of an imam in a Muslim country:

> *The mosque has always been a big part of Muslims' religious and social activity. The imam is usually a volunteer. Especially because the majority of mosques are built by local financial assistance of local communities and philanthropists, the imams are chosen from the same communities. Imams volunteer to lead prayers, deliver sermons during Friday, or [lead] Eid prayers. They are usually highly honorable and respected people who do not expect any financial gains in return to their religious service. They expect only reward in heaven.*

In the United States, most immigrant congregation members work long hours to make ends meet, and thus they have little time to assume the responsibility of being a volunteer imam. These immigrant work realities necessitated the establishment of a professional Muslim clergy "to help promote the spiritual principles of Islam, perpetuate faith and foster better understanding between the Muslim community and people of other religious faiths." The fact that this statement appeared in the *Masjid News,* the Mission's monthly newsletter, in October 1995 demonstrates an attempt to justify, through the printed word and perhaps in other domains, the emergence of professional imamhood. Further, in the United States now, imams, like their Christian and Jewish counterparts, are expected to be educated professionals. Thus, the imam is recruited from outside the congregation. Haj Tantawi, the imam who left the Mission in 1996, was a professor of religion in Egypt, and the newly selected one, a Yemeni, has a university degree in business administration. When I asked a member to explain why the former imam was an Egyptian and not a Yemeni, he answered, "Egyptian imams are very learned in Islam. Of course to have a knowledgeable imam is very important here, because they do a lot of things. But also the Yemenis know that the Azhar Seminary [in Egypt, where the Mission's imam had taught,] is the best in the world for Islamic studies. They wanted to bring someone [in] who knows what he is doing." The imam of the Mission is elected, formally appointed, and fully remunerated by the Mission's board of directors, a practice that would be virtually unthinkable in a Muslim country.

According to Raymond Brady Williams (1988, 93), immigrants' mosques are increasingly hiring full-time imams who are trained in Islamic subjects. Several factors in the receiving society create the need for expanded uses of the mosque and therefore of the imam. The mosque now is a place where members carry out their individual and communal religious duties, hold social occasions pertaining to nonmosque business, conduct marriage ceremonies, perform funeral services, and teach Sunday religious school—none of which happens in mosques in Muslim societies. Thus, the making of a professional Islamic ministry resembling that of the denominationally ordained clergy reflects the capacity of Muslims to respond to their surrounding environment. The Mission's imam perceives his increasingly professionalized role as a reflection of the immigrant community's heightened awareness of the importance of their congregation not only as a place of worship but as a site where the group is reconstituting itself and its ideologies.

Looking back to the days of Sheik Daoud, the Sudanese Babikir explains his view of the changed Mission leadership:

> *When the mosque was established, we did not hire an imam. Whoever was able to volunteer to lead prayer did so. . . . In the 1940s we were tired after serving for a long time in the war. The mosque was a good place to come together to worship, and exchange information*

Rogaia Mustafa Abusharaf

*and chat. We did not have Sunday religious classes or a board of
directors. There weren't as many mosques then as there are now.
Our mosque was very similar to those you find at home based on
one's willingness to volunteer. We did not have to pay anybody to
do anything.*

The situation is vastly different now. Sheik Daoud is no longer alive
to provide, to lead, and to serve as he thought necessary. The imam
now is dependent on his congregation for his livelihood and therefore
has to respond to the desires of the board of directors. His role continues to expand beyond the already expanded one adopted by Sheik
Daoud.

Haj Mukhtar Al Tantawi, the Egyptian imam, reflected on his role
in the Mission:

> *I was hired by the Mission to be the resident imam in 1993. The
> Mission Board of Directors knew of my background as professor of
> religious studies from the imam who used to be here before me but
> who chose to return to Egypt after serving for three years. My job
> here is to lead prayer during* jumaa *and Eid, to deliver the sermon,
> to conduct marriage contracts, and to perform funeral services.
> Being resident in the* masjid *also makes me responsible for every-
> thing that goes on here. Also I make sure that Sunday school runs
> smoothly. I have invited many speakers to give lectures at several oc-
> casions, and we also organize pilgrimage trips to Saudi Arabia. I in-
> troduced a lot of activities and events in the Mission. In* Ramadan
> *[the Muslim month of fasting] I started a* maidat elrahaman *[soup
> kitchen] and a clothes drive for the needy people in Brooklyn. It
> does not matter what their religion is: we serve dinners for everyone
> during that month, and all year round we try to help. Muslims are
> trying to be helpful to those who are in need.*

One of the main activities of any imam is leading the congregational prayer, which remains the most significant ritual for the hundreds who attend every Friday afternoon. Prayer is preceded by an
Arabic *khutba* (sermon), in which Haj Tantawi, for example, addressed
a variety of issues ranging from politics, theology, and history to a
more transnational discussion of the global Muslim community. Following the Arabic *khutba,* Haj Ali delivered an English version before
announcements or commentaries were communicated. (Tantawi did
not speak any English but encouraged a bilingual khutba.)

Through sermons, the Mission community comments upon prevailing antipathies and negative imagery of Muslims in their host environment. *Khutbas* are reflective of Muslims' experience as immigrants and

as adherents of a markedly politicized faith. These commentaries range from resistance to the increased proliferation of stereotypical perceptions of Muslims as violent and oppressive to expression of deep-seated discontents with human rights violations in the Balkans, an exceptionally important issue for the congregation. A sermon about the Balkans provides a time for reflecting on and for mourning the massacres and ethnic cleansing of the Bosnians "while the entire international community was watching," as one immigrant put it. These events had significant reverberations on the Muslim world in general and on this congregation in particular, since the Mission has been a strong advocate for the Bosnian cause. At the end of each prayer, members are reminded to make donations to be sent by nongovernmental and human rights organizations for relief operations.

According to Haj Tantawi, the new role he had taken on as a community activist through outreach efforts "in time of need" reflects the mosque's intention to counterbalance the negative public image associated with Muslims in North America. The soup kitchen program is one example of such activities.

In addition to guiding the community, the imam plays a pivotal role in *dawaa* (missionary) efforts in the United States. Several mosque members indicated that conversions in the Mission happen with predictable regularity. This is hardly the role an imam assumes in a Muslim society even where there are sizable non-Muslim communities, but in North America imams are increasingly walking in the path of Western evangelists. Not only does the imam's newly acquired authority enhance his ability to undertake a balancing role between the congregation and the larger society, but it legitimizes his status as a religious figure in the North American religious world.

Haj Tantawi's role in religious instruction was also substantial. Sunday religious school falls under the imam's jurisdiction because he selects the curriculum for Arabic and Qur'anic instruction. Haj Tantawi's background as a religious studies professor before his migration to Brooklyn enhanced the role of the congregation as a vehicle for socialization of children. On Sundays children ages six to sixteen attend multiage classes instructed by male teachers. I was informed that most of the girls who are not enrolled in the Sunday Islamic schools are already attending the Islamic school system sponsored by the Muslim immigrant and nonimmigrant community in New York.

The adoption of Sunday as an important day for religious activities, as Warner (1994, 81) has indicated, is one of the noticeable calendrical adjustments that immigrants are undertaking. In the United States,

Sunday becomes a day for family-oriented activities even though Friday is the Muslim sacred day. Haj Tantawi indicated that

> *since everybody works on Friday we cannot adhere to it as a formal day of religious classes. Even for* jumaa *I am obligated to keep the* khutba *and prayer rather short, so people can go back to work. For the Sunday school, we decided that since all religious classes are held on Sunday, we did not want to choose a separate day. It is easier just to do what everybody else does here.*

In the process of teaching Yemeni children the principles of Islam and the Arabic language, the Mission, like so many other immigrant mosques, is striving to sustain Muslim identities. Warner (1993a, 13) argues that

> *as religion becomes less taken for granted under the conditions prevailing in the U.S., adherents become more conscious of their tradition, and many become more determined about its transmission. Religious identities that had been ascriptive from birth may become objects of active conversion, in order to counter actual or potential losses by defection.*

Religious education in general and in the Mission in particular allows the congregation to serve as a mediator between the host and immigrant culture. Hence, education aims at transmitting both revealed and cultural knowledge to the new generation of American Muslims, whose educators spare no effort in promoting the moral, spiritual, and cultural foundations of conceptions of accountability to God and the community in which they live at an early age. Religious instruction, including Qur'anic education, offers one means for inculcating "memorizable truth" and passing it from one generation to another. In the face of the dramatic influences of the larger society on young children, the Mission education reflects the determination of the congregation to preserve the identity of immigrants. As Haj Ali observes:

> *Sunday school is a great contribution to teach children about their religion and their purpose in life as responsible, virtuous adults. When you bring children to the mosque, you create an understanding of who they are, and where they came from. Some people like to send their children to religious schools. But they are very few, and at some point they have to join public schools. We have to understand that these are American-born children, and they could be pressured by their peers, especially in big cities. So, if children go to public schools and come once a week to the mosque, that will still be good, because they just want to be reminded.*

The greatest change that the Mission has made in adapting itself to its foreign environment, then, has been in the increasingly wide-ranging and professionalized role of its religious leader. But this adaptation has gone hand in hand with several other changes, including the adoption of the host country's organizational forms (nonprofit status and board governance) and religious norms (Sunday school and congregational membership).

Conclusion

The purpose of this chapter has been to highlight the changes in the Islamic Mission's ethnic membership as well as in its organizational form through examining the interrelated processes of ethnicization and religious professionalization. The objective has been to understand the way in which this congregation has changed through the years.

This social history of the Mission provides an excellent example of how congregational structures are shaped by the overall context of the immigrant-host relationship. The Islamic Mission has given Muslim immigrants an opportunity to rearticulate their faith through distinctive adaptations to the host environment's dominant culture, while still struggling to maintain the essentials of their faith and the desirable attributes of their own culture. Throughout this ongoing effort, immigrants stress their determination to retain their culture and way of life even as they rework some roles and adopt some new ones. The Mission, like other Muslim congregations in North America, adopted native organizational structures that parallel those of churches and synagogues. The fine line between adaptation and assimilation is important for immigrants who have "learned that much of their impact and effectiveness depends on [their group's] effective leadership and organization" (Abul Fadl 1991, 59).

What is interesting about the Mission is that the more modifications and adjustments the immigrants accomplished, the more aware they became of their distinctive identity in contrast with other groups. Their adaptation therefore is not a "linear progression" toward Americanization or an incidence of cultural assimilation, but rather a modification and a renegotiation of roles.

ACKNOWLEDGMENTS

Many people have given me help and support. Dr. Terry Schmitt offered excellent editorial comments, and I benefited immensely from his insight and knowledge. I owe a great debt to Professor Larry Mamiya of Vassar College for providing invaluable information, including correspondence and newspaper clippings pertaining to Sheik Daoud Ahmed Faisal. Thanks go also to Professors Jim Faris and Dennison Nash at the University of Connecticut. Versions of this chapter were presented to the New England Religious Discussion Seminar at Hartford Seminary; I am especially grateful to Reverend Dr. Carl Dudley and Richard Chiola of Yale Divinity School, who participated in the seminar. I must likewise express many thanks to the New Ethnic and Immigrant Congregations Project, especially to R. Stephen Warner and Judith G. Wittner, for their constructive comments. I am grateful to Adila Abusharaf and Eva Beerman for their company during much of my fieldwork. Last but not least, I would like to acknowledge the help and generosity of the Mission congregation, the imam, and the many people who offered information, all of whom made the completion of this chapter possible.

NOTES

1. Imam means religious leader, one who leads the congregation in prayer. Haj refers to a Muslim who has performed the annual pilgrimage to Mecca.

2. The pilgrimage (*Hajj*) is one of the five pillars of the Islamic faith, which are (1) *alshahada,* the confession of faith; (2) *salat,* performing prayers five times a day; (3) *zakat,* almsgiving; (4) *Siyam,* fasting; and (5) the pilgrimage to Mecca. The performance of the annual pilgrimage is a religious obligation that every-able bodied Muslim has to undertake once in one's life-time. Millions of Muslims from all walks of life perform the annual rite, which is believed to be "the culmination of an act of faith" as Abul Fadl (1991, 34) argues. The Hajj consolidates the Muslim sense of community. Purity, piety, and community are all brought into focus during the pilgrimage.

3. Muslims perceive daily prayer as a link between God and the individual. The Arabic word (*salat*) literally means link. Since salat is often performed communally, it strengths community consciousness as well as God consciousness.

4. The origins of the Ahmadiyya movement can be traced back to the nineteenth century, when this sect was founded in India to propagate Islam all over the world, including the United States. The migration of Ahmadiyya missionaries took place during the nineteenth century, and most of their activities were focused on converting African-Americans, who saw Islam as a way of circumventing alienation and ethnic oppression.

5. *Omra* denotes a visit to Mecca. It is not obligatory like the *Hajj.*

REFERENCES

Abul Fadl, Mona. 1988. "Islamization as a Force of Global Cultural Renewal." *American Journal of Islamic Social Sciences* 5 (2): 163–179.

————. 1991. *Introducing Islam from Within: Alternative Perspectives.* Leicester, England: Cromwell Press.

Arebi, Saddeka. 1994. *Women and Words in Saudi Arabia: The Politics of Literary Discourse.* New York: Columbia University Press.

Aswad, Barbara. 1991. "Yemeni and Lebanese Muslim Immigrant Women in Southeast Dearborn, Michigan." Pp. 256–281 in *Muslim Families in North America,* edited by Earle H. Waugh, Sharon McIrvin Abu-Laban, and Regula Burckhardt Qureshi. Edmonton, Alberta: The University of Alberta Press.

Eickelman, Dale F. 1989. *The Middle East: An Anthropological Approach.* Englewood Cliffs, N.J.: Prentice Hall.

Farrant, Lawrence. 1965. "The Days of Ramadan." *Brooklyn World Telegram,* January 5, p. B1.

Fernea, Robert. 1961. *Nubian Ethnographies.* Prospect Heights, Ill.: Waveland Press.

Geertz, Clifford. 1971. *Islam Observed.* Chicago: University of Chicago Press.

————. 1973. *The Interpretation of Cultures.* New York: Basic Books.

Handlin, Oscar. 1973. *The Uprooted.* 2nd ed. New York: Atlantic Monthly Press.

Held, Colbert. 1989. *Middle East Patterns: Places, Peoples, and Politics.* Boulder, Colo.: Westview.

Klass, Morton. 1961. *East Indians in Trinidad: A Study of Cultural Persistence.* Prospect Heights, Ill.: Waveland Press.

Makhlouf, Carla. 1979. *Changing Veils: Women and Modernization in North Yemen.* Austin: University of Texas Press.

Mamiya, Lawrence. 1995. "A Historical Overview of African American Sunni Muslim Movements, 1929 to 1975." Paper presented at the Islam in America Conference, De Paul University, Chicago.

McLaughlin, Virginia, ed. 1992. *Immigration Reconsidered.* Oxford: Oxford University Press.

Murphy, Joseph. 1994. *Working the Spirit: Ceremonies of the African Diaspora.* Boston: Beacon Press.

Richmond, Anthony. 1974. "Migration, Ethnicity and Race Relations." Pp. 192–203 in *International Migration,* edited by G. Tapino. Proceedings of a Seminar on Demographic Research in Relation to International Migration. Buenos Aires: CICRED.

Roof, Wade Clark. 1993. *Generation of Seekers: The Spiritual Journey of the Baby Boom Generation.* San Francisco: Harper.

Scott, David. 1991. "That Event, This Memory: Notes on the Anthropology of African Diasporas in the New World." *Diaspora: Journal of Transnational Studies* 1 (3): 261–285.

Sowell, Thomas. 1996. *Migrations and Cultures.* San Francisco: Harper Collins.

Toomey, Jeanne. 1951. "Arabs Find Welcome in Boro." *Brooklyn Eagle,* August 16, p. 10.

Turner, Richard. 1986. *Islam in New York in the 1920s: A New Quest in Afro-American Religion.* Ph.D. dissertation, Princeton University.

Warner, R. Stephen. 1993a. "Introduction to the New Ethnic and Immigrant Congregations Project." Working paper, Office of Social Science Research, University of Illinois at Chicago.

———. 1993b. "Work in Progress Toward a New Paradigm for the Sociological Study of Religion in the United States." *American Journal of Sociology* 98 (March): 1044–1093.

———. 1994. "The Place of the Congregation in the Contemporary American Religious Configuration." Pp. 54–99 in *American Congregations,* vol. 2, edited by James P. Wind and James W. Lewis. Chicago: University of Chicago Press.

Waugh, Earle H. 1991. "North America and the Adaptation of the Muslim Tradition: Religion, Ethnicity, and the Family." Pp. 68–101 in *Muslim Families in North America,* edited by Earle H. Waugh, Sharon McIrvin Abu-Laban, and Regula Burckhardt Qureshi. Edmonton, Alberta: University of Alberta Press.

———. 1994. "Reducing the Distance: A Muslim Congregation in the Canadian North." Pp. 572–612 in *American Congregations,* vol. 1, edited by James P. Wind and James W. Lewis. Chicago: University of Chicago Press.

Weekes, Richard. 1984. *Muslim Peoples: A World Ethnographic Survey,* 2nd ed. Westport, Conn.: Greenwood Press.

Williams, Raymond Brady. 1988. *Religions of Immigrants from India and Pakistan: New Threads in the American Tapestry.* Cambridge: Cambridge University Press.

IV

Internal Differentiation

8 | Caroling with the Keralites: The
Negotiation of Gendered Space
in an Indian Immigrant Church

Sheba George

*There was a tense moment of silence as the fifteen young people of Saint
George's Orthodox Church[1]—mostly teenage girls clutching their head
coverings—faced their fathers, who were practicing songs in their native
language, Malayalam, that they were planning to sing during the church's
annual caroling party. The youngsters of this congregation of immigrants
from the state of Kerala in south India had gathered with a purpose. They
wanted to go Christmas caroling with their fathers. The men seemed
surprised that the young people wanted to accompany them. Anna, one of
the older girls, approached her father, a drummer in the group, to explain.
As her peers watched, he brushed her off saying, "Not now. We'll talk
about it later." The men continued their practice session as if the teenagers
were not present in the sanctuary. Ironically, although the first generation
of immigrants often worries about how they will keep their children involved in the congregation, in this instance they clearly did not want to
include their children.*

The change of seasons was in full swing that early November, heralding
the fast-approaching Advent season in the church. The priest's announcements at the end of the service for the first Sunday in November
included an invitation for those interested to participate in the church's
Christmas caroling party. I had been attending the church as a visiting
researcher only since June, and I was unfamiliar with their practice of
caroling. I turned to Anna, sitting next to me, to ask if she were going
caroling. She smiled and replied that she would like to go but that it
was only the men who caroled in their church. I expressed my surprise

at this information, since I had never heard of any such restrictions on caroling participation in the Indian Orthodox tradition.

After the service that day, I found myself with Anna and some of the other teenage girls who had gathered together as usual in the basement of the church for the weekly social hour. Caroling became the topic of conversation when an announcement over the loudspeaker called all prospective carolers to the sanctuary. Anna was still interested in the outing and said she thought caroling would be fun. Some of the other girls agreed, seeing it as a chance to get out of the house at night, stay out late with friends, and go to the homes of friends from other churches in the community. I suggested to Anna that she talk to the priest, himself a newcomer, who seemed enthusiastic about increasing the participation of members in the church.

Over the next two Sundays, Anna and her friends discussed among themselves as well as with the priest their desire to participate in the caroling. It was these conversations that led them to approach the men during the practice session. Although the men were still reluctant to comply with the girls' request, in the end the priest intervened to persuade them to take the young women along. Nonetheless, the men resisted their participation every step of the way.

Many immigrant communities in the United States face the problem of maintaining their ethnic traditions and connections as their children absorb American culture. Indian Christians manifest just such a concern, which they express as the fear that their children will succumb to what they see as the secularism and immorality of American society (Williams 1988, 104). Unlike the majority of Indian immigrants, Indian Christians come to the United States with the expectation of being a part of the majority in a "Christian land," but instead find themselves alienated from the morals of "Christian America." These fears, as well as the desire to re-create a community in a land of strangers, propel Indian Christians to "attempt to preserve personal and group Christian identity by establishing Indian churches in the United States" (Williams 1988, 104).

Immigrant religious institutions tend to have special classes and programs to teach the next generation about their religion and culture and to motivate them to participate in and maintain the religious institutions into the future. To judge by the Sunday school classes, the vacation Bible schools, and other special programs organized for the socialization of its youth, the Saint George Orthodox congregation is no exception.[2]

Consequently, I was surprised to observe the anomalous adult resistance to the teenagers' desire to participate in the caroling, a church-sponsored social event without any special ritual or cultural restrictions.[3] Why did these parents, who normally insist on involving their children in the ethnic space of the immigrant church, resist their participation in caroling? I think that the answer lies in the fact that it was mostly young girls, not boys, who asked to be included.

The men's attempt to keep caroling as an adult, male preserve has to do with this congregation's specific immigration history, which involves the relative shift in status between men and women within their families. Despite sociological literature that points to the unique nature of U.S. congregational space, which affords gendered leverage and increased participation for immigrant women, Saint George's is one congregation where the young girls, like their mothers, do not have many participatory roles.

For sociologist R. Stephen Warner, one of the unique attributes of religious institutions in the United States is that they play an important role in the empowerment of marginalized groups such as women. He argues that "If the religious community simply mirrors the local patriarchy (or the local gerontocracy), women (or young people) will have reason to escape it" (Warner 1993b, 1072). Functioning as extrafamilial organizational leverages, religious institutions allow women to play one patriarchal institution against another through the formation of women's organizations.

In her study of women in the black sanctified churches, Cheryl Townsend Gilkes (1985) provides evidence for such religious organizational space in American religion. Similar to the Indian immigrant women, many black women are the breadwinners for their families, and as such are able to harness their substantial organizational and financial capacities in the formation and running of women's departments in their churches.

Furthermore, in the case of immigrant congregations, there is some evidence that women have greater levels of participation in the U.S. setting than in their native countries. For example, Yvonne Yazbeck Haddad and Adair Lumis (1987, 55) argue that the Islamic centers in the United States play an important role in the social integration of women whose lives might be isolated and lonely without the social events at the mosque. Won Moo Hurh and Kwang Chung Kim (1990) find that greater numbers of immigrant Koreans become churchgoers in the United States than in Korea and that Korean immigrant women's mental health is significantly associated with church involvement. Similarly, Pyong Gap Min (1992) finds that many Korean immigrant women, who cannot continue their preimmigration occupation of teaching in the United States, find it meaningful to teach Korean-language classes in immigrant congregations.

The literature would lead one to hypothesize, as does Warner (1993a, 5), that "typically, [immigrant] women assume a more prominent role in the congregation in the U.S. than they did in the country of origin." One would expect the participation in the religious sphere to be even more accentuated in the case of the women of the immigrant Kerala Christian community because of their greater economic and social status relative to the men. Yet, the adult male resistance against the mostly female teenagers' desire to go caroling points to the patrolled borders of gendered territory. In voicing their desire to go caroling, the girls had crossed the boundaries that afford only a minimal level of participation to their mothers.

My own interest in this research topic stems from my experiences growing up in an immigrant Indian Orthodox church. Having come to the United States as a young girl with my family, I spent a good part of my childhood involved in a church community similar to the one at Saint George's. As a result, entrée into the research site was relatively easy, although I often found myself in the classic liminal position during my fieldwork. Owing to my sometimes conflicting identities, I was variously perceived as both researcher and community member, and as neither adult nor child (although adulthood is attained by marriage, I, an unmarried woman in my late twenties, was too old to be a child). But this liminality also gave me room to maneuver among my different identities. For example, I could associate with both the adults and the teenagers without having to belong to either group.[4]

Rather than adopting a dichotomized view of the ethnographer as either insider or outsider, or native or other, I, along with anthropologist Kirin Narayan (1993, 671), believe that it is more useful to look at the fieldworker in terms of "shifting identifications amid a field of interpenetrating communities and power relations." From this experience, I can attest to the constant challenge of having to decide how to position myself in the face of conflicting demands, as occurred in the case of the caroling.

To attempt to understand the paradoxical adult resistance to the participation of the young people, I will first examine the gendered nature of the immigration of this Indian group and the social structure of the church, including the conventional assignment of gender roles in the Indian Orthodox church. Then I will look at how the propagation and creation of male roles in the church, as well as the redefinition of roles, all work together to extend male participation in the U.S. congregation. And while both the propagation and the creation of roles are essential to the expansion of male participation, I will focus on the redefinition of roles by examining the caroling incident and show that the adult resistance to the young people's desire to go caroling can be seen as a battle over gendered territory. To begin the analysis, I turn to the story of the immigration of Kerala Christians to the United States.

Primary Female Immigration and Its Impact on Gender Relations

The shortage of nurses in the United States in the 1960s resulted in the increasing recruitment of foreign nurses, especially from Asian countries. Whereas only 7 percent of the foreign nurses licensed in the United States were from Asia in 1960, this number went up to 63 percent by 1972 (Mejia et al. 1979, 74).

The immigration of Indian nurses increased substantially after the 1965 Immigration Act lifted restrictive national quotas. By the late 1970s, their numbers were exceeded only by those of Filipina nurses, closely followed by those of Koreans. From 1975 to 1979, 11.9 percent of the nurses admitted to the United States as permanent residents were from India, 11.2 percent were from Korea and 27.6 percent were from the Philippines (Ishi 1987, 288). Despite the increasing immigration of foreign nurses, there were continuing reports of severe shortages in the number of nurses.[5] The U.S. Immigration Nursing Relief Act of 1989 was enacted to allow the immigration of approximately 16,000 nurses to help relieve the shortage (McQuaid-Dvorak and Waymack 1991).

In 1914, the first Indian nurses were recruited by the British colonial forces under the guidance of Florence Nightingale and eventually were organized into the Indian Military Nursing Service. According to sociologist Ranjana Ragavachari (1990), the nurses were mostly recruited from the Indian Christian communities in the state of Kerala or from the Anglo-Indian communities, which were relatively more open to allowing women to work outside the home, especially in a low-status profession such as nursing. Ragavachari (1990, 15) attributes the low status of the profession to "existing cultural norms deeply rooted in Hindu philosophy" that relegated nursing to the realm of the polluting and the impure. Additionally, given that Nightingale's model of nursing was based on explicitly Christian principles, it seems probable that Christian nurses were more easily trained and therefore perhaps more aggressively recruited by the British colonial powers.

Consequently, there has been a history of nurse migration from the rural areas of Kerala to the more urban areas of India since the early 1900s, a phenomenon that developed as a survival strategy in the Kerala Christian community.[6] Kerala nurses also make up an important part of the global labor pool for nurses. As part of a global step-migration process, Kerala nurses worked, for example, in Middle Eastern countries before immigration to the United States began.

The Kerala Indian Christian community in the United States is unique among Asian Indian immigrants in the prominent role that women played in the immigration process. Unlike most immigrant groups, Kerala Christian nurses arrived first and later sponsored the immigration of their husbands and families. Typically, the men waited in India with the children until they were allowed to join their wives, who were already working in the United States and supporting the household through remittances. In other cases, single women went back to India with their green cards and found husbands with whom they could return. In this immigration experience, conventional roles were thus partially reversed for men and women (Williams 1988).

Since women were primary agents of immigration, their husbands and male kin were dependent on them when they joined them in the United States. This dependence of the men on the women often went beyond finances. Because they had immigrated prior to the men, the women of the community had become more proficient in dealing with American society.

Furthermore, the jobs most men obtained were of lower status and income than those held by their wives. They typically had to relocate for their wives' job convenience and to reeducate themselves in new trades and professions to become employable. In his study on immigrant groups from India and Pakistan, Raymond Brady Williams (1988, 108) describes the Kerala Christian men as follows: "Most of the men who followed their wives took positions in machine shops or factories, or used the connections their wives had in the hospitals to get training as medical technicians."

Although many of the women had worked in India and had contributed financially to the household income, they had not played the primary role there that they had after immigrating. And while the traditional gender roles of their parents' generation may have altered for these couples in India, there were two important differences that marked their U.S. immigration experience. First, even though the women had worked outside the home in India, their husbands were not as likely to have taken an active role in household work because of the availability

Sheba George

of inexpensive help and the presence of relatives. Furthermore, the women who were in nursing were unlikely to earn more than their husbands in India. Thus whereas the women experienced upward mobility and an increase in general status after immigrating, many men in their community became downwardly mobile and lost status.

Orthodox Christianity and Gender Roles in Kerala and the United States

Since most of the Kerala nurses in the United States are Syrian Christians,[7] it is important to take a brief look at the history of Syrian Christianity in India. Syrian Christians from Kerala, the state at the southernmost tip of India, claim their descent from the early converts of the apostle Thomas, who, tradition has it, was martyred in southern India in 72 A.D. These Christians of Kerala are called Syrian not because they have Syrian ancestry but rather because they use Syrian liturgy. Syrian missionary influences starting in the seventh century led to the establishment of the church under the patriarch of Antioch with a liturgy that still retains some Syriac.

Over the centuries the Syrian Christians became divided into different denominations. There are now Catholics, Eastern Orthodox, and Protestants of every stripe who claim a Syrian Christian ancestry. The Orthodox Syrian Christian church of India is one such denomination within this tradition. It broke off ties with Antioch in 1912 and is currently led by a patriarch from Kerala.[8]

With the new wave of Kerala immigration to the United States in the late 1960s, there was also an increasing need for religious institutions among the new arrivals. Many of these pioneer immigrants became actively involved in renting churches or community halls and organizing makeshift congregations.[9] Faced with the problem of a shortage of clergy, they paid for priests from other congregations in sometimes distant areas in the United States to come once a month—often on Saturdays—to conduct the liturgy. But since priests in the Orthodox tradition are allowed to marry, and since their wives are often nurses, there were frequently more immigrant priests than congregations in the main U.S. immigration centers.[10] Whereas in India priests are engaged in their vocation on a full-time basis and are supported by the parish, in the United States they usually must work in secular jobs to supplement their income from their congregations.

With the number of North American congregations increasing, the mother church in India placed them into the newly formed North

American diocese and assigned a bishop to oversee it on behalf of the patriarch in Kerala. Saint George's is one of fifty-nine such congregations in the United States and Canada.

The Service at St. George's

The majority of the congregation at Saint George's are Indian-born adults from Kerala.[11] Their children include both the American-born and the "1.5 generation" of those born in India but raised in the United States. The majority of the congregation seem to be between the ages of thirty and fifty. There are equal numbers of men and women. The youth who attend church range from the very young to those in high school. The college-age and postcollege group is conspicuously absent.[12]

The congregation stands with bare feet in the sanctuary, since it is considered to be a holy space, much in the tradition of Indian religious spaces. They leave their shoes in the foyer or in the basement. The church building is shaped in a T-formation. The altar is at the end of the leg of the T, and the priest faces the front, away from the congregation. The wall behind the altar that the priest and the congregation face has a stained-glass window in which a cross and white dove figure prominently. The chancel is veiled and unveiled with an ornately decorated curtain at particular times in the service. Both this curtain and the priest's vestments are made of the same, highly embroidered material.

The main altar is flanked by two mini-altars with shrines dedicated respectively to the Virgin Mary and Saint George, a bishop of the church. Devotees can light votive candles and donate money in the collection boxes placed in front of the approximately 5-by-5-foot paintings of Mary with the baby Jesus on the left and Saint George on the right. The altar area; the ornate curtain and garments of the priest; the paintings; the twelve tall candles on the altar, symbols of the twelve disciples, surrounding a prominent cross; the incense; the chalice and plate used for communion; and the bells and other noise-making devices heard at various parts of the service, all make for a sensually and aesthetically evocative experience.

The whole service can take from three-and-a-half to four hours. Most of the service is either chanted or sung, and is conducted with the congregation standing. While the traditional church in Kerala does not have chairs or pews, with people standing and sitting on carpeted floors, most churches in the United States, such as Saint George's, have pews. A male member at Saint George's plays a synthesizer, but there is no official choir. Traditionally, the churches in Kerala have not had separate choirs, although it is no longer uncommon to find them there. At Saint George's, it is the women who seem to be unofficially responsible to carry the singing during the service.

The service does not change from Sunday to Sunday. The liturgy remains the same, although the translation of most of the service into Malayalam from Syriac is a relatively recent event. While neither Bibles nor hymnals are necessary, since most people know the service by heart, copies of the service book in Malayalam and English transliterations of the service are available. After the service, the congregation files by the priest—first the boys and girls, followed by the men and women, respectively. They place their offering on a plate, and the priest blesses them by touching the cross he holds to each one's forehead as they cross themselves.

During the service, the sexes are physically separated by a long carpet that runs down the center of the church. The younger boys and girls must stand at the front of their respective sides. The women and girls have their heads covered. Almost all the women wears saris, the traditional Indian garment that allows them to cover their heads easily. Some visiting grandmothers wear the traditional women's outfit from Kerala, which predates the sari. The young girls also tend to wear either *salwaar kameezes* (a North Indian outfit made up of pants, a loose top, and a long scarf) or Western-style skirts and dresses with scarves to cover their heads. In contrast, the men and boys almost exclusively wear pants and shirts, with the occasional visiting grandfather in the typical Keralite white sarong and shirt.

The gender roles and ideology in the Orthodox church are starkly delineated and enforced, as best exemplified by the physical separation of the congregation by sex. Women do not have any official roles in the Sunday service other than joining in communal responses and hymns. Furthermore, women and girls receive communion and final blessings only after all the men and boys have taken their turn.

Only men and boys can be altar helpers or assistants, after they have been consecrated as deacons or acolytes. They also can formally lead the congregation in responses and enter the altar area, which is off limits to women and girls, who are considered polluting because of menstruation and who are therefore barred from contact with all that is holy.[13] My own experience with a priest in another church who almost dropped a heavy table on my foot while I was helping him move it because I had accidently stepped on the altar illustrates the importance of this traditional prohibition.

Women also do not have many leadership positions available to them in the administration of the church. In fact, only males over twenty-one years of age have a vote in the general meetings. Typically, women serve in no administrative capacities except in the areas of child education, food production, and church-sponsored women's groups. For instance, women may become Sunday school teachers but they cannot be elected to the managing committee of the congregation. There is, however, a service/prayer group for women called the Martha Mariam Samajam (group) that involves offices for women. In U.S. congregations such as Saint George's, the gendered nature of the immigration clearly contributes to the creation of an almost exclusively male-run sphere. Nonetheless, women slightly outnumber the men on Sunday morning both in numbers and in volume of sound.

The U.S. Congregation as Male Turf

For most Kerala men who are sponsored by their wives or other female kin, the immigration experience brings a painful loss of status in two ways: relative to the women in the community and relative to their social positions before immigration. Whereas their nurse wives and sisters experience upward economic mobility as well as an increase in status in the immigration process, the men face the prospect of perhaps never making as much money or gaining equivalent professional status as the women. This situation helps explain why there is a greater male need for recognition and power in such a communal sphere as the immigrant congregation, where male leadership is reinforced. In an interview, Mr. Mathen, whose wife is not a nurse, explained the reason for the importance of church roles when he said:

> *Most of our people came here as a spouse—rather, most of the men—as a spouse of a nurse. Nurses over here make good bucks and the men go for a clerical job—whatever—and the women make more money. Women have this thing [feeling] that "I am the breadwinner or I make more money." This is not just my opinion. Several people, even the husbands of nurses, who are my friends—this is their opinion too. Now in the house there is nothing [for the men]. Husbands don't have the feeling that "I make more money than you." In the house, the husband does not have his proper status. In the society, you are an Indian—what status do you have? For men—where are they going to show their "macho" nature? That's why they play in the church. This is what is going on in our churches, and I am not just talking about St. George's.*[14]

A second way that loss of status occurs for the immigrant men is with respect to their social and economic positions before immigration. The difficulty in transferring Indian degrees, credentials, and work skills and experience to the U.S. context often leaves them in the position of having to start all over again. As immigrants, they have less access to the political and social structures of the wider society in the United States. Low incomes and unstable employment in usually secondary labor market jobs leave many with few opportunities for public participation and access to leadership positions. In both an informal survey and in interviews conducted at Saint George's, many men who were initially hesitant to disclose the exact nature of their work used such vague terms as "business" or "office." This gap in their social lives leads to a greater male need for public participation and leadership opportunities. The immigrant congregation thus becomes an arena par excellence to meet such a need.[15]

Two factors contribute to the creation of the immigrant congregation as an ideal space for male leadership. First, Orthodox gender ideology and practices in Kerala allocate church administration to men. Because leadership roles in the Kerala congregations are reserved for socially and economically prominent members of the community, lay leadership is inherently associated with high status for Kerala Christians. Mr. Markos emphasized his status back in Kerala when he said that he was from a family that had held leadership positions in the first churches of Indian Orthodoxy in the seventh century. Talking to him made me realize the unique and complicated relationship of the church and identity for Syrian Christians of Kerala. Because families are the unit of identity, the church family becomes the mega-umbrella under which family and individual identities can be traced. For the immigrant male members suffering from a loss of status, Saint George's becomes a logical space to exercise leadership that is communally associated with high status.

Second, many immigrant congregations are conservative institutions whose highest priority is often the creation of a social and religious space that approximates and compensates for what the immigrant has lost of the imagined homeland (Herberg 1960). In many ways, Saint George's attempts to reproduce an untainted "little Kerala" for its members suffering from alienation in the wider U.S. society. Mrs. Mani's complaint about her husband exemplifies why church participation is so important for immigrant men. "As for me," she said, "I told my husband, 'Don't join all these parties and groups in the church. Just go to church, pray, and come back. Why go for these parties? I don't like that.' He [her husband] says, 'I have to have a niche here somehow. What should I say to all these guys that turned against me? At least I have three to four people with whom I can talk now.'" Without extended family or friends, having such a niche as the church becomes crucial for the men.

For the immigrant women, the gender ideology and practices of the Indian Orthodox church limit their participation in the congregation. Additionally, irregular nursing work schedules make it difficult for most of them to attend church and affiliated activities, such as the women's group meetings. From my interviews, it is clear that the female members' opinions about their level of participation range from those who are satisfied with the status quo to those who would like to have more active roles and a voice in the decision-making processes of the congregation. Mrs. Philip, who is of the latter opinion, explains why she curtails her own inclination to participate vocally in the general body meetings: "In fact, I have felt like talking at times, but I know that [the men] are going to talk about me. . . . They will talk to the husband and say, 'See how your wife is.' This leads to a fight at home. But when they [the women] are at work, they argue and talk, but because they don't want a fight with their husbands or people talking, they just keep quiet [in church]."

The immigrant congregation is more than a mere reflection of the native congregation organized around Indian Orthodox conventions of gender roles. The greater male need for institutional roles in the United States has shaped the group's particular development and organization. This increased male need for participation may be part of the impetus behind the prevalence of schisms as well as the creation and redefinition of new male roles within congregations that allow for greater male participation.

Congregational Splits: The Propagation of Male Roles

The prevalent splitting of Kerala congregations in the United States results in the formation of new congregations and consequently increases leadership opportunities for the men.[16] At the local level, these splits serve the needs of both laity and immigrant priests. At the national and international levels, the proliferation of congregations appears to benefit both the bishop of the immigrant diocese and the mother church.

Splits in immigrant congregations allow more male members to participate actively in church affairs.[17] Because the newly formed groups tend to be small, the vigorous participation of male members becomes crucial to their survival. Mrs. Mani told me that her family had left their first congregation to join a split-off group because her husband was given the chance to serve at the altar there. She elaborated that he had not been getting along with the priest at their home congregation and was therefore not serving at the altar, and that the priest in the new congregation had "compelled" them to join due to the small numbers there.

The people involved in such splits probably feel a sense of importance as key players shaping events. For example, Mr. Kuriakose, who was hesitant at first to speak openly of his involvement in the group that eventually split off from Saint George's, became markedly animated as he gave the following account of the prominence of his own role:

> Mr. K: *Well, before the split they came here. Everybody was in this room. Mathen Achen [Father Mathen] was sitting there. All the people who left—they were all here. And Achen told us what he was going to do. Of course Mathen Achen suffered a lot. He said, "I am going to resign." At that time, I suggested that we will buy some time—one or two weeks. But Achen's very strong supporters in the group made him resign [to start a new congregation]. The same day, in one conversation, one of the people in this group [the splitting group] was telling that we might again split. Even after going [from Saint George's], we will again split.*
>
> SG: *Why did that person say that?*
>
> Mr. K: *Well, that is the pattern. That's how this history [goes]. It was like that every time we split.*

The phenomenon of the increased numbers of schisms is also facilitated by the manner in which the mother church in India handles the immigration of priests. Instead of being sent for a specified period of time to serve a congregation, the priests come like other immigrants, sponsored by relatives. Often priests are married to nurses and suffer a loss in status similar to that of other immigrant men in the congregations. Furthermore, because most congregations cannot afford their upkeep, they cannot be full-time priests and must find other work during the week. In several interviews, respondents suggested that the priests were partly responsible for the prevalence of splits, since it becomes a very important identity issue for them to have a congregation where they can conduct Mass, maintain their vocation, and receive the income that comes from both the monthly congregational contribution as well the individual donations accompanying the administration of priestly duties. Thus if there is a thriving congregation in a particular area and a new priest arrives, chances are that within a few years he will find a dissatisfied group of people in the existing congregation who will precipitate a split.

The immigration of Indian Orthodox priests differs from that of priests in the Marthoma church, a Protestant Indian church whose administration in India sends a priest to a particular U.S. congregation for a three-year period, during which the congregation usually must support the priest. Typically, for the three to four smaller Orthodox congregations in a large U.S. metropolitan area, there tends to be one large Protestant congregation.

Interestingly, the macrolevel politics of the Indian Orthodox church also appear to have played a part in the phenomenal incidence of congregational splitting in the United States. Father Elias, a veteran in the American diocese, gave this opinion on congregational splits:

> Fr. E: *Most of them—a number of congregations—started because the priest had a problem with the congregation, so they went away with a number of people and started it, which is because of a lack of discipline in the church. And the bishop encouraged it, unfortunately because of ulterior motives.*
>
> SG: *What do you think this was?*
>
> Fr. E: *To tell the world that he has so many congregations in his jurisdiction. I have not seen any effort on his part—again not to be considered as a negative criticism, just my observation—to resolve a situation where a congregation was going to be split. He indirectly encouraged splitting. He always said, "The more you have, the better you are."*

The bishop who resigned from his office as head of the U.S. diocese in 1992 was allegedly attempting to promote a separation from the mother church in India so that he could become the leader of an independent church in the United States. Part of his alleged strategy was to encourage the splitting of congregations so that he would have a greater number under his jurisdiction.[18] The mother church in India apparently did not discourage congregational splits, since they meant more mandatory revenues for the church.

Collective Cooking: The Creation of
New Male Roles

Besides forming new congregations, another means of increasing opportunities for male participation is to create new, informal roles within the existing congregation. For example, activities that are typically seen as female responsibilities, such as the cooking and serving of food, are taken over by the men on a weekly basis as well as on the major feast and festival days at Saint George's.

In Kerala there is a tradition of male leadership in cooking for wedding banquets and other such social events where food must be prepared for large groups of people. However, there are few occasions for the serving of food in the congregational setting. The typically large congregations in Kerala do not have weekly refreshments after the service. But because worshipers in the United States often travel a great distance to come to Sunday service, and because the social and fellowship aspects of congregational life are much more central in the immigrant church, refreshments and whole meals after the service are the norm in this country.

In the context of this newly arisen need in the immigrant setting, the men assume relatively greater responsibilities for the food production at a public level. The men at Saint George's appear to control the public part of this process from the planning of meals to the collective preparation and serving of the food in the church.

On a weekly basis, it is usually the men who make the coffee and serve refreshments and meals. Typically, there are six or seven men discussing politics and other matters in the basement kitchen while they wait for the coffee to brew. While clearly so many men are not needed to make coffee or to put out the snacks, those gathered in the kitchen are ostensibly taking care of this need.

When the priest announced one Sunday that people were needed to bring food for a particular festival Sunday, it was the men who volunteered. On other special occasions, such as Christmas, when a meal had to be prepared for the worshipers, it was the men who gathered to cook.

A number of women were present near the kitchen as they waited for the Christmas Eve social program to begin later that evening. As some quietly sat talking among themselves, others peeled onions or cut garlic while watching the men cook. These women appeared to be more of an audience as they watched and joked as the men cooked, cleaned and decorated the hall for the festivities.

At one point, there was one man left alone in the kitchen, and he lamented in jest that he had been deserted, much like Jesus on the cross, to take the blame for cooking. He reminisced about the days before the most recent split at Saint George's and how they had lost a couple of expert male cooks to the new group. Clearly, cooking for church functions had become institutionalized as another opportunity for male participation.

The women's lack of public participation in the cooking does not mean that they do not cook for church functions. In fact, in the case of potluck dinners or other occasions where food is not prepared in the church kitchen, it is likely that the women are the ones cooking at home, even if it is their husbands who stand up to volunteer what will be brought. For example, one festival Sunday, Molly Patrose arrived with her husband in tow, and he was carrying a pot of food for a communal meal taking place that day. I was standing with a group of women when one of them teasingly suggested that it was he who was doing the cooking these days. Molly immediately assured us that she had done the cooking and that he was only carrying the heavy pot because of her bad back.

Male initiative in the serving and preparation of food seems to be present to the extent that it occurs in a collective public process that allows for male participation in a group of their peers. In addition to the propagation of existing male roles via the splitting of new congregations and the creation of new roles within congregations, the redefinition of caroling as a male activity is another way that the church sphere becomes more firmly established as male territory.

Caroling: The Redefinition of a Role

While Christmas caroling in the United States is an activity traditionally available to individuals and groups without institutional affiliations, in Kerala it is mainly a church-sponsored activity. Besides the overt function of spreading the "good news" of Christmas, caroling is also a means of raising money for the church. In Kerala, caroling groups from different churches make the rounds of the neighborhood, visiting the homes of both members and nonmembers, where donations are expected.

In the United States, the Kerala Christian congregations continue the practice of forming caroling groups that go to the homes of both members and nonmembers, including Hindus in the Kerala immigrant community. They are bringing the "good news" in the form of songs often written to the tunes of Malayalam film songs.[19] The tacit understanding is that each home they visit will donate money to the congregation. Because donations from caroling are an important source of income, the caroling groups put in long hours and cover extended areas of a typical metropolitan area.[20]

For example, Saint George's schedule for caroling stretched over a period of three weeks, during which the group went out caroling on Thursdays and Fridays from early evening to the early hours of the next morning, even though many carolers had to work the next day. On weekends, the group started caroling as early as two in the afternoon and often did not finish until two the next morning. They covered large distances in a single night, going out to distant suburbs.

Members of the congregation in particular areas took responsibility for obtaining invitations for the caroling group to perform at the homes of other Malayalee immigrants in their neighborhood. The hosts in each home usually offered refreshments, and the hosts of the first and last homes, usually Saint George's members, prepared meals for the carolers.

I learned that caroling at Saint George's, besides being an opportunity for passing on the "good news" and raising funds, promotes exclusive male participation and camaraderie. In Kerala, the caroling groups of the Orthodox congregation tend to be made up of young people from the Sunday school chaperoned by Sunday school teachers. The caroling group at Saint George's departed from this Kerala convention in that only men took part in this activity, until the youth voiced their desire to participate. Thus in making caroling an exclusively adult male activity, members of Saint George's had redefined a role traditionally assigned to youth in Kerala.

Caroling by Men for Men

In my work with the Saint George congregation, I had to make the difficult decision to accept the priest's request to organize the young people's caroling venture. While I sympathized with the teenagers and wanted to help the priest increase participation, as a researcher I did not want to undertake a controversial leadership position. After the young people first made public their interest in caroling, the priest asked me to organize the group and direct their singing.[21] By accompanying the youth and directing their singing, I was able to observe the way that caroling was primarily a male bonding experience not only for the men singing but also for those listening. Because of my gender, relative youth and role as organizer, I became the object of some sanctions that gave me insight into the manner in which boundaries were drawn around male participation. Additionally, I was able to witness how caroling was organized by men for men. The camaraderie of the carolers came from the group's exclusive male membership, from the style of the singing, and from the illicit drinking among some of the carolers that had to be hidden from the priest who accompanied them. In addition to building the bond of fraternity among the singers, caroling also seemed to be directed to meet the approval of the male heads of the households visited and to inspire their benevolence in the form of donations.

The size of a caroling party varied from twenty to twenty-five men, including a couple of drummers and tambourine players, someone dressed as Santa Claus, and the priest. The men were extremely animated as they clapped their hands and sang at the top of their voices. They usually stood around in a circle, rhythmically moving together, and at the critical moments throwing their bodies forward to match the beat. They seemed to value volume over singing in tune. It was a highly physical experience, and the carolers appeared exhilarated as each song inevitably built to a crescendo. The style of their performance seemed reminiscent of a type of Kerala folk singing that accompanies boat races in which only men participate.

Part of the source of their animation may have been the liquor that some of them were secretly imbibing. In Kerala Christian society, the consumption of liquor is strongly disapproved; there is no acceptable form of social drinking. In the United States, alcohol may be more freely used by Kerala immigrants, but it is never present in the congregational setting other than as part of the communion. Consequently, the carolers had to go to great lengths to conceal their drinking.

As I waited with the youth in the basement of the house from which we started caroling, I noticed adult male carolers discreetly entering a small room, one or two at a time. I investigated this room when I had a chance and found that it was the laundry room set up as a makeshift bar with a few bottles of liquor. Again, I noticed similar setups in the basements in some of the homes of other congregation members. Having to orchestrate this forbidden activity collectively not only increased the camaraderie among the singers but also extended fraternal membership to those male hosts facilitating the libationary adventures.

At the typical home, the family was usually awaiting our arrival, given that the caroling coordinators had called ahead to notify them of our itinerary. Usually the priest and other leaders of the caroling party would shake hands with the men in the household and address them for all matters. The women and children remained in the background, listening and preparing refreshments for the group. It was also the men of the households who in turn addressed the carolers and communicated the good wishes of the family. Finally, it was the men who gave the donation check to the leader of the group at the end of the singing.

In the homes of congregation members, the male hosts often had additional duties. Besides facilitating the basement consumption of alcohol, they sometimes would personally direct the carolers to the homes of those Kerala immigrant neighbors, often not church members, who had agreed to a visit from the group. Thus the men of the congregation were intimately involved as both performers and hosts in the success of the caroling venture.

Caroling also gave each participant a yearly opportunity to display, compare and measure their progress, especially financial, in the wider Kerala immigrant community. Discussions about property values, long-term plans for return to India, and the pain of losing children to extracommunity marriages made up the exchange of male hosts and carolers.

The importance of the man of the house being present for the visit became evident one night when, despite an appointment, the male householder was absent, and the carolers decided to change plans. Upon finding out that this man would not be home for another half-hour, they altered their itinerary despite the inconvenience. Even though his wife and the rest of the household were perfectly capable of receiving the glad tidings and making a donation, the fact that the carolers decided to wait suggests the significance of this man's presence as host and audience.

It became clear that caroling was male turf only when the girls pushed the invisible boundaries by asking to be included. It is interesting that there was resistance not only because they were impinging on adult territory but also because the youth were mostly young women. The varying forms of the expression of resistance point to ways in which the battle over caroling was part of a war over the very meaning of gender.

Vocabularies of Motive in the Battle Over Gendered Turf

The possibility that the youth would go caroling with the men incited various reactions that ranged from the unwavering support of the priest to the warnings of possible danger to the young people from one caroler. Because of the staunch backing of the priest, the young people were able to accompany the men a few times.

There were nine teenage girls, but only three preadolescent boys who were enthusiastic about caroling. The girls appeared eager to have a chance to be with their friends and stay out late. In contrast, the older teenage boys made jokes about how they didn't sing and how they had more important things to do besides caroling. Although about seven boys came to the first practice at church, most appeared apathetic and ridiculed the adult male singing style as if they were trying to distance themselves from the men. One boy described the men as "drinking and jumping around so much that they shake the ornaments right off the Christmas trees." Two of the three boys who did go caroling were part of a Christmas Eve skit that caricatured the animation of the adult male singers, thus indicating their ambivalence about their own participation.

The reticence of the boys was matched by parental concern about their lack of interest. One woman told me that her son had a beautiful voice but did not want to participate. She asked me if I would ask him to join the group. One man asked the priest if he would talk to his sons about participating. Even though the priest asked and the two high school boys agreed to participate, they never came. While the girls were never applauded as a group for their interest in participating, they were asked to recruit some boys to come along.

Throughout the caroling, there were varying expressions of adult concern about the presence of the girls. First, it was strongly felt that it was inappropriate—both logistically and socially—for the girls to be out late at night. Then it was suggested that it would be dangerous for the girls to be out caroling. One night, one of the leading male carolers told the van full of mostly girls that it was shameful that the girls were taking more initiative than the boys. Another night, the presence of the girls was characterized as a sign that the men had lost their usefulness and that a female takeover had occurred.

The Inappropriate Presence of Women and Children

At the news that the young people desired to go caroling, no adult other than the priest expressed complete support for the plan. The underlying consensus seemed to be that it was inappropriate to take them along. Perhaps because they were mostly young girls, the discourse surrounding the logistical feasibility of including them became one that equated the youth with women and children. Some argued that the cold weather would be too much for women and children, while others brought up the danger of slippery winter roads. There was also the alleged difficulty of having too many cars following each other and the extra liability of minors getting lost at night in unfamiliar areas.

The discussion surrounding the propriety of including the teenagers in the caroling came to be based on certain arguments about gender. Opponents claimed that girls were too frail and lacked stamina, invoking gendered images of the troubles that would befall an integrated caroling party.

The Dangers of Female Sexuality

Soon after the public announcement of the youth participation, I received a phone call from a male caroler with whom I was acquainted. He informed me that he did not think that it was a good idea for the girls to go. He asked me if I knew that at times there might only be one van for the entire group and how I felt about squeezing into the van with a bunch of men. I responded by saying something to the effect that the young people were very accommodating.

At this point, he interjected that although he had not wanted to raise the issue, he did believe that it was dangerous for girls to go caroling. He alluded to the possibilities of sexually inappropriate behavior, since sometimes the men get drunk and act rowdy. He concluded that he would not let his own daughter go with the men, and since he regarded me as a daughter, he thought that he should warn me.

While most of the general resistance to caroling had centered around its inappropriateness for the girls because of such factors as the bitter cold, inconvenience, gender roles, and bad driving conditions, the caller had introduced a new objection: that it was dangerous for the girls to be in such close, crowded conditions with a bunch of men who might verbally or sexually abuse them, even though most of the men were the fathers of these girls. He was saying that, on one hand, it was dangerous for the girls, but on the other hand that there was also an implication that the sexuality of the girls becomes dangerous at night in a crowded van when the men are intoxicated. He seemed to be saying that if the men were intoxicated, they could not be held responsible for their actions, and that it was up to the girls not to put the men in such a dangerous position by coming along at night.

It is possible that this man may not have actually thought that the girls were in danger or dangerous to the men. He may have just wanted to drink in peace without his daughter around. However, the fact that he could appeal to the discourse of dangerous female sexuality implies the primacy of the male prerogative and the legitimacy of male space.

It is the discourse around the potential danger of female sexuality to men that requires women and girls to cover their heads during the service so as not to distract men and to remain indoors after dark so as not to tempt them.

The Shameful Presence of the "Girls Who Are Better"

The first time that the young people were taken caroling, the nine girls and three boys were put into a van along with me and a couple of adult men. Besides the man driving the van, we were also accompanied by Mr. Philip, who was one of the coordinators of the caroling party. At one point in the journey, he turned around and asked the teenagers why more boys had not joined them. One of the girls responded that they were lazy. He ignored the girl's opinion and reiterated the question to the three boys in the van. When they did not say anything, he said, "Shame on you that the girls are better than you." At this remark, one of the girls asked, "Why is that? Why can't girls be better?" Mr. Philip went to great lengths to justify his position that indeed boys ought to be better than girls. He appealed to the authority of a misunderstood statement made by the priest as cultural rationale and then fortified his position with a scriptural defense to justify why boys should be better.

Earlier that Sunday morning, the priest had given a sermon on the birth of John the Baptist. He veered off on a tangent to point out to the congregation that the parents of John were especially happy to be told by the angel that they were going to have a son (Luke 1: 14). He observed that, much like the people of biblical times, Keralites are also overjoyed to have boys. "Why is this?" he asked rhetorically. His answer was that boys are seen as bringing money to the family, whereas girls are perceived as the cause of money lost as dowry. He added that while it may not be true in this congregation, some Kerala immigrants ask for thousands of dollars as dowry for their sons. Clearly, in this context, he was being critical of the practice of dowry and of valuing boys over girls.

Mr. Philip, in responding to the question of why girls should not be better than boys, interpreted the priest's descriptive statement that Keralites prefer baby boys as prescriptive. He then connected this interpretation of the priest's statement to the fact that God had created Adam first and that boys should therefore be first and better at all things. The girl who asked the question gave me a frustrated look. Mr. Philip said to me in a low voice, as if explaining himself, "I just said that to lift the spirits of the boys." The three boys in question, however, did not appear to need to have their spirits lifted.

Mr. Philip's concern over the absence of the boys mirrored that of other adults in the congregation. Their concern seems to come from their expectation that boys should be natural-born leaders, especially in church affairs. For the girls who were questioned about the boys' whereabouts and were told that their presence was shameful, the message was not only that their ability to contribute is inherently deficient but also that their insistence on participating is cause for disgrace. The look on the young girl's face indicated that the message had been received loud and clear.

Indira Gandhi and Violated Turf Boundaries

In order to accompany the adults, the young people had to agree to the terms laid out by the caroling coordinators, which ensured that the adults would have total control over them and that their presence would not be a direct infringement of territorial boundaries. That is, the youngsters were allowed to carol only for a couple of the nights and on a Sunday afternoon. They were expected to leave earlier than the adults at a specified time, travel in a separate van, and follow directions. Whereas the men typically sang two Malayalam songs in each household, the teens were allowed only one. Despite these controls, there were clear signs that the men felt their boundaries had been violated.

After the second practice, at which I taught the young people a Malayalam song, the adults asked for a trial performance. The young people were aware that this was a test to see if they were presentable as a group. They had worked especially hard on learning the song, given that none of them could read Malayalam or speak it very well. I transliterated the song into English so that they could learn it. With a short amount of practice, they had learned it quite well, judging from the praise they received the following week in the homes where we caroled.

The main reactions from the men were critical, and their praise was very hard to come by. One man said that the young people's singing lacked volume. A couple of the men suggested that they stick to English songs. Others gave some sparse indications of approval. While it is possible that the second generation's singing did not meet the men's standards in terms of volume and style, the adults' lack of enthusiasm was not simply over missing aesthetic elements of the performance. It appeared that they were at least ambivalent toward, if not bothered by, their children's ability to sing the Malayalam songs. That the teenagers were stepping on the men's linguistic turf became evident in the suggestion from more than one man that the children stick to singing in English.[22]

Besides their discomfort over the challenge to their domain, the men also appeared quite uneasy with the gender of those challenging the boundaries, as an incident that occurred while we were traveling between homes in the van demonstrates. About six men were packed into the front seats of the rather large van. The girls, boys, and I were jammed together in the back. We did not have proper seats, since the back seats had been folded over to make additional room. I was trying to teach the young people a new Malayalam carol that they could add to their repertoire. They did not have much trouble picking up the carol, which was sung to the tune of a Malayalam film classic. I noticed that a few of the men were paying attention to our singing in between their own conversations. The words of the song were unfamiliar to them, but they started chiming in at the refrain, since it was a classic and a very catchy tune. Then one of the men said, "Next year the kids will be able to do it [caroling] on their own." Another said, "Yup! That's all we are good for now—to sing the refrain." After a while, he added, "I guess Indira Gandhi is still in power."[23]

As the young people continued to practice the new Malayalam song, the man who had made the comment about Indira Gandhi spontaneously began to sing one of the adults' caroling staples. All the other men joined in. There was an awkward silence in the back of the van as the rudely interrupted teenagers had to stop learning the new song, at least for the time being.

The interaction in the van demonstrates the men's awareness that their territory was being infringed upon when the young people started learning the Malayalam songs. On the one hand, many of them complain about their children not speaking Malayalam.[24] Yet in this instance, some of them appeared intensely uncomfortable listening to their offspring singing in the language. The comment "that's all we are good for now—to sing the refrain" sounded like a lament about losing the last foothold. The subsequent comment about Indira Gandhi may have been directly inspired by the majority female presence and especially by my role as the organizer. That the men spontaneously burst into their own song while the youth were still singing perhaps attests to the level of their discomfort. It was also an assertion of their dominance and their right to intervene at any point. While on one hand their musical outburst temporarily stopped the young people from learning the new song, it also established their prerogative over shared space and assuaged their fear of Indira Gandhi being back in power. Or perhaps Indira Gandhi was indeed still in power for most of the men, including the one who made the comment, given that their wives are nurses.

Conclusion

Because many of the adult generation at Saint George's consistently express concern about increasing their children's participation in church activities, the second generation's desire to go caroling, and especially to sing in their native language, ought to have been welcomed by their parents. Additionally, because there are apparently no religious restrictions or rigid conventions from Kerala that prohibit young people from caroling, the resistance expressed by Saint George's adults appeared anomalous and required explanation.

It appears that the impetus to preserve and expand male power in the communal sphere of the church is at odds with the aim of cultural transmission and the retention of the second generation in the church. On one hand, for the men who are both economically and socially marginalized in the wider society, the church and its affiliated activities, such as caroling, become precious space where they feel a sense of belonging and ownership. That they are particularly threatened that it is their daughters and not their sons who want to participate points to the gendered nature of the conflict.

On the other hand, many of the men realize that in order to pass on their religious and cultural practices to their children, they have to give up some of this space for the sake of the young people. There is a resulting ambivalence on the part of the fathers at their children's success that was vividly apparent during the caroling expeditions. Despite their resistance to the young people's participation, even when we were en route to the homes, it was the fathers who were beaming proudly as the various listeners expressed admiration that children could sing so well in Malayalam.

That invisible gendered boundaries were at stake became clear when the young people's desire to go caroling provoked adult (and mainly male) discourses about the meaning of gender. The varying expressions of resistance from the carolers rely on these discourses, which, I believe, while drawing on religious and cultural sources for legitimation, were grounded in the historically specific, gendered immigration experience of these men.

The discussion about the inappropriateness of the girls' participation in the caroling depended on a discourse about female frailty and weakness. The man who phoned me to talk about the danger of young women going caroling also invoked a discourse about the danger of female sexuality. Interestingly, while he argued that the girls had to be protected from the potentially intoxicated men, the obverse side of the discourse was the legitimation of exclusively male space as protection for men who are potential victims of feminine wiles. The man who cried shame on the boys was banking his argument on the discourse of naturally and divinely decreed male leadership over women. The musical interruption in the van was possible only because of the existence of an underlying discourse that allows adult men control over shared space. The telling comment about Indira Gandhi underlines the reality of a female-led immigration process that serves as the framework within which these boundaries are negotiated.

It is easy to be critical of the men for exercising their patriarchal authority in attempting to exclude the teenage girls. However, in light of the losses they suffered in the immigration experience, especially along gender lines, it is understandable why the congregational space and their roles there are so critical for them.

Nevertheless, judging by the high attrition rate of young people over high school age at Saint George's, the parents' fears that they are losing the second generation are quite justified. By failing to incorporate the young people successfully into the church, they are ensuring their own early demise as an institution. Interventions such as funding a special youth worker[25] and increasing the opportunities for participation for young people in church activities may stem the flow temporarily. However, I believe that the American diocese needs to map out a long-term vision that addresses such issues as offering consistent English-language services and training clergy to meet the needs of both the first generation and the American-born. Finally, the church needs to reevaluate the sexist bases of its gendered practices that are bound to continue alienating the second generation—both young men and women—who live in a world where the sight of Indira Gandhi in power is at least not unusual and sometimes even welcomed.

ACKNOWLEDGMENTS

I am indebted to the New Ethnic and Immigrant Congregations Project for support in the initiation and completion of this paper, and especially to R. Stephen Warner and Judith G. Wittner for their editorial suggestions as well as for all their generosities. I am also grateful to Michael Burawoy and Raymond Williams, whose suggestions were critical to the formation of my argument and its final presentation. Last but not least, I thank the priest and members of Saint George's, who shall remain anonymous but without whose cooperation I could not have undertaken this project.

NOTES

1. All the names of the institutions and individuals mentioned here are pseudonyms.

2. At the 1995 national Indian Orthodox church family conference that I attended, a main topic of discussion was how to keep young people in the church. At the concluding session of the conference, in response to a young college graduate who had expressed interest in the ministry, a spontaneous collection was taken up for his financial support, and the priest at Saint George's offered him free room and board in return for working with the young people at his church.

3. I have received conflicting reports from interviews about the gender of carolers in Kerala. Some people report that both boys and girls go, while the majority claim that it is only young boys. But all accounts agree that it is not an exclusively adult activity in Kerala, even though there are no official church regulations about who is allowed to go caroling.

4. My ability to move between the youth and adult identities also points to the difficulty of sustaining these traditional social definitions in the American context. Part of the conflict around who gets to go caroling may be related to the tension surrounding the challenge of the Indian definitions of these categories in an American environment where eighteen-year-olds are adults.

5. The American Hospital Association reported a 12.7% vacancy rate in nursing positions in 1989. The American Nursing Association (ANA) reported a 18.9% vacancy rate in nursing-home positions (Friedman 1990).

6. Saskia Sassen-Koob (1984) notes that the large influx of women into the labor market may disrupt unwaged work structures in the community, thereby minimizing the possibilities of returning to the communities of origin and consequently inducing a pool of migrant workers.

7. While no accurate figures exist on the number of Kerala immigrants, a directory on Keralites in the United States (Andrews 1983) indicates that 85% are Christians, which make up only one-fifth of Kerala's population. As Raymond Brady Williams (1988, 108) explains, "That astounding figure results from the recruitment of nurses from Kerala and from the fact that the nursing profession is heavily populated by Christians." Williams's (1988) own survey of the Kerala Christian community in Dallas found that 49% of adults reported nursing as their occupation.

8. For an in-depth description of the history and organization of various Christian groups in Kerala as well as the immigrant congregations in the United States, see Williams (1996).

9. I make the distinction between the parish in India and the congregation in the United States since the former tends to be ascriptively organized around geographical divisions, whereas the latter is formed on the basis of convenience and political splits.

10. The main immigration centers have been major urban areas such as

New York and Chicago as well as cities in Texas, Florida, California, and New Jersey. For a complete description, see Williams (1996).

11. The Indian Orthodox church categorizes membership per nuclear family unit and not per adult. The adult males in the family are the official representatives of the family, and it is typically the man's name that appears on the church roster. In the very rare cases where there is no male representative, the woman's name appears on the roster but she is still ineligible to vote in public meetings, despite being a contributing member. It is hard to give an exact head count for Saint George's, but I estimate that about 400 people—adults and children—attend the services; 101 families are listed on the roster.

12. When using the term "youth," I am including teenagers and all unmarried men and women into their late twenties. In the Indian context, one attains adulthood upon marriage, which has historically happened for most people in their late teens or early twenties. Thus potential marriage partners are referred to as "suitable boys or girls."

13. In 1987, the church synod revised the constituton to permit girls under the age of 5 to be brought along with male children to kiss the altar during the baptism ceremony. That the church chose the age of 5 is not accidental, since it sees females under that age as nonsexual.

14. I conducted interviews in both Malayalm and English. I often asked the person being interviewed which language he or she preferred. Most often, we switched back and forth through the interview. As a result, the quotes in this paper were sometimes translated from Malayalam.

15. Won Moo Hurh and Kwang Chung Kim (1990) also found the same phenomenon among Korean American male immigrants in Korean American churches.

16. The tendency for congregations to split over nondoctrinal issues is a growing concern among many church leaders. While I do not have the exact numbers of congregations that have formed from splits, informed church members at national meetings indicate that it is a common pattern in most metropolitan areas where there is more than one congregation. Further research is necessary to ascertain the exact numbers.

17. Eui Hang Shin and Hyung Park (1988) find schisms to be prevalent in Korean immigrant congregations as well. Furthermore, they find that competition for status-enhancing staff positions is one of the major reasons for such splits.

18. While he is no longer the diocesan bishop, Bishop Mar Gregorios holds the title of "Senior Bishop" and is in charge of "renegade" congregations and priests who refuse to be under the supervision of the new bishop. Since his resignation, Bishop Gregorios has presided over an annual family conference that has been consistently scheduled for the same weekend as the official national conference of the U.S. diocese.

19. These songs are sometimes written by members of the community in the United States using the tunes of film songs from Kerala. Christian songs

from the growing Christian popular music scene in Kerala are also used. Having songs in the latest tunes with instrumental accompaniment becomes a matter of pride among the caroling groups from the different Kerala congregations as they try to outdo each other in the caroling and at the annual ecumenical Christmas program.

20. For example, in 1994, the donations from caroling made up one-third of Saint George's total income for the year, according to the financial report presented at the general body meeting.

21. The priest, who was new to Saint George's, was very enthusiastic about increasing the participation of all members. He saw me as a resource for the young people, and asked me to take leadership in organizing retreats and teaching Sunday school. The priest's sponsorship legitimated my presence in the church and facilitated my research immensely.

22. Language is a point of tension in immigrant congregations such as Saint George's, where the first generation prefers the service in Malayalam, which is not accessible to most members of the second generation. Ironically, in this case, the young people's attempt to sing in Malayalam was not welcomed by those same parents who otherwise insist that their children learn Malayalam.

23. Indira Gandhi, the first and only female prime minister of India, is a symbol of female leadership in India.

24. Because I speak Malayalam fluently, the adults often expressed surprise and approval.

25. See n. 2.

REFERENCES

Andrews, Kunnuparampil Punnoose. 1983. *Keralites in America: Community Reference Book*. New York: Literary Market Review.

Friedman, Emily. 1990. "Nursing: New Power, Old Problems." *Journal of the American Medical Association* 264 (December 19): 2977–2978.

Gilkes, Cheryl Townsend. 1985. "'Together and in Harness': Women's Traditions in the Sanctified Church." *Signs: Journal of Women in Culture and Society* 10 (Summer): 678–699.

Haddad, Yvonne Yazbeck, and Adair Lummis. 1987. *Islamic Values in the United States: A Comparative Study*. New York: Oxford University Press.

Herberg, Will. 1960. *Protestant-Catholic-Jew: An Essay in American Religious Sociology*. Garden City, N.Y.: Anchor.

Hurh, Won Moo, and Kwang Chung Kim. 1990. "Religious Participation of Korean Immigrants in the United States." *Journal for the Scientific Study of Religion* 29 (March): 19–34.

Ishi, Tomoji. 1987. "Class Conflict, the State, and Linkage: The International Migration of Nurses from the Philippines." *Berkeley Journal of Sociology* 32: 281–312.

McQuaid-Dvorak, Eileen, and Mark Waymack. 1991. "Is It Ethical to Recruit Foreign Nurses?" *Nursing Outlook* 39 (May–June): 120–123.

Mejia, Alfonso, Helena Pizurki, and Erica Royston. 1979. *Physician and Nurse Migration: Analysis and Policy Implications.* Geneva: World Health Organization.

Min, Pyong Gap. 1992. "The Structures and Social Functions of Korean Immigrant Churches in the United States." *International Migration Review* 26 (Winter): 1370–1394.

Narayan, Kirin. 1993. "How Native Is a 'Native' Anthropologist?" *American Anthropologist* 95 (September): 671–686.

Ragavachari, Ranjana. 1990. *Conflicts and Adjustments: Indian Nurses in an Urban Milieu.* Delhi: Academic Foundation.

Sassen-Koob, Saskia. 1984. "Notes on the Incorporation of Third World Women into Wage-Labor Through Immigration and Off-Shore Production." *International Migration Review* 18 (Winter): 1144–1167.

Shin, Eui Hang, and Hyung Park. 1988. "An Analysis of Causes of Schisms in Ethnic Churches: The Case of Korean-American Churches." *Sociological Analysis* 49 (Fall): 234–248.

Visvanathan, Susan. 1989. "Marriage, Birth, and Death: Property Rights and Domestic Relationships of the Orthodox/Jacobite Syrian Christians of Kerala." *Economic and Political Weekly,* June 17.

———. 1993. *The Christians of Kerala: History, Belief, and Ritual Among the Yakoba.* Delhi: Oxford University Press.

Warner, R. Stephen. 1993a. "Introduction of the New Ethnic and Immigrant Congregations Project." Working Paper, Office of Social Science Research, University of Illinois at Chicago.

———. 1993b. "Work in Progress Toward a New Paradigm for the Sociological Study of Religion in the United States." *American Journal of Sociology* 98 (March): 1044–93.

Williams, Raymond Brady. 1988. *Religions of Immigrants from India and Pakistan: New Threads in the American Tapestry.* Cambridge: Cambridge University Press.

———. 1996. *Christian Pluralism in the U.S.: The Indian Immigrant Experience.* Cambridge: Cambridge University Press.

9 | Competing for the Second Generation: English-Language Ministry at a Korean Protestant Church

Karen J. Chai

> *The red-brick, white-pillared . . . church sitting on a well-tended green might well grace a standard-issue postcard of picturesque New England. Inside, a minister preaches from an imposing pulpit, jabbing the air with his fingers as his voice rises and his congregation bows deeply in the shining oak pews before him.*
>
> *When the pastor steps down, about 200 worshipers—most of them middle class, middle aged, and dressed in their Sunday best—reach for their hymnals. A choir rises as Protestant liturgical music played by a string ensemble swells to the church rafters.*
>
> *But despite its setting, the scene is far from typical. The minister is . . . preaching in Korean. The congregation is Korean—and the Protestant hymns are sung in Korean.*
>
> *An hour after this service, a van packed with Wellesley College Korean Americans pulls up outside the church. A yellow school bus that has stopped at Harvard, BU [Boston University] and MIT to pick up dozens of Korean students arrives as well. The pews, empty only briefly, fill again with Koreans of the so-called "second-generation"—students and young professionals born to immigrant parents in the United States.*
>
> *This congregation ignores the hymnals, and kicks off the service with a half-hour of finger-snapping, singing, and foot-stamping to plugged-in, folk-rock spirituals. The worshipers are here to praise the Lord and pay homage to their Korean heritage in the language they know best: English. (Dezell 1995)*

On August 22, 1986, I first walked into the small library of the church described above. Dragged kicking and screaming to Friday-night Bible study at this Korean church by my parents, my seventeen-year-old

Americanized self was horrified to find thirty people, mostly in their mid-twenties, singing a gospel song in *Korean*. My parents, eager to lessen their anxiety about their daughter going away to college, had hoped that this church would connect me to a caring Korean community. Unfortunately, there were only two other college students in attendance, and unlike myself, it seemed that all of the members had spent their formative years in Korea. Despite these differences and my initial resistance, I stayed. Over the course of the next ten years, I was to see this 30-member group of young adults at Paxton Korean Church (PKC)[1] evolve into a 250-member body with its own English worship service and budget—what R. Stephen Warner (1993, 1994) would call a "de facto congregation." The Korean gospel songbooks and acoustic guitars have since given way to overhead projectors and songs in English accompanied by electric guitars, bass, keyboards, and drums. This group no longer meets in the library on Friday nights. It has moved into the sanctuary.

In this chapter, I tell the story of Paxton Korean Church, a Protestant[2] church located in Paxton, Massachusetts, an affluent suburb of Boston, and its English-language ministry. I draw from data obtained through participant observation, interviews,[3] and reviews of relevant literature and archival records. Being fluent in Korean, I conducted the research in Korean as well as in English. (Translations from Korean are noted.) Of course, my familiarity with PKC also stems from my personal involvement as a member since 1986. In fact, it is my experience there that first sparked my interest in the sociology of religion. While my membership has sometimes presented challenges to me as a researcher, it has been an invaluable asset to my work overall. My perspective as both an "insider" and a researcher has enabled me to develop a deep appreciation for the complex dynamics at work in this church.[4] I also gained a broader understanding of these dynamics by conducting ethnographic research at other ethnic churches and community organizations around the country.[5]

After presenting a historical and theoretical overview of the Korean immigrant church and the issue of generational transition, I will trace the internal and external factors that contributed to the establishment of PKC's English worship service. I will then discuss generational differences at PKC and identify some of the social functions that church membership serves for the second generation. Next, I will examine the ways in which commitment and boundaries are maintained among PKC's second-generation Korean American members, noting especially the other organizations that compete with PKC. I will then con-

Karen J. Chai

clude with an analysis of factors contributing to PKC's English-ministry success and a discussion of the challenges that it will face in the future. In the process of reaching out to the second generation, PKC has evolved into a church of two co-existing, de facto congregations. Not only do these congregations differ in membership demographics, but they have markedly different worship styles, somewhat different beliefs, and potentially different trajectories.

Korean Churches in the United States

> *When the Chinese go abroad, they open a restaurant. When the Japanese go abroad, they open a factory. When the Koreans go abroad, they start a church.*[6]

The ethnic church has historically been an integral part of American life for immigrant groups, and Koreans are no exception. Beginning with the very first Korean plantation workers who arrived in Hawaii in 1903, the church has been the focal point of the Korean immigrant community. Its initial prominence can be attributed to the fact that 40 percent of the early immigrants to Hawaii were either Christian upon arrival or had at least been exposed to Christianity in Korea (Choy 1979, Patterson 1988, Min 1992).[7] This is because Protestant missionaries encouraged Korean converts to emigrate to the United States, which they promoted as a Christian nation. American churches also helped sponsor immigrants. According to Won Moo Hurh and Kwang Chung Kim (1990, 29), "the transplanted Korean church in Hawaii left a legacy of providing Koreans with both Christian and ethnic fellowship." This legacy prevented secular ethnic organizations from approaching the importance of ethnic churches in the Korean immigrant community. In contrast, the predominantly non-Christian early immigrants from China and Japan developed strong secular ethnic organizations based on regional and kinship ties (Hurh and Kim 1990).

Later Korean immigrants, half of whom were Christian prior to arrival, reinforced the tradition established by the early Korean immigrants (Hurh and Kim 1984, 1990).[8] Two factors account for the high percentage of Christians among post-1965 Korean immigrants: the appeal of Christianity to certain classes and the nature of the U.S. Immigration Act of 1965. Christianity's association with Western progress as well as with advanced science and technology tended to attract members of the urban middle class (Kim 1981). Conversion was often seen as a means to upward mobility by means of Westernization.

Furthermore, among urban Christians, it was the middle-class converts who were able to immigrate because the 1965 Immigration Act promoted family reunion and favored professional and technical workers (Hurh and Kim 1984, 1990).

The fact that some 25 percent of non-Christian Korean immigrants affiliate with Korean churches after arriving in the United States further bolsters the church's prominence in the Korean American community (Hurh and Kim 1990). According to Min (1992, 1371), "many probably began attending the ethnic church primarily because it met their practical needs associated with immigrant adjustment." Smith (1978, 1175) states that migration itself is "often a theologizing experience." Therefore, religious affiliation may be more "salient for both individuals and the group after immigration than it had been before immigration" (Warner 1993, 1062). The practical needs met by the ethnic church fall into four categories, all of which would be appealing even to nonbelievers: fellowship, maintenance of cultural tradition, social services, and social status and positions (Min 1992).

First, churches bring individuals together, binding them into a community with regular face-to-face interaction and rituals (Durkheim [1915] 1965). Of course the church serves a number of functions for all groups, not only for immigrants. However, the need for community is heightened among immigrants, who face the "complex conditions of uprooting, existential marginality, and sociocultural adaptation for rerooting" (Hurh and Kim 1990, 31). The church offers, at minimum, weekly opportunities for interaction with other immigrants and instills in members a sense of belonging, comfort, and meaning. It also serves as a microcosm for Korean society, a place where one can meet old friends and also see new faces (Hurh and Kim 1990). Because anyone can join regardless of background, there is widespread participation in the church. Other voluntary ethnic associations, which meet less frequently, often have specific requirements for membership based on school, age, or occupation.

Second, the church helps immigrants maintain their cultural traditions. For example, Korean churches often celebrate holidays by serving Korean food or sponsoring traditional Korean activities and games. Furthermore, immigrants hope to pass down Korean culture to their children by enrolling them in church-sponsored Korean language and culture programs. For many Korean American children, church is the only place where they can meet other children with the same cultural heritage. As a result, Christianity and Koreanness often become very closely associated in their lives.

Third, the church provides social services for members. It offers help to families in need through financial donations or personal support. Pastors and leaders counsel members on such matters as family relations, employment, housing, health care, and education. Church members also share information on those issues, as membership provides access to a well-established personal network that can yield helpful tips and opportunities.

Fourth, the ethnic church plays an important role in satisfying the needs for social status, prestige, power, and recognition within the immigrant community (Hurh and Kim 1990, Min 1992, Shin and Park 1988). This is particularly important in compensating for the downward mobility that usually accompanies immigration. Hurh and Kim (1990) find that this function is more significant for Korean male immigrants, for whom holding a staff position in the church is positively correlated with mental health. Similarly, Sheba George's study of Indian immigrants at a Syrian Orthodox church highlights the relationship between gender and the status function of the immigrant church (see Chapter 8). It is no surprise that Korean immigrant churches have a more hierarchical leadership structure than American churches. In fact, Korean churches that decide to affiliate with American Protestant denominations have encountered difficulty, because Korean pastors insist on maintaining leadership titles that do not exist in American congregations.[9] The Korean immigrant church "provides a hierarchical structure which can serve as a ladder of achievement for church members" (Park 1989, 62).

Beyond particular group characteristics and functions, Koreans' high degree of participation in the ethnic church can also be seen as a manifestation of American pluralism. According to Raymond Brady Williams (1988, 3), religion in the United States "is an accepted mode both of establishing distinct identity and of intercommunal negotiation." Hurh and Kim (1984) note that while racial and ethnic separation is not encouraged in the United States, religious distinctiveness is promoted. Ethnic churches are therefore convenient vehicles for preserving ethnic culture and identity with the support of most Americans. In fact, many Korean ethnic churches became established with the generous contributions of white American churches (Hurh and Kim 1984, 1990).

Since 90 percent of the Koreans in the United States today are either post-1965 immigrants or their descendants, most studies of Korean immigrant churches have focused on the dynamics within the first-generation Korean-language ministry (Hurh and Kim 1990, Min 1992, Shin and Park 1988). At the time of these studies, the first generation was busy establishing the over two thousand Korean churches in the United States, and their young children were in Sunday school (Hurh and Kim 1990, Warner 1994). As long as more Koreans immigrate to the United States, more Korean-speaking churches will be planted and maintained.[10]

As the children of these immigrants come of age, however, will they continue the legacy begun by the first generation? In what direction—if any—will these Americanized, second-generation Korean Americans take the ethnic churches? I have identified the important functions that ethnic churches serve for the first generation. What are their functions in the lives of the second generation? For a group that has been immersed in American culture and feels most comfortable speaking English, the significance of attending a Korean ethnic church is quite different. These are some of the issues I will discuss with respect to Paxton Korean Church.

The "Silent Exodus"?

Although there are no official data on the number of second-generation Korean Americans who attend church—Korean or non-Korean—community leaders and scholars estimate that the figure is quite low. Pai et al. (1987) find that the alienation of second-generation youth from immigrant churches is widespread. Kwang Chung Kim and Shin Kim (1996) observe that most "grown-up" second-generation Korean Americans do not attend their parents' church, even if they reside in the same city. As a result, many of these immigrant churches are gradually transforming from a "church of family members" into a "church of parents" (Kim and Kim 1996, 14). According to some estimates, 90 percent of postcollege Korean Americans are no longer attending church.[11] Similarly, a study of Korean Americans in the New York City area found that while up to 75 percent of the first generation attend church, only 5 percent of the second generation remain in the church after college.[12]

Church leaders argue that traditional Korean churches have been ineffective in addressing the real needs of the second generation, whose members still desire an affirmation of their heritage. One Korean Canadian pastor warns church leaders that if nothing is done in the near future, a whole generation of Korean Americans will be lost through "the silent exodus" (Song 1994). He terms it an "exodus" because the number of those exiting is "staggering." It is "silent" because the exit of the second generation is often unnoticed or not given serious attention within Korean churches. In addition to the language and cultural barriers between the generations, there is a problem of "ownership":

> *Many second-generation members think of the Korean immigrant church as merely a church for their parents, and not for [sic] theirs to identify with, even though they have practically grown up in the Korean church setting. These second-generation Koreans sometimes feel "homeless" as they find themselves neither fitting in with the Korean immigrant churches nor integrating into the mainstream [Anglo-Saxon] churches. (Song 1994, 1)*

As assimilation processes[13] inevitably alter the character of the Korean ethnic group over generations, ethnic churches must adapt to these changes in order to secure organizational survival.

Based on his studies of Japanese congregations in Canada, Mark Mullins (1987) presents an ideal-typical model of ethnic church development to secure survival. During the first stage of ethnic church evolution, the church is dominated by the language and clergy from the country of origin. However, the church soon encounters dilemmas primarily related to the tension between language and culture in the old society and the new. As members age and their descendants become structurally assimilated into the host society, the unique language and social needs that motivated the first generation are no longer relevant. In response, the church must develop new goals. Mullins (1987, 327) writes:

> *If ethnic churches de-ethnicize their religious tradition and broaden their base of relevance, organizational survival is a possibility. In order to recruit non-ethnics (as well as acculturated members of the ethnic group), churches must broaden their original goal to include these "outsiders" and create an environment which would be equally attractive to them.*

Mullins believes that even if congregations do not consciously modify their original goals, the process of accommodating English-speaking members and mixed marriages will eventually lead to their transition from "ethnic" to "multiethnic" congregations.

This model implies that the solution to the silent exodus is the transition from a monolingual immigrant church to a second stage with a bilingual minister who also conducts English-language services. The third and final stage of Mullins's model is a monolingual congregation that has been de-ethnicized and transformed into a multiethnic church. By adapting to the inevitabilities of assimilation, the church can insure survival.

On one hand, Paxton Korean Church seems to fit into the second stage of the model in that it has expanded its programming to better incorporate members of the second generation as well as non-Koreans. PKC's English ministry has been growing in membership at a rate of nearly 25 percent per year for the past eight years. It has grown so much, in fact, that its members now outnumber the first-generation members. The English ministry even sponsors outreach programs to Cambodian youth in Lowell and the homeless in Boston. It also coordinates its own missions program, sending teams to work with a Korean missionary in Thailand. On the other hand, what has emerged at PKC is not one unified church, but two co-existing de facto congregations with different styles, priorities, and visions for the future.

"A Service of Our Own": Paxton Korean Church and Its English Ministry

The purpose of [Paxton Korean Church] English Ministry is to build a community of believers who love God and one another, and to make disciples of Christ."[14]

Founded in 1974 with just thirty members, Paxton Korean Church is among the largest Korean churches in New England, with 600 members. Each Sunday, 200 people attend the 11:30 A.M. Korean worship service, 150 children attend Sunday school, and 250 attend its 1:45 P.M. English worship service. While the Korean-speaking congregation maintains its size through recruiting students from Korea who are attending nearby schools in addition to the first-generation immigrants in the Boston area, the main source of PKC's growth has been the explosion in the membership of its English-language ministry.

Unlike most churches, PKC has had only one pastor in its history, Reverend Kim, who came to the United States in 1968 to receive further seminary training. Although he had intended to return to Korea upon the completion of his studies, he eventually decided to establish his ministry in Greater Boston. PKC rented the facilities of predominantly white churches for the first fifteen years, moving three times. In 1988, after renting Community Church of Paxton for seven years, PKC negotiated an arrangement for joint ownership with that church. The arrangement grew out of PKC's desire for a church "home" and Community Church's struggle to maintain its large facilities in the face of dwindling membership. Financial support from the Korean congregation saved Community Church from reducing its pastoral ministry to half-time.[15] In turn, PKC secured a large, conveniently located building. Paxton is a particularly suitable location for a Korean church, since it is the fourth largest population center for Korean Americans in New England, with Asian Americans accounting for 6.5 percent of the town population. In fact, Paxton has recently been classified as a "suburban enclave" for Asians (Chung 1995).

Although PKC's Korean ministry has been successful in many ways, it has not been immune to some of the problems that plague immigrant churches. In 1992, a group of elders at the church registered a complaint with the denomination, citing "dissatisfaction . . . in the direction and philosophy of Reverend Kim's ministry." Several elders and members eventually decided to leave PKC to plant their own church. The conflict ended peacefully, however, as remaining PKC members sent them forth with a bittersweet time of blessing and prayer during their last worship service at PKC. Since that time, some of those elders have moved away from greater Boston, and others have returned to PKC. Their new church has since experienced its own schism, with only one family remaining and yet another break-off church newly formed by three families.[16]

The English ministry at PKC was formed in the early 1980s as the Young Adults Group under the guidance of a middle-aged, first-generation deacon. At the center of this ministry was the Friday-night Bible study, which consisted of thirty minutes of singing, two hours of small-group studies, and thirty minutes of refreshments and fellowship. This fellowship attracted Korean American college students, graduate students, and professionals who were interested in learning more about Christianity while meeting others like themselves. Although there were no seminary-trained staff members, the group was led by a core group of committed members and annually elected officers. Although English was the preferred language, most members were bilingual. The Young Adults Group was created in response to the need for a ministry to a specific culture and age group, but its members were still comfortable interacting in Korean and worshiping in the Korean-language services on Sundays.[17]

As the years went on, however, the incoming college students were progressively more Americanized. English became the sole language for many in the Young Adults Group, who, unlike the original members, had been born in the United States. Because of the language barrier, some Friday-night Bible study attendees could not attend the Korean worship service on Sundays.

Thus, Paxton's English ministry essentially functioned as a parachurch, and its monolingual members could not consider Paxton Korean Church as their true "home" church. The leaders of the Young Adults Group recognized that if they could not expand their programming, they would lose members to other groups. Indeed, all of the four other Korean churches in the Boston area at the time had either established or were planning their own English-language worship services. They were also becoming more aggressive, postering campuses and sending letters to incoming college students over the summer. Furthermore, secular Korean student organizations on campus were continuing to dominate the social scene among Boston's Korean American students. The most significant change at PKC came as a response to this growing competition and the increasing Americanization of the second generation.[18]

PKC's pastor and elders first attempted to resolve the language issue in 1987 by introducing a simultaneous translation system during the Korean worship service (see Fenggang Yang's essay [Chapter 10] for a description of such a system in a Chinese church). Second-generation Korean Americans listened to English translations through small radio headsets. Although this system enabled more people to participate, the translations, done by inexperienced staff, were often slow, inaccurate, and uninspiring. Furthermore, the content of the sermons was more appropriate for an older generation—one that was more Korean, and one whose main concerns were making a living and raising children in a "foreign land." The simultaneous translation system proved inadequate in bridging the language and culture gap, and was gradually discarded over three years.

Some of the second-generation members also felt uncomfortable with the idea of an ethnically limited church. They saw the Korean church as a place in which to explore their ethnic roots within the context of Christianity. The main element was Christianity, and Korean culture was a secondary bonus. With the emphasis on evangelism, the members had to confront the problem of trying to witness to their non-Korean, non-Christian friends. If a Korean friend wanted to attend PKC, it would be no problem. However, if a non-Korean friend were interested in Christianity, members could not hope to have him or her join PKC. This illuminated the inherent paradox in an exclusive church that also promotes proselytization. The second generation increasingly called for its own English worship service—one that would be inviting and open to non-Koreans while providing Korean Americans with an opportunity to express their ethnic identity.

The greatest obstacle in the establishment of the English worship service at PKC was the lack of an ordained, English-speaking pastor to lead the service. Starting in 1989, however, a significant series of events occurred at PKC. Four of its members—all well-educated professionals—felt the call to leave their promising careers and go into the ministry. One by one, they enrolled in nearby Gordon-Conwell Theological Seminary. Soon, these seminarians began planning an English-language worship service at PKC.

Before their plans were approved by the leaders of PKC and the Community Church of Paxton, these seminarians and leaders had to explain why they wanted to start their own worship service, even without an ordained pastor. The pastor of Community Church of Paxton did not understand why they wanted to go through the trouble of creating another Sunday service, when an English service was already being offered by his church at 9:30 A.M. in the same building. The leaders noted that language was not the only issue—rather, second-generation Korean Americans desired ethnic fellowship and a service designed to help them overcome the challenges and conflicts that are unique to their experience.

Their goal was finally realized on September 15, 1991, when PKC held its first English worship service at 1:30 P.M., with 120 people in attendance. Although each of the three seminarians who remained at PKC felt unable to lead by himself, they joined forces to preside over services and deliver the sermons in rotation. At first, PKC's English worship service followed established conventions, opening with an organ prelude and the lighting of candles by two children dressed in robes. The group used Community Church's hymnals, singing in English the same traditional Protestant hymns that the first generation would sing in Korean. Although the order of events was changed slightly, the program was essentially an English version of the Korean worship service, except that the sermons were tailored to the concerns of second-generation Korean Americans. While the Friday night program was casual, upbeat, and contemporary, the Sunday service was calm and reflective, echoing the richness of tradition.

Toward the end of each ninety-minute Sunday service, Reverend Kim would enter the sanctuary to give the final benediction and greet members as they exited. Although he gave the leaders a large degree of autonomy in planning the English worship service, he also recognized that visitors and parents might question the legitimacy of a service that was not led by an ordained pastor. He continues this practice today. His presence for at least part of the service, however short, is one of the few elements that the Korean and English services have in common.

Soon after the inaugural English worship service, leaders began talking about adding a short time of singing before the service, much like the informal period that preceded each Korean worship service. This was designed to keep members occupied in case of last-minute delays and to help them "prepare their hearts for worship." The English worship service committee, which consisted of seminarians and lay leaders, then decided to bring in the Gospel songs, instruments, and overhead projector that had previously been relegated to Friday nights. This ten-minute prelude gradually grew into a thirty-minute segment that is now a favorite and integral part of worship, becoming PKC's "trademark" and blurring the style line between Friday nights and Sunday afternoons.

As new members and seminarians have brought songs and ideas to PKC's English ministry, the English worship service has become more akin to a new-style evangelical church. Gone are the candle-lighting rituals and hymnals, steeped in old, main-line Protestant tradition. They have been replaced by the rituals of hand-clapping and bopping to the beat of contemporary Gospel songs from Vineyard Christian Fellowship and Hosanna Integrity Music, reminiscent of members' days in the youth group and consistent with current trends in American evangelicalism.[19]

Ironically, the language barrier that divided generations facilitated the success of PKC's English worship service in the end. This language barrier had given the second generation an important reason to break away from the first and create its own worship service. Without this language difference, the second generation would not have had an excuse to create a whole new worship service within the same church— a service that appeals to their generation, yet is different from what everyone might have imagined.

Friendly Rivalry: Other Korean Churches

There are currently four other Boston-area Korean American Protestant churches with English worship services, all evangelical. Prospective members engage in church "shopping" to compare such factors as size, quality of ministry staff, doctrine, location, and service time.[20] Until 1995, all of the English-language ministries had essentially been departments of existing Korean immigrant churches. Since then, three new predominantly second-generation Korean American churches have been established—two planted by recent Gordon-Conwell graduates, and another that broke off from a suburban first-generation church and moved to an urban location. All of PKC's "rival" churches are accessible by public transportation, and some boast convenient morning worship service times.

PKC's suburban location, while ideal for immigrant families, has been a mixed blessing for the English ministry. The English worship service is the third service in the church building every Sunday, and members complain that its current starting time of 1:45 P.M. cuts into the day. Because most live in the city and do not own cars, they must also rely on rides from friends or on the church van and bus service. Three vans transport members from surrounding suburbs, but the largest group of members spends up to one hour on the yellow school bus hired by the church to bring in members from Boston and Cambridge. Bus service was begun in 1991 to accommodate the sudden growth in membership that came with the establishment of the English service. Transportation continues to be an area of major concern for PKC, especially because the English ministry has had to devote thirteen percent of its annual budget to transportation costs.

Although PKC's location and worship time discourage some prospective members, they have proven to be beneficial for the church in part by raising barriers to entry. One former PKC member notes that she saw "more commitment at PKC." People at her current church come and go as they please, and they do not always stay for all of the activities. She admits, "At PKC, it was a pain that I had to stay for such a long time because of my ride, but now I think that was good." Although there are still people who "come and go as they please" at PKC, the problem of free-riders, those who benefit from the organization while contributing little to the common good, is reduced, because the time commitment required often attracts more enthusiastic members.[21]

As membership has grown considerably in a short period, however, PKC has lost some members and potential members to smaller, rival churches. PKC is sometimes criticized as being "too big" and "too impersonal." Although its membership is still growing, the rate of growth at PKC has dropped slightly from that of the earlier years. Heightened competition has forced leaders to recognize that the church is becoming structurally saturated and can no longer grow on the basis of informal relationships. In response, PKC's postcollege group followed the lead of Korean and American evangelical churches by trying out a cell-group system in 1996. These ten-member cell groups form an intentionally created network of cohesive subgroups within the church, so that members can simultaneously enjoy small-church intimacy along with large-church diversity.[22]

The coming of age of the second generation has also created demands beyond the English worship service. Since 1990, PKC has maintained an English-speaking couples' ministry within the Young Adults Group. Currently there are fourteen couples, nine of whom have children. Each Friday and Sunday, mothers, volunteers, and paid babysitters staff a nursery on a rotating basis, watching the service over closed-circuit television. In 1996, parents who attend English worship service also established a small Sunday school program for their children.

Sunday school is one area in which programming needs to be expanded. Couples Group leaders warn that because the other Korean American churches have begun their own Sunday school programs, more settled families will go elsewhere if PKC does not offer an appealing children's ministry. Although the English-speaking ministry initially catered specifically to students, it now finds that its membership also comprises growing families, with parents seeking Christian education for their children. The failure to retain settled families would, in turn, prevent the congregation from maturing into membership stability and financial security.

Generational Differences

How do the priorities and beliefs of second-generation Korean Americans differ from those of the first generation? It is difficult to generalize on these issues, as there are certainly in-group differences. In the course of the interviews, however, some interesting contrasts emerged. First-generation interviewees tended to see Christianity as an ascribed characteristic that comes with family church membership. Immigrant churches are strict in observing traditions and rituals, preserving hierarchy, and financially supporting the church. Several prominent families serve as cornerstones of the church, contributing large amounts, serving as leaders, and opening their homes to newcomers and guests. Confucian elements of duty, respect, and protection pervade the workings of the church.

The second generation, however, is less concerned with formal structures and processes, and instead stresses Christian ethics and evangelism. One college student remarks that the first generation is more "fervent" and faithful in activities such as prayer. At the same time, he feels that the first-generation leadership puts more emphasis on outward characteristics such as numbers: "The leaders like you to bring friends to church just to have the church grow in size." The

Karen J. Chai

second generation thinks of itself as more individualistic and views Christianity as an achieved characteristic that comes through "accepting Jesus Christ as one's personal savior."

As it is with other evangelicals, the notion of being "born again" is key in the second-generation conception of Christianity at PKC. More than demonstrating loyalty and commitment to the church, it is important that one have experienced a personal encounter with God. For the first generation, the immigrant congregation is a "Gemeinschaft within the Gesellschaft, a remembrance of Zion in the midst of Babylon" (Warner 1993, 1063). Ethnic particularism binds first-generation congregation members, who follow the mainline, ascribed model of recruitment. What the second-generation congregation chooses as the basis of its identity, however, is no longer Korean culture and language, but evangelical Christianity.

The subject of marriage vividly illustrates generational differences in attitudes toward religion and ethnicity. Several second-generation PKC members state that while they themselves would like to marry committed, "born-again" Korean American Christians, their parents, some of whom are active churchgoers, emphasize the Korean over the Christian criterion. That is, some "religious" parents would not object to their son or daughter marrying a non-Christian, but they would definitely object to him or her marrying a non-Korean. This inconsistency often causes the children to doubt the sincerity of their parents' faith. Members express frustration about receiving pressure from their "Christian" parents to settle for a non-Christian spouse. A married woman explains:

> Church is different for me and my parents. I like to think that I separate Koreanness from Christianity. My parents think it's more important to marry a Korean. They think that someone is Christian if he grew up in a Christian household. . . . When I was younger, I was more under my parents' cultural influence, but as I developed a more Christian outlook, [the ethnicity of my spouse] didn't matter. That only changed right before I met my husband—I wanted to please my parents more.

Embedded in this conflict is the children's desire to please their parents. They also recognize the status hierarchy within the Korean American community that favors those who marry others of Korean descent: "Because I married a Korean, I'm considered by all of my elders as being successful. Because of his status, it makes my parents' status higher. My cousins who didn't marry Koreans are looked down upon."

Generational differences can be attributed to several factors. First, ministry needs of people in their twenties differ from those of a group in their forties and fifties, as the types of challenges that one faces vary according to one's stage in life. Second, immigrants generally lack integration into American society and depend heavily on contact with others from their native country. In contrast, members of the second generation can choose from more organizational options. Because they generally feel more comfortable in American society, their "comfort zone" is not restricted to ethnic organizations.

Third, I have found that, in many cases, the generations have had separate religious educations and experiences. With the first-generation parents struggling to adjust to a new society and many even to a new religion, there were few resources available for their children's Sunday school programs. Most adults were ill-equipped to implement a Christian education curriculum, let alone one in English. In response, Korean churches sometimes recruited "a mission-minded adult from a Caucasian church . . . or a college student from a nearby Christian college" (Goette 1993, 241) or a local seminary student to teach the children. In other cases, parents enrolled their children in the "Sunday school of the Caucasian church from which they [were] renting their facilities" (Goette 1993, 241) or sent them to Bible programs at local evangelical churches.

The result was a two-tiered Christian educational system in which the second generation essentially received teachings from a tradition different from that of their parents, and parents had little direct involvement in what was being taught to their children. The evangelical seminarians introduced excited youth to guitar-accompanied contemporary Gospel songs. Non-Korean evangelical churches also initiated the children into their own brand of American Christianity and provided youth with Christian role models who, unlike many of their parents, were fluent in English.

Thus, most second-generation children did not grow up worshiping with their parents. Even if a family attended a Korean church together, religious experiences were difficult for the different generations to discuss. This system set the stage for the second generation's questioning of their parents' faith, as well as the first generation's concern that their children had become "too religious" in some cases.

The Role of PKC in Korean American Lives

Given that second-generation Korean Americans have a different religious experience from their parents and face no language barrier in American society, why do some still choose to attend a Korean church?

Many of the reasons that second-generation PKC members give are the same practical reasons for which first-generation members attend church, as outlined earlier in this chapter. What is different between generations, however, is the nature of struggles and challenges that they face. Furthermore, the first generation is forced to choose the ethnic church, but the second generation makes the choice not because it has no other options, but because the church is a safe space where ethnicity and spirituality merge into one.

Although some interviewees expressed ambivalence about their social motives for attending PKC, the most consistently cited reason was the opportunity to be with people who share their cultural background. One young professional explains why it is important for her to attend a Korean church:

> *I still feel that for some reason my identity hasn't jelled. I think I would be able to attend an American church and receive the same kind of spiritual food that I would get at a Korean church. The only thing that would be different would be the cultural aspect. . . . Yes, it was comforting to see people who looked just like me, who I can talk to about kimchee or [other] Korean food or how to make it—that side of me.*

The second generation finds that PKC can meet a deeper sense of spirituality and impart a strong sense of Christian identity. They are able to form close relationships with others who have been shaped by the same Korean cultural forces. Church becomes the place where they find their all-consuming identity—an identity whose boundaries are constantly reinforced. As another member puts it, "social and spiritual experiences [are] mixed . . . inadvertently" at PKC. She adds that she feels "more comfortable with Koreans and [finds it] easier to get along with them."

PKC English-ministry members also cite the importance of the status function of the church. One woman admits that, in retrospect, church was "the place where [she] could feel important, worthwhile," especially because of her position as a Young Adults Group officer. PKC was also a haven in which she did not feel forced to compromise her Korean and Christian identities, because she was surrounded by others in the same situation

Second-generation Korean Americans often struggle with their marginality with respect to both Korean and American societies. Some have characterized Christianity as a way of having one new identity supersede the other, thereby relinquishing them from their struggle

(Kim 1993). Others note that the second generation sometimes establishes its identity not with respect to the conflict between the society of origin and the host society, but in contrast to the first generation.[23] That is, they are most concerned with differentiating themselves from their parents. I found support for both perspectives at PKC.

Many second-generation members stated that their parents have always been active in a local Korean church in the United States. However, they also grew up seeing their parents get into conflicts and splits over church matters, which did not appear so "Christian." They also felt parental pressure to seek high-paying, high-status occupations in order to elevate their family status. Furthermore, parents stressed the importance of marrying a Korean, with hardly any mention of Christianity. These seemingly contradictory messages led the second generation to believe that their parents' version of Christianity is not what Christianity is supposed to be. Consequently, the second-generation ministry has adopted a more casual worship style, and emphasizes missions and sacrifice rather than prosperity.

In a close-knit community such as PKC, where members spend endless hours together, intrachurch relationships are inevitable. Dating and marriage are hot topics, discussed at virtually every gathering. Regardless of age group, members talk about their relationships, gossip about potential couples, and even poke fun at those who "really need" to get married. Countless sermons have touched upon this topic, and one member notes that church is a "[sexually] charged" environment for him. It is no surprise that several of the married couples within the group first started dating as PKC members. An important function of church membership is that Korean Americans are meeting friends—and spouses.

The fact that many PKC members have met their spouses at the church is not lost on the first generation. For instance, one Korean immigrant from Connecticut approached Reverend Kim at the 1996 wedding of a couple that had met at PKC. He said, "I hear that your church is the place to go if you want your children to marry well. It seems that a lot of young people go to your church. I have a son who is working in Boston" (translated from Korean). He then listed his son's credentials, implying that he would like Reverend Kim to introduce his son to a suitable mate from the church, even though his son does not attend church. Indeed, in a 1995 sermon, Reverend Kim had recounted numerous cases of marriage between individuals who had met at PKC or through his introduction. He had noted that parents from all over the country ask him to introduce their children to suitable mates. Rev-

Karen J. Chai

erend Kim had concluded his sermon by urging the Korean-speaking congregation to attend church faithfully so that their children could marry well.

Instead of forcing the second-generation members to integrate themselves into the first-generation model of the Korean church, the first generation at PKC has given them the autonomy to create their own programs. Relinquishing control has ironically enabled the first generation to see two of their greatest wishes come true. First, it has led to an English ministry that brings together like-minded members, yielding friendship networks that in turn, foster intragroup marriage. Second, intragroup marriage contributes to the persistence of the Christian legacy among Korean Americans as well as to the persistence of Korean American ethnic and racial identity. As church membership grows more diverse, intermarriage with non-Koreans is likely to increase. For the time being, however, PKC continues to be an ideal place for Korean parents to send their children to find Korean mates.

"The Fast Track": Organizational Commitment and Boundary Maintenance

It is difficult to generalize about which factors lead to a greater commitment to the church, especially since members themselves often attribute differences to spiritual forces. It does seem, nevertheless, that the committed members have been recruited through social networks and have become embedded into the Christian social community. Whether they became embedded because of their commitment or whether they became committed because of their dependence on the social community is unclear.

One factor to consider is age. In general, most of the college students who choose to become involved in church tend to become very involved, whereas graduate students and professionals exhibit more variation. Perhaps college is a unique time that fosters spiritual quests, or perhaps PKC programming appeals more to college students. Perhaps postcollege members are just maintaining their level of commitment from their college years, or perhaps they view PKC merely as a place where they can perform a weekly religious ritual and meet other Korean Americans. After all, the church also serves as a convenient method of entrée into the Korean American community.

Another potential explanation for the differing levels of involvement is car ownership. Some members must ride the provided transportation, while others drive their own cars to PKC. Those with cars can come and go as they choose, but those who ride the buses and vans must walk to bus stops and remain at PKC for the entire duration of its programs on a given day. Most of the college students do not own cars, so attending PKC simply takes more effort for them.

A third factor in commitment is the number of alternatives that members have if they want to meet fellow Korean Americans or Christians. If college students want to meet people like themselves, they can often find close friends on campus with the same ethnic background, or they can join a campus organization. For people who are not in college or who attend schools that have only a few Korean Americans, church is their main option. For example, a large number of students from a local single-sex college are very active members of PKC, as are students of another school with very few Korean Americans.

Although there are different views about what it means to be a "good Christian," several indicators are used by PKC members to gauge commitment to the church, commitment to God, and fitness for leadership. One obvious measure of commitment to PKC is the degree of involvement in church activities, and some members spend sixteen hours per week in church-related activities. These include Friday-night Bible studies, Sunday worship services, campus or cell-group meetings, planning meetings, and various fellowship events. This does not include time spent socializing with Christian friends. For this subgroup, all of their activities are oriented around Christianity. In fact, one member estimates that she spends 60 to 75 percent of her free time in church-related activities.

Among college students, involvement in the Korean Students Association (KSA) has delineated moral boundaries and has often raised questions about one's commitment to God. All of the college students I interviewed—in Boston and other cities—agree that on their campuses, the main competition of Korean churches is the KSA. There has traditionally been a bit of tension between the two organizations, because church members tend to regard the KSA as a self-serving social organization whose primary purpose is to hold intercollegiate dance parties.

A very active PKC woman admits, "I culturally associate spirituality with certain behaviors, and there is a stigma attached to KSA people [as opposed to] church people." She adds that part of this stigma stems from the fact that missionaries who went to Korea were conservative Presbyterians and Methodists, who instilled in Korean Christians beliefs against the evils of smoking, drinking, and dancing that immigrants brought with them to the United States. In turn, the immigrants passed these attitudes down to their children. While the second-generation Korean American Christians have worked to distance themselves from the sometimes ascetic traditions of their parents, some influences seem to persist. These attitudes, however, reinforce boundaries between the Christians and their KSA counterparts, often bolstering commitment to the church and identifying potential leaders.

With respect to the church-KSA tension, a Gordon-Conwell seminarian serving at one of PKC's rival churches declares:

> The number-one problem for Korean American college students is the KSA. It is the single most detriment[al organization]. . . . They [the church and KSA] are fundamentally incompatible, because the KSA and the church have different goals. One is to glorify Korean culture, and the other is to glorify God. . . . The KSA provides an alternative for Korean American college students instead of joining a Korean church.

In turn, KSA members sometimes view churchgoers as self-righteous and narrow-minded in their pursuit of "holiness" while ignoring important issues pertaining to the Korean community. Interviewees who try to be active in both the church and the KSA complain of the stress that they encounter due to the polarization of the two groups, as one woman explained: "Whenever there is a KSA event or party, it seems that there is a PKC retreat. I always felt like I had to choose between the two. . . . There is nothing wrong with the KSA. It is just a social group. I don't see why the church has to treat it as such a negative organization." This woman confesses that she often resents her fellow churchgoers, because they seem to frown upon her participation in non-Christian activities. She adds that she has served as president of her school's KSA and has dated a non-Korean, non-Christian man.

In effect, the church and the KSA have created a dilemma for Korean American students on many campuses, since both compete for unwavering commitment. In the past five years, another organization has entered the college scene: Korean Christian Fellowship (KCF), a student group that holds Bible studies and fellowship activities on campus.[24] At some schools, KCF is led by seminary students who also serve at local Korean churches. In fact, one of PKC's seminarians also leads a campus KCF, and often brings KCF members to PKC programs. At other schools, however, missionaries affiliated with parachurch groups such as InterVarsity or Campus Crusade for Christ lead the KCFs. On these campuses, the KCF fellowship events take place on Friday nights at the same time as church-sponsored Bible studies. Consequently, students must choose between attending Bible study at a local Korean church or attending campus fellowship. Even though KCF members still attend local churches on Sundays, active KCF members are often so committed to the KCF community that their involvement in the churches is minimal.

Therefore, on some campuses, commitment to KCF complements church commitment and even draws new members to PKC. On others, however, time conflicts and the divergent membership constituencies take away commitment from the churches. In the latter case, KCF offers the advantage of easier access to close interaction with other members. Daily accountability and fellowship are available without having to venture off-campus. However, one student who chose to join PKC Bible studies rather than KCF Bible studies notes that he was drawn to the diversity of PKC's membership as well as to the superior rigor and depth of its Bible studies.

In order to keep up with the potential competition from KCF, PKC has altered and expanded its college ministry. For example, there are more campus-based fellowship activities, and the college group has been divided into smaller subgroups by year in school. Freshmen through seniors now have their own elected class officers who coordinate spirit-building group activities. The establishment of smaller subgroups facilitates a greater degree of accountability and maintains enthusiasm among the growing number of college students. Like cell groups, they benefit the church, because small groups of people are more cohesive and more effective in keeping members in check.

Boundaries and codes of conduct also exist for postcollege members and leaders who are judged to be "good Christians." For instance, some members like to go dancing, while others see it as a "stumbling block" for younger Christians. In the winter of 1994, a few postcollege leaders attended a dance club with other members. When word of this spread, it caused a great deal of controversy about what is acceptable behavior for leaders and "good Christians." It evoked resentment from those who went, because they felt as if they were being judged for merely trying to have an active social life. A former PKC member living in another state heard about the leaders going to a dance club and even sent them letters of rebuke. A "guilty" member recounts:

> There were other people who received letters from someone in . . . [another state] who heard about it third hand. . . . We were all encouraged [by one of the seminarians] to go to the first leaders' retreat, and that's when [the trip to the club] was brought out. It wasn't the primary issue, though things leading up to it made it seem like it would be the primary issue. I mean, we were all guilty.

Although they were not addressed individually, the seminarian leader, who had found out about the excursion, raised the issue at a leaders' retreat, attended only by the most committed members. He advised those present to be careful about what they chose to do, because they could send confusing messages about the Christian lifestyle to younger Christians who look to them for spiritual leadership. Alhough they had been previously tapped as suitable leaders, these individuals are still susceptible to the draw of alternative pastimes and sometimes stray from the ideal. When they exhibit a desire for a lifestyle other than that advocated by the church, they experience conflict and guilt.

Outside the realm of leadership, some members are quite content to limit their involvement at PKC and actively attend dance parties and clubs. Others choose to attend Sunday services only, forgoing the other seemingly peripheral church activities. They see church mainly as a place to go to every week for service and do not necessarily want more, even though they are aware of their own marginality and the fact that they may be missing out on important experiences. One interviewee explains how he feels about his peripheral role in the church:

> *The purpose of the church is to evangelize, proselytize. . . . So in that sense, [PKC] is very actively involved in doing the right thing. But again, it's something that you can't necessarily force upon someone else. . . . [Although I] might not feel comfortable being on the "fast track" [to heaven], . . . I can see that there's something more to be gained by being on the "fast track." I can see that they [people on the "fast track"] have a much deeper understanding of the personal issues as such . . . , [but] I'd rather at this point be on the remedial track. . . . Maybe over time, things might change. But I don't feel left out at this point, no, not at all. I don't feel pressured to join the fast track, either.*

This individual does not feel like a full member of the church, yet every week he drives to the suburbs to attend services. There is something that still draws him to be with other Korean Americans in this context. His statement also illustrates the fact that while PKC has a core of very committed active members, its size still accommodates those who are content to stay on the borders.

Factors in PKC's English-Ministry Success

The main reason for the success of Paxton Korean Church's English-language ministry is the degree to which the church has met the ethnic, social, and spiritual needs of second generation Korean Americans through its expanded programs. Although second-generation members still enforce boundary distinctions, they do so on their own terms. It is carried out within the context of programming that has been set by them, not by the first generation.

Several important factors have made it possible for this effective programming to be developed at PKC. First, its location in the Boston area means that there is an abundant supply of highly motivated and well-educated Korean American students and professionals from which to draw. Since these young people come from all over the country, they often bring with them training and personal connections from their home churches. In turn, this provides a fertile environment for networking and cross-pollenization.[25] These network ties have led to a degree of isomorphism among Korean American churches, as programming ideas, songs, news, members, and guest speakers travel along the church circuit.

Second, Boston-area educational institutions not only provide potential members, but also maintain a most crucial supply of second-generation seminary students who serve as church leaders. These seminarians, who also bring with them the practices and zeal of their various home churches, have been the visionaries and spiritual authorities among the Korean American Christians. Without the initiative and dedicated labor of these seminarians at PKC, the English ministry could not have emerged. All of PKC's seminarians, as well as the majority of staff at other second-generation Korean American ministries in Boston, have attended nearby evangelical Gordon-Conwell Theological Seminary.

Third, the fact that Boston has never been a major destination for Korean immigrants means that the ratio of local first-generation Korean immigrants to second-generation students and professionals is quite low. Korean pastors in the area are well aware of the large numbers of second-generation students that they can potentially reach, while they also maintain an eye on the crucial function that these students could serve as Sunday school and youth group teachers. PKC leaders have paid close attention to the changing needs of the second generation, because they recognize that if they lose them, they have fewer first-generation immigrants to keep the church going.

Fourth, PKC's second-generation Korean American members are generally not the children of its first-generation members. This is another result of Boston's drawing power for students and young professionals from around the world. Because the first-generation members meet the second-generation members when they come to Boston as adults, they entrust them with more autonomy in ministry. The increased autonomy also means that the second-generation members do not regularly interact with first-generation members. Consequently, the second-generation members do not feel the same Confucian sense of duty toward the first-generation members as they would toward a congregation comprised of their own parents. With the relative dominance and independence of the second-generation Korean Americans in the Boston area, events at PKC offer insight into issues that Korean ethnic churches around the country will eventually confront.

Fifth, the senior pastor's ministry style has afforded leaders a great deal of autonomy over PKC's second-generation ministry. Realizing early on that his ability to minister to the second generation was limited by a generational and cultural gap, he enthusiastically supported the efforts of second-generation members to build their own ministry. His laissez-faire approach gave the English-ministry leaders the space to develop and realize their own vision and programs within PKC. Their autonomy has given second-generation leaders a crucial sense of ownership.[26]

Finally, the critical mass of second-generation Korean American students and professionals in the Boston area has given rise to a number of alternative settings in which Korean Americans can affirm their ethnic heritage. Groups competing with PKC for the time of second-generation Korean Americans include other Korean American churches, Korean American young professionals societies, the campus-based Korean Christian Fellowship, and the Korean Students Association. Furthermore, a host of businesses marketed toward Korean and Asian Americans, including nightclubs and bars, have recently sprung up, beckoning for the time of the second generation. These alternative settings push PKC's English-ministry leaders and members to reassess constantly their goals, boundaries, and strategies in order to compete more effectively for the second generation.

Challenges Ahead in the "Gilded Cage"

The result of the unique Boston mix is a Christian program at PKC designed and implemented by second-generation Korean Americans that is relevant to their experiences and consistent with their worldview. PKC has succeeded in drawing the second generation to the church by giving them a space in which they can build their own ministry—one that is very different from that of the first generation. As the English-language ministry comes into maturity, however, the first and second generations must eventually address the reality of their differences.

One English ministry leader notes that the English ministry has been kept in a "gilded cage," reaping the benefits of remaining within a financially supportive larger church but finding itself severely restricted in implementing its own vision. The benefits offered by the Korean-speaking congregation at PKC do carry with them drawbacks, however, such as association with a liberal denomination as well as reliance on costly transportation services. PKC's English-ministry leaders sometimes express frustration at the first-generation leaders' reluctance to support the English ministry's decision to devote a large percentage of its annual budget to funding missions. At the same time, some first-generation members complain that the second generation, "spoiled" by not having had to worry about the "bottom line," is too quick to judge. One woman notes that, after all, the first generation's "raising up" and support of the English worship service can also be considered as missionary work (translated from Korean).

PKC's English ministry has financial autonomy in terms of budget allocation and could potentially support its operations with the funds raised from the tithes and offerings of the English-speaking congregation. Nevertheless, it still accepts subsidies from the Korean-speaking congregation for such costs as building maintenance, denominational apportionment, and van payments. Otherwise, there are virtually no joint activities, and members of one group rarely know members of the other. The Korean- and English-language ministries at PKC are officially part of the same church and share the same head pastor, but finance is what seems to link these organizations on a practical level.

At PKC, the first-generation congregation did not change its own ministry to incorporate the second. Rather, it tried to incorporate English speakers through simultaneous-translation services. When that effort failed, it continued its Korean ministry but supported the second generation in their creation of a new de facto congregation within the same walls. While many immigrant churches accommodate English speakers because they face certain extinction if they do not, PKC has enough new arrivals for the time being and is unlikely to significantly alter its programming to accommodate more Americanized members. If anything, PKC's Korean ministry is more likely to attempt to alter its programming vertically rather than horizontally—to reach the younger group of foreign students from Korea.

The PKC case can be considered an example of de facto congregationalism on three levels (Warner 1993, 1994). On one level, the denomination recognizes PKC's crucial position within the district and allows it a degree of flexibility in its practices. The denomination must respect the fact that Korean pastors and congregation members are accustomed to certain Christian conventions practiced in Korea that are not followed in the United States, including life terms for ruling elders, exclusion of women from ordination, and a more literal reading of the Bible.[27]

On another level, PKC's Korean congregation recognizes its English-speaking congregation as the most promising group within the church. As a result, first-generation PKC leaders are willing to grant the group a large degree of autonomy and to support the English ministry to the fullest of their abilities. This willingness has enabled the English ministry to grow even further apart from the denominational mold.

In turn, the unique style of PKC's English ministry allows for de facto congregationalism on a third level. Denominational affiliation is not a major factor in deciding whether to join PKC. Some English-ministry members feel uncomfortable being affiliated with PKC's denomination, but they realize that the denomination has little impact on the daily ministry of the church from their perspective. In effect, PKC's English-ministry members choose to join PKC *in spite of* its denominational affiliation.

Despite the de facto congregationalism of PKC, denominational affiliation will still present an important challenge for PKC's English ministry. Although the English worship service is now in its sixth year, there is still no permanent ordained pastor to lead the congregation. In the meantime, an enthusiastic white Gordon-Conwell professor ordained in another denomination has been serving part-time as interim associate pastor.[28] He has proven to be quite popular in his first four months of service, but the continuing lack of a permanent pastor, despite repeated search efforts, has frustrated many members.[29] Furthermore, members of PKC's English ministry tend to have beliefs consistent with more conservative evangelical movements, and therefore have little loyalty to PKC's denomination. The fact that an acceptable associate pastoral candidate will most likely not be ordained in PKC's denomination poses a potentially larger problem.[30]

This will once again raise issues within the denominational leadership, which would be reluctant to lose PKC's English-speaking congregation, a large church in its own right. If an associate pastor ordained by another denomination is found, Reverend Kim and denominational leaders may worry that this person would lead the congregation out of PKC and into a newly independent church of another denomination.

Even without a permanent associate pastor, membership growth continues, and the number of non-Korean members has been steadily rising ever since the creation of the English worship service. Many of these members are of Asian ancestry—Chinese, Japanese, Vietnamese, Filipino—but others are of European or African descent. These non-Korean members now comprise about 10 percent of the total English-language ministry, and several hold important leadership positions. The willingness of the congregation to recruit non-Koreans reflects their determination to shun ethnic exclusivity, focusing instead on Christian doctrine. Since these non-Koreans started attending PKC as friends of members, it reflects the growing diversity in members' social networks and even in their dating relationships. This is consistent with Mullins's ideal type of the ethnic church over generations, as the congregation is now more interested in characterizing itself as a new-style evangelical church rather than as a Korean ethnic church. At the same time, it is very evident from interviews that being with co-ethnics is a cherished and important part of Korean Americans' Christian experience.

Therefore, an underlying issue at PKC and at other Korean ethnic churches is the dilemma of "identity and mission: whether their principal role is to serve new immigrants, to disciple an Americanized next generation, to blend their congregations into Christian America, or to move their churches into some yet undiscovered form and function" (Lee 1996, 51). Paxton Korean Church is doing all three to some extent. For the foreseeable future, it seems that PKC's Korean ministry will continue on its own course, drawing members from new first-generation immigrant families and students from Korea. As long as there remains at least some supply of these groups, the ministry is likely to continue as is.

Will the runaway success of the English ministry enable the second generation to move out of Paxton to be closer to its current target population of young urban students and professionals? The fact that even its most dedicated leaders are young students and professionals who do not necessarily plan to settle permanently in Boston means that the future is quite uncertain. Of course, all of this can change if a capable bilingual pastor suddenly steps in upon Reverend Kim's eventual retirement to unite both congregations in doctrine and goals.

Conclusion

Rather than incorporating second-generation Korean Americans into their first-generation ministry, as Mullins's model suggests, the first generation at PKC has helped the second generation plant a new church within the existing structure. This new congregation has become very successful in its own right. However, it has been nurtured quite apart from first-generation influence, so it is unclear whether this second-generation congregation will ever supplant the first generation in the Paxton church building. Can the two groups really eventually mesh into one de-ethnicized church, or will this second-generation congregation move away from the "gilded cage" and toward a future as a multiethnic, missions-minded church? The answer will depend on many of the same factors that will determine the fate of the Korean ethnic church in general in the United States.

One factor is the rate of Korean immigration to the United States and the number of Korean students who come to study in American schools. Another factor is the degree to which Korean Americans will desire ethnic fellowship. As they become increasingly acculturated and increasingly intermarry, Korean Americans may not feel a particular desire to join a Korean church or may come to prefer a multiethnic church. Third, the Korean American community may choose to become more politically active or to form more secular organizations, which would be alternative settings for experiencing ethnic fellowship. Much also depends on the changing nature of American society and the degree of acceptance of racial and ethnic minority groups. In the case of a sudden wave of racial discrimination or exclusion from non-ethnic institutions, Korean Americans may once again flock to the ethnic churches. On the other hand, Korean ethnic churches may themselves become multiethnic, following the model put forth by Mullins.

All of the above possibilities have already occurred. The future depends on the strategy that each church adopts and the unique environment in which it exists. The success of these strategies will determine the fate of each Korean American church.

NOTES

1. The names of the town, churches, and leaders have been changed.

2. PKC is a member of a national, main-line Protestant denomination. Although its denominational affiliation shapes many facets of the church, PKC's denomination has granted it a large degree of autonomy with respect to its English-language ministry. Because it essentially considers the English ministry to be a department of the church, much like a Sunday school, the denomination is more concerned with the running of the Korean-language ministry. I also found that denominational affiliation was not an important factor in members' decisions to join PKC, as long as it was Protestant. It is, however, an area of growing concern as the English ministry matures and

considers whether it wishes to support a denomination with a liberal central bureaucracy. For further discussion of denominations, see Eui Hang Shin and Hyung Park (1988), R. Stephen Warner (1994), and Robert Wuthnow (1988).

3. For this study, I interviewed over 20 individuals in the Boston area (from September 1994 to September 1995). Although the majority were second-generation Korean American PKC members, others were first-generation immigrants, college students, and professionals. The interviews lasted between 45 and 90 minutes. Because the interviewees were contacted through church and school networks, the sample may be skewed. It is also important to note that PKC members as a whole are well educated and come from solid middle- to upper-middle-class backgrounds. Their attitudes and experiences speak only for a subset of Korean Americans, but they do suggest worthwhile conclusions about the Korean ethnic church in the United States.

4. As a member, I have participated in most of the major activities of both the Korean- and English-speaking congregations of the church for the past 10 years. I have had access to information that a nonmember simply would not have been told or could not have learned through short-term participant observations. For further discussion of the insider as researcher, see Kirin Narayan (1993).

5. For example, I studied an independent second-generation Korean American church in the Chicago area for 2 months during my residence at the 1994 summer institute of the New Ethnic and Immigrant Congregations Project. In the summer of 1996, I conducted ethnographic research on the Portuguese American community in the Boston area for a pilot study on transnationalism.

6. One version of a popular saying among Koreans (see Shin and Park, 1988, 234; Park 1989, 56; Dezell 1995, 32).

7. To understand fully the preeminence of the ethnic church for Koreans in the United States, one must look back at the history of Christianity in Korea. Although Christianity was introduced only a hundred years ago, it has had a major impact on Korean society because of a variety of factors. First, Christianity was introduced at a time when the traditional faiths of Buddhism and Confucianism were being associated with corruption and exploitation of the peasants. Second, much of the growth in Christianity occurred during a period of domestic turmoil created by wars and the threat of Japanese annexation. Rodney Stark and William Sims Bainbridge (1985) note that people tend to look toward new religious systems during such crises, seeking answers that are not being provided by their current religions. Third, Christian missionaries established hospitals and universities in Korea, and they won the favor of Korean leaders with their medical expertise and care.

Furthermore, Presbyterian missionaries aided in the resistance against Japanese annexation (Kitano and Daniels 1988). Because the missionaries came from the West, some Koreans saw Christianity as a vehicle for modernization and upward mobility. By allying themselves with a foreign faith, they believed that they would gain knowledge about other countries. This association of Christianity with modernization and Westernization still pervades Korean churches in the United States.

8. In Korea, Buddhists are the largest religious group, with 24.4% of the population. Christians are the second largest group, with approximately 22%. Of the Korean Christians, 76% are Protestants. Although Christianity is a minority religion in Korea, it is more active than Buddhism in social, political, and educational activities and service (Min 1992, Dearman 1982).

9. For example, Korean Presbyterian churches offer lay leader titles such as *chipsa* (deacon), *ansu chipsa* (hand-laying deacon), and *changno* (elder) in order of increasing importance.

10. According to U.S. census data, 25,618 Koreans immigrated to the United States from 1966 to 1970; 112,493 from 1971 to 1975; 159,463 from 1976 to 1980; 166,021 from 1981 to 1985; and 172,851 from 1986 to 1990 (Barringer et al. 1993, 25–26). In 1990, there were approximately 814,495 people of Korean descent in the United States, and this figure is projected to rise to 1,320,759 in 2000 (Barringer et al. 1993, 50).

11. Peter Cha (1994) presented this figure at Katalyst, an annual conference of church leaders involved in ministries to second-generation Korean Americans.

12. Interview with Dr. Stephen Linton, Research Associate at the Center for Korean Research, Columbia University, New York, January 3, 1997. During his 10 years as a Christian educator, Linton traced the religious participation of 200 young Korean Americans.

13. In this chapter, I use the term "assimilation" broadly to refer to the process through which immigrants and their descendants can become incorporated into the host society through intermarriage, adoption of host language and culture, etc. I recognize that assimilation is the topic of much current debate, and that it can involve mutual adjustments between the immigrant and host communities. The process of assimilation also varies greatly according to the specific characteristics of the immigrant group and host society (see Mittelberg and Waters 1992; Gans 1979; Portes and Zhou 1993).

14. This is the purpose statement of PKC's English worship service as it appears on the weekly Sunday bulletin.

15. The arrangement between the two congregations called for PKC to underwrite a major portion of the church renovations and construction, which involved mostly the expansion and creation of more classroom and office space. The two churches then created a joint corporation, whose board would consist of 6 members from each church. That corporation subsequently became the owner of the church building. The contract encourages mutual cooperation between PKC and Community Church. If, for any reason, one congregation were to move elsewhere, the remaining congregation would become the sole owner of the church building.

16. This case illustrates Shin and Park's (1988) finding that organizational

schisms are largely responsible for the dramatic increase in the number of Korean immigrant churches. They identify several causes for the frequency of schisms in ethnic churches. First, there is fierce competition for lay leadership positions among immigrants who seek status often denied them by American society. Second, there is an abundant supply of ambitious ministers to lead break-off churches. Third, heterogeneity within immigrant congregations is conducive to factions along economic, political, and social lines. Causes of schisms continue to change over time as churches enter new stages of development and maturity.

17. In fact, the very name of the group reflects a more Korean-language orientation. It is a literal translation for *chong nyon hweh,* which is a common Korean term for associations of younger people.

18. With the improvement of the Korean economy, increasing numbers of young Koreans were also coming to the United States to study. When the Young Adults Group became more decidedly monolingual, the Korean-speakers formed their own program in 1990 to cater specifically to the needs of the students from Korea. Although the group attends the Korean worship service with the older first-generation immigrants, it holds its own fellowship events, retreats, and Bible studies. The Korean-speaking young adults are now completely segregated from the English-speaking young adults, and no joint activities are sponsored.

19. At the same time, the influence of the Korean Christian tradition can still be observed in some aspects of PKC's English ministry. For example, second-generation members refer to seminary interns as *jundosa* and address them with the honorific form, *jundosanim.* Commonly used in Korean churches, the terms mean "evangelist" and are used in many second-generation congregations due to the lack of a satisfactory English equivalent. The English worship service also appoints lay leaders to the position of deacon, which is typical of Korean churches but atypical of churches in the denomination. Finally, in 1996 second-generation leaders decided to add a time of corporate prayer to the Friday and Sunday programs in order to highlight the importance of prayer to the congregation. This distinct brand of prayer is referred to as *tongsung gido* in Korean, meaning "crying out prayer." After the worship leader presents the congregation with a specific prayer request, members simultaneously pray aloud, filling the sanctuary with their voices and cries until the leader ends the period with a prayer.

20. Until 1989, the church encouraged PKC members to form close relationships with members of other churches. For example, there were joint retreats as well as monthly fellowship meetings called United Korean Christian Fellowship, sponsored by the second-generation groups at five Korean churches between 1987 and 1989. As the individual congregations grew in number, however, they chose to focus on unity within their own churches. Although some churches invite other churches for praise nights (sing-along gospel music concerts) and other events, joint activities essentially disappeared.

In fact, the leaders of the churches have become so independent that they often disagree on important issues and question one another's practices. For example, leaders of one church drew criticism when they discouraged their members from joining campus Bible studies or any other events that were not sponsored by their church. Within the past year, however, pastors of Korean American and Chinese American churches coordinated a joint sunrise Easter service in English.

21. For a discussion of the "strict-churches-grow" hypothesis, see Lawrence Iannaccone (1994).

22. The cell-group system can be considered a feature of both Korean and American evangelical Christianity. It is an integral part of many large churches in Korea and of Korean immigrant churches as well as of Vineyard Christian Fellowship churches (see Min, 1992, 1382; Warner 1994, 87).

23. Jean Bacon (1996) discusses second-generation Indian Americans in this context.

24. At some schools, the student organizations have slightly different names and/or memberships. For instance, some campuses have a Korean American Students Association (KASA) and an Asian American Christian Fellowship (AACF). For the purposes of this paper, I will group those organizations with the KSA and KCF, which are their counterparts at other schools.

25. For example, high school students in Seattle may hear about PKC through older friends from their Seattle church who have moved to Boston for college. If they decide to attend college in Boston as well, they are likely to attend PKC with their Seattle friends. The network also yields a "chain migration" of members from one church to another, in both directions.

26. Church historian Tim Tseng was quoted by Helen Lee as stating that "unless the first-generation leaders are able to give second-generation pastors the freedom to lead, their young people will not go to these churches. First-generation pastors need to be aware of their dynamic" (Lee 1996, 52).

27. For example, most Presbyterians from Korea are accustomed to a tradition more conservative than the Presbyterian Church (U.S.A.). However, their lack of familiarity with the denomination's constitution and their desire to stay true to their own strong tradition means that "Koreans 'tend not to [follow] the line on the Book of Orders'" (Lee 1989). Disputes with denominations are not limited to Korean churches, but Korean churches tend to wield more bargaining power simply because of their size. Ministers of other ethnic congregations acknowledge that they share feelings of being discriminated against and manipulated by the denomination, but most are afraid to speak out for fear of falling out of favor with the denomination (Lee 1989).

28. The interim pastor is the academic adviser to one of PKC's seminary interns and was asked to serve at PKC after the main English-ministry leader suddenly announced his resignation. So far, members say that they enjoy having the wisdom and sophistication of an experienced, ordained pastor.

Because his position is only temporary, the pastor often comments that he does not wish to alter PKC's ministry, but that he wants to support members in continuing to do the things that they have been doing so well. I would expect that there would be more changes in the ministry if a full-time, non-Korean pastor were to be appointed.

29. In 1995, 4,253 Asians were enrolled at member institutions of the Association of Theological Schools (Lee 1996, 51). Although Koreans are the fastest-growing ethnic group among seminary students, many are students from Korea, not Korean Americans. While there is an adequate supply of Korean-speaking pastors, there is a lack of experienced second-generation pastors. Furthermore, many of those who are qualified to lead second-generation congregations seek the autonomy of starting their own churches, rather than submitting to the authority of a first-generation pastor with a potentially different style and vision.

30. After years of searching for a permanent associate pastor, the English ministry finally hired a full-time pastor, who started in August 1997. True to PKC's history of finding leaders from within its own congregation, this pastor, John Lim, was found in the ranks of its own members. In fact, John Lim had been the very English ministry leader who had resigned in September 1996 after serving for several years part-time as the main English ministry leader. During his time off from PKC, he decided to give up a career in medicine and pursue ministry full-time while finishing up his seminary education at Gordon-Conwell Theological Seminary.

Pastor Lim has made several important structural changes in the English ministry, modeled largely on the principles outlined in Rick Warren's (1995) *Purpose-Driven Church*. The Sunday English worship service has become decidedly more "seeker-sensitive," replacing Christian jargon with more straightforward terms, making the service much more accessible to those who did not grow up in a Christian tradition. Pastor Lim has been able to shift staff member roles and appoint new leaders, largely because of the legitimacy and authority that he had already established with the congregation during his previous years of service. His personal affinity with Reverend Kim has also helped him get off to a running start. Although Pastor Lim has brought much-needed stability and leadership to the English ministry, issues of denominational affiliation remain unsettled, since Pastor Lim is not yet ordained in any denomination.

REFERENCES

Bacon, Jean. 1996. *Life Lines: Community, Family, and Assimilation Among Asian Indian Immigrants*. New York: Oxford University Press.

Barringer, Herbert R., Robert W. Gardner, and Michael J. Levin. 1993. *Asians and Pacific Islanders in the United States*. New York: Russell Sage Foundation.

Cha, Peter, 1994. "Towards a Vision for Second Generation Korean American Ministry," Paper presented at Katalyst 1994, Sandy Cove, Md., March 21–24.

Choy, Bong Youn. 1979. *Koreans in America*. Chicago: Nelson Hall.

Chung, Tom L. 1995. "Asian Americans in Enclaves—They Are Not One Community: New Modes of Asian American Settlement." *Asian American Policy Review* 5 (Spring): 78–94.

Dearman, Marion. 1982. "Structure and Function of Religion in the Los Angeles Korean Community: Some Aspects." Pp. 165–183 in *Koreans in Los Angeles: Prospects and Promises*, edited by Eui-Young Yu, Earl H. Phillips, and Eun Sik Yang. Los Angeles: California State University, Center for Korean-American and Korean Studies.

Dezell, Maureen. 1995. "Koreans Keep the Faith." *The Boston Globe,* January 12, pp. 25, 32.

Durkheim, Emile. [1915] 1965. *The Elementary Forms of the Religious Life*. Reprint, New York: The Free Press.

Gans, Herbert. 1979. "Symbolic Ethnicity: The Future of Ethnic Groups and Cultures in America." *Ethnic and Racial Studies* 2: 1–20.

Goette, Robert D. 1993. "The Transformation of a First-Generation Church into a Bilingual Second-Generation Church." Pp. 237–257 in *The Emerging Generation of Korean-Americans,* edited by Ho-Youn Kwon and Shin Kim. Seoul, Korea: Kyung Hee University Press.

Hurh, Won Moo, and Kwang Chung Kim. 1984. *Korean Immigrants in America: A Structural Analysis of Ethnic Confinement and Adhesive Adaptation*. Madison, N.J.: Fairleigh Dickinson University Press.

———. 1990. "Religious Participation of Korean Immigrants in the U.S." *Journal for the Scientific Study of Religion* 29 (March):19–34.

Iannaccone, Lawrence. 1994. "Why Strict Churches Are Strong." *American Journal of Sociology* 99 (March): 1180–1211.

Kim, David Kyuman. 1993. "Becoming: Korean Americans, Faith, and Identity—Observations on an Emerging Culture." Master of Divinity thesis, Harvard Divinity School.

Kim, Hyung-chan, and Wayne Patterson. 1974. The Koreans in America, 1882–1974: A Chronology and Fact Book. Dobbs Ferry, N.Y.: Oceana Publications.

Kim, Illsoo. 1981. *New Urban Immigrants: The Korean Community in New York*. Princeton: Princeton University Press.

Kim, Kwang Chung, and Shin Kim. 1996. "Ethnic Meanings of Korean Immigrant Churches." Paper presented at the Sixth North Park College Korean Symposium, Chicago, October 12.

Kitano, Harry H. L., and Roger Daniels. 1988. *Asian Americans: Emerging Minorities*. Englewood Cliffs, N.J.: Prentice-Hall.

Lee, Helen. 1996. "Silent Exodous." *Christianity Today,* August 12, pp. 51–52.

Lee, John H. 1989. "Koreans Sue Presbytery, Allege Bias, Deceit, Theft (Part II)." *Los Angeles Times,* February 5, pp. 1–2.

Min, Pyong Gap. 1992. "The Structure and Social Functions of Korean Immigrant Churches in the U.S." *International Migration Review* 26 (Winter): 1370–1394.

Mittelberg, David, and Mary C. Waters. 1992. "The Process of Ethnogenesis Among Haitian and Israeli Immigrants in the United States." *Ethnic and Racial Studies* 15 (July): 412–435.

Mullins, Mark. 1987. "The Life-Cycle of Ethnic Churches in Sociological Perspective." *Japanese Journal of Religious Studies* 14 (4): 321–334.

Narayan, Kirin. 1993. "How Native Is a 'Native' Anthropologist?" *American Anthropologist* 95 (September): 671–686.

Pai, Young, Delores Pemberton, and John Worley. 1987. *Findings on Korean-American Early Adolescents and Adolescents.* Kansas City: University of Missouri School of Education.

Park, Kyeyoung. 1989. "'Born Again': What It Means to Korean Americans in New York City." Pp. 56–78 in *Worship and Community: Christianity and Hinduism in Contemporary Queens,* edited by Roger Sanjek. New York: Asian/American Center, Queens College/CUNY.

Patterson, Wayne. 1988. *Korean Frontier in America: Immigration to Hawaii, 1886–1910.* Honolulu: University of Hawaii Press.

Portes, Alejandro, and Min Zhou. 1993. "The New Second Generation: Segmented Assimilation and Its Variants." *The Annals of the American Academy of Political and Social Science* 530 (November): 74–97.

Shin, Eui Hang, and Hyung Park. 1988. "An Analysis of Causes of Schisms in Ethnic Churches: The Case of Korean-American Churches." *Sociological Analysis* 49 (Fall): 234–248.

Smith, Timothy. 1978. "Religion and Ethnicity in America." *American Historical Review* 83 (December): 1155–1185.

Song, Minho. 1994. "Towards the Successful Movement of the English-Speaking Ministry Within the Korean Immigrant Church." Paper presented at Katalyst 1994, Sandy Cove, Md., March 21–24.

Stark, Rodney, and William Sims Bainbridge. 1985. *The Future of Religion: Secularization, Revival, and Cult Formation.* Berkeley and Los Angeles: University of California Press.

Warner, R. Stephen. 1990. "The Korean Immigrant Church: A Comparative Perspective." Paper presented at colloquium at the Princeton Theological Seminary, February 16–18.

Warren, Rick. 1993. "Work in Progress Toward a New Paradigm for the Sociological Study of Religion in the United States." *American Journal of Sociology* 98 (March 1993): 1044–1093.

———. 1994. "The Place of the Congregation in the Contemporary American Religious Configuration." Pp. 54–99 in *American Congregations,* vol. 2, edited by James P. Wind and James W. Lewis. Chicago: University of Chicago Press.

———. 1995. *Purpose-Driven Church.* Grand Rapids, Mich. Zondervan.

Williams, Raymond Brady. 1988. *Religions of Immigrants from India and Pakistan: New Threads in the American Tapestry*. Cambridge: Cambridge University Press.

Wuthnow, Robert. 1988. *The Restructuring of American Religion: Society and Faith Since World War II*. Princeton: Princeton University Press.

10 | Tenacious Unity in a Contentious Community: Cultural and Religious Dynamics in a Chinese Christian Church

Fenggang Yang

May they be brought to complete unity to let the world know that you sent me and have loved them even as you have loved me.—Jesus, The Gospel of John 17: 23[1]

致中和, 天地位焉, 万物育焉.
Once Equilibrium and Harmony are realized, Heaven and Earth will take their proper places and all things will receive their full nourishment.—Confucius, *Zhong Yong* 1: 5[2]

Unity is an appealing ideal in both Christianity and Chinese culture. According to the New Testament, Christians ought to become one organic body in Christ: "The body is a unit, though it is made up of many parts; and though all its parts are many, they form one body. So it is with Christ. For we were all baptized by one Spirit into one body—whether Jews or Greeks, slave or free—and we were all given the one Spirit to drink" (I Corinthians, 12: 12–13). In ancient Chinese classics, unity and harmony are highly valued.[3] Many observers are fascinated by the magnetic unity of the heterogeneous Chinese people.[4]

However, history exhibits a different reality, one of numerous divisions, for both Christianity and Chinese society. In the history of Christianity, especially Protestantism, schisms are myriad. And Chinese society, especially in modern times, reveals the bloodshed of warlords, civil wars, and violent political struggles. Overseas Chinese communities are likewise notoriously fragmented (Lyman 1974, Chen 1992). When Christian religion and Chinese culture come together, as they do in Chinese Christian churches, will unity or division prevail? This question is pertinent to understanding the conflicts, unity, and cultural diversity in churches, as well as "the clash of civilizations."[5]

Christianity is growing fast among the Chinese in the United States and in China, but Chinese Christians remain a small proportion of the Chinese populations in both countries.[6] Research on Chinese Christian churches in the United States has been scarce, so I must draw my theoretical references mainly from studies of American Protestant churches and certain other ethnic churches.

Most studies of polarization among Protestants have focused on the denominational level. However, the dynamics at the congregational level can be different from those at the denomenational level (see Warner 1988). Moreover, the problem of division may be better understood by a comparison with its opposite—unity. In this chapter I describe and analyze the religious and cultural dynamics in a Chinese immigrant church. I find that the most important sources of division were cultural group differences rather than socioeconomic factors (Niebuhr 1929), because church members are socioeconomically homogeneous. Status competition was more often between cultural groups than between deprived immigrant individuals (cf. Palinkas 1984, Shin and Park 1988). Furthermore, although theological disagreements are potential factors of division in this Chinese church, there were none of the contending parties of theological liberals and conservatives found in mainline American churches (Hoge 1976, Warner 1988).

The central findings of my study are as follows: (1) there was a complex, multidimensional diversity in this ethnic Chinese church; (2) even though the heterogeneous groups within the church were often contentious, the church itself maintained a tenacious unity; and (3) the forces that promoted this unity were the ideal of unity in Christianity and Chinese culture, a respect for diversity, and an emphasis on harmonious relationships.

The Ethnographic Field and the Plan of Study

The church under study here, which I call the Chinese Fellowship Church (CFC),[7] is one of about twenty Chinese churches in a metropolitan area on the east coast, where the Chinese population has become substantial.[8] The CFC is typical of today's Chinese churches in many ways: it grew out of a fellowship group and is conservative, nondenominational, and mid-sized.[9] In 1995 weekly church attendance was about 270.

In 1992 I was baptized and became a CFC member, following more than three years of contact with members who were evangelizing to mainland Chinese students and visiting scholars (like myself). A year and half later I decided to focus on this church for the New Ethnic and Immigration Congregations Project and my dissertation research.[10] I determined to be a watchful member,[11] a silent observer in church meetings, and an empathetic listener in informal conversations and formal interviews. I made it clear that my stay in this area would be transient and that I had no intention of becoming a leader or power-player in the church. I have been well received as both a participant and an observer. Beginning in September of 1993, I conducted (1) extensive participant observation in various gatherings and meetings; (2) many informal conversations and formal interviews with members, ex-members, and former pastors; and (3) a thorough search and close readings of several boxes of church documents.[12]

In this chapter I will provide a brief history of the church before demarcating the complex diversity of its members. Then I describe the various subgroups and their contentiousness, and compare the church's two pastors. Following this I offer a focused discussion of major factors promoting church unity. I conclude the chapter with a reflection on, or perhaps a hope for, the possibility of extending some principles drawn from this case study to the larger society. First however, let me start by describing an event at the church that vividly illustrates many elements of division and unity at work in the congregation, and the characteristically circumspect conduct of its conflict.

A Showdown After a "Love Banquet"

It was the last Sunday of June 1995, sunny and humid. After worship services people crowded into the CFC's Fellowship Hall to have lunch. This had become a tradition of the church, fondly called the "Love Banquet." A dozen old men and women sat quietly at the tables in a corner, waiting to be served. Children were running around. About two hundred people, from teenagers to those in their sixties, formed a loose line winding around the tables and chairs, chatting as they waited. Voices buzzed in Mandarin, Cantonese, and English, mixed with laughter. Suddenly strong strokes of piano keys permeated the hall and brought the voices into a singing stream. Then a man stood up and called on people to bow their heads before saying grace. He particularly prayed for God's presence and guidance in the congregational meeting that afternoon. After the meeting was mentioned, conversations resumed in much lower tones, while the laughter faded away. One by one, everyone moved to the kitchen window, got a plastic plate filled with rice, vegetables, and meat, and then sat at a table or wandered around. The Love Banquet was unusually quiet. I happened upon the chairwoman of the Ark Fellowship, one of several fellowship groups in the church. She was walking around with her plate in hand, informing fellowship co-workers that their planned meeting was canceled due to the sensitive timing, that is, before the congregational meeting.

Walking into the sanctuary well in time for the meeting, I had to search to find a seat. A man next to me remarked with a grimace: "There are more people now than in the worship service." The attendance was indeed unusually large. The last congregational meeting in January was attended by 56 members. This time there were at least 150.

A man in a dark suit, Mr. David Lee, the chairman of the Official Board, called the meeting to order. He asked nonmembers and junior members less than eighteen years old to sit to the back in the overflow area, and reminded them that they had no right to vote. Then he asked for two "brothers" and two "sisters" to say prayers for the meeting. This was followed by an awkward silence, after which Chairman Lee said: "Please don't waste time. . . . You may use any language, English, or Mandarin, or Cantonese, or any other. A one or two-word prayer is fine, as long as you are moved to." Upon repeated encouragements and urging, two men and two women offered short generic prayers with reluctance and overlong pauses. The air was tense.

As routinely done in congregational meetings, the pastor first presented his report. Reverend Daniel Tang, senior pastor for the past four years, proceeded to paint a rosy picture of church attendance and finance. "What we need," he concluded with confidence, "is to pray more in unity, to establish the Elders Board, and to make long-range goals." However, his contrived calm looked edgy.

Then Chairman Lee and several deacons reported on church ministries. Some of them presented proposals and asked for approval by vote. All this proceeded smoothly without much discussion.

Finally, the real agenda for most of the day's participants—to vote on the proposal to reappoint the senior pastor—was discussed. Chairman Lee reiterated, in English and Mandarin, that, according to the church constitution and bylaws, the pastor's reappointment was subject to an anonymous vote in a congregational meeting every two years, requiring a two-thirds majority of positive votes. He then urged, "If you don't understand the issues, you may want to refrain from casting a vote." He added, "If you want to vote but don't have a clear opinion of either approving or opposing, you may choose a vote of abstention.

Abstention does not mean opposition, but the ballot has to be cast in order to be counted. However, only 'yes' votes will be counted as positive votes. Is this clear?"

An old woman called out, "Before casting the ballot, we should have a time of praying first. Let's follow what God wants us to do." This seemed a righteous request, even though a round of outspoken spontaneous prayers, as are frequently offered in group meetings, might trigger heated debates or occasion another awkward silence like the one at the beginning of the meeting. The chairman treated her plea as a motion, which was then seconded and unanimously approved. The assistant pastor's wife quickly suggested that everyone pray silently before a concluding prayer was offered by one person. Without going through another round of seconding and voting, Mr. Lee immediately appointed "Uncle Yao," the most senior member of the church, to conclude the silent prayer.

The sanctuary became very quiet. Rain was rustling on the roof, and muffled thunder was heard. It seemed that it was not until this moment that many people took notice of the storm. Mr. Yao slowly rose and prayed loudly in a husky voice: "This is the family of God. Pray to God our Lord. Give us power to make this church able to glorify your name in this region." Four assigned men immediately distributed ballots and, after the voting was done, collected them. While they were counting the ballots in another room, the deacon of the treasury presented a detailed budget report, but people paid little attention. They were anxious for the result of the vote. Finally it came. "Let's receive the result of the vote with calm," Mr. Lee admonished. "No matter what happens, we believe everything is under God's control." The result: one-third opposed the reappointment, and a large number cast ballots of abstention. The proposal to reappoint the senior pastor for another term failed to pass. Reverend Tang had to leave in three months.

This was not the first time a pastor was voted out in this church, although the proportion of negative votes was unprecedentedly high. The vote showed that church members were divided in their opinions. It reflected not only the dissatisfaction of many members with Reverend Tang, but also the contention among various groups in the church. Nonetheless, everybody acted with composure and great caution, and the chairman handled the proceedings firmly, avoiding open debate. These are indications of the length to which church members were willing to go to protect unity. To understand this situation, we need to take a look at the history of the church.

A Brief History

The Chinese Fellowship Church is the second oldest Chinese church in its metropolitan area. The first, which I call the Interdenominational Mission Church (IMC), was incorporated in 1935 out of several denominational missions to Chinese immigrants under the leadership of the City Council of Churches. Its participants were immigrant laborers and merchants from rural areas of Guangdong Province who came to this city during the Chinese Exclusion period (1882–1943).[13] The lingua franca was Cantonese. CFC began with Chinese refugees[14] and students of the 1950s and early 1960s. Before coming to the United States, most had fled first to Taiwan or Hong Kong from the wars and the communists on the mainland. About a dozen new Chinese Christian immigrants and students formed a fellowship group in 1957. After a year of gathering in homes, they started a Sunday worship service in a downtown office building, which marked the birth of CFC. They adopted Mandarin as their official language and named their church *Guoyu Libaitang* (Mandarin Worship Hall). They also decided to make it independent, without denominational affiliation.

As Chinese students and immigrants continued to arrive, attendance at CFC kept increasing and reached a hundred by the end of the 1960s. In the early 1970s the church moved to a prime suburb, where it constructed its own sanctuary and education buildings. There followed a period of rapid growth during which the church received forty to eighty new members every year, nearly half of them newly baptized adult converts. Sunday service attendance peaked at more than four hundred in the mid-1970s. Then, in 1976, there was an abrupt split.

Beneath suspicions of financial mismanagement by pastors, the deep conflict was centered on church polity and the authority of the pastors. CFC was a lay-initiated church, and members were highly educated. Democracy and the equality of all members were the norms. Until the end of the 1960s, the congregation annually elected three to seven lay leaders, called "co-workers" or "deacons," to take care of routine management. In 1969 Reverend Frank Chao became the pastor. He had a Presbyterian background and was a graduate of a conservative Presbyterian seminary in the Midwest. Reverend Chao pushed hard and successfully ordained three permanent lay elders; reduced the power of the Deacons Board; and reduced the frequency and functions of the congregational meeting. He pressed on to centralize power despite rising resistance from some lay leaders and active members. Finally, in 1976, some members openly confronted him. They questioned his authority and asked to restore the democratic congregational polity. However, many others took the pastor's side, arguing that mass democracy was not biblical and that pastors were sent by God to lead, rather than to be led. A series of special congregational meetings was held to "clarify" the controversies, in which heated debates and direct confrontations eclipsed any attempt to reconcile disputes. Eventually, Reverend Chao was forced to resign. A few months later, about half of the members suddenly withdrew from CFC and started another independent Chinese church with a church polity designed by Reverend Chao.

After the schism, CFC restored the highest authority to the congregational meeting, and explicitly limited the power and the term of the pastor. The revised constitution kept the clauses authorizing an Elders Board, but these positions have remained unfilled. It also adopted Robert's Rules of Order for deliberations at congregational meetings to maintain order in the face of emotional arguments. After several years of instability, church attendance recovered and stabilized around 250.

In 1982 the church began to hold annual summer retreats for all members on a remote seminary campus, started a quarterly magazine as a public forum for church members, and hired Reverend Philip Hung as the pastor. After eight years of service, Reverend Hung resigned and left for a Chinese church in the South. During this period, twelve fellowship groups emerged one by one. These groupings, based on social and cultural backgrounds, had a profound impact on the church in the 1990s.

Multidimensional Diversity

CFC is a Chinese church. With the exception of a very few Caucasians, its participants are all Chinese. However, behind this homogeneous appearance is a complex diversity with multiple boundaries defined by the very different religious, cultural, and social backgrounds of the members.

Denominational Diversity

Because CFC is an independent evangelical church, it is open to any and every prospective member, including non-Christians, nominal Christians, and Christians with various denominational backgrounds. Thus, denominational diversity has been a characteristic of church members since the beginning. Over the years, the proportion of con-

Table 1. Chinese Fellowship Church: Denominational Backgrounds of Members, 1976 and 1995[a]

Denominational Background	1976 N	1976 Percent	1995 N	1995 Percent
Baptized at CFC	145	32.6	170	58.4
Transferred members	300	67.4	121	41.6
Baptists	58	19.3	24	19.8
Presbyterians	35	11.7	11	9.1
Lingliang Tang[b]	18	6.0	2	1.7
Episcopalian/Anglican	17	5.7	8	6.6
Methodists	15	5.0	7	5.8
Lutherans	15	5.0	8	6.6
Little Flock[c]	13	4.3	6	5.0
Other[d]	62	20.7	24	19.8
Unknown	67	22.3	31	25.6
Total transferred	300	100.0	121	100.0
Total members	445	100.0	291	100.0

a. Members in 1976 include all those who had joined the church by 1976 (some had left by then but there was no systematic pattern among them). Members in 1995 include all those who were marked as current members in the 1996 Church Directory (21 names had no membership record, but I found no systematic pattern among them).

b. Lingliang Tang is an indigenous Chinese church with Presbyterian influence.

c. Little Flock (*Xiaoqun*), also known as the Assembly Hall (*Juhuisuo*) or the Local Church (*Difang Jiaohui*), is an indigenous Chinese church with Plymouth Brethren influence.

d. Other denominations include the Adventist, Assemblies of God, Catholic, Christian and Missionary Alliance, Church of Christ in China (*Zhonghua Jidu Jiaohui*), Congregationalist, Church of Nazarene, Free Evangelical Church, Reformed, United Church of Christ, and some independent Chinese churches or protodenominations.

verts who were baptized at this church has increased. But the number of transferred members remains large, and their denominational backgrounds differ remarkably (see Table 1).

Among members with a denominational background in 1995, Baptists were the largest group, at 20 percent, with Presbyterians second, at about 9 percent. There were also significant numbers of people from such Western denominations as Episcopalian, Anglican, Lutheran, and Methodist, and from the indigenous Chinese churches of Lingliang Tang and Little Flock. Lingliang Tang had Presbyterian roots. Little

Fenggang Yang

Flock was influenced by the Plymouth Brethren tradition, and had strong anticlerical and antidenominational tendencies. Watchman Nee, the founder of Little Flock who was martyred by the Chinese communists, has enormous influence among many Chinese Christians, and some non-Chinese Christians as well, through the wide circulation of writings by and about him.

Theologically CFC is dominated by fundamentalists and evangelicals. In rituals, the church follows the Reformed tradition with a Baptist accent. The main sanctuary has little ornament—no icons, sculptures, or stained-glass windows. The organ pipes are the most eye-catching feature on the front wall; below them is a recessed hollow, where a large metal cross hangs above the baptismal pool. Sunday services always center on the preaching. There is no recitation of a creed and no altar call. The church observes only two ordinances or sacraments—baptism and communion. Baptism is conducted only for adults or youths, and immersion is clearly preferred. However, transferees who received other forms of baptism, including infant baptism, are not required to be baptized again. Communion is celebrated once a month as a time of commemoration, reminding believers of Jesus' death and grace for sinners and of the need of forgiveness and reconciliation.

Denominational backgrounds are usually downplayed in this independent church, but when it is time to form opinions, the latent denominational differences can become crucial. This showed up in the frequent disagreements over the form of church polity. Baptists and Little Flock people favor a democratic congregational polity and emphasize the equality of all members. In contrast, Presbyterians and other connectionalists tend to endorse more authority for ordained pastors and elders.

Thus, it is hard to achieve a consensus in CFC due to denominational and other differences. Even if a consensus is achieved, it is difficut to hold it for long because of the constant flow of members. Only 17 percent of present members joined the church before 1976. Many have left the area to follow job opportunities, while many others came and joined. When new members arrive, they sometimes question polity and policies that are different from what they have known. The 1976 schism resulted in a *de jure* congregationalistic polity for the last twenty years. But every once in a while some members request the restoration of the Elders Board or challenge the system of congregational democracy. In the 1990s, Reverend Tang, with background in the Evangelical Free and United Methodist churches, pushed to select elders, but he failed. Today the Official Board, led by Chairman Lee, a Presbyterian, is again making efforts to install lay elders. Will they succeed this time? No one can predict. Only one thing is sure—even if a consensus is achieved, it may not be long before challenges emerge in opposition.

Linguistic Diversity

Language problems are common to immigrant churches. When the original language of the immigrant group is not English, eventually the American-born generation will bring up the issue of adopting English in the church. However, ethnic Chinese churches have not followed the straight-line evolutionary pattern of linguistic and cultural changes proposed by Mark Mullins (1987),[15] because, in addition to tensions between English and Chinese, there have been more complicated problems because of the numerous Chinese dialects. Although the written Chinese characters and grammar are much the same across the country, the spoken dialects are many and often mutually unintelligible.

Chinese Fellowship Church was established as a Mandarin church. Mandarin was chosen because it was the "national language" that every educated Chinese should be able to speak, a language that "signifies the unity of the Chinese and the importance of Chinese culture."[16] After less than ten years, however, "Mandarin" was dropped from the name of the church, which became instead a more inclusive "Chinese" church.[17]

Among Chinese immigrants in the United States, there have been many speakers of the Taishanese, Cantonese, Swato, Hakka, Mandarin, Taiwanese (Southern Fukianese), and Shanghai dialects, among others. Some ethnic Chinese from Southeast Asia speak none of these dialects but, say, Vietnamese or Indonesian. CFC has received members of most of these dialect groups, as the "place of origin"[18] data in church records indicate (see Table 2).

Probably no other ethnic group in the United States has experienced language problems on the same scale as the Chinese. American Jews are similarly heterogeneous, but at the synagogue there is the common ritual language of Hebrew. Asian Indians have multiple dialects or languages, but they do not hold an expectation that all Indians should stick together. Koreans and Japanese, like Chinese people, do hold such an expectation, but they are linguistically homogeneous compared to the Chinese in the United States. In Chinese churches, various dialect groups often become contentious about linguistic usages, yet they try to remain in the same church with their Chinese compatriots.

Fenggang Yang

Table 2. Chinese Fellowship Church: Place of Birth or Place of Origin of Members, 1976 and 1995[a]

Place of Origin	Main Dialect	1976		1995	
		N	Percent	N	Percent
China (not specified)	Mandarin(?)	17	3.8	15	5.2
Guangdong[b]	Cantonese	95	21.3	32	11.0
Hong Kong	Cantonese	31	7.0	25	8.6
Taiwan[c]	Mandarin/Minnan	48	10.8	40	13.7
Fujian	Minnan/other local	26	5.8	11	3.8
Zhejiang	Local[d]	34	7.7	24	8.2
Jiangsu	Local	27	6.1	8	2.7
Shanghai	Local	24	5.4	13	4.5
Shandong	Local(Mandarin)	18	4.0	1	0.3
Sichuan	Local (Mandarin)	12	2.7	3	1.0
Other provinces[e]	Various	69	15.5	34	11.7
Diaspora Chinese[f]	Various	16	3.6	12	4.1
USA and Canada	English	23	5.2	69	23.7
Unknown		5	1.1	4	1.4
Total		445	100.0	291	100.0

a. Either birthplace, ancestral place, or place from whence one came to the United States (see n. 18).

b. Some people were from Hainan and Chaozhou (Swato), in Guangdong Province, and their dialects were unintelligible to Cantonese-speaking people.

c. Major Taiwan dialects are Taiwanese (Minnan, or Southern Fujian dialect) and Hakka. Many people from Taiwan were mainland-born Chinese who went to Taiwan in the 1940s and the 1950s. They may speak no Taiwan dialect but rather Mandarin and their original dialects.

d. Zhejiang, Jiangsu, Shanghai, and many provinces south of the Yellow River have unique and mutually unintelligible local dialects. Dialects in Shandong, Sichuan, and most provinces north of the Yellow River are distinctive variants of Mandarin.

e. Including southern provinces, with mutually unintelligible dialects: Anhui, Guangxi, Guizhou, Hubei, Hunan, Jiangxi, Macao, and Yunnan; and northern provinces, with local dialects of Mandarin variants: Beijing, Gansu, Hebei, Heilongjiang, Henan, Jilin, Liaoning, Shaanxi, Shanxi, Tianjin, and Xinjiang. Each of these provinces were represented by fewer than 10 CFC members in 1976 and 1995.

f. Including Indonesia, Japan, Malaysia, Peru, Philippines, Singapore, Thailand, and Vietnam.

Language problems go beyond linguistic differences. Some languages and dialects are associated with cultural and social status or political leanings. Before World War II, for example, Taishanese, as commonly spoken by the dominant immigrants from certain rural districts of Guangdong, was regarded as the *true* Chinese language in American Chinatowns. Later, "Standard Cantonese, as spoken in the cities of Hong Kong, Macau, and Guangzhou, replaced Taishan [dialect] as the common language," because it was thought to signify more genteel urban origins (Wong 1994, 238–241). As mentioned, Mandarin is the official language of China that every educated Chinese is expected to be able to speak. Since the 1970s the rising Taiwan independence movement has become associated with an insistence on speaking Taiwanese. Above all this, though, English fluency is indicative of an immigrant's success in entering mainstream American society. On the other hand, for second-generation Chinese, speaking Chinese may show the extent of their Chinese identity.

CFC changed its Sunday service from monolingual (Mandarin) to bilingual (Mandarin and Cantonese) in 1967, and to trilingual (Mandarin, Cantonese, and English) in the early 1970s. In the trilingual service, the sermon and announcements are all spoken or translated in three languages. Very often, the worship leader and the preacher speak Mandarin, which is translated into English, sentence by sentence, by a person standing side by side with the preacher behind the pulpit. Another person, invisible to the congregation, simultaneously translates every word into Cantonese, which is transmitted wirelessly to earphones in the designated pews.

Given the technical complications, three languages/dialects seem the maximum that a Sunday service can adopt; a fourth language translation is one too many. In 1973 some Taiwanese-speaking CFC members asked for a separate Sunday school class in Taiwanese, claiming that the existing classes in Mandarin, Cantonese, and English could not meet their spiritual needs. In 1975 and 1976, the church also hosted a Sunday service in Vietnamese for refugees from that country. Both experiments were short-lived.

The trilingual pattern can be found in Chinese churches across the United States today. Many churches started as monolingual, but in five to ten years, English and another Chinese dialect had to be added. The Interdenominational Mission Church in Chinatown was a Cantonese-speaking church. After half a century, however, instead of becoming an English-speaking church, it has turned into a trilingual church. Both English and Mandarin have been added. In the mid-1970s, a

Taiwanese-speaking church was founded in this area. When I visited it in 1994, the Sunday service was also trilingual—Taiwanese, Mandarin, and English. Continued immigration, a sense of peoplehood of all Chinese in spite of linguistic obstacles, and technical limitations may be the reasons for the dominant trilingual pattern of Chinese churches in the United States today.

One solution to the demands of various dialect/language groups would be to break the congregation into several Sunday services, as some large churches do. However, such differentiation requires an increase of staff, space, and facilities, and a relatively large membership. Even more importantly, it requires psychological adjustment to separate a church into two or more congregations, a step that is often resisted for various reasons. First, many Chinese church members as well as leaders fear that separate Sunday services may lead to a split of the church. Second, some parents want to sit beside their teenage children in the same service. Third, some members appreciate the bilingual translation, and find it helps them to learn English or Chinese.

At CFC, the first request for a separate English service was recorded in the early 1970s, but it did not become a reality until 1986. Since then, a combined Sunday communion service for all church members, intended to preserve and signify CFC's unity, has been held on the first Sunday of each month. In the combined service the sermon and announcements are all translated consecutively in Mandarin and English, while Cantonese has been sacrificed. Hymns are often sung bilingually with one stanza in Mandarin and the next in English, or simultaneously in Mandarin, English, Cantonese, or whatever language one chooses. After he was elected chairman of the Official Board in 1995, David Lee tried to recover the sense of being "one big family" that this church had once had. He pushed to make the English service bulletins available to Chinese service participants and the Chinese service bulletins to English service participants. Still, some English-speaking people feel the combined service is inefficient, whereas some Cantonese-speaking people are not happy about the absence of Cantonese. Nevertheless, most people participate in this monthly ritual of symbolic unity.

Sociocultural and Sociopolitical Diversity

The vast majority of CFC members share a similar socioeconomic status. Most are highly educated, middle-class professionals. However, they do have different sociocultural and sociopolitical backgrounds.

Socioculturally, CFC members are from different provinces of

China and from various countries (see Table 2). In addition to linguistic diversity, these places often have distinctive cultural customs and social norms. These provincial differences and various diasporic experiences were *not* insignificant for many Chinese. In fact, most members wrote the name of their county in addition to the province for the "place of origin" item on the membership application form; some even gave their district or village of origin. This is an indication of their attachment to their specific ancestral locality.

Interestingly, this Chinese church has had a white, American-born assistant pastor since 1989. Reverend Allan Houston and his wife, both in their mid-thirties, grew up in the American South.[19] They have learned no Chinese and show little interest in Chinese culture, although they have been in this church for more than seven years. CFC also has a few non-Chinese members, who are married to Chinese.

The various immigrant cohorts also differ sociopolitically. For example, among the Mandarin-speaking members, there have been three cohorts of immigration. Most of those who came in the 1950s and 1960s were "sojourners," that is, they were born in mainland China but forced to go to Taiwan, Hong Kong, or other places due to wars and the victory of the Chinese communists on the mainland. They were followed by their children's generation, who were either born or raised in Taiwan or Hong Kong. People in both cohorts generally hold anti-communist views. Compared to the first cohort, the second cohort has less attachment to the mainland and mainland Chinese, although their Chinese identity may be similarly strong. Beginning in 1980, immigrants and students from the People's Republic of China arrived. While they are often sharply critical of aspects in Chinese society under the rule of the communists, they tend to resent the same comments when spoken by any member of the first two cohorts. Some church members who were born or grew up in Taiwan are sympathetic to the Taiwan independence movement or to the Kuomintang's position of resisting quick unification with mainland China. However, most mainland Chinese are deeply opposed to Taiwan independence.

Fellowship Groups

Multiple diversity in CFC is inescapable. Over the years, leaders of the church have tried to deal with this fact in very different ways with very different consequences. In the 1970s they tried to suppress cultural pluralism. In spite of the increasing heterogeneity of the membership, or perhaps exactly because of it, Reverend Chao discouraged cultural groupings, fearing that these might lead to division in the church and pose a contradiction to the spirit of Christian unity. With attendance up to four hundred in the overcrowded sanctuary, many people still resisted the idea of holding a separate, English Sunday service. In the whole church there were only two adult fellowship groups, one for women and one for men. Instead of groupings based on social and cultural background, informal prayer meetings based on residential neighborhoods were promoted. "The purposes of the regional prayer meetings," said the pastor, as recorded in the minutes of a congregational meeting, "are to get brothers and sisters acquainted with each other, to make people feel close in the family of the Lord, and to forge a sense of belonging to a group." However, a sense of intimacy and belonging was hardly achievable because people had very diverse backgrounds, in language, customs, and cultural habits. This policy of suppressing cultural pluralism ended in 1976 with the split described above.

In the 1980s, under the leadership of Pastor Hung, fellowship groups were encouraged based on language/dialect, age, sex, and social background (see Table 3).[20] There were twelve such groups by 1995.

Each fellowship group has its own leadership core, activity plans, and even an independent budget. Most groups have a biblical name. They hold meetings weekly, biweekly, or monthly for Bible study or social purposes at members' homes on a rotating basis. Fellowship members do not necessarily live in the same neighborhood, so often they have to drive a long way to attend meetings. The fellowship groups can be outspokenly contentious in church deliberation, but they also help to stabilize the church in critical times, such as during the unhappy process of voting out the pastor.

There are four Mandarin-speaking groups. The Evergreen Fellowship has about thirty elderly "sojourners" who came to the United States as immigrants or as family members of the immigrant professionals. Many speak little or no English. They do not hold deaconship positions on the Official Board and give little input on church affairs. Because elderly status itself is revered in the Chinese tradition, however, their opinions bear important weight when they do speak out. This was evidenced in a conflict with Assistant Pastor Houston about hiring a second non-Chinese-speaking pastor in 1990 (see below). Canaan Fellowship members are also "sojourners" who came to the United States in the 1960s and 1970s as students or as immigrants. They are engineers and government technocrats, speak fluent English, and live in affluent suburbs. Most of them joined the CFC before the 1976 schism, and have served as deacons and deaconesses; some even chaired the Official

Table 3. Chinese Fellowship Church: Fellowship Groups and Their Characteristics, 1995

Fellowship	Official Member-ship	Regular Attend-ance	Age Range	Social Backgrounds	Dominant Language
Evergreen	31	31	65+	China, "sojourners"[a]	Mandarin
Canaan	26	26	50–65	China, "sojourners"	Mandarin
Living Water	20	20	30–50	Taiwan or Hong Kong	Mandarin
Ark	56	100–200	20–60	PRC[b] and "co-workers"[c]	Mandarin
BSG[d] A		20			
BSG B		20			
BSG C		35			
BSG D		25			
Elim	20	15	50–65	Hong Kong, Guangdong, and Southeast Asia	Cantonese
Carmel	33	20	30–50	Hong Kong and Southeast Asia	Cantonese
Bethel	15	15	25–55	Intermarried Couples, ABC,[e] ARC,[f] and others	English
Couples'	16	16	25–40	ABC and ARC	English
Emmanuel	60	40	18–30	ABC and ARC	English
Teens'	17	25	13–17	ABC and ARC	English
Career	16	16	25–35	non-U.S.-born young people	English/ Chinese
Women's[g]	2	8	30–60	Women, single or married	Chinese/ English
Nonaffiliated	77			Varied[h]	

a. "Sojourners": people who were born in mainland China and fled to Taiwan, Hong Kong, and/or other places before coming to the United States.

b. PRC: People's Republic of China

c. "Co-workers": lay volunteers in the evangelistic ministry to mainland Chinese. They have various backgrounds, many from the Canaan and Living Water Fellowships.

d. BSG: evangelistic Bible Study Groups within the Ark Fellowship. Participants include prospective converts.

e. ABC: American-born Chinese

f. ARC: American-raised Chinese

g. The Women's Fellowship does not hold regular meetings.

h. Includes people born in Taiwan in the 1930s and descendants of Chinese immigrants who came to the U.S. before World War II.

Board. Many became dissatisfied with Reverend Tang, whereas a few people who had joined the church after 1976 dissented from the seemingly harsh treatment of the senior pastor. Living Water Fellowship members are a generation younger than Canaan people. Many have parents from mainland China, but they themselves were born or grew up in Taiwan or Hong Kong. Several come from families with a history of several generations in Taiwan or Hong Kong. Computer programming is the dominant occupation among them, and they speak English well. Except for one couple, all joined the church after 1976. Some have served as deacons, but their influence in the decision-making process is still limited due to the powerful presence of the older people. Several frustrated Living Water members openly dissented over the vote on Pastor Tang and indeed on any vote on a pastor. However, unable to criticize the older people, the dissenters pointed their fingers at the newcomers—mainland Chinese—accusing them of immature spirituality and lack of respect for the authority of the pastor. In response, some Canaan and other older members stood up for the legitimacy of the vote and spoke in defense of the newcomers.

There are two Cantonese-speaking groups, Elim and Carmel. In terms of age, time of immigration, career or employment, and English-language ability, the Elim members are comparable to the Canaan people, and the Carmel members to the Living Water people. Most can understand and speak at least passable Mandarin, but they value their Cantonese dialect dearly. Recently some members of each group requested an improvement in the use of Cantonese in Sunday services. Some also complained that the evangelism ministry to mainland (Mandarin-speaking) Chinese took too much time and money, while ignoring Cantonese-speaking Chinese. Mandarin-speaking people refuted this claim and suggested that the Cantonese speakers should do the evangelizing themselves instead of complaining about others' work. Some dissatisfied Cantonese-speaking members have also become inactive, so that the numbers of regular participants in these two groups are fewer than their official membership. In addition, some Cantonese-speaking members on the Official Board were contentious. When they complained loudly, others had to listen, and then would either yield to or pacify them for the sole purpose of maintaining church unity and harmony. Cantonese-speaking people were also disappointed with Reverend Tang for his poor sermons and his failure to visit church members, and some confronted him about his theological views. In self-defense Pastor Tang made what one member called "mulish" responses. One time he even stood up to exorcize the demons of a confronting man. This action had grave consequences that affected the relationship between the pastor and many church members.

There are four English-speaking groups—Bethel, Couples', Emmanuel, and Teens.' Bethel Fellowship is a loose group lacking internal uniformity and strength. The majority of members in the Couples', Emmanuel and Teens Fellowships are children of the older members. Emmanuel members are college graduates or graduate students. The regular attendance is lower than the official membership because many study or work far away from home, and only come back during holidays and vacations. Some teens bring their middle-school friends to the group, so their attendance figure is higher than the actual membership. These American-born Chinese or American-raised Chinese either prefer to speak or only speak English. Some members who are in their thirties or late twenties wanted more participation in the decisions of the church, but often found themselves alienated from the power center. In 1993 a frustrated young man who had once served as a deacon on the Official Board circulated a six-page letter among church leaders. He complained that young people had few opportunities to participate in church leadership and that their opinions were never taken seriously. He resented the "politics" of the older people on the board, and called for a separate and independent English board. Although the demand for an independent board failed, young people did achieve more autonomy and made significant changes in the English service with the help of Assistant Pastor Houston. During the recent controversies concerning Senior Pastor Tang, some of the English-speaking young people voiced their disagreement about the vote on a pastor, and argued that the authority of the pastor should be respected, not decided by church members. However, parents and church leaders asked these young people to refrain from voting due to their lack of knowledge about the church or the Chinese-speaking congregation. Some complied but expressed frustration and regret afterward.

Career Fellowship members are busy with their studies or jobs, and have not much time or energy for the church, and the Women's Fellowship likewise meets infrequently and is not really functional in the church.

There are seventy-seven members without fellowship affiliation. They either cannot find a good fit in any group or do not want to join one. These include descendants of pre-World War II immigrants and older Taiwan-born people. For example, the present chairman of the Official Board, Mr. Lee, and his wife, belong to no fellowship group. They were both born in Taiwan in the 1930s. They are the third or fourth generation of Christians in their families, which have had a long history in Taiwan. Mr. Lee came to the United States as a graduate student and then became a university professor. Free from constraints of fellowship groups, he skillfully played a leadership role during the controversies surrounding the ouster of Pastor Tang.

The most recently formed group is the Ark Fellowship. This Mandarin-speaking fellowship includes the newly baptized mainland Chinese and the "co-workers," lay volunteers in the evangelistic ministry who have various social backgrounds. Several Canaan or Living Water members regularly participate in Ark Fellowship activities as well but still remain in the other groups. This evangelistic ministry for mainland Chinese was initiated in 1989 by Mandarin-speaking church members. They organized evangelism lectures, picnics, and festival celebrations. These activities attracted a hundred or more students and visiting scholars from the People's Republic of China. To make their evangelism more effective, regular participants are organized into four Bible study groups, each comparable in size to other fellowships.

Disillusioned with the communist utopia and trying to make sense of life in this new and strange land, these mainland Chinese are compelled toward new values and worldviews, which the church helps them to construct. Meanwhile, these newcomers also shape the church in new ways. The enthusiastic responses of mainland Chinese to Christian evangelism excited many church members, yet, the thinking and behavioral patterns of these mainland Chinese are challenging to the co-workers and others. For example, because they prefer sermons and lectures that provide rational explanations of the world and moral guidance for everyday life, they found Reverend Tang's preaching disappointing. He made blunt demands for money offerings, which were often out of context and regarded as vulgar. Once he led a Bible study group, but he was soon ejected by the annoyed participants who complained that his talks were monotonous, his Bible interpretations poor, and his attitudes arrogant. After that Ark co-workers effectively kept him out of the Ark Fellowship.

After experiencing Maoist ritualism during the Cultural Revolution (1966–76), most of the mainlanders tend to detest rituals. They prefer informal discussions at fellowship meetings to Sunday worship service and Sunday school. They like dialectical debates and express more political and nationalistic concerns. As newcomers, they expect to be welcomed by other members. But these tendencies made other church members uncomfortable, who were hesitant and reluctant to befriend the mainland Chinese; some even blamed them for the ouster of Reverend Tang. However, the Ark co-workers and some other older members spoke in defense of the newcomers, and tried to promote understanding and integration between mainland Chinese and others. As the emotions aroused over the removal of Reverend Tang diminish, some older members have begun to initiate integration efforts.

Two Pastors in the 1990s

The Chinese Fellowship Church has had two pastors in the 1990s, one a white American, Allan Houston, and one Chinese, Daniel Tang. Their different backgrounds and different fates in the church also illustrate the cultural and religious dynamics of this Chinese Christian church.

Reverend Houston holds degrees from a small Christian college in the South and a conservative seminary in this metropolitan area; he also studied at Dallas Theological Seminary. In 1982–83, when he was a seminarian in this area, he served as a youth intern at CFC. He was also the English speaker at two CFC summer retreats in the mid-1980s. In 1986 CFC began the separate English Sunday service under the leadership of an American-born Chinese assistant pastor. When that young man resigned in 1988 to continue his graduate study, the Pastor Search Committee recruited Reverend Houston, who by then had been ordained and was working in the South.

One year after Reverend Houston came, Reverend Philip Hung, senior pastor since 1982, left for a Chinese church in the South. For a time, Assistant Pastor Houston became the only pastor of the church. To maintain normal operations, he assumed greater responsibility and pushed to hire another Caucasian man as the youth pastor. Chinese-speaking seniors, threatened by the increasing presence of non-Chinese-speaking pastors, voiced strong opposition. Subsequently, Reverend Houston was confined to ministering to English-speaking young people, and the second Caucasian man left the church after a few months' service without a pastor's title.

In 1991 the church hired Reverend Tang as the senior pastor. He could speak several Chinese dialects as well as English. With the backing of some members, and working on the basis of his own interest as the senior pastor, he tried to control both the English and Chinese Sunday services. He insisted on preaching at both on a given Sunday at least once a month, and he wanted Reverend Houston to act as his assistant. However, since Reverend Houston was hired by the congregation and thus was responsible to it, not to the senior pastor, he resisted Reverend Tang's push for authority and power.

Then, in early 1993, there was the six-page letter from the English-speaking young man, which Reverend Houston supported. In the name of the Couples' Fellowship, Reverend Houston drafted a proposal to establish an "English-Ministry Leadership Team" independent of the Official Board, and to change the place and time of the English service from before the Chinese service to simultaneous with it. Some older people worried about this apparently divisive move. One man commented that this proposal "is one of the most unbiblical documents I have ever seen," for it seemed to him that the authors were totally obsessed with being leaders. He questioned, "Where is the biblical teaching of stewardship?" He and some other members argued that the church was one congregation, although it had two Sunday services; that both pastors were hired by and for the entire church rather than one for the Chinese service and the other for the English service; and that many members were fully bilingual and could attend either service. The deacons held a special meeting to discuss how to stop the centrifugal development by helping the senior pastor to take control and uphold unity. However, by that time many lay leaders had either lost confidence in Reverend Tang or found fault with him.

Reverend Houston mobilized support from key members as well as from English-speaking people in the name of Christian evangelism. Representing the young people, he claimed that changing the start of the English Sunday service from 9:30 A.M. to 10:30 A.M. (thirty minutes before the Chinese service) would make it possible for members to invite non-Christian friends. Thus he successfully changed the time and space of the English service while also developing his own leadership team. Since the English service was now overlapping with the Chinese service, it was practically impossible for the senior pastor to preach at both services on a given Sunday. These changes worried many members.

Pastor Tang was expected by lay leaders to harmonize group relationships. However, he failed to realize the complexity of the relationships in such an organizational structure. Within a short time he unwisely confronted the assistant pastor, the chairmen of the Official Board, and some key members.

Reverend Tang's theological views also caused concern to many people. Some believed that he was not conservative enough, pointing to his training at insufficiently evangelical seminaries, his previous pastoral service to mainline churches, and his calling for a greater role for women in CFC. Fundamentalist members also bluntly challenged his seemingly charismatic views on exorcism and spiritual healing.[21] The ouster of Pastor Tang in the summer of 1995 followed these events.

Given the structure of the church as well as his background and actions, it came as no surprise to me.

In the meantime, Reverend Houston, a non-Chinese who speaks no Chinese, has had his tenure renewed by four biennial congregational votes. Today (summer 1996) he remains in the position of assistant pastor, and he is the only pastor on staff. Both the church and he understand that he serves CFC not because it is a *Chinese church,* but because it is a *conservative Christian church.* He has been generously treated and well respected, not because he is a white American, but because of his theological match with the church and his effective ministry to the young people. On the other hand, he has only limited power. These limits are both imposed by church members and self-chosen by him, because he has shown little interest in Chinese culture.

Tenacious Unity

Thus far I have elaborated the remarkable diversity and contentiousness in this church, but have only mentioned the tenacious protection of unity in passing. I will now closely examine the forces making for this unity in the final section of this chapter.

First, there is socioeconomic homogeneity among CFC members. Most adults are college graduates, many with master's or doctoral degrees, and work as professionals. Among the American-born or -raised youth, every one expects to attend college. Entrepreneurs and laborers are few. This is thus a uniformly salaried, middle-class church.

Second, unity as an ideal in both Christianity and Chinese culture is repeatedly invoked in Sunday services and fellowship meetings. These gatherings often highlight the condemnation of divisiveness in the New Testament and proclaim that true Christians should be united into one organic body in spite of, indeed exactly because of, differences among them. They emphasize in addition that Chinese culture has always highly valued unity and harmony, and believe that without unity and harmony little can be achieved.

Cultural heterogeneity is the most prevalent potentially dividing factor in the church. But cultural homogeneity is also CFC's strongest cement, for this is a *Chinese* church. The Chinese identity is clear. The Chinese (written) language and cultural values provide the base for a sense of peoplehood, without which the members would have not come together. Although the understanding of "Chineseness" may vary, the Chinese as an ethnic minority in the United States are indeed distinctive. Many church members are aware of the history of the Chinese

Exclusion Acts. They are also proud of being members of a successful minority in contemporary American society.

Interestingly, in this *Chinese Christian* church, the ideals of Christian unity and Chinese unity complement and supplement each other.[22] Both can be evoked at once in order to stress the need for unity. In the real world, an insistence on either certain Christian doctrines, such as the form of baptism, or certain aspects of Chinese culture, such as a particular dialect, might lead to conflicts. When divisive tendencies do occur due to sociocultural or sociopolitical differences, CFC members are reminded, by leaders or by themselves, that they are Christians. As Christians they should be united in the same God, the same Christ, and the same Spirit. Worldly differences should not become excuses for the very division the Bible condemns. On the other hand, when there are theological disagreements, they are reminded that they are all Chinese and thus should be united as a people. Myths of unity among Jews or Koreans are used to stress the need for unity among Chinese. Insistence on certain potentially divisive Christian doctrines is criticized as sectarianism and ridiculed as dogmatism. Some people have denominational backgrounds, but they have chosen to congregate with other Chinese despite any expectations of superordinate denominational loyalty.

Of course, both being Chinese and being Christian have limits. Because a majority of church members are adult converts to the Christian faith, they tend to emphasize Christian unity and often criticize aspects of Chinese cultural traditions. This may distance them from non-Christian Chinese. This Christian unity also helps inclusiveness extend to non-Chinese Christians, although it is still quite limited at present. On the other hand, as evangelical Christians they are compelled to evangelize. Because of cultural affinity, their priority is to evangelize other Chinese first, both locally and abroad. In short, the sense of Chinese peoplehood and the will for Christian unity are mutually reinforcing forces for unity of Chinese Christians.

Third, the diversity within the church is respected. The groupings based on social and cultural backgrounds might appear to be manifestations of division against unity, tensions among groups that might seem to be dangerous, conflict-inducing forces. In fact, however, the subgroups actually help to stabilize the church and maintain unity. Exactly because these intimate groupings exist, people can achieve a sense of security and intimacy, out of which grows a need for reaching out to other people. This principle may also be extended to higher layers of society. As professionals, most of these Chinese work among non-Chinese. Because their ethnic church meets their needs for intimacy and psychological security, they are able to be confident and comfortable with non-Chinese in their work and in the larger society. In contrast, the policy of discouraging cultural groupings before 1976 led to all kinds of anxiety and dissatisfaction, and eventually ended with the bitter split. A respect for cultural differences is thus important to uphold unity.

Of course, there is an actual danger of compartmentalization of the close-knit subgroups. To maintain cohesion, it is necessary to enhance the communication between the groups and to proclaim a higher level of universalism that reaches beyond the narrow boundaries. To promote communication across subgroups, the church has energetically promoted the Sunday "Love Banquet" and has held annual summer retreats on a remote seminary campus since 1982. These measures provide opportunities for church members to share life stories and to know each other better. The active and capable lay leaders also work to promote unity. Equipped with linguistic capabilities—fully bilingual or trilingual—broad understanding and sensitivities, and networking experiences, they are able to move across several fellowships. They participate in their meetings as members or guest speakers, weaving strings through the net of the church to help hold it together. Some family ties and friendship bonds that stretch across fellowship boundaries contribute to unity as well.

Lastly, cultural resources help maintain church unity. Chinese culture highly values harmony. Soft approaches and behind-the-scene maneuvers are preferred to direct confrontations and public debates. Writing about Asian American churches, Birstan Choy (1995) puts this metaphorically: "acupuncture is preferred to surgery." Because of this approach, there was no public discussion or debate during the 1995 congregational meeting before the vote. Everyone maintained an air of calm. To avoid any trouble, the Ark Fellowship canceled its planned co-workers meeting. When newcomers ask about the 1976 schism and other past conflicts, long-time members often respond with silence. They believe that the best way to protect unity is to forget the unpleasant past and look forward, that open debates and direct confrontations did not work in 1976 and would not work today. When being confronted, people may fear to lose face (*diu mianzi*), and consequently become emotionally stony. "We Chinese are often not large-minded enough to bear direct confrontation and open discussions," an Ark Fellowship co-worker said, "so a better approach is to keep a harmonious atmosphere and be considerate of others who need to save face."

Reflection

Many Chinese American churches can boast of having successfully forged "unity out of diversity." Religiously, every declared Christian could be accepted in their congregation, regardless of denominational background or theological position. Ethnically, any Chinese could find a niche in the church. Probably no other type of ethnic Chinese organization or association in North America today has achieved such a unity of such a heterogeneous people. Within the boundaries of "Chineseness" and Christianity the church has realized a unity out of diversity.

The empirical findings of this study may have greater significance. The Chinese Christian church is one place where East and West meet. The church succeeds in integrating Chinese (Confucian) values and Christian beliefs, and this integration helps create a united community out of diversity. It shows that the East and the West, or the Eastern Confucian civilization and the Western Christian civilization, can be symbiotically integrated. "The clash of civilizations" prophesied by Samuel Huntington (1993) may be avoidable; the principles found at work in CFC may lead to hope for unity on higher levels. When diversity is respected, a vision of unity is held, and harmony is maintained, the United States of America, as the "nation of nations," and the world of diverse civilizations in which it exists can be similarly hopeful.

ACKNOWLEDGMENTS

I am very grateful to Stephen Warner and Judith Wittner for their tireless readings and critical comments of earlier drafts. I also appreciate helpful comments by other fellows at the New Ethnic and Immigrant Congregations Project as well as Dean H. Hoge, Che-Fu Lee, William V. D'Antonio, Pyong Gap Min, and Carol Dupre. I especially want to thank CFC members for all their help.

NOTES

1. All biblical verses in this chapter are from the Holy Bible, New International Version.

2. *Zhong Yong,* commonly known as the *Doctrine of the Mean,* is a central document in the Confucian tradition. This verse is my own translation based on James Legge (1893) and William Theodore De Bary et al. (1964).

3. See, for example, *Yi Jing (Book of Change),* Qian: Zhuan; *Lun Yu (Analects)* 1: 12; *Zhong Yong (Doctrine of the Mean)* 1: 4.

4. Anthropologist James L. Watson (1993) described Chinese unity as "a question that has preoccupied Western observers since the early Jesuits first began to write about the Central Kingdom: What held Chinese society together for so many centuries? Put another way, how was it possible for a country of continental dimensions, inhabited by people who speak mutually unintelligible languages and exhibit an amazing array of ethnic differences, to be molded into a unified culture?" It is also well recognized that China has tremendous magnetism as a cultural center to both Chinese in China and in diaspora (see Tu 1994).

5. Samuel P. Huntington (1993) proposed that after the Cold War, "the clash of civilizations will dominate global politics." He envisioned that the conflicts will be between "the West and the Rest," that is, between "Western Christian civilization," on the one hand, and Islamic civilization and Confucian civilization, on the other hand. This article has stirred up great debate.

6. No reliable data are available about the proportion of Christians among Chinese in the United States and other countries. In Taiwan, Hong Kong, and mainland China, estimates put the proportion between 2% to 5%. Chinese Christian leaders estimated that Christians were 5% to 10% of the Chinese in America, whereas some surveys indicate that the proportion could be as high as 32% (Hurh and Kim 1990, 20).

7. Pseudonyms are used in this chapter for several reasons. First, the populations and the dynamics in this church are quite common among Chinese churches. The particularities in this chapter, although they are presented accurately and factually to the best of my ability, serve only the purpose of illustration. Second, many of the church people and some scholars may see personality conflicts as major determinants of church division, but I find that these conflicts were more likely results than causes and were secondary problems compared to other factors discussed here. Adopting pseudonyms will, I hope, minimize the attention given to the particular personalities of the subjects in this church. Third, pseudonyms protect the privacy of the church members.

8. According to the U.S. census, the Chinese population has doubled every decade since 1960 in this metropolitan area as well as in the whole country. The 1990 census counted 39,034 Chinese in this area, which probably did not include all Chinese students and visiting scholars. But these temporary residents on several large campuses in this area are important to the Chinese church because it recruits members from them too. In addition, many new Chinese immigrants have arrived since 1990. Taken all together, the Chinese population in this metropolitan area today can be as many as 80,000.

9. Most of the about 700 Chinese Protestant churches in the United States in 1994 were conservative in theology and about half were nondenominational. For a discussion of overall characteristics and trends of Chinese churches, see Fenggang Yang (1995).

10. One of the reasons I chose this particular church for in-depth research was its accessibility to me as a member. Being a sociology student from the

People's Republic of China, I had experienced some difficulties in my 1993–94 study of all Chinese churches in this area. After I introduced that proposed project at a monthly gathering of their pastors, one pastor immediately questioned, "How could we know that you are not doing the investigation for the Chinese communist government?" This pastor, who had served in the Chinese Nationalist (Kuomintang) army and seemed to have a continuing fear of mainland Chinese, later expressed reluctance to be interviewed and refused to show me any church documents. Some fundamentalist leaders often questioned the usefulness of a sociological study.

11. I, like many new converts from the mainland, was invited to be involved in "co-workers" meetings of the evangelistic ministry to mainland Chinese. In business meetings I refrained from initiating actions, but in Bible study or evangelism meetings, I did often ask questions. When I was approached to take up leadership responsibilities at this or another ministry I declined, but I did accept a volunteer task of editing the newsletter for the Ark Fellowship (see text below). I also contributed essays to the quarterly church magazine.

12. Interviews were conducted either in Mandarin or English. Most church documents were in Chinese. Many quotations throughout this chapter are my translation.

13. In 1882 Congress passed the Chinese Exclusion Act, which prohibited Chinese laborers from entering the United States. This was followed by several other anti-Chinese acts, which were not repealed until 1943. See Sucheng Chan (1991) on the life of Chinese immigrants during the exclusion period.

14. After 1943, the United States allowed 105 Chinese immigrants each year. However, many Chinese came in the 1940s and 1950s under special refugee acts (Chinn et al. 1969).

15. Mullins's theory was based on his research on a linguistically homogeneous group—Japanese in Canada—with a single, large immigrant cohort.

16. Quotations are taken from the official history of CFC, printed in a special memorial collection on the occasion of the thirtieth anniversary of the church in 1988.

17. "Chinese" is used by the church to indicate a people, not the language. A "Mandarin church" may exclude non-Mandarin-speaking Chinese, whereas a "Chinese church" means to be open toward all Chinese people. This is clear in Chinese.

18. The item in the church membership record is "place of origin" (*jiguan*, in Chinese). It can be understood as either ancestral place, birthplace, or place from whence one came to the United States. People may choose whatever they want to put here, but the choice indicates a certain significance of the place to the person. For example, in Table 2 the numbers of people who recorded that they were born in or came from Taiwan, Hong Kong, and Southeast Asian countries would be higher if people had not been able to record their ancestral places. Similarly, not all those who listed their place of origin as Taiwan or Hong Kong were born there.

19. Reverend Houston is often referred as "the American pastor" or "the white American pastor" by church members, both immigrants and the American-born Chinese. Some Chinese immigrants habitually refer to any non-Chinese as *waiguoren* (person of foreign country or foreigner) and every Chinese as *zhongguoren* (person of the Central Country, or the Middle Kingdom). This distinction of us versus others is more cultural or ethnic than political (modern nation-state), just as Jews distinguish themselves from gentiles. This indicates a strong sense of peoplehood among all Chinese.

20. The church updates its roster every year. The 1996 Church Directory lists 392 people (not including preteen children), among whom 312 are members, most classified into one of the 12 fellowship groups. The fellowship names reported here are the actual titles, which are quite common in many Chinese churches. At the same time, they are carefully chosen and thus indicative of the members' intentions. For example, "Canaan" was selected because its members compared themselves to the ancient Jews who arrived in Canaan after 40 years of wandering in the wilds. This label may also reflect a self-perceived sense of assurance, maturity, and elder status. People who initiated the Ark Fellowship expressed a sense of urgency to save souls following the model of the righteous and obedient Noah.

21. Fundamentalists and charismatics, although both conservative in theology, hold different views on certain religious practices. Unlike charismatics, for example, fundamentalists frown on manifestations of pentecostal gifts, such as speaking in tongues and spiritual healing (see Warner 1988, 132–134, 170).

22. Many people perceive Chinese culture and Christianity to be incompatible with each other, and Chinese identity and Christian identity to be incongruous. However, I find that conversion to Christianity and the church seem to serve Chinese identity in many ways for Chinese in America (see Yang 1996).

REFERENCES

Chan, Sucheng, ed. 1991. *Entry Denied: Exclusion and the Chinese Community in America, 1882–1943*. Philadelphia: Temple University Press.

Chen, Hsiang-shui. 1992. *Chinatown No More: Taiwan Immigrants in Contemporary New York*. Ithaca, N.Y.: Cornell University Press.

Chinese-English Bible. 1990. Berkeley, Calif.: Hymnody and Bible House.

Chinn, Thomas W., H. Mark Lai, and Philip P. Choy, eds. 1969. *A History of the Chinese in California: A Syllabus*. San Francisco: Chinese Historical Society of America.

Choy, Birstan B. Y. 1995. "From Surgery to Acupuncture: An Alternative Approach to Managing Church Conflict from an Asian American Perspective." *Congregations: The Alban Journal* November–December: 16–19.

De Bary, William Theodore, Wing-tsit Chan, and Chester Tan, eds. 1964. *Sources of Chinese Tradition*. New York: Columbia University Press.

Hoge, Dean R. 1976. *Division in the Protestant House: The Basic Reasons Behind Intra-Church Conflicts*. Philadelphia: Westminster Press.

Huntington, Samuel P. 1993. "The Clash of Civilizations?" *Foreign Affairs* 72 (Summer): 22–49.

Hurh, Won Moo, and Kwang Chung Kim. 1990. "Religious Participation of Korean Immigrants in the United States." *Journal for the Scientific Study of Religion* 29 (March): 19–34.

Legge, James. 1893. *Chinese Classics*, vol. I. Oxford: Clarendon Press.

Lyman, Stanford M. 1974. *Chinese Americans*. New York: Random House.

Mullins, Mark. 1987. "The Life-Cycle of Ethnic Churches in Sociological Perspective." *Japanese Journal of Religious Studies* 14 (4): 321–334.

Niebuhr, H. Richard. 1929. *Social Sources of Denominationalism*. New York: World.

Palinkas, Lawrence A. 1984. "Social Fission and Cultural Change in an Ethnic Chinese Church." *Ethnic Groups* 5 (4): 255–277.

Shin, Eui Hang, and Hyung Park. 1988. "An Analysis of Causes of Schisms in Ethnic Churches: The Case of Korean-American Churches." *Sociological Analysis* 49 (Fall): 234–248.

Tu, Wei-ming, ed. 1994. *The Living Tree: The Changing Meaning of Being Chinese Today*. Stanford, Calif.: Stanford University Press.

Warner, R. Stephen. 1988. *New Wine in Old Wineskins: Evangelicals and Liberals in a Small-Town Church*. Berkeley and Los Angeles: University of California Press.

Watson, James L. 1993. "Rites or Beliefs? The Construction of a Unified Culture in Late Imperial China." Pp. 80–103 in *China's Quest for National Identity*, edited by Lowell Dittmer and Samuel S. Kim. Ithaca, N.Y.: Cornell University Press.

Wong, Bernard P. 1994. "Hong Kong Immigrants in San Francisco." Pp. 235–255 in *Reluctant Exiles? Migration from Hong Kong and the New Overseas Chinese*, edited by Ronald Skeldon. Armonk, N.Y.: M. E. Sharpe.

Yang, Fenggang. 1995. "Chinese Protestant Churches in the United States: Explanations for Their Growth and Their Conservative and Independent Tendencies." Paper presented at the annual meeting of the Society for Scientific Study of Religion, St. Louis.

———. 1996. "Religious Conversion and Identity Construction: A Study of a Chinese Christian Church in the United States." Ph.D. dissertation, Catholic University of America.

Conclusion

A Reader Among Fieldworkers

Judith G. Wittner

When Steve Warner invited me to join him in leading the fieldwork seminar that launched the studies reported here, I knew little about the sociology of religion and less about the varieties of religious practice and experience among immigrant populations in the United States. My contribution to the New Ethnic and Immigrant Congregations Project was to be my fieldwork experience and my knowledge of feminist scholarship. Most of what I know about studying religious practices I learned in the five years since we began these studies by reading the successive drafts of the essays that make up this book. As reader I observed from a distance. I learned about the sites—places I never visited, people I never met—as they were presented on the page. Of course no description, however detailed, can capture more than a fraction of the experienced world, so I was left to imagine relationships, to impute motives, and to bring my own understandings to the reading.

As readers do, I drew on my own experiences and current interests to fill in the blanks. Raised in a secular Jewish home by parents who put their own immigrant parents' religious practices aside to embrace the antifascist, socialist, and labor struggles of their day, I had no childhood memories that might help me to understand religious motivations. Moved by the politics of my youth—civil rights, the opposition to the Vietnam War, community organizing, and feminism—I dismissed religious involvement as a distraction from struggles for justice, peace, and community connection. As a sociologist, a profession to which I came late, I remained interested in the power relations of race, class, and gender, and learned to respect the everyday world as a site for inquiry. But the sociology of religion, like its practice, didn't interest me. I was content to remain an outsider professionally as well as personally, only occasionally puzzling over what motivated religious sentiment, what propelled people into regular religious practice.

All of the rich ethnographies presented in this volume, grounded as they are in everyday religious practices, introduced me to religion from the inside. Instead of calling up my cherished stereotypes of religion, the studies revealed a range of religious practices with much to tell about political action at the religious grass roots. There are stories here about the work that goes into building a religious community: encouraging nonkin to take responsibility for each other and organizing individuals to pursue common goals, some as intangible as attaining "success" or "respectability," others as concrete as sending cash to communities back home. By looking at the everyday practices of religion and focusing on the actualities of community-building—on what members of religious groups *do* as well as what they say—the essays show how religious gatherings identify and try to meet the needs of their individual members, how families band together to survive in a foreign setting, and how strangers recast themselves as comrades and collaborators to make the world they envision.

Comments scattered throughout Luís León's essay (Chapter 5) awakened me to the politics of religious community-building. Here was a lengthy description of "born-again" religion directed to the conversion of members of Chicano gangs. How different this focus was from that seen a generation ago, when groups such as the Black Panthers identified involvement in radical political struggles as the road to salvation for gang youth. The Panthers' radical analyses and strategies for building a new society coexisted with a violent, patriarchal internal culture (Brown 1992). In contrast, a radical practice underpins the conservative message of Victory Outreach, as converts are exhorted to think critically about and then renounce violent or "cool" versions of masculinity and instead make "physical, emotional, and spiritual contact with other men," take time with their children, and forgive their fathers for abandoning them. León's essay opened my eyes to the attraction of a religious community growing out of congregants' everyday needs and realities: the promise of attachment and love to immigrants far from homes and families left behind in Mexico, of acceptance to young men adrift on the streets of Los Angeles, and of worldly success through faith, work, and education to people struggling to make a living (how Harvard has captured the imagination of these and other immigrants!). Victory Outreach gives shape and legitimacy to these longings and offers blueprints to guide members toward their fulfillment.

As my work with the project expanded from co-teaching the fieldwork seminar with newly selected project fellows to discussing research sites and editing drafts of their papers for the book, I learned more details about each community. It soon became clear that these were not the backwaters and retreats from the world I had imagined. Instead members of the religious gatherings, associations, and congregations described here were caught up in major currents of contemporary political, economic, and cultural life. I began to see their attempts to strengthen their community ties with one another, to position themselves favorably in terms of class and race, and to resolve growing internal divisions of gender and generation as important experiments, with lessons for anyone interested in how people make their worlds together.

I

Seen from outside, solidarity among immigrant groups seems both spontaneous and inevitable. After all, don't immigrants naturally concentrate in particular regions, cities, and neighborhoods, and, because of their common history and current proximity, create distinct communities of their own (see, for example, Rumbaut 1991)? Not really, according to the evidence presented here. Seen from inside, community-building, involving the creation of mutually responsible relations and ties beyond blood and marriage, requires great effort. It means rewriting a group's history or constructing it anew, refashioning long-standing practices ranging from religious worship to daily habits of association, and overcoming, among other things, internal divisions of gender and generation. It means doing all these things and more by resolving dilemmas never before confronted and by giving up past futures for visions still being negotiated among members of the community.

However, I don't intend in this chapter to abstract from these accounts only the general and generic, to find what is common among these ethnographies. That would defeat the goal of this project, which is to discover the specific details of daily life that make religious communities what they are.

The essays here describe a diverse array of congregations and religious associations. Some religious associations drew on a remembered past and its traditions of solidarity to replicate an old community in the new. The saints associations of the Maya in exile and the Iranian culture preserved by the first generation of Persian Jews, both groups forced by political events to leave their homelands, re-created former religious and cultural practices in the United States. Members of the Maya FEMAQ' community, one of the poorest groups in this book and in this country, and Jewish Iranians, members of one of the wealthiest, each found ways that enabled them to resurrect their homeland in exile. In both cases, changes are in the offing. As Shoshanah Feher (Chapter 2) explains, the first generation of Persian Jews could keep to themselves because they had the resources that allowed them to do so. But they weren't rich or powerful enough to maintain those conditions for their children and grandchildren, who must search for other ways to live in a world not of their making. A similar process may be in its early stages among the Maya. As Nancy J. Wellmeier writes (Chapter 3), some members of the community are beginning to put down roots in this country, and some children raised here are not so eager to leave it for a home they have never known.

Other congregations, whose members have, perhaps, more freely chosen to journey here, recombined past practices and developed new ways drawn from American culture and religious organization to transform relationships and build their communities. Elizabeth McAlister (Chapter 4) reports on how New York fashions symbolized a new status among Haitians. Prema Kurien (Chapter 1) describes how the religious communities of Indians she observed modified Hindu traditions and borrow American congregational forms to produce a unique patchwork of religious practices and organization out of an incongruous variety of pieces: a "secular" deity not likely to divide the community; new songs and prayers written by members of the congregation to supplement traditional *bhajans*; and classes to transmit Hindu culture.

As different as the details may be, each of these essays shows the "hows" of congregation-building. How does a disparate group of individuals become a unified congregation? Fenggang Yang's (Chapter 10) careful analysis of the centrifugal and centripetal forces working in his Chinese Christian church shows how the members created a fragile unity out of a fractious, diverse assemblage of peoples. Rogaia Mustafa Abusharaf (Chapter 7) shows in detail how Yemeni Muslims adapted religious practice to the demands of work and worship in the United States. Rather than presume that communities are natural groupings based on biological ties of race or psychological bonds of language and nation, both Yang and Abusharaf demonstrate empirically how people produce a congregational community in a concrete setting.

Most striking to me in these stories of congregational creation is the organizational wisdom of religious actors in promoting community solidarity. A congregation is not an undifferentiated mass of members connected in uniform fashion to the whole. Often it has a cell-like structure, with small units agglomerating into a coalition of believers.

Judith G. Wittner

The members of the Chinese Fellowship Church studied by Yang learned through conflict and schism that solidarity could best be won by respecting diversity, a respect enacted in and through their small, culturally and linguistically homogeneous fellowship groups. Although they adhered to the ideal of wider unity, the members of the congregation did not invoke that ideal to eradicate difference. Instead, unity emerged as an outcome of cross-cutting ties of family and friendship, the shared cultural value of harmony, and the sense of peoplehood engendered by the history of the Chinese in the United States, a unity symbolically marked by the monthly meetings of the whole. Likewise, León's Alcance Victorians met in small groups, no larger than fifteen. These small gatherings helped newcomers to overcome their alienation from each other and to recognize and respect one another as unique and important contributors to the collective. The fact that the congregation was embedded in a global network gave their fellowship added significance. Randal L. Hepner (Chapter 6) also refers to the ways that members of his congregation, like the populations from which they came, both "transcend and preserve their particular national identities."

Like families, small, face-to-face religious assemblies make it possible for members to know one another's unique qualities and special interests, to learn her or his wants and needs; this in turn produces solidarity as co-religionists come to act and feel mutually responsible for each other. Feminist theorists have discussed these dynamics as the relations of "caring." The organization of caring in this society, they maintain, is based on the work women do ("caring for"), which has neither been recognized as work nor valued. The feelings and emotions surrounding caring work, or "caring about," are compelling courses of action making women feel responsible for the work, which leads men and children to expect it from them (DeVault 1991). Using caring as a sensitizing concept (Blumer 1969), I could see in these essays the many ways that members of religious communities institutionalized collective and nongendered forms of care for each other. In principle, at least, they did not organize caring simply along lines of gender or solely within privatized family households.

Congregations offered their members many types of caring relationships and assistance. In their respective studies, Kurien and Feher give examples of the material aid that resource-rich congregations made available to their constituents, supplementing private resources and promoting collective responsibility. Such aid included access to the skills, knowledge, and services of its doctors, lawyers, teachers, and businesspeople. Resource-poor congregations pooled other kinds of skills and knowledge. Wellmeier reports that the FEMAQ' community helped newcomers tap into the stream of possibilities that made for success in California: housing, job leads, and important information about immigration law. Similarly, Hepner suggests that regular participation in the Church of Haile Selassie I helped members develop organizational experience and competence in speaking in public, intangible skills, perhaps, but ones that are useful in a variety of ways.

In addition to material aid, members of congregations and religious groups undertook the emotion-work that many have habitually associated with families, and channeled these feelings into specific courses of action for the benefit of the group and its members. A "fear of falling" (Ehrenreich 1989) in racial or class terms seemed to have animated many of the people described here. Caribbean immigrants, part of the racial majority in their homelands, feared the indignities, disfranchisement, and other burdens heaped upon an ill-treated black minority in a white-majority, racist society. Rastafarian congregations, according to Hepner, have been sites of resistance to being identified with African Americans, a situation quite different from that seen in earlier years, when Rastas empathized with "sufferahs," advocated political struggle, and made common cause with Africans in diaspora. As Sheba George (Chapter 8) describes, the men of Saint George's Church feared a future in which they were displaced as the dominant authorities in their church and in their families. The solidary men's group, a source of support and a place to develop new relationships among men, was the response of these well-to-do Indians, who were eager to negotiate preferred racial and class statuses, and who feared the loss of their children to depraved Americanism. Feher reported that Jewish Iranians, down to the "1.5 generation," worried that their children were attracted to gangs, drugs, and crime. Such fears mobilized projects designed to bind the next generation more closely to its ethnic/religious community of origin.

Other emotions drove other courses of action. Emotions linked the young men of Alcance Victoria to the idea that they *could* be part of the world of "respectable" and affluent families by channeling their rage against the inequality that spawns gang life into commitment to the church and its principles of action (Chapter 5). The public performances celebrating Maya communities in exile simultaneously evoked and assuaged emotional memories of home and kept community feeling alive (Chapter 3). Indigenous music also helped Maya immigrants maintain their emotional attachment to home, so the reported divisions within the community over the "Latinoization" of marimba concerts shows a weakening consensus about the community's cultural markers. The desire to find community with others who shared their experiences as the children of immigrants kept Indian American college students within their parents' religious orbit (Chapter 1), but drove Korean American college students to build their own congregations and associations, as Karen J. Chai (Chapter 9) explains. In Chai's Korean church, the passions music aroused became vehicles for creating a service more reflective of the interests and concerns of the younger generation. Haitian Catholics tapped into the the heightened emotions of another group's public religious gathering to maintain and extend their own celebrations (Chapter 4). Kurien's informant called the emotion stimulated by familiar rituals "peace of mind." In these many ways, emotions helped to mobilize collective action, keeping men's place intact in the congregation; rescuing young men from drugs and life on the streets; tying young people to their community; maintaining commitments to homes and villages far away; transforming religious worship to express the unique experiences and culture of the second generation.

Emotion-work creates more solidarity within congregations. As do housewives and mothers and all others who provide caretaking services individually and privately, congregations bring and keep people together with their focus on their needs, desires, visions, and dreams. Emotions motivate people to take responsibility for the well-being of others. Emotions support expectations of care and love from certain caretakers. Emotions connect people more strongly to each other. By generalizing the emotions of caring to the community and taking public responsibility for supporting their members, congregations, whatever else they do, challenge the privatization of care and prefigure a more equitable society.

II

I wrote at the outset that I did not wish to abstract from the chapters that which was common to them all. However, another fruitful way of generalizing is to connect local relations with relations that extend beyond the locality and that structure what can be seen, known, and acted upon there.

Building connections in times of great change must always be conflictual. Power relations are threatened from below by changes that leave some traditions of ruling unsupported and that simultaneously threaten myths justifying the status quo. If men aren't so powerful outside home, what keeps them powerful inside? If children are more comfortable with American culture and can navigate their parents' adopted world with greater ease, what is parental authority about? It's not difficult to see these challenges to authority growing out of structural and cultural realignments that have deeply affected the members of these religious associations. These were small communities nested within regional, national, international, and global structures. The restructuring of production on a world scale, the national and international politics of war and diplomacy, the state and national laws and policies governing immigration and settlement, the cultural products disseminated worldwide by mass media, the rightward political turn in the United States and elsewhere, all these and more constituted the world in which these small religious bodies formed. The globalization of production was the main impetus to the immigration of all but the first-generation members of the Iranian Jewish community (although one could trace the overthrow of the shah in 1979, which prompted the migration of Jews from Iran, to the global pressures of international capitalism). Working-class women from the Caribbean, Indian nurses, Chinese and Indian professionals, family men and youths from Central America and Mexico, all were responding to the specific pushes and pulls of their various economic and political situations, as well as to the more general social forces of race, class, and gender. Women of the Haitian (Chapter 4) and Rastafarian (Chapter 6) congregations, learning that they could earn dollars as domestics, office clerks, garment workers, or child carers in New York, might be the first in their families to migrate north (see Sutton 1992). Workers with the education and skills to pursue medical and technical careers—here Indian nurses (Chapter 8) and Chinese computer specialists (Chapter 10)—were no doubt attracted to a country where their prospects seemed brighter than they would have been at home. This mobile labor force was divided within by the pull of jobs and careers differentially on women and men, on occupants of different racial categories, and on persons with particular skills, differences that produced a range of possibilities for and constraints on religious association.

Globalized culture also played a role in setting the stage for congregational action (see, for example, Appadurai and Breckenridge 1988). Hollywood films and American television transmit American race and gender stereotypes and fears around the world, orienting potential immigrants to American versions of race, class, gender, and generational politics. The discourse on family values that several of the studies document, I believe, had such a foundation, drawing as it did on a widely disseminated popular analysis of American social problems that holds poor communities of color morally responsible for the poverty and violence they experience. The immigrants described here seemed to share these concerns about family disintegration, community disorder, and moral decline in the United States.

Conventional perspectives on class and race that support a blame-the-victim analysis may be widespread among newcomers to the United States at the present time. However, the picture is more complex when it comes to women and gender. True, Hollywood films and commercial television often trivialize and misrepresent women's lives and concerns, but these media also communicate feminist ideas and conceptual resources by publicizing the international women's movement and by introducing immigrant audiences to the ways women around the world have brought their concerns and interests onto a public stage. Certainly, such ideas have played an important role in inspiring activity, analysis, and vision among many of the communities described in this book.

Inside views of religious gatherings reveal the contested politics within these communities-in-the-making. As traditions and past practices became more difficult to maintain under the pressures of immigrant life, internal divisions emerged. When women or children objected to their exclusion from church business, when they demanded that their concerns and interests be publicly recognized by the congregation, or when they called for collective resources to be apportioned to their projects, they were disputing the priorities of men or of an older generation and seeking to reset the collective agenda, to redefine the collective vision. Seeing another option, many Muslim women deserted the Mission for mosques that promised to accept them more fully as members (Chapter 7). Often, however, dissatisfied women and children either did not perceive or could not take the option to exit. In these cases, congregations became public arenas where emergent constituencies such as women or members of the second generation made claims and where people used to exercising control tried to hold the line against their demands for resources and recognition.

Class and racial locations—how a group was situated in terms of the global, regional, and local divisions of labor and consumption—set the stage for many of these internal divisions to emerge. That immigration is first and foremost a survival strategy within the context of globalized economic relations and the restructuring of worldwide divisions of labor is a fact brought home to readers most directly in the chapters by Wellmeier, George, Hepner, McAlister, and León, who write of working-class communities that originated in their international income-producing strategies (see Rodriguez 1995). Among the trained professionals and technical workers described by Yang and Kurien and the Korean parents of members of Chai's congregation, immigration was less a matter of individual and family survival, and more clearly a mobility strategy.

Once newcomers are positioned by global (and national and regional) forces in the new setting, once they become engaged in the work of congregation- and community-construction, what more is there to be said about class relations? For me, two aspects of class relations stand out in these portraits of religious communities. First, these studies describe relationships that have been hidden by or shoehorned into statistical categories—race, age, country of origin. These categories are not simply neutral, but rather are part of a system of accountability to administrative bodies that regulate and control immigration and labor (Smith 1990, 107–138). Here some of the actualities of their momentous transition, as immigrants themselves experience it, are recorded and the relevancies of their lives foregrounded. Second, these essays show in detail how class operates in everyday relations. For example, some congregations strategized to situate themselves favorably (however understood) within the new society. Professionals and businessmen in the Hindu (Chapter 1) and Iranian Jewish (Chapter 2) communities identified methods to preserve their privileges and respectability as unassimilated ethnic groups within the American professional-managerial class. Alcance Victorians (Chapter 5) tried to move gang members from permanent unemployment into entrepreneurship; the young, "First Second Generation," raised in the same church, looked forward to careers instead, no doubt aware of their declining opportunities in small business and their new opportunities in education and the professions.

In these instances of class action, the "family values" discourse and the model of the breadwinner/housewife family were used to mobilize particular actions and projects. For example, the Hindu strategy for economic success was built around family and community solidarity, a practice that included parents' financial, social, and educational support of their children, backed up with community resources (Chapter 1). These parents hoped this strategy would tie their children firmly enough to the Hindu community to enable them to pass their class position and its privileges on to their children's generation (see Portes and Zhou 1993). Among Iranian Jews of the "1.5 generation," the concept of family values helped to shape and legitimize their project to make their community into an extended family (Chapter 2). Their

Judith G. Wittner

plan was to keep the threatened community alive by creating fictive "aunts and uncles" to take the place of Jewish youngsters' wage-earning mothers and fathers during the long working day. By these means they would prevent another "holocaust of our young people," this time by protecting Jewish Iranian children from abandoning Judaism and casting their lot with those on the wrong side of the class/race divide in Los Angeles.

In the class drama among the men of Victory Outreach (Chapter 5), the family values discourse was a blueprint for achieving class status instead of passing down a way of life already achieved, as was the case among Hindus and Jews. Here family solidarity was a vision and a model, not a lived reality. Celebrating "good" family life was a call to act in the service of this ideal and a promise that it could be achieved by following the teachings of the church and its leaders. In the Rastafarian congregation (Chapter 6), by contrast, the concept of family values seemed to fuel and justify a revolution from the ranks by helping the Daughters of Zion to articulate and organize their claims. As Sister Sonia pointed out in her manifesto on the need for women to take central roles in church governance, "the family is the cornerstone of civilization."

In the United States, race tends to distribute groups among occupations and has been a framework for class formation (Winant 1995, 36). Recognizing this fact, several communities feared being lumped with African Americans and were eager to establish a distinct ethnic identity that distanced them from the troubles and deprivations of life at the bottom of the racial pecking order in the United States. Kurien claims that developing an Indian ethnic identity helped Hindus to avoid being assigned to a more problematic racial identity, and Feher describes how Persian Jews chose to emphasize their religious identity with American Jews over their national origins to avoid the difficult status of Iranians in the United States. These racial/ethnic strategies were simultaneously class strategies. Jobs, housing, and education, as well as respect, were among the prizes to be won by groups on the right side of the color line.

Hepner refers to another aspect of the process of racialization: its role in organizing the racialized community internally. He suggests that West Indian identity (in contrast to Jamaican, Barbadian, Dominican, and other national identities) could only develop away from homelands in the Caribbean, in a country where differences among various nationals are practically invisible and where black West Indians are in danger of joining the end of the queue for access to jobs, housing, and neighborhood resources. On the other hand, Wellmeier's Maya community in California, coded "Hispanic" by the Catholic parishes it entered, worked to maintain its Native American identity and its distinctive style of life. Still, the Maya way of life is even now undergoing transformations that may undermine its present "old country" Mayaism, changes that presage emerging struggles over problems of racial/ethnic identity.

Like class and race, class and gender relations also mix in ways that make it difficult to speak of each separately. Worldwide social and economic changes have increased the demand for women's labor, while demand from the traditional sources of men's employment—manufacturing, unskilled and semiskilled labor, craft production—has declined. In the wake of these global changes in the workforce, women around the world have been challenging patriarchal ideologies that they find at odds with their new situations.

Reading between the lines of Kurien's essay suggests that Hindu women's talk about women's place, an "ideal wife," and women's importance marks an emerging conflict between the kind of family presupposed by their discourse on family values and the difficulties of realizing that ideal in the face of the realities of Hindu women's and children's lives in the United States. Such talk suggests uncertainty about a set of understandings that once went without saying, but that are now coming up for discussion. Simply to raise this issue, to begin talking to one another about their place in the community, is in itself a radical move because it puts women's interests *qua* women into public discourse. Hindu wives initiated talk about their own importance in their families and in the community; their daughters, educated in the United States, introduced feminist ideas into these discussions. From brief comments in Feher's and Wellmeier's papers, it seems only a matter of time before the women of IJF/SIAMAK and the women of the Maya community, respectively, who are increasingly less dependent on male wages and increasingly likely to participate in the worlds of school and work outside their home, also begin to raise questions about the forms of male supremacy in their communities.

Hepner alludes to a more full-blown reshaping of women's power in the congregation. Women have managed to make the congregation at the church of Haile Selassie I a place where their practical interests—family well-being, women's partipation in governance—have taken their place beside and, perhaps, above men's. Church leaders praised family life and women's work. As women's interests and projects became institutionalized within the congregation, church re-

Judith G. Wittner

sources were redirected toward providing child care, religious education of children by women, and the participation of women in church governance. Did Abuna Asento Foxe's new perspective encourage this development, or have women's demands here and elsewhere pushed him to rethink the place of women in the movement? Whatever the answer, women's growing economic importance and centrality in the family are reflected in their push to become members of the congregation in their own right.

There is the possibility that León was able to tell only part of the story of his congregation, because as a man he was excluded from the women's world there. We suspect this would also be true of the Yemeni men interviewed by Abusharaf. Possibly women's public verbal support of female submissiveness and male dominance in Victory Outreach is not borne out in women's actual activities in the church (see also Stacey 1991). And while the women may not be quite as docile as they themselves claim, other changes in the makeup of the congregation suggest that the patriarchal project will not enjoy pride of place in the future. The idealized image of the retiring, supportive, virgin wife reconstructed out of the dreams of young street men will not do for the dreams of single women in the congregation or of the young men and women focused on university educations and careers. Whether or not these shifts in membership will lead to a rethinking of congregational goals, one thing is certain: gender relations were the focus of the work of this congregation, whose members believed that the journey from hard to settled living required that they reshape their everyday lives around a particular gender order.

Generational divisions, forcefully described by Feher, George, and Chai, and hinted at in the studies by Yang, Wellmeier, León, and Abusharaf, also were intertwined with class issues. Feher's informant voiced his class- and race-based fears that the generation of Jewish Iranians born in the United States. were in danger of succumbing to gangs, drugs, crime, pregnancy, prostitution, and AIDS. As George explains, the second generation at St. George's made concrete the men's apprehension over the radical shifts in their lives and in the lives of their wives and daughters. The second-generation Korean Americans Chai studied wanted a mix of ethnicity, religion, class, and culture that is different from what their parents offered and more like who they were: young people uncomfortable with their Koreanness and eager to establish a congregation more reflective of their Christian spirit and their music. They wanted to shape this project with people like themselves, those who shared memories of a Korean upbringing in an immigrant household, who were students away from home, who were immersed in and comfortable with American culture.

The stirrings of generational divisions are reported by Yang, Wellmeier, and León. Yang notes that there were differences between younger and older members of the congregation. Young people complained they were shut out of church governance, and they disagreed with the positions and tactics of the older members of the congregation. Wellmeier hints at troubles to come between the generations, as years in exile lengthen and as young Maya Americans begin to see their future in their adopted homeland. And, as I have just noted, the congregation of Victory Outreach that León studied is changing, as single women and Mexican families join, and as a second generation, hooked on education and professional work, comes of age.

George's account of the conflict over caroling begins with the men's seemingly strange behavior and explores the intertwined politics of class, generation, and gender in the struggle over who was to join the caroling group. The story about the attempts of these Indian men to shore up their patriarchal privilege by, among other things, keeping their daughters from caroling, provides a close-up view of the men's responses to their economic decline and to their shaky hold on their patriarchal power. Neither breadwinners nor cultural authorities in this new world, their strategy—to preserve and enhance their position as leaders of the community and the congregation—seems destined to promote an exodus of their children from the church. From the men's perspective, the girls' interest in caroling must appear to echo the emergence of women as public actors elsewhere—in politics, in the work world—and poses yet another threat to the men's solidarity and control. In a few years, however, their children may complain that the church belongs to and speaks for their parents, not them, as did the second-generation Koreans that Chai described. It is less likely that the second-generation Indian American girls will continue as their mothers seem to have done, supporting men's control over the church while the women go about their business elsewhere. These changes suggest one way that a younger generation may begin their "silent exodus" from parents' congregations and help to explain precisely how generational relations can sour. In reading these essays, I wondered if the Korean American members of Chai's church would tell similar stories when asked about growing up in their parents' congregations, and whether the Jewish American grandchildren of the Persian Jews of Los Angeles in Feher's study would construct their religious biographies in a similar fashion.

George's study, although focused on a small event in a small world, adds depth and complexity to the story of generational change in immigrant religious communities. Her very presence, her act of organizing the girls for caroling, provoked the relations that she studied. By contrast, Yang reports on men's worlds in the Chinese Fellowship Church from within the community of men. He says little about women's part in this congregation, thus reflecting, no doubt, the marginality of women to the men's deliberations. However, if one of the complaints against the dismissed pastor was that he was too liberal on women's issues, doesn't that suggest that women's place is an emerging question at this Chinese church? The history of women uniting within male-dominated organizations to make public their demands for parity suggests that women's concerns will continue to intrude into the deliberations of the male congregation, and perhaps more insistently. As the men discuss their own hopes for a church organized according to their needs and interests, it is possible that women in the congregation may, like others before them have done, begin to think about the ways the congregation could serve them as well.

III

The relationships that the authors of these chapters entered into in the course of their research resonate in the essays they produced. Advancing far beyond the traditional ethnographic concern with "getting in" and "getting on," the researchers situate themselves in the sites they are studying and write about their part in the generation of data. Because they have written about themselves as well as others, and because they write of their participation in the very relations they study, the contributors illuminate many connections between who they are, where they stand, and the kind of knowledge to which their biography and their local identities give them access. As those who have tried fieldwork know, researchers form particular relationships with the people they study that affect what they see and how they interpret it. By clarifying their connections to the worlds they explored, the authors have made it possible for readers to assess the quality of the information they present. In this way, reflexivity becomes a useful substitute for distanced and decontextualized objectivity.

Perhaps only George could have uncovered the particular struggles she did as she stood with the young women who wanted to go caroling and was positioned by the men of the community as the "prodigal" daughter free from marital and parental constraints. By playing this role, which was partly her doing and partly theirs, she made it necessary for the men to articulate their opposition and to bring into the open some otherwise unspoken tensions between themselves and the young second-generation women. Wellmeier is neither a Catholic priest nor a Maya woman, two groups that were normally excluded from the ceremonies and meetings that she attended with the men. As a Catholic nun, her position, within the community but not of it, fit her work as a go-between who mediated, at the behest of community leaders, among the community, the Catholic church, and the state. From this stance, she was able to represent the community both in her advocacy work for them and in her academic writing. In George's case, her gender/ethnic/religious identity was central in her positioning in the community. In Wellmeier's, her position betwixt and between communities overrode her race/gender identity.

Several of the authors were members of the communities they studied, but others were not. Did this matter? Not in the direct way I expected it would, because of the multiple aspects of identity salient in the researchers' particular relationships in the field and because of the situated and fluid character of these relationships. In fact, because a number of the contributors were members of the groups they studied, they were able to offer more information than we would have known otherwise.

For example, Yang and Chai were in some ways complete insiders, long-term members of the congregations they observed. Still, from time to time they had to adopt the critical distance necessary for ethnographic work, which set them apart from their co-worshipers. Moreover, as graduate students, Chai and Yang were participants in an academic community as well as a religious one. At times the conflicts between these positions surfaced, reminding us all that we are both insiders and outsiders, never fully one or the other, and never completely in either place once and for all.

Racially, McAlister and Hepner were outsiders, whites who studied black congregations. However, the close relationships they were able to build with members of their respective communities suggest that an insider need not always be someone who shares genes or an upbringing with others, but can also be a person who knows how to do the relational work of the community. Such knowledge is obtained not by engaging in a passive intellectual exercise but rather by actively taking a part in the community. Both McAlister and Hepner possessed insider knowledge based on their immersion in their adopted worlds. They were fluent in the dialects of the people they studied, and they knew well—

and lived by—their rules of conduct and other everyday practices. Mc-Alister made her first of many trips to Haiti with Haitian friends from New York, migrants who traveled continually between the two places, maintaining active relationships in both poles of their transnational circuit. She learned their music and was invited to participate in their religious worship and in their everyday lives. Hepner lived among the brothers in Brooklyn and in Kingston, spoke their language, and absorbed their ways and thoughts. His blond dreadlocks and island talk showed him to be more of an insider than anyone focused on racial difference would have guessed possible. McAlister's and Hepner's experience-based knowledge, what Dorothy Smith (1990, 206) calls "insider's materialism," allowed them to shape their stories to describe their subjects' meanings, concerns, and relevances, and not simply to satisfy disciplinary or professional requirements, real and imagined.

From her years of residence in the home communities of the Maya in Guatemala as a member of a Catholic religious order, her competence in their Indian language as well as her fluent Spanish, and her deep commitment to the well-being of the Maya community, Wellmeier, too, had insider's knowledge. But from the community's point of view, a more important relationship was constructed on the basis of her status as a partial *outsider*. Wellmeier's respectful approach to the Maya community and her firsthand experience of their lives positioned her as a knowledgeable and sympathetic ally. It is significant that the FEMAQ' community was interested not only in her services but also in the knowledge about them she was going to produce. Their demand to see her research reports seemed to be a way for the Maya to "talk back" by holding scholars accountable to the people they study, as well as to institute what Michael Burawoy (1991, 4–5) has called an "I-Thou" research relationship, shaped by dialogue among relative equals rather than by distance or immersion. Beyond activating a more egalitarian relationship between the scholars and the communities they study, acquiring the right to see ethnographers' research reports helps members of these communities to develop their own, grassroots reflexivity, thereby enhancing their ability to pick and choose more knowledgeably from among a range of alternatives that will shape their future (see Chapter 2; Lash and Urry 1994, 50–51). This is how the imam interviewed by Abusharaf interpreted the growing professionalization of the Yemeni clergy: as a function of the immigrant community's increased awareness of a congregation as a site where, according to Abusharaf, the group is "reconstituting itself and its ideologies."

In relation to the women of the congregation he studied, León presents the limiting case, a multiple outsider who has access only to women's public speech and acts of devotion. Any private words or subversive acts by the women seem beyond the boundaries of what León can observe. But this is, after all, the point of this project. Every one of these ethnographies is necessarily situated in the standpoint of its author and draws on the relationships he or she entered into in doing research. This means that all of these studies are necessarily partial stories. They tell readers about religious worlds as they are illuminated through the lived relationships between scholars and members of communities. Other scholars and other informants, working together, will show us different aspects of these worlds.

ACKNOWLEDGMENTS

I wish to thank Michael Ames, Arlene Kaplan Daniels, Anne Figert, Mary Jo Neitz, and R. Stephen Warner for their helpful comments and suggestions. My thanks also go to the New Ethic and immigrant Congregations Project's very competent graduate assistants, Elise Martel and Linda Andes, and to my graduate assistant at Loyola University, Rebecca Burwell. I am especially grateful to Steve Warner for inviting me into this project, to Katherine Pyne Addelson for getting me started, and to Kathleen Adams for her willingness to read and reread several drafts of this chapter.

REFERENCES

Appadurai, Arjun, and Carol Breckenridge. 1988. "Why Public Culture." *Public Culture* 1 (1): 5–9.

Blumer, Herbert. 1969. *Symbolic Interactionism: Perspective and Method.* Englewood Cliffs, N.J.: Prentice-Hall.

Brown, Elaine. 1992. *A Taste of Power: A Black Woman's Story.* New York: Pantheon.

Burawoy, Michael. 1991. *Ethnography Unbound.* Berkeley: University of California Press.

DeVault, Marjorie L. 1991. *Feeding the Family: The Social Organization of Caring as Gendered Work.* Chicago: The University of Chicago Press.

Ehrenreich, Barbara. 1989. *Fear of Falling: The Inner Life of the Middle Class.* New York: Pantheon.

Lash, Scott, and John Urry. 1994. *Economies of Signs and Space.* London: Sage.

Portes, Alejandro, and Min Zhou. 1993. "The New Second Generation: Segmented Assimilation and Its Variants." *Annals of the American Association of Political and Social Science* 530 (November): 74–96.

Rodriguez, Nestor. 1995. "The Real 'New World Order': The Globalization of Racial and Ethnic Relations in the Later Twentieth Century." Pp. 211–225 in *The Bubbling Cauldron: Race, Ethnicity, and the Urban Crisis,* edited by Michael Peter Smith and Joe R. Feagin. Mineapolis: The University of Minnesota Press.

Rumbaut, Rubén G. 1991. "Passages to America: Perspectives on the New Immigration." Pp. 208–244 in *America at Century's End,* edited by Alan Wolfe. Berkeley: University of California Press.

Smith, Dorothy. 1990. *The Conceptual Practices of Power.* Boston: Northeastern University Press.

Smith, Michael Peter, and Joe R. Feagin, eds. *The Bubbling Cauldron: Race, Ethnicity, and the Urban Crisis.* Minneapolis: The University of Minnesota Press.

Stacey, Judith. 1991. *Brave New Families: Stories of Domestic Upheaval in Late Twentieth-Century America.* New York: Basic Books.

Sutton, Constance R. 1992. "Some Thoughts on Gendering and Internationalizing Our Thinking About Transnational Migrations." Pp. 241–249 in *Towards a Transnational Perspective on Migration: Race, Class, Ethnicity, and Nationalism Reconsidered,* edited by Nina Glick Schiller, Linda Basch, and Cristina Blanc-Szanton. New York: New York Academy of Sciences.

Winant, Howard. 1995. "Dictatorship, Democracy, and Difference: The Historical Construction of Racial Identity." Pp. 31–49 in *The Bubbling Cauldron: Race, Ethnicity, and the Urban Crisis,* edited by Michael Peter Smith and Joe R. Feagin. Minneapolis: The University of Minnesota Press.

Project Director's Acknowledgments

The New Ethnic and Immigrant Congregations Project, whose fruit this book is, was supported by generous grants from the Lilly Endowment, Inc., and the Pew Charitable Trusts. Judith Wittner and the chapter authors join me in expressing our deep gratitude to these foundations and to our program officers, James P. Wind, Craig Dykstra, and Christopher Coble at Lilly, and Joel Carpenter, Darryl G. Hart, and Luis Lugo at Pew. At Lilly, Olga Villa Parra shared her wisdom about Hispanic religion, and James Lewis, Director of the Lilly-funded Louisville Institute, gave helpful advice on the timing of proposals.

The project itself was inspired in 1991 by separate conversations with Nancy T. Ammerman, James P. Wind, John A. Gardiner, and Edwin Hernández, and I am delighted to remind each of them of my gratitude for their timely contributions.

The foundation of that inspiration was laid a decade before in field trips to the congregations of my students at the University of Illinois at Chicago; conversations during 1986–88 with Marilyn Fernandez and Kwang Chung Kim, then affiliated with the Pacific/Asian-American Mental Health Research Center at UIC, helped to firm it up. I am happy to record these long-standing debts, but I know that the debt to my students cannot be so easily discharged. In 1988–89, Sang Hyun Lee, Earle H. Waugh, and Raymond Brady Williams continued my education on the religions of immigrants. My brother, the late Michael R. Warner, supported these early efforts in many ways, not least by faithfully clipping John Dart's columns from the Los Angeles *Times*, and Janet Lever helped me take advantage of the southern California leads Mike gave me.

In subsequent years and in various ways many other individuals shared their knowledge of ethnic and immigrant religion with me, among them were Edwin Aponte, Ruben Armendariz, Hyunjung Bae, Ihsan Bagby, Carl L. Bankston III, Anne Blackburn, Mehdi Bozorgmehr, Peter Cha, Carmel Chiswick, Kevin J. Christiano, Fr. Charles Dahm, Karen Davalos, Frederick Denny, Ven. Karuna Dharma, Ana-María Díaz-Stevens, Jay Dolan, Helen Rose Ebaugh and RENIR (the Religion, Ethnicity, New Immigrant Research project), Diana Eck and the Pluralism Project, Fr. Virgilio Elizondo, Gaston Espinosa, Marcia Farr, Henry Finney, Jonathan Friedlander, Steven J. Gold, Yooshik Gong, Justo L. González, Asim Hafeezullah, Vijay Kamath S. J.,

385

Young-Il Kim, Peter Kivisto, Barry Kosmin, Peggy Levitt, Rev. Samuel Ling, Lowell W. Livezey, Lawrence Mamiya, Timothy Matovina, Gordon Melton, Ewa Morawska, Patricio Navia, Paul D. Numrich, Ana María Pineda R.S.M., Leslie Ramos, Ven. Havanpola Ratanasara, Timothy L. Smith, Tom W. Smith, Samuel Solivan, Anthony M. Stevens-Arroyo, Ismail Sumaira, Araceli Suzara, Donald Swearer, Thomas Tweed, Eldin Villafaña, Harold Vogelaar, Jack Wertheimer, Paul C. Yang, David Yoo, and Eui-Young Yu. I thank them all, especially Paul Numrich, to whom my indebtedness is particularly profound.

The staff of the UIC Office of Social Science Research—John Gardiner, Iris Tillman, Nina Smith, and Johnetta Stevens—provided intelligent and understanding administrative support throughout the five years of the project, and the succession of NEICP project coordinators—Angela Mascareñas, Linda Andes, and Elise Martel—kept things running smoothly, setting up meetings with consultants, keeping track of fellows, processing the flow of manuscripts, and much more. In the most intense phase of the project—1994–95—Linda Andes was the heart of the NEICP; Elise Martel helped bring the book to publication.

The NEICP Advisory Committee—David Badillo, Richard E. Barrett, Assad N. Busool, Xiangming Chen, Hearn Chun, Kathleen S. Crittenden, Luin Goldring, James C. Hall, Lansiné Kaba, Lowell Livezey, A. G. Roeber, Sylvia Vatuk, and Judith G. Wittner—shared the work involved in and the responsibility for choosing the fellows. Lowell Livezey's parallel Religion in Urban America Program provided valuable synergy.

Members of the Chicago Area Group for the Study of Religious Communities were the first to respond to the early plans for the project, and I thank them for their interest. The Project Team for Congregational Studies—Nancy Ammerman, Jackson Carroll, Carl Dudley, Nancy Eiesland, Ardith Hayes, Lawrence Mamiya, William McKinney, Robert Schreiter, Jack Wertheimer, and Barbara Wheeler—constituted a valued sounding board for the developing project from 1992 on. Members of the Program for the Analysis of Religion among Latinos listened to our emerging ideas and offered their advice during a meeting in November 1992; thanks to PARAL members Gilbert Cadena, Ana-María Díaz-Stevens, Lara Medina, Segundo Pantoja, Milagros Peña, Andrés Pérez y Mena, Caleb Rosado, and Anthony Stevens-Arroyo.

For the design of the project, the recruitment of the fellows, and the conduct of the training program, we drew on the advice of many consultants in addition to those mentioned above: thanks to Karen McCarthy Brown, Joy Charlton, David Daniels, Lynn Davidman, Lien Du, Roger Finke, Steven Glazier, Michael Hirsley, Albert Hunter, Ray Hutchison, Ai Ra Kim, Jung Ha Kim, Fred Kniss, Frances Kostarelos, Lionel Maldonado, Carol Maxwell, Mary McGee, Donald Miller, Mark Mullins, Mary Jo Neitz, Amparo Ojeda, Robert Orsi, Daniel Rodriguez Diaz, Wade Clark Roof, Russell Spittler, Shobha Srinivasan, K. Peter Takayama, Ruth Wallace, and Gisela Webb.

In the last stages of the project, Ana-María Díaz-Stevens, Mary Waters, Lawrence Mamiya, and Pyong Gap Min provided valuable comments on the fellows' draft chapters. Michael Ames, our sponsoring editor at Temple University Press, alternately encouraged and challenged us; the book is better for his involvement.

None of the persons and institutions mentioned above bears responsibility for the findings and interpretations presented in the chapters herein; responsibility is borne by the respective authors and the editors.

As project director, my greatest debt is to those authors, the NEICP fellows and Judy Wittner. As recounted in the introduction, Judy and the fellows (including summer fellows Haider Bhuiyan and Brian Steensland) shaped the project's agenda during the 1994 summer institute and then again during the 1995 writing workshop. (We all want to thank the cordial staff of the Bonnie View Plantation Hotel, Port Antonio, Jamaica.) Site visits with the fellows during 1994–95 provided much food for thought, and I am grateful to the respective communities for including me in the welcome they extended to the fellows. A long-term reward of the project for me was the opportunity to work with Professor Wittner. For four years, the project and I benefited from her seasoned field research experience, mastery of literatures, sociological conscience, and commitment to clear writing. Thank you, Judy.

Finally, I must acknowledge that this project, like everything I do, would not have been conceived, let alone accomplished, without the constant support, wise counsel, and inspiring example of my wife, Anne Heider.

R. Stephen Warner

About the Contributors
and Editors

Rogaia Mustafa Abusharaf is a visiting scholar at the Pembroke Center for Teaching and Research on Women at Brown University and teaches anthropology at the University of Connecticut, Storrs.

Karen J. Chai is a Ph.D. candidate in sociology at Harvard University.

Shoshanah Feher is currently on the research faculty of the School of Medicine at the University of California, Los Angeles.

Sheba George is a Ph.D. candidate in sociology at the University of California at Berkeley.

Randal L. Hepner is Visiting Assistant Professor of Anthropology at Michigan State University and Research Associate with the Metropolitan Detroit Congregational Study Project.

Prema Kurien is Assistant Professor of Sociology at the University of Southern California.

Luís León is Assistant Professor of Religion at Carleton College.

Elizabeth McAlister is Assistant Professor of Religion at Wesleyan University.

R. Stephen Warner is Professor of Sociology at the University of Illinois at Chicago.

Nancy J. Wellmeier is a special consultant on Guatemalan Catholics for the National Conference of Catholic Bishops.

Judith G. Wittner is Associate Professor of Sociology at Loyola University of Chicago.

Fenggang Yang is Research Associate at the Center for Immigration Research, University of Houston.

Index

Azhar Seminary (Egypt), 254

Bainbridge, William Sims, 324
bala vihar (child development meeting), 39
  as de facto congregation, 45
  educational focus, 41, 45
  and ethnic identity, 61
  as religious innovation in U.S., 42, 57
  as "Sunday schools," 57
  of Tamils in Los Angeles, 39–41, 51–54
    cultural programs in, 40–41, 52–53
    "family values" in, 57
    gender ideals in, 53–54
    socioeconomic status of members, 54
Balmer, Randal, 11
Bhagavad Gita, 38–39, 57
Bhuiyan, Haider, 29n. 9
Bible
  King James Version, among Rastafari, 221
  literal reading of, among Korean Christians, 321
  studies, 303, 315–316, 347
  use of, in religious meetings, 109, 172, 218
biculturalism, 83–85, 138–139
  See also code-switching
borderlands, religious
  Alcance Victoria, 189, 192
  115th Street, New York, 125
  See also languages in religious communities
Buddhists
  in Korea, 324–325n. 7, 325n. 8
  Japanese, in U.S., 4, 26
  literature on, 8
Bones, Jah, 203, 225
Boston, Massachusetts
  Korean immigrants in, 302

  drawing power for Korean-American students and educated professionals, 318
  ratio of first and second generation in, 318
Boyle Heights (Los Angeles district), 165
  birthplace of Alcance Victoria, 168
  birthplace of Victory Outreach, 167
  as gang territory, 170
  population of, 195n. 2
  See also East Los Angeles
Brooklyn, New York
  diocese of, 145
  as U.S. home to Haitians, 127, 142, 144–145
Brown, Karen McCarthy, 141
Burawoy, Michael, 381

Casanova, José, 224
Catholic Church
  apostolates (ministry projects) of, 10, 113, 144–145
  challenges to, 116
  Chicanos lapsed from, 187–188
  Haitian parishes, 145
  inculturation of Maya practices, 105–106
  legitimacy of, 12, 100, 109
  Maryknoll order, 105
  Pallotine order, 125, 145, 150
  Spanish speaking parishes, 5
  variation within, in reception of Maya, 113, 114–115, 119n. 22
Cedras, General Raoul, 157n. 21
cell groups, cell units
  in Alcance Victoria, 174, 195n. 5
  in Korean immigrant churches, 307, 314, 316, 327n. 22
CFC (Chinese Fellowship Church) (pseudonym for east coast congregation)
  age groups in, 335
  circumspect conduct of conflict in, 335, 337, 356

Creole *(continued)*
theories of, 156n. 17
creolization, 137, 138, 156n. 17
See also cultural coalescence; cultural oxymorons; Haitian religious continuum; inculturation; syncretism
Cruz, Nicky, 166
cultural coalescence, 194
See also creolization; cultural oxymorons; inculturation; syncretism
cultural oxymorons, 173–174
See also inculturation; syncretism
Czestochowa, Our Lady of, 136, 142, 156n. 10

Dallas Theological Seminary, 352
Daoud, Sheikh Ahmed Faisal (founder and leader of Islamic Mission), 236, 244–245, 252, 254
biography, 239–240, 247
and Islam in America, 244
as "zealous missionary," 241–242
Davidman, Lynn, 11
de-ethnicization
and institutional survival, 63–64, 301, 323
and Korean second generation, 304, 309, 322
See also ethnicization
Denny, Frederick, 28n. 4
diasporas
African, 202
Chinese, 346
Haitian, 125, 134, 135
Hindu, 55
in Islam, 240, 241
in Rastafari teaching, 222
religious identities in, 3
Sudanese, 242
Díaz-Stevens, Ana-María, 29n. 10
djaspora, Haitian conception of, 132
Dolan, Jay, 11, 12

Duvalier, Jean-Claude, fall of in 1986, 125, 131, 140, 146, 149, 156n. 12

East Los Angeles, 165
street names in, 169–170
See also Boyle Heights
Eck, Diana, 12
entrepreneurs, religious, 22–23, 177
See also specific religious leaders: Arguinzoni, Sonny; Figueroa, Jesus; Foxe, Abuna Asento
Ethiopia, history of, 198–202
Ethiopian Orthodox Church, 204
and Rastafarians, 229–230n. 11
ethnicization, 375
in Hindu organizations, 45–46, 59
among Iranian Jews, 83–86
in Islamic Mission, 235–236
among Rastafari, 211–212
See also de-ethnicization; race; racialization
ethnographic research
authors' accounts of
Abusharaf, Rogaia Mustafa, 236–238
Chai, Karen J., 296–297, 324n. 3
Feher, Shoshanah, 75, 78–79
George, Sheba, 268, 281, 283–284
Hepner, Randal L., 229n. 2
Kurien, Prema, 46–47, 51–52, 67n. 18
León, Luís, 169–170, 194–195, 195n. 2
McAlister, Elizabeth, 124, 140–141
Wellmeier, Nancy J., 98–100, 117n. 4
Yang, Fenggang, 334–335, 358n. 3, 358–359n. 10, 359nn. 11, 12
reflexivity in, 379–382
requisites for, 11
evangelical conversion
as "the change" among Chicanos, 169, 177, 178–179, 182, 189

Huehuetenango (department of, Guatemala), 100
Huntington, Samuel P., 357, 358n. 5
  theory of "clash of civilizations," 333, 357, 358n. 5
Hurh, Won Moo, 28n. 4, 267, 297–300, 392n. 15

identities
  negotiation of, 17, 165
    Chicano, 165–166, 192
    Haitian, 29n. 6, 125, 153–154
    Hindu, 44, 63, 375
    Jewish, 79–85, 89–90
    Maya, 107, 115
    pan–West Indian, 211–212
  reproduction of ethnic, 299
    Chinese, 354–355, 355–356, 360n. 22
    Indian, 59, 61
    Keralite, 275
    Korean, 298, 304, 311
    Yemeni, 247, 258
  reproduction of religious (*see also* Sunday schools)
    Hindu, 39, 45, 50, 62
    Jewish, 84–85, 87
    Muslim, 257
  transnational
    Haitian, 132, 381
    Rastafari, 212
  See also evangelical conversion
IJF (International Judea Foundation), 71, 74–75
  and American Jewish community, 78, 86–87
  assimilation as concern in, 89
  Chashm Andaaz (bimonthly magazine), 71, 78, 87
  family values in, 80–81
  generational relations in, 76, 87–88, 89
  generations in, 81–82
  history of, 77–78

identities, negotiation of, in, 75, 79–80
  Jewish, 84
  Iranian, 85–86
  integrationist strategy of, 86, 87
  among Iranian Jewish organizations in Los Angeles, 75
  leadership, 76–77
  marriage, out-group, as concern, 83, 84
  occupations of members, 75–76, 79
  outreach of, 78
  proximal host of, American Jews as, 83–84, 86, 88
  religious involvement and, 76
  SIAMAK, Farsi name of, 91n. 7
  social service provision of, 77, 88
  socioeconomic status of members, 75–76
  See also Fakheri, Dariush; Iranian Jews
immigration
  cohorts in, 26, 42–43, 66n. 8, 73–74, 346, 347–352
  gendered, 270
  "new," defined, 5–6
  patterns compared, 297
  refugees and, 5–6, 8 (*see also* refugees)
immigration legislation
  California Proposition 187, 115, 181, 182
  Chinese Exclusion Act of 1882, 7, 338, 354–355, 359n. 13
  Immigration Reform and Control Act (1986), 103–104
  Immigration Reform and Responsibility Act (1996), 156n. 8
  1965 law (Hart-Celler Act), 6–7, 8
    effects of, 42, 132, 211, 271
    provisions of, 28–29n. 5
inculturation, 9
  in Catholic church policy, 113
  among Maya, 105–106

inculturation *(continued)*

See also cultural coalescence; creolization; languages in religious communities; syncretism; Christianity, among Chinese; Confucianism, in Korean immigrant churches; evangelical Protestantism, and Catholicism; Korean culture, and Christianity; Vodou, and Catholicism

Indian Orthodox Church

family status and, in India, 275

North American bishops of, 271–272, 278, 292n. 18

and other Indian Christian denominations, 271

schism from Antioch, 271

schisms in North America in, 276–278

Iranian Jews

and American Jews, 74, 83–84

immigrant generations among, 81–82

"in limbo" generation of, 76, 81

in Iran, 72–73

and Iranian politics, 76–77

in Los Angeles, 73–74

occupations of, 73

as sojourners, 71–72, 77–78

tricultural strain among, 79–83, 84

See also IJF

Islam

adaptation and preservation of identity in, 258

stereotypes of, in North America, 255–256

theology of, role of congregation in, 238–239

women, variation of roles in, 248–250

Islamic Mission (mosque in Brooklyn), 235

Africans in, 241–242

African Americans in, 243–244, 245

board of directors, 252

congregationalism in, 252, 257

contrast to other mosques, 248–250

ethnic succession in, 245–247

khutbas (sermons) in, 238, 255–256

missionary activity of, 256

professionalization of clergy in, 252–256

Sunday activities, 256–257

Sudanese in, 242–243, 245

women in

early inclusion, 244

later exclusion, 238, 247–248

Yemenis in, 246–247, 258

See also Daoud, Sheik Ahmed Faisal

Iannaccone, Lawrence R., 231n. 20, 327n. 21

Italians

as ethnic group, 126, 127–128, 129, 150

hostility toward Puerto Ricans, 150

as immigrants, 125–126, 131–132

symbiosis with Haitians, 151

Jamaica

history of, 198–202

political parties in, 201, 203, 206–207, 230n. 14

Jews, American

immigration of, 26

as reference group

for Chinese, 355, 360nn. 19, 20

for Indians, 63

for Iranian Jews, 83, 85–86, 87–88

Kasinitz, Phillip, 211

Kerala Christians

Christmas caroling among, 280, 291n. 3

history of, in India, 271

production-oriented religion *(continued)*
  contrasted with consumer-orientation, 107, 151
  of Haitians, 142
  of Hindu Malayalees, 111
  of Italians in New York, 126–128, 150–151
  of Maya, 107, 111, 114
proselytization
  activity of second generation Korean Americans, 304, 308, 312, 317
  See also evangelical conversion; evangelical Protestantism; missions; missionaries
proximal host, 83
  concept of, 10, 18–19, 84, 119n. 21
  of Haitians, in New York, 146–147, 153
  of Iranian Jews, in Los Angeles, 83–87
  of Maya
    in Los Angeles, 108
    in United States, 115
  See also ethnicization; racialization
Puerto Ricans
  and drug trade in New York, 157n. 23
  as immigrants, 28n. 3, 126, 149–150
  and Italians, 149–150
  "Nuyoricans," 126, 166
  Yoruba-based religion of (*La Regla de Ocho*), 151

Q'anjob'al (Maya Language)
  affectionate address to father in, 109
  basic to culture, 101
  Bible translation in, 119n. 23
  as first language, 107–108, 108–109
  orthography of, 117–118n. 5
  and other Maya languages, 100

race
  in CFC, 360n. 19

and color consciousness, among Chicanos, 169, 176, 186
  in ethnographic research, 380–381
  "*La Raza*," 174
  in sociological analysis, 14
  See also ethnicization; racialization
racialization, 375–376
  and Haitians in the U.S., 146–149, 155n. 2
  and Indians in the U.S., 44, 62
  and Koreans in the U.S., 211–212
  and Rastafari in the U.S., 323
  See also ethnicization; proximal host; race
Ragavachari, Ranjana, 269
Rajagopal, Arvind, 62
Rastafari attire, 135
Rastafarian movement
  history of, 198–202
  ganja use in, 200, 208, 229n. 10, 231n. 19
  lion, symbol of, in, 230–231n. 18
  mansions in, 228–229n. 1
  See also CHSI; Foxe, Abuna Asento; Selassie, Haile I
Rastafarian organizations
  Ethiopian World Federation, 204, 205, 209, 230n. 12
  Imperial Ethiopian World Federation, 205, 207, 208, 210, 214
  See also CHSI; Foxe, Abuna Asento
rational-choice humanism, contrasted with Marxist social determinism, 164–165, 192, 193–194
refugees
  category of immigrants, 5–6
  Chinese "sojourners," 347
  from El Salvador, 8
  from Guatemala, 8, 103, 104
  Iranian Jewish "sojourners," 71–72, 77–78
  traditionalism among, 27
religions. *See* specific religions

Williams, Raymond Brady *(continued)*
  quoted, 44–45, 56–57, 64, 72, 87,
    254, 270
Wittner, Judith G., 12, 13, 14, 15, 27
women
  in global division of labor, 269–
    271, 372
  idealization of
    as mothers, 216–217
    as wives, 53–54, 171, 178
  networks of, 250
  religious participation of, 38, 40,
    53, 102, 126, 170–171, 172–
    173, 214–215, 244

religious restrictions on, 111, 168,
    183, 248–249, 268–269, 273–
    274
Wossen, Merd Asmatch Asfa, 205,
    230n. 13
  pictures of, in CHSI, 210

Yang, Fenggang, 18, 27, 101, 111,
    304, 368, 369, 374, 377, 378,
    379, 380
  See also ethnographic research,
    authors' accounts of